TO THE HORIZON AND BEYOND

A Life of Service to the Red Cross

Hansrudi Brawand

The publisher wishes to acknowledge and thank Dr. Douglas H. Johnson for his invaluable help and support for Africa World Books and its mission of preserving and promoting African cultural and literary traditions and history. Dr. Johnson and fellow historians have been instrumental in ensuring that African people remain connected to their past and their identity. Africa World Books is proud to carry on this mission.

Copyright © 2022 Hansrudi Brawand

ISBN: 9780645583250

No part of this publication may be reproduced, stored in a retrieval system, or transmitted, in any form, or by any means, electronic, mechanical, photocopying, recording or otherwise, without the prior permission of the publishers.

This book is sold subject to the conditions that it shall not, by way of trade or otherwise, be lent, re-sold, hired out or otherwise circulated without the publisher's prior consent in any form of binding or cover other than in which it is published and without a similar condition including the condition being imposed on the subsequent purchaser.

Cover design, typesetting and layout: Africa World Books
Unit 3, 57 Frobisher St, Osborne Park, WA 6017
P.O. Box 1106 Osborne Park, WA 6916

I DEDICATE THIS BOOK TO MY WIFE ANN,
THE LOVE OF MY LIFE

CONTENTS

About the Author   7
Acknowledgments   9

1. The Distance Calls: Biafra, Nigeria, 1969   11
2. From Nigeria to South- and East Africa: 1969-1970   91
3. Anatolia – The Asian Part of Turkey, 1970-1971   106
4. Bangladesh, 1971-1973: Life Changes   191
5. Sudan and Southern Sudan, 1973-1976   301
6. Zurich, Switzerland, 1976-1979: Native Soil   345
7. Perth, Western Australia, 1979-1980: To New Shores   363
8. Mogadishu, Somalia, 1980-1981   376
9. Perth, 1982-1984: New Perspectives   405
10. Kassala, Sudan, 1985-1986   417
11. Dhaka, Chittagong, Bangladesh, 1986-1989: A Homecoming   438
12. Kassala, Sudan & Perth, 1989-1991: At Home – with Wanderlust   481
13. Ljubljana, Slovenia & Zagreb, Croatia: 1992-1993   502
14. Kassala, Sudan, 1993-1994: The Last Mission   524

Afterword   537
Index   540

ABOUT THE AUTHOR

Hansrudi Brawand was born on 14 February 1932 in the famous tourist resort of Grindelwald, surrounded by high mountains, in the so-called Glacier valley of Switzerland. His parents had a plant nursery and at the age of 16 he moved to the border town of Basel, on the river Rhine, where he became an apprentice baker and pastry chef. In 1951, after passing his exams, due to a disturbing flour allergy, he reluctantly decided to quit that profession. He could have chosen to become a policeman, border guard or customs officer but preferred working as chemistry worker in the famous company Roche.

At the age of twenty, during compulsory military training, he liscensed as a truck driver and that became his next profession. For a few years he drove tankers with heating oil from the Rhine port to many destinations around Switzerland. Travelling through his beautiful homeland became a passion. Still, he knew it was impossible to discover his hidden potential while driving trucks.

When he discovered the International Committee of the Red Cross (ICRC) was looking for people to serve in civil war-torn Nigeria-Biafra, he quickly applied and several months later he was on his way to Africa. The work there quickly changed his life forever.

That was the beginning of a life-long career with the Red Cross. Whether fighting against starvation, refugee misery, diseases, or building houses for the poorest of the poor, Brawand remained dedicated to the Red Cross cause of alleviating human suffering.

ACKNOWLEDGMENTS

Without my loyal friend in Perth, Peter Deng, the founder of Africa World Books, this book would never have been translated into English and published in Australia. Peter grew up in South Sudan and later became a refugee for many years in Kenya before coming to Australia. I want to express my heartfelt gratitude for his efforts, support, and encouragement to publish the English language version of this book. I would also like to extend my gratitude and thanks to Dr. Sara Maher, an outstanding editor, who ensured that the stories of my work with the Red Cross, so many years ago, came back to life again.

CHAPTER ONE

THE DISTANCE CALLS: BIAFRA, NIGERIA, 1969

SPOTLIGHT ON NIGERIA

Nigeria is a multi-ethnic country with two main religions: Christianity in the south in the north of the country. Since Nigeria's independence from Britain in the state1960, some people of Nigeria were vying for supremacy. In particular, the Christian Igbo living in the province of Biafra felt disadvantaged compared to the Muslim Haussa and Fulani of the north. The conflict was exacerbated by the oil fields in the Niger Delta, near the Igbo settlement area. This oil was economically very important for Nigeria and thus a central bone of contention between the opposing groups and their armies.

On January 15, 1966, the first serious incident occurred when Igbo officers seized power. Nigerian Prime Minister Abubakar Tafawa Balewa was killed in the attack. General Johnson Aguiyi-Ironsi took over from the Igbo officers. Large sections of the

Nigerian population feared that the Igbos would oppress them in the future. A few months later, in July 1966, a countercoup restored the supremacy of the north, and a devastating persecution of the Igbo began. A pogrom ensued, in which tens of thousands of these people died.

At the end of May 1967, the Nigerian central government also passed a territorial reform, as a result of which Nigeria was divided into twelve federal states. The administrative borders were set in such a way that the oil areas were outside the Igbo access. The persecution of tens of thousands of south-east Nigerians living in the north-west of the country, many of them Igbo, continued. Those who did not fall victim to a massacre were forced to flee to their region of origin, Biafra. Now the military governor of the south-eastern region of Chukwuemeka, Odumegwu Ojukwu, himself an Igbo, acted promptly. On May 30, 1967, he proclaimed the independence of the Biafra region. The actual war then escalated in the early morning hours of July 6, 1967, when Nigerian troops crossed the Biafra border. Despite fierce resistance, it soon became apparent in the course of this civil war that Biafra was militarily inferior. The decisive factor here was not least that the former colonial power, Great Britain, supported the central government. Other arms suppliers to Nigeria were the USA, the Soviet Union, Spain, Poland, Czechoslovakia, Belgium, and the Netherlands; the latter three states stopped their arms deliveries in the course of 1968. Half of the weapons available to the Republic of Biafra came from its production and the other half from the People's Republic of China. Other suppliers were Portugal, France, and Switzerland. However, Biafra was not recognized diplomatically by any of these states.

On May 18, 1968, Nigerian troops captured the important port city of Port Harcourt. Biafra thus lost access to the sea and thus free supply from the outside world. Biafra was now two-thirds occupied. The remaining territory could only be supplied by air.

An increasingly important role was played by the humanitarian aid flights that began in 1968. These flights were only able to head for Biafra at night from the islands of São Tomé and Fernando Po. As Biafra no longer had an airport after the loss of their most important cities, an improvised runway at Uli-Ihiala, (in today's Anambra state), became the main transhipment point for relief goods and arms deliveries. When the International Committee of the Red Cross, (ICRC) stopped the relief flights in June 1969 after one of its planes was shot down, the supply situation deteriorated dramatically. For a year after the fall of 1968, it looked like a military standoff. The Nigerian army was unable to finally take the remaining Igbo heartland. Smaller counter-offensives by members of the army and guerrilla activities behind the front prevented this again and again. However, a weakened Biafra was no longer able to cope with the final offensive that began in December 1969 and finally had to capitulate on January 15, 1970. Biafra became affiliated with the state of Nigeria again. However, the Igbo were ostracized for decades and no longer received important posts, neither in the military nor in the administration. Biafra's economy, for its part, was destroyed by this devastating civil war. It took several years before an economic recovery occurred.[1]

---

1   In an article in the Wiener Zeitung, on February 28, 1992, this war event was discussed under the title "Genocide with assistance." Author Harald Steiner wrote that by imposing a hunger blockade, Nigeria resorted to

HANSRUDI BRAWAND

THE DISTANCE CALLS

It was late October 1968 when I heard on the midday news on Swiss radio that the International Committee of the Red Cross (ICRC) was looking for new staff to work in Biafra, in Nigeria, West Africa. I listened, immediately wide awake. Was this finally my chance to go abroad? It was also in the newspaper the next day: Yes, the ICRC was looking for people for Biafra. There had been a bitter war since 1967 after this eastern region broke away from the federal state of Nigeria and proclaimed the Republic of Biafra. Countless people, especially children, had starved to death. The ICRC needed more staff to expand its on-the-ground assistance. I felt sure. This was my chance to turn my life around the way I wanted.

That same day I called the ICRC in Geneva, expressed my interest, and asked for an interview. They listened to me and told me they would call me back in a few days. So the first step was taken and it was time to keep my fingers crossed. However, deep inside I also heard a quiet and cautious voice, worried about whether it was wise to leave peaceful Switzerland and go to work in a dangerous war zone in unfamiliar Africa. But my longing for going overseas, the search for a real change that held new, unknown challenges in store for me, silenced this somewhat despondent little voice and rigorously brushed its concerns aside. The desire for a good dose of

---

"genocidal means" in order to conquer what remained of Biafra. Two million people died, mostly children. Another 750,000people, most of them Igbo, died in combat or were massacred by Nigerian troops. This has been described as genocide. The author stated: "Genocide is the most appropriate term for it." Source: Wikipedia/compiled by Heidi Jaberg-Zwahlen.

adventure also played a part. Switzerland had become too narrow. The vastness and the foreignness of Africa lured me.

A job with the ICRC seemed a long way off for the time being, but the promised call back said that some new employees had recently flown to Biafra, and I got the appointment I had hoped for, an interview in Geneva. This was of central importance to me – the ICRC was still looking for people who could be sent to Biafra in a few months – maybe even sooner. After said interview, which was positive, the ICRC man promised to put me on that list. I returned happily to the waiting room. I met another applicant there, Guido Müller from Zurich. We immediately liked each other and took the next train back to Zurich together. We had more than enough to talk about.

Guido had already been in action in Biafra a year before. He talked about his work there, the difficulties, changing, unforeseeable situations, the war, and the misery of the civilian population. We kept in touch from that day on.

In February 1969, Guido informed me that he would be flying back to Biafra for the ICRC in a few weeks, but I still had to wait. The situation could change at any time, I was reassured on the phone. However, according to the ICRC's admonition, I should be ready to leave within a month if they requested me. When I told my boss at the time and my colleagues about my Biafra plans, everyone was horrified and found it difficult to understand that I wanted to go there. This unfortunate war in West Africa, which had claimed so many lives was heard of every day in the news. Several ICRC employees had died there.

At the end of April, the long-awaited call came from Geneva:

"Mr. Brawand, are you still willing to go to Biafra for us?" "Yes of course!" was my answer. "You know Guido Müller. He is coming back to Switzerland in June for family reasons. We want you to replace him in Enugu, in Nigerian-held Biafra. However, you need to depart on May 24th. Is that possible?" "I will make it possible!" I said firmly. "Please send us your passport as soon as possible, please also confirm that you will arrive in Geneva ready to travel on May 19." In those minutes I could hardly believe that I was making progress. "Will do, thank you very much, goodbye!" I ended the call. I was jubilant, screaming my joy out into the world: "Yes, yes, yes!" I did it! Finally! Now things happened in quick succession. With this call, the gateway to the world had opened a crack for me. I was certain my life would change from the ground up. An eventful future awaited me. How eventful that would be was beyond my imagination and that was definitely a good thing. The company showed understanding of my imminent departure. I was able to take another week's vacation, deregister from the townhouse in Zürich, and pay my taxes, and rent, three months in advance, for my one-room apartment. I was also given military leave abroad from the district command. Now it was time to say goodbye to the company and my friends. For some, it seemed like goodbye forever. They didn't think they'd ever see me alive again. But everyone wished me the best. My parents were even more worried about my safety. My mother cried when I said goodbye in Interlaken. Arriving in Geneva, I changed to the bus to Grand-Saconnex, where I checked into a room reserved by the ICRC.

The four-day preparatory course for our assignment in Biafra began the next morning. There were five participants whom, were introduced to the history, structures, tasks, and goals of the ICRC by a friendly, German-speaking instructor. The Geneva Red Cross Convention was also an important part of this introduction. The Red Cross and the Geneva Conventions were born when Henry Dunant witnessed the devastating consequences of war at a battlefield in Italy. In the aftermath of that battle, Dunant urged successfully for the creation of a civilian relief corps to respond to human suffering during conflict, and for rules to set limits on how war was waged. The Geneva Conventions have been ratified by 196 countries.

The main focus, however, was on the practical work that awaited us on site. Administration, reporting, responsibility, behavior, transport, storage, distribution of aid supplies, relationships with local authorities, cooperation with the Nigerian Red Cross, personal safety, and wearing the large ICRC badge, were of considerable importance. Our heads were spinning, and we asked a lot of questions. This course was extremely interesting and instructive for me, and the days flew by.

One of the participants was the nurse, Monika Stalder from Lucerne, another was the car mechanic, Harry Metzger. We were the team of three that boarded the Swissair flight to Accra in West Africa on May 23rd at Geneva Cointrin airport. For me, it was the first flight over the Alps and the Mediterranean! As the North African coast came into view far below, my heart pounded with joy. Red Cross people were allowed to go forward into the cockpit individually. The flight captain was very interested in our adventure and asked questions about where we came from and where we were going. The visit to the cockpit made a big impression on me. I thought I was floating in a spaceship and looked spellbound down at the endless expanse of the light brown Sahara. I discovered fine, dead-straight lines that must have been desert paths or dirt roads, lost somewhere in the haze. Up there, 10,000 meters above the ground, I realized that my new future had begun.

Towards evening we landed in Accra, the capital of Ghana, and I set foot on African soil full of expectations and full of energy. But when we got into a taxi at the airport, I got a fright for the first time. I had to catch my breath as we drove at full speed on the wrong side of the road into my first African left turn. But Monika laughed uproariously and cried: "It's left-hand traffic here, Hansrudi!"

My first night was restless. The many new impressions had thrown me off course, literally shaking me. I was glad when the next day dawned. We had to go to the airport early. With the same Swissair plane, we flew along the West African coast on a short connecting flight. At 9 a.m. we landed at the airport in Lagos, the capital of Nigeria. Thanks to the Red Cross emblems, we didn't have to open our suitcases at customs. We were welcomed by Mr. Pfister, the ICRC's head of human resources in Nigeria, and we drove 15 kilometers into a Lagos traffic jam, in the ICRC's VW bus. It was pure chaos with car horns constantly honking from all sides. Shaky buses and trucks emitted dark clouds of exhaust fumes. The sidewalks were full of people, with no pale faces anywhere. That was a whole new perception for me.

We drove over the Carter bridge, the connection between the port and the city, because Lagos is on an island. On the right was the large port of Apapa. We saw countless freighters at the docks, ready to unload their cargo. Some had hoisted Red Cross flags;

aid supplies were waiting there to be unloaded. Finally, we reached the two-storey ICRC building in the suburb of Ikoy and were greeted warmly by the staff. Monika, Harry, and I each received fifty Nigerian pounds from the cashier so that we wouldn't be left completely destitute. We had to stay in Lagos for a few days until a ride to Enugu arose, about 800 kilometers away. Flights there were disrupted because the Enugu airfield had been mistakenly attacked by Biafran planes a few days earlier. The attack had been aimed at destroying enemy Nigerian jet fighters.

We stayed at the Hotel Jkoyi, which was beautifully situated in the middle of a large garden area with palm trees, exotic bushes, and flowers. We even had a large swimming pool at our disposal. I had not imagined my Red Cross mission to be so peaceful. However, Monika and Harry, who had been to Biafra before, did not like Lagos. They wanted to continue to Biafra in the bush as quickly as possible and would have preferred to leave immediately. But we had to be patient for a few more days. In Switzerland, Pentecost was being celebrated that weekend and I dwelled on my thoughts. My friends from the New Alpine Club in Zurich would be packing their rucksacks or were already on the way up to a summit, while I was busy cramming the English language under palm trees.

We were in the middle of the rainy season, with thunderstorms unloading large amounts of warm rain every day. This resulted in high humidity, which I still had to get used to. For dinner, we took a taxi into town and sat down in a restaurant with Nigerian and Lebanese specialties. The next evening, our beautiful Monika met a rich Lebanese man named George. She only accepted his invitation to dinner on the condition that Harry and I were invited as well. That was okay with George. So, the three of us unexpectedly came to a sumptuous dinner on the open roof restaurant of a highrise building, with a great view of the illuminated harbor. Several freighters were being unloaded at the piers. The many lights were reflected in the water, creating an almost Christmas-like atmosphere for us Swiss. All three of us thanked our host warmly. Bad luck for him that Monika kept her distance. However, George did not give up and invited her to lunch the next day, but when he went to pick her up, she pretended to have a headache and other minor aches and pains. But George had already ordered lunch. So, he asked me if I would like to dine with him. Of course, I did and enjoyed another great meal. George then took me back to the hotel and expressed concern about Monika's state of health. He continued to court her and appeared to be deeply in love. But Monika kept coming up with more excuses. Finally, George threw in the towel and said goodbye to her, a little offended. He had been a truly charming and generous host; but there was nothing for Monika, who was impatiently waiting for the onward journey to Biafra.

It took two more days until Guido Müller finally arrived from Enugu. We greeted each other warmly in the hotel lobby. He wished that the three of us would move to the Federal Hotel with him. This was right on the harbour across from the docks. Here I was able to marvel at the incoming and outgoing cargo ships with their flags and names, as well as the goods being unloaded from the docked ships, which was a 24-hour around-the-clock operation. Memories of my visits to the Basel Rhine port surfaced. But here everything was much bigger, more foreign, and took place in the tropical heat. We had to wait another three days before we could start.

Guido had much to discuss with Jean-Pierre Hocké, our ICRC Head of Mission. In addition, Guido had brought a very long shopping list because Enugu had become a ghost town. There was very little to buy there. So I accompanied him for two days on his shopping spree through Lagos. Harry, who was supposed to have gone to Enugu with us, was told to stay in Lagos as head of the auto mechanics. He refused to work in Lagos. He wanted to go back to Enugu, where he liked it better. However, that was rejected. So, Harry decided to break off his assignment and return to Switzerland at his own expense.

On the eve of our departure for Enugu, a lot was going on at the Federal Hotel. We were introduced to August Lindt, the ICRC's Plenipotentiary Minister for Nigeria and Biafra. He was a friendly, humorous older gentleman who chatted freely with us. When he heard that my name was Brawand, he spontaneously said that I must be from Grindelwald and be related to his friend, the former national and Berne government councilor Samuel Brawand. I proudly said yes and reverted to my most original Grindelwald dialect, which he obviously enjoyed. There was no sign that he had been arrested by the airfield commander the night before and had spent the night in a barracks with the two pilots. The reason for this: his plane had allegedly not had permission to land.

The next day at lunchtime we were finally able to drive off in the big, fully packed Land Rover. Guido Müller steered the vehicle marked with the Red Cross safely and practiced through the heavy traffic out of Lagos. A small Red Cross flag fluttered in the wind on the front fender. There were four of us in the car. In addition to Guido, Monika, and me, Mr. Mennel, originally from Eastern

Switzerland, also traveled with us. He was married to a Nigerian, had lived in the country for many years, and owned a pest control company in Lagos. The Red Cross had commissioned him to smoke out several warehouses in Enugu because the supplies stored there were infested with ants, beetles, and other insects. The heavy traffic only slowly eased off after about 50 kilometers. On the way, I marveled at the large banana trees and the many termite piles. The latter lined the road like milestones. You couldn't see far, however, because dense vegetation blocked the view. The paved road was just wide enough for two trucks to cross and there was a meter-wide unpaved strip on both sides.

Guido set a brisk pace. We regularly passed villages, some of whose names I wrote down, such as Igode, Fhagamo, and Shaguro. In every village, the children waved and laughed at us as soon as they saw our Red Cross vehicle. Of course, we waved back happily. The landscape was now getting hillier. We reached the top of a hill and quickly went down again in the direction of a small valley, where a narrow, single-lane wooden bridge awaited us. Guido gripped the steering wheel tightly as we sped down the dead-straight road at accelerating speed. All the passengers stared spellbound at the narrow bridge without railings and hoped our chauffeur had aimed correctly. The momentum of the high speed helped to overcome the subsequent incline quickly. We saw rusted and burned-out truck wrecks lying in the creek bed next to the bridge. They had lost the competition to cross the single-lane bridge faster than oncoming traffic.

Shortly after Jelese, Guido stopped and handed the wheel over to me so that I could get used to driving on the left. Initially, my heart began to pound as I entered a confusing left-hand bend at a speed of 80 kilometers per hour and an hour later, I ran over a chicken in Ugpogu. In the rear-view mirror, I saw a man pick up the flattened hen and angrily shake his fist at us. I sped off at full speed! Towards evening Guido asked me to stop and buy five pineapples from a woman on the side of the road. Each fruit weighed at least four kilos. The anticipation of this treat was great for all of us.

Shortly afterward we reached Benin, the day's destination. The city is still famous throughout Africa for its bronze art. After dinner at a hotel, we set out to admire these works of art. As tired as we were, after a short tour, we returned to our rooms knowing full well that the rather arduous journey would continue the next day. We wanted to be fit and well rested so that we were prepared for unknown hardships.

The next morning, we filled our vehicle with petrol for the first time. The atmosphere in the city was tense and quite frightening, especially for me as a newcomer. Military trucks came from everywhere and drove through the city. An anti-aircraft gun was mounted on the rear of the front of each vehicle with a gunner sitting behind, ready to shoot down the Biafran planes that had (allegedly) attacked the city in the previous few days.

Benin was soon behind us, which gave me a sigh of relief. Again, we drove through hilly landscapes that showed us the beauty of the country. We were able to enjoy the breathtaking view, and get an idea of the varied, green landscapes, exotic trees, bushes, and flowers. Above all this, white clouds were passing above. We were met by herds of skinny white cows with huge horns. A surprising picture, especially for me as a Bernese "Oberlander." Mr. Mennel, who had long been a resident, explained to me that these migrant herds were common. The Fulani tribe practices this type of cattle breeding. The herds of cows from northern Nigeria would thus be driven as far as Lagos, where all cows were used for slaughter: "These herds usually covered one 1,000 kilometers of road. Often a whole year. Sometimes there are pregnant animals among them, which then calve on the way," said the eastern Swiss. There was more than enough grass along the roads and paths. Now and then the shepherds in a village would also sell a cow: "After selling the cows in Lagos, the shepherds return north; this time by truck," my compatriot reported. Meanwhile, we were traveling in the Nigerian state of the Midwest, which is famous for its abundance of wood; mainly mahogany. We saw huge, cleared forest areas. The trunks were transported by truck to the lagoon near Lagos and thrown into the water. Tugboats then hauled them to Apapa, the huge port opposite Lagos and there the wood finally disappeared into the bellies of freighters to be shipped overseas.

We reached Ekpoma shortly before noon, where it was market day. Colorfully dressed women walked between the stalls, carrying enamel basins on their heads, filled with fruit and vegetables. This bustling market looked picturesque, with all these brightly colored clothes, because the men were also dressed in bright colors. I could hardly get enough of it and also found it amusing to listen to the haggling in a foreign language. This seemed to be a kind of game because there was a lot of laughter. Sometimes they also pointed their fingers at us strangers or scrutinized us secretly. I liked this new world, which was so different, surprising, exciting, and fascinating.

As we continued our journey, I encountered a flock of vultures for the first time in my life. Around a bend, more than ten of these scary-looking birds sat in the middle of the road and ate a small animal that had been killed by traffic. We slowly drove past these fellows, who looked very strange to me. I also learned straight away that vultures are protected in Africa and therefore must not be killed because they are Africa's health police.

When we reached Auchy, one of the larger towns, a policeman informed us that the ferry in the neighbouring town of Idah had sunk in the Niger river. So, the river was not passable for us there, which would have been the shortest way to our destination of Enugu. This information caused some deep sighs in our group. For better or worse, we now had to make a detour of 200 kilometers to Lokoja and hope that the Niger was passable there. This journey became more and more adventurous. Guido and I now took regularly turns at the steering wheel. For me, it was the best exercise ever to get used to the conditions there.

Two hours later we reached the state of Kwate. Here we came to an area that gave us one impressive long-distance view after another. We drove through open country, then over hill ranges again, and even through rocky regions. In the meantime, it had gotten pretty hot, and we appreciated the constant headwind, which cooled us. During the course of the afternoon, we reached Lokoja and drove straight down to the ferry, hoping a little tensely that the Niger was passable here. That seemed to be the case, but many vehicles were still waiting on the shore, and the ferry was already occupied by trucks and other vehicles. Guido chatted briefly but convincingly with the captain and was awarded a place. But only because the Red Cross was given the right of way. Lucky! But we rejoiced too soon.

The ferry suffered an engine failure and had to be repaired. So, we sat down in the shade behind the boathouse and looked out over the brown, lazily rolling waters of the river which was probably a kilometer wide and where the Niger and Benue rivers met.

At 5 p.m. the captain announced that the ferry would not be able to leave until 6 a.m. the next day. Not so bad, Guido and Mr. Mennel decided. Trucks sometimes have to wait a whole week for the crossing here. So, we drove our Land Rover back off the ferry and registered at the nearby inn, which was set in a small, well-kept park. The stately inn was probably built during the British colonial period. Here we treated ourselves to a hearty dinner, which we deserved. Later we relocated to an outbuilding that consisted of one large room. To our delight, there was a magnificent pool table in the middle. Everyone immediately grabbed a billiard cue, pressed light blue chalk onto the tip, placed the balls in the triangular frame, and put on a poker face. Guido was the first to aim. The colored balls were already rolling on the green surface, moving everywhere but not where they were supposed to. However, that didn't matter. We were all "greenhorns" and comforted each other after a bad game with the beer we had brought with us.

Later in the evening, it got warmer and warmer, the air more and more oppressive - a thunderstorm was brewing. Suddenly the rain came, pattering loudly on the tin roof. Lightning flashed, followed every second by thunderbolts. Surprisingly, the light didn't go out, instead, the wind blew a lot of rain into the chimney just above our pool table. The large playing area was suddenly underwater with the rainwater running into the six side pockets. We continued to play anyway because now it was getting really exciting. Every time the stick hit the cue ball, a fountain of water splashed over the waiting players. We had a great time. One of us began to sing: "Such a day, as wonderful as today." Exactly half past five the next morning we were back at the landing stage in front of the ferry with our Land Rover. Many other vehicles were already there. The drivers of military trucks immediately tried to challenge us for our place on the ferry. But Guido, who knew his stuff very well, waved his arms vigorously in the cool morning air and spoke resolutely to the captain. Blonde Monika offered support by giving him a beaming smile. That worked! We got our place on the ferry.

Around a dozen, military and civilian trucks were now parked on the old ferry, along with legions of infantry, traders, and colourfully dressed women with children. We left on time just as a beautiful sunrise appeared on the horizon, which lifted the spirits on the ferry significantly. Zigzagging to avoid sandbanks, the heavy ferry slowly moved downstream. A Nigerian gunner sat on the roof of the ferry house with a rotating twin anti-aircraft gun. Together with a comrade, he searched the sky for any attacking Biafran aircraft. After about 45 minutes we docked at Shintaku on the far bank, a few miles downstream, and breathed a sigh of relief.

The next challenge that awaited us was driving about 100 kilometers of bumpy, wet, and sometimes muddy dirt road. We were thoroughly shaken by the drive and two and a half hours later we finally reached a paved road near Otukpa. We still had about 90 kilometers to drive to Enugu, but it quickly became clear to us that we were getting closer and closer to the war zone. Every few kilometers we were stopped at a roadblock. Suspicious soldiers with automatic weapons at the ready asked us where we were coming from and where we were going and sometimes checked our luggage. Luckily, they overlooked my camera wrapped in newspaper.

We found ourselves in East Central State – occupied Biafra, the actual homeland of the Igbo. This Nigerian federal state was proclaimed as the new state of Biafra when the war broke out. In the meantime, however, a large part of Biafra had been recaptured by the Federals, i.e., the Nigerian troops. The landscape became more open and then we came across shot-up tanks or burned-out military trucks on the side of the road. We also knew that on the right-hand side, far from the road, Biafrans were sitting in the bush and organizing occasional raids as guerrillas. Around noon we reached the Nine Miles Corner crossroads, one of the big roadblocks. Military personnel and black-uniformed police officers checked passers-by here. We were recognized as ICRC people and were able to drive through the barrier without major controls.

Shortly thereafter, the road led us over a high plateau. Here we had a magnificent view over the wide, open, green country. Biafra was literally at our feet. From this perspective, this beautiful landscape looked so peaceful and tranquil. Yet, for two years, there had been such a bitter, merciless war down there in the bush, resulting in a terrible famine with countless victims with hundreds of thousands of children affected.

Suddenly Guido shouted: "Look! Down there is Enugu!" My heart was pounding. There, far below, I saw the rather small town for the first time, surrounded by greenery and without high-rise buildings. Now, this long-awaited place was finally there before my eyes. My first ICRC assignment and at the same time the center of my own life for an indefinite period. A strange, indescribable feeling came over me; overwhelming joy, coupled with a good dose of insecurity and a pinch of doubt. Would I be up to the task? We drove on, down a narrow, winding, steep road. Guido showed us the curve where, on Christmas 1968, a huge military articulated lorry carrying over 120 soldiers fell down the gorge, and about 60 soldiers lost their lives.

Finally, we reached our destination, Enugu. Guido drove straight to a two-story apartment building, which was the ICRC building. I was allocated a spacious room on the second floor with air conditioning and a small fridge. A few other ICRC people lived here, mostly Swiss. In the afternoon, Guido took me on the first tour of the 18 warehouses with the thousands of tons of relief supplies that were constantly being stored and retrieved. The many workers had already finished work because working hours began at 7:30 a.m. and ended at 2 p.m. Guido then drove me to some of the suburban residential areas that were now deserted, and in doing so introduced me to the war-torn side of the city. Before the war, approximately 140,000 people had lived in Enugu, around 1,000 of whom were white. But when the Nigerian troops attacked the capital of Biafra, most people fled and only six to eight thousand people had remained in Enugu.

About 95 percent of the residential and commercial buildings were empty, entire suburbs were deserted. I was shocked when we drove through the streets of the residential areas or when we were looking for passage on a street overgrown with plants. Most of the single-family houses were no longer visible. They had disappeared up to the roofs, under the luxuriantly rampant creepers and climbing plants. Even tarred neighbourhood streets were covered with this vegetation, which grew rapidly during the rainy season. Only in the middle of the street was there, if at all, a strip of asphalt one to three meters wide. Later I entered some of these green, haunted houses. I had to be wary of possible new residents, especially snakes. There was great disorder everywhere in the rooms, everything was full of dirt. Rats had rampaged, tearing up mattresses and leaving their droppings. Plants had come in through broken windows, and furniture was scarce. Nigerian soldiers had collected it and stored it somewhere. The battle for Enugu had also left its mark. You could see bullet holes in house walls, and cartridge cases with a verdi gris patina were still lying around. Some buildings were destroyed, their ruins overgrown. In Enugu's center, however, life pulsated. A fair number of shops were open, but supply was poor. Everywhere I saw soldiers patrolling, armed with automatic guns or assault rifles, dressed in camouflage fatigues and with a green slouch hat on their heads.

There were checkpoints on all the bridges. As everywhere in Nigeria, many Igbo women were out and about in brightly colored robes, proudly walking upright, carrying goods of some kind on their heads. I was told that these colorful dresses were a single piece of cloth about two meters long that was cleverly wrapped around the body to rest just above the ground. A blouse and an elegantly wrapped headscarf were worn with it. They were pretty, those Igbo women. They didn't need lipstick or make-up.

When I climbed wearily into my freshly made bed that first evening in Enugu, I couldn't think of falling asleep, because from outside a thousand-voiced concert of croaking frogs reached me at full volume. However, I quickly got used to this night music. Every evening they lulled me into a refreshing sleep with the window open. On that first evening, however, everything was still unreal, and I still couldn't quite grasp it: I had finally arrived at the place I had longed for.

On June 3rd, my first day at work, I drove with Guido to the office building, which was next to the three largest warehouses. There were also some walls full of bullet holes. The approximately 130 workers and administrative staff - all Igbos - were expecting us. Guido introduced me to them as his successor. I first talked a little about my long journey and then stated how much I looked forward to working there and the good cooperation with all of them and also that I depended on their support. It seemed like I hit the right note. Some laughed at me, others promised to support me. To my relief, Guido stayed here for another three weeks to introduce me to all the tasks. Gerhard Penka, a German, also worked there. He was responsible for the satellite stores just under a kilometer away. He would leave with Guido. So I had to work really hard to soon be able to run this big shop on my own. We were sitting at Guido's desk when Sam, the dispatcher, came into the office. Guido gave instructions on what had to be delivered by truck that day. For example, the Irish mission station in Uturu should receive 20 sacks of dried beans, 20 sacks of rice, 10 bales of cod, and five cans of palm oil. Enugu was the ICRC central warehouse with around 3,000 tons of food. Up to nine medical teams and mission stations, some of which worked more than 100 kilometers away, were supplied from there. These teams helped hundreds of thousands of people in need in the war zones with our supplies.

Challenging tasks lay ahead of me. I had a bit of a bad feeling about it because my English was still poor. Another problem was obtaining rice, beans, and palm oil. All of this had to be bought locally, primarily from traders from the north. It was cheaper and quicker than carting these goods from distant Lagos to Enugu. But we had to fill out purchase contract forms with precise and quality information, the weight and number of bags, and the delivery deadlines to be met.

Guido warned me about these traders from the northern tribe of the Hausas and explained what to watch out for and how to check. The Hausas were Muslims in wide, flowing robes and were shrewd businessmen. We simply called them contractors but unfortunately, they could also be rascals. On my first detailed tour of the central warehouse, I became aware of what was stored here in very large quantities. There was cod in 50-kilo sacks, salt, flour, wheat, rice, soy flour, dried milk, corn, beans, rolled oats, sugar, dried yeast, egg powder, children's food, emergency rations, palm oil, and butter fat, but also wool blankets, tents, clothes, soap and much more. Unfortunately, most of the flour was infected by insects and beetles thrived in the cold store. The first thing I did was arrange for the 1,100 tons of Australian flour to be shifted onto pallets. All the sacks were piled up in several square towers reaching under the roof of the flour warehouse. This work was very exhausting, the dusty workers sweating profusely in the humid heat under the corrugated iron roofs. I kept praising them, understanding when they took a breather. Finally, our pest controller Mennel was able to take action. He had all the flour sack towers carefully wrapped in plastic and sealed. Then he laid plastic tubing lines, tucked their ends under the plastic covers, and poured gas into them. All gates were locked in a flash. No one was allowed to enter the flour warehouse until the next day. This gassing process was the only remaining possibility to save the precious flour from total loss. Around 150 tons of dried cod fish were stored in another building and those small, voracious beetles also appreciated this important protein food. We could even hear these parasites when we stood in front of the stacked bales. A soft nibble was clearly audible and uninterrupted, day and night. A noise that annoyed us greatly. There were bales that came to weigh 30 kilos instead of 50 because of these beetles. So, there was a need to hurry if we didn't want to end up with empty sacks one day! Here, too, the expert Mennel was the savior. He had brought smoke candles from Lagos. Some of them were lit after work and the gates were hermetically sealed. The effect could be seen the next morning. The beetles had left the stockfish and now lay dead in their tens of thousands on the cement floor, needing to be swept up. Unfortunately, we had to repeat this smoke candle procedure a few more times to get rid of the bugs completely. The dried cod had now been smoked, but that didn't detract from its popularity in any way.

I slowly got to know the local management staff better. The most important employee was Gabriel Nnam: reliable, competent, and respected by everyone. He had been working in these warehouses, which belonged to the United African Company (UAC), before the war broke out. The ICRC was now allowed to use them for this humanitarian action. Daniel Quovo, the Chief Security man, also worked here. You could also rely on him completely, he was indispensable. Later, when I opened a Red Cross bakery in Enugu, it would have been impossible without him and his support.

Hezekia Nnamchi, our accountant, also sat in our own office. He conscientiously wrote down all the incoming and outgoing stocks in his big book. Careful records were also kept of the deliveries and maintenance of the trucks and Land Rovers. Every two weeks, together with Mrs. Johnson, we collected the pay for all local employees from our American area coordinator Allan Platt. Mrs. Johnson was the ICRC Treasurer in Enugu and was the wife of the Rev. Kingsley Johnson, an English Methodist minister. Our typist Emanuel Nnamani was also in another office. He wrote the letters to the medical teams, the police, the ICRC in Lagos, and whatever other correspondence arose. Mike, a 14-year-old boy who was on his own was the receptionist. He had marched through the Biafran bush, snuck through front lines, and finally reached Enugu. His father was a seaman on a British ship. His mother and siblings still lived in Owerri, in enclosed Biafra.

It was important to have good local cadres you could rely on, but we had many workers and they often had to be encouraged to work. Some of them kept trying to steal goods. We also employed two tailors and three carpenters to do all kinds of repairs. Apart from defective sacks, the tailors mainly repaired truck tarpaulins that had been torn by the wind. An important task to prevent the transported relief supplies from getting wet in sudden torrential downpours. These severe thunderstorms were always a great experience for me. The large masses of water fell from the sky, with a loud roar on the huge tin roofs, falling in torrents, rushing over the forecourts, and flooding them. I asked the warehouse managers to report any leaks in the roofs to me so that they could be sealed immediately. One of the workers proved to be very skilled for this task. Under no circumstances was the water allowed to drip onto the precious, life-saving food. I also made sure that all goods in all warehouses were placed on pallets to avoid any water damage from the floor. This order made me rather unpopular with the workers. This is understandable because shifting goods for days in the greenhouse heat was extremely tedious work.

Every week there was a meeting, with representatives of other aid organizations working there. The goal was to improve cooperation together to be able to look after the starving, war-disabled population even better. These meetings always took place on Wednesday mornings in the International House, which before the war was the seat of an embassy and sometimes a consulate. Andy Okoro of the Nigerian Red Cross was the Chair. A charming man with a lot of charisma and humor, which was extremely good for these meetings. In the beginning, however, I felt quite uncomfortable with my bumpy English. I still didn't understand certain words and expressions. So, I wrote them down in my notebook without anyone noticing and consulted my pocket dictionary in English/German after work. There were days when I felt as if I had been pushed into deep, cold water, but every day I was kicking hard, and gasping for air and more English.

At these intensive meetings, around 20 people sat at a large, long table. All of our field teams were represented here, as well as the police, the military, a senior doctor, the professor from a British organization, the ICRC coordinator, the transport chief, and myself, as chief of warehouses. We reported back on our activities, and the resulting problems made suggestions and asked questions. Everyone had problems that united us. We looked for solutions together or at least tried to achieve improvements, and especially to learn from mistakes made. Once I had an embarrassing incident to report. We had delivered Swiss cheese to two field teams, which had become inedible in the tropical climate. For the long journey to us in West Africa, the company which sent this cheese had cut it into long blocks and wrapped it in aluminum foil. Unnoticed by us, the cheese, had turned into mouldy, stinky cheese, a kind of inedible Limburger. So, we decided at our Wednesday meeting to bury the remaining cheese as soon as possible. At least the Biafran worms got their money's worth.

In the first days of June, on a Sunday, Guido, Monika, and I went on a trip to Achy with our area coordinator Allan Platt. After about ten kilometers, two drunken soldiers stopped us at a roadblock and refused to let us through, Red Cross emblems notwithstanding. They waved their guns in front of our Land Rover and yelled at us. It was an uncomfortable situation. Drunk soldiers in a war zone were not to be trifled with. These two were thoroughly enjoying their performance and power, which luckily for us was short-lived. Suddenly an officer drove up in a military Land Rover. He snapped at the two heroes to let us through. The two seemed sober in a flash, threw themselves into position, and shouted: "Yes sir, yes sir!"

Our Sunday excursion was not under a lucky star. As soon as we arrived in Achy, the noise of battle could be heard nearby. Behind the settlement, it sounded very similar to one of the traditional field shootings in Switzerland, only more intense. A friendly officer ran up to us, quickly explained the situation, and urged us to leave for our safety. Without discussion, we turned our Land Rover as fast as we could.

We used the way back to visit the bush clinic in Udi. It was here that I met Fred Zerfas, an experienced, kind Australian doctor. We liked each other right away. He later told me a few things about his native Australia. At the time, I had no idea, that many years later Australia would also become my new home. Fred was in the process of examining a few dozen sick Igbo patients that Sunday. Outside the clinic, I took a closer look at the trenches that had been dug and were now thickly overgrown with grass, and I was shocked. In each ditch, snakes, very venomous young green mambas a meter long, crawled slowly through the grass. All the doors would have to be closed properly at once. The nurses told me they had long since gotten used to these dangerous creatures.

On the way home, Allan, who knew the area well, drove us along an overgrown side road to the most beautiful vantage point in this area. Enugu lay at our feet. We could see a good 50 kilometers across the hilly, green country. Later I came up here alone several times, sat on a stone, and enjoyed the fantastic view, and apparent peace in this so hard-fought country. I listened to the wind in the trees and bushes, gently cooling me. And despite all the beauty, being alone up there, I always felt uneasy. I often looked over my shoulder, there was war in the country after all. The wonderful view could not hide it. This was shown by the condition of the now peaceful and large vantage point. Barely two years ago, when Enugu was still the capital of all Biafra, there was desperate fighting there. Lots of shell casings were still lying around. Enugu was attacked from there on October 4, 1967, and overtaken the same day. Many civilians were killed by the bullets when they were unable to flee quickly enough.

Just days later, Guido informed me that Magdalena and Gertrude, the two nurses from the Swiss Medical Team in Ihe, had received permission to relax on a cattle ranch for a few days. But since the women couldn't go there alone, he thought I should accompany them. "I'm going home soon, and you won't have time for such a trip after that," Guido said. I didn't need to be told twice, I eagerly prepared for the four-day trip.

We started around noon and after 100 kilometers made a brief stop at the Abakaliki mission station with the Irish priest, Father O'Connor. A few hours later we reached the village of Obudu, where we continued our journey on a bad, dirt road. This meandered through a narrow, seemingly endless valley, then rose more and more into no man's land. We hadn't seen a vehicle for a long time, and we didn't even see any soldiers. Meanwhile, night had fallen. Undeterred, I drove with my two passengers at a brisk pace around a right-hand bend when suddenly, out of nowhere, three soldiers appeared in the headlights. They jumped in the air, their automatic weapons at the ready, and roared: "STOP!" Magdalena and Gertrude cried out in shock. My foot slammed on the brake pedal, the wheels locked, while the car slid down the narrow gravel road towards the three national defenders. Finally, no more than two meters in front of them, the car stopped. The only sound I heard came from my heart. It was stuck high in my throat, throbbing loudly and wildly. I had to swallow several times. The three soldiers came to the car window; pointing guns at us, they told us to get out. They asked harshly and suspiciously for ID and our destination and skimmed the luggage. They only gradually calmed down when they finally noticed the red crosses painted on the luggage.

Now an officer came along. He explained to us that it wasn't usual to drive through here after 6 p.m. Then he politely apologized for the shock he had caused and let us move on. Magdalena and Gertrude doubted whether the idea of going to the cattle ranch had been a good one. A little later, again after another right-hand bend, another moment of shock! A large black snake, probably two meters long, slowly crossed the road. This time I accelerated and drove over it as braking was too dangerous – "close your eyes and through," was the motto here because snakes can immediately go inside a vehicle and ride along. We didn't need a black mamba, one of the most dangerous snakes in Africa, as a stowaway. Our thirst for adventure had been satisfied for the time being.

We were fed up with the remote valley, which was even more ominous in the black of night. All three of us longed for a cozy bed, away from all dangers. But we had to grit our teeth and get through the rest of the journey. The road now climbed steeper and steeper. We climbed 1,000 meters in altitude, via 22 hairpin bends, in a short time and were now at about 2000 meters above sea level. As I drove up to a large gate at the entrance to the ranch I heard, "land in sight" in my head. A boy immediately sprayed our vehicle to kill any bugs, then we were warmly welcomed to the ranch and shown to a small chalet. One room for the two women, the other for me. A familiar picture hung above the small fireplace in my rustic room: the Church of Grindelwald with the Wetterhorn Mountain – my church. My heart opened up. Nothing could happen to me now, peace reigned here. After a hearty dinner with huge steaks and vegetables, I soon fell into a long, refreshing sleep, without the usual frog concert.

For the next two days, we went on excursions on foot, wearing boots because of the snakes. We carefully walked through the almost knee-high, light green, lush grass, always expecting one snake or another. The cattle ranch was a sprawling hilly alp broken up by tree-covered indentations. The ranch, named Obudu Cattle Ranch and was noted on the Michelin Africa map, had around 2,000 cattle.

We arrived at the highest point of the alp, at almost 2,000 meters, and we once again had an exceptional view. In the distance, we saw several herds of grazing cows. Far below, no more than five kilometers away, in a deep valley, lay the border with Cameroon. The green hills and pastures on the Cameroon side offered us the same picture as here: lush vegetation, grazing cows. A peaceful, tranquil world, but on this side of the border, surrounded by a horrid civil war.

A deep, tree-covered incision in the terrain aroused our interest. As we got closer, we heard water rushing. Curious, we walked on and saw a small waterfall through the foliage of the trees. We cautiously felt our way down to its source. A natural pool of water almost tempted us to take a quick dip. With the emphasis on almost, because on the ranch we had heard that gorillas still lived in this area, albeit very shy. I, therefore, suggested we leave, I did not want to risk a handsome gorilla suddenly kidnapping Gertrude and Magdalena to add to his hairy harem.

On Monday morning we drove back towards Enugu, well rested, and with our cooling boxes full of fresh beef for the team kitchen. It took two hours before we came across another car. In Ogoja, we took the opportunity and bought stamps at the post office as the post office in Enugu was still closed. That way we could at least stamp our letters and give them to those who went to Lagos.

Our next stop was at Abakaliki Mission Station, 100 kilometers from Enugu. The Irish team leader and coordinator Father O'Connor invited us to tea and handed me a list of much-needed groceries. The Irish medical team worked there in their own bush clinic, and also organized the distribution of food. Judy Baker, a Nurse of the American Red Cross also worked there. Father O'Connor was an impressive character who liked to smoke his pipe and had lived in Abakaliki for 20 years. He knew the country like no other. A wise, interesting man and shrewd advisor: I listened to him spellbound. In the late afternoon, we drove on, having to stop briefly at every roadblock. Again and again, we passed heavily armed Nigerian Federal soldiers, marching single file to their nighttime positions. Their enemies, the Biafrans, liked to raid at night, if possible, during a thunderstorm. They withdrew just as quickly afterward. The Nigerians defended the roads while the Biafrans controlled the bush.

A week later it was time. As agreed, Guido Müller and Gerhard Penka returned to Europe. They said goodbye to me and wished me success. From then on, I had to find my way on my own, but I also gave the local managers more responsibility. I started doing this immediately, and it worked quickly and well. Agbo, my first man in camp 2, was aware of his responsibility when the suppliers delivered rice or beans by the truckload. He knew that every fifth sack had to be weighed and that poor quality or defective sacks had to be rejected. Two men per truck counted the sacks; and independently of each other. They had to be responsible for their work, had to keep accurate lists, and sign them. The same system was applied to outsourcing. I kept making random checks, counting sacks, boxes, and cans. In the case of blatant, presumably intentional mistakes, I showed no mercy and dismissed them immediately. That was important to show that sloppiness and trickery would not be tolerated. For me, Red Cross goods were never just any goods. In all my years of service around the world, I always saw the countless donors behind this, who made help for the needy possible in the first place. Many of these donors, perhaps not wealthy themselves, helped to alleviate great hardship. Because of this, I had zero tolerance for poor behavior. The security men: Daniel, Felix, Amos, and Emmanuel, were careful and checked meticulously. But even they sometimes underestimated the ingenuity of those who stole. To my great satisfaction, we usually found them out. The police also worked meticulously, asked for several copies of the criminal complaint in writing, and then we had to trot up to the police building with witnesses. It was important for us to maintain a good and relaxed relationship with the police. During one of my visits to the station, I had a very special experience. As I walked through the yard a door opened. Three police officers came out, along with a boy of about eighteen in gym shorts and a T-shirt. Two police officers grabbed him and laid him face down on a wooden table in the yard. Then they pulled his pants down. Now the third policeman took up a long rod, stood by, and, while another counted slowly, began to smack the boy's bare bottom; twelve times, fortunately not too strongly. But with every hit, the boy screamed: "Ouch!" I smiled: he could speak Swiss German! That made me like him. I had to grin whether I wanted to or not. With an offended face but hardly any visible traces, the boy then climbed down from the table and quickly pulled his gym shorts back up to make his slightly damaged buttocks disappear. When I asked why one of the police officers replied: "The guy lied to us. That was the payoff." Tough but fair and hopefully educational.

A little later, one of our warehouses was broken into. Our check showed that four sacks of salt were missing. The perpetrator was caught trying to sell the salt in the market. Unfortunately, one of our carpenters was the culprit, which I deeply regretted. As a result, I had to testify several times at the main police station and finally even appear in court. In Enugu at this time the banks closed, the post office and the prison were nothing but ruined walls, but the judiciary functioned. When the judge appeared in court at 10:00 a.m. that day, in robes and sunglasses, everyone present immediately stood up in awe. A police officer urged the judge to try our case first because the Red Cross was providing humanitarian aid here. The judge complied with this request and waved me forward to the witness stand. There a woman took my right hand and placed it on a Bible. I had to repeat after her to tell nothing but the truth and only the truth. Then it started. Everything they wanted to know from me: the judge, the prosecutor, the defence attorney. Other witnesses were questioned. Finally, after an hour of interrogation, I was able to leave. A week later, the carpenter was found guilty and sentenced to two years in prison. A harsh penalty for stealing four sacks of salt. For me, however, it was an impressive experience in a country shaken by civil war.

No sooner had this theft been filed, during a routine check after work, I noticed that most of the hinge screws on the inside of a warehouse door were missing. Probably in preparation for a night-time burglary. The Chief of Police authorized three additional police officers to lurk in this warehouse at night. As early as daybreak I came back myself and yelled very loudly: "I'm the Red Cross chief. I am coming in now!" Then I slowly opened the big gate and announced myself loudly a second time, just to be on the safe side. But I could already hear gun breechblocks being locked in the semi-darkness. In shock, I looked up at a pile of rice sacks where three-gun barrels were pointed at me as the cops yelled, "Hands up!" My arms shot up like something out of a gangster movie. Now they finally recognized me. Quite shocked, I was allowed to put my hands down again. The three guards carefully climbed down the sacks and said, in embarrassed voices: "Sorry, sir." I swallowed hard. That could easily have gone wrong. No burglars had come that night, but from then on, I didn't send any more police officers on the lookout and I replaced the missing screws at the door hinges.

The longer the more than a thousand tons of flour from Australia remained in storage, the more urgent it became to use it. We sent flour samples from different bags to the laboratory in Lagos for analysis. The answer was positive: the flour, even if it was no longer of the best quality, could still be used after being sieved. But there was a lack of flour orders from the teams. Even an appeal by correspondence to everyone was of little use. Still, I started to take action. My original job as a baker helped me with this. First, I sent Daniel, the former Enugu taxi driver, to look for empty bakeries. I had the idea of getting into Red Cross bread production myself. Daniel found two such properties within a very short time. Although he knew the street on which three other bakeries had been located, he could no longer find them under the jungle of overgrown plants. The very next day, accompanied by a police officer and four workers armed with machetes, we set off, determined to find the remaining three bakeries that had disappeared. Our search was rewarded. But all five bakery buildings were completely covered and overgrown with climbing plants, practically disappearing under a blanket of green. The workers immediately started hacking with machetes, looking under the thicket on the wall of the house for a bakery sign. A true task of Sisyphus in the sultry atmosphere, but adventurous, exotic, and exciting - everything to my liking. Surprises and failures presented us as we hacked away climbing plants. It felt like we were on a treasure hunt for Solomon's diamonds. The plants had entered the houses through open windows and doors and had even put down new roots here and there in the dirt. After hours of searching, hacking, and sweating in these uninhabited ghost quarters, where rats, mice, snakes, and other unwelcome creatures felt at home, we finally brought "our" five bakeries back to light. Now it was time to weigh up and decide which of these bakeries was most useful to us. I decided on the one that was best preserved, which was the "States Bakery," on Umonovo Street, in the uninhabited Ogui district. The wood-burning oven had to be repaired first because of a crack in the wall, and some rusted-through roof panels and two rotten ceiling beams also had to be replaced. The cleaning of the rooms littered with dirt and rubbish was more than a *tour-de-force*. Mucking out and scrubbing was done with a lot of energy and even more enthusiasm. "My" bakery had to be clean! To our great delight, in one of the rooms, we found hundreds of rectangular black baking pans that were perfect for getting into the bread business.

Next, I applied in writing to the Chief of Police for an operating licence. He took a look at our bakery himself, agreed immediately, and off we went. But then the owner of the property suddenly got in touch, demanding compensation or rent. Andy Okoro from the Nigerian Red Cross in Enugu drew up the relevant contract. As rent, the bakery owner received an agreed percentage of flour for his own use. That was fine with us and a cost-effective solution since the flour had to be used up quickly one way or another. While the carpenters and a bricklayer carried out the necessary repairs, workers cleared the building of overgrown plants and dirt, cleaned the equipment and I called for a few bakers. At least 200 men were already standing in front of my office the next morning. Each of them claimed to be a baker. However, they had no certificates - unfortunately, these were lost in the war. I smiled to myself because I recognized some of these "bakers" immediately. When I was looking for carpenters, they presented as carpenters. When I was looking for tailors, they had pretended to be tailors. Nevertheless, I found real bakers among these many applicants - despite the lack of certificates. It was enough to ask technical questions to separate the wheat from the chaff. First of all, of the four bakers that were hired, one spoke English. He was appointed boss. Then I had flour, salt, and dry yeast brought to the now fully functional and spotlessly clean bakery. In addition to the water in plastic barrels, firewood also had to be carted in to heat the oven. First, all the flour was time-consumingly hand-sifted to eliminate the dead insects, which looked like small black ants. The making of the bread dough was also done by hand. We had a large rectangular wooden trough available for this purpose. Then we all waited

TO THE HORIZON AND BEYOND

anxiously for the moment when the first Red Cross Biafra bread could be taken out of the oven. It smelled like a bakery now, and the bread had that nice brown crust, but the loaves were flat and heavy, almost like bricks. Quite a disappointment for us bakers. The long journey and the prolonged storage in the heat did not do the Australian flour any good. So we started tinkering, trying more yeast, heating the water more, and letting it ferment longer. Little by little, we were rewarded for our efforts with better and better bread quality. Soon we were able to hire additional bakers and two helpers to utilize the bakery even better and make more bread. Eight hundred to a thousand loaves were being made every day, six days a week. But really good, tasty bread, the way I liked and dreamed of, unfortunately never happened. The quality of the aged flour was too poor. Even all the tinkering didn't help. But surprisingly with the medical teams and their distribution points in the front area, in the Enugu hospital, and in the two orphanages, our bread was very popular and a welcome additional source of food. We got some praise for it. But just as important for us journeyman bakers were the deep satisfaction that this vast amount of flour could be saved from spoiling and helped to alleviate the famine far and wide. We were only able to achieve this thanks to my experience as a baker, which I had learned many years before.

In addition to baking bread, there was another way to process flour. Kpoff-kpoff (pronounced poff-poff), is a popular dish in Nigeria. For this purpose, a dough is made from flour, egg, milk powder, a little sugar, and yeast, and formed into balls. These balls are fried in hot palm oil. Nigerian-style donuts are sold in shops and markets. One day an Igbo woman came to my office with a bright idea. She offered to make kpoff-kpoffs like this for the Red Cross if we provided the ingredients. The usual margin was fifty-fifty. In other words, we got half the kpoff-kpoff, and she was allowed to sell her half in the market as a reward. Since we had the ingredients, in stock, we gave it a try. It worked so well that I signed a contract with this woman. She delivered us our share of kpoff-kpoffs every day, punctual as clockwork. Soon I had five women under kpoff-kpoff contracts.

* * * * *

The business prospered to the great delight of all of us. From then on, we delivered the kpoff-kpoff together with the bread to our people. The five women – three of whom were war widows – all had several children. They had to work hard to get them fed and grow. These women started before four o'clock in the morning to make the kpoff-kpoff, deliver half to us and sell the other half at the market.

The development of our bakery brought me closer to the population. The co-operation with the kpoff-kpoff market women resulted in a reliable give and take that was good for all of us. I received the proof of this unexpectedly.

One day I was sick in bed, unable to get up and I sent Seppli, as we called our reliable house boy, to the warehouse with the heavy bunch of keys to take a message to the entire workforce: "Today you can and must show that you can do it without Hansrudi." For my part, I began to shiver miserably. Francis, our Igbo cook, brought more and more blankets and covered me completely. Although it was hot outside, I continued to shake and felt freezing cold. So, I put on socks, pulled a cap over my ears, and crept deep under the mountain of blankets. But I couldn't get the extreme shivering cold under control. Presumably, somewhere along the way, an infected Biafran mosquito had chosen me as a blood donor, bit me, and triggered a hearty dose of malaria. Early in the morning, Monika Stalder quickly put some aspirins on my bedside table before she drove to the bush clinic in Udi. At 8 a.m. a doctor came to examine me. I was happy that this tall, slim American Dr. Jim Shonkwiler from Indianapolis – who everyone just called Jungle Jim – was standing in front of me as I was shaking with fever. He was an original, a joker always full of mischief. He walked around all day with a stethoscope in his breast pocket, smiling mischievously when teased about it. But today I was glad to see Jungle Jim standing in front of me with his stethoscope. I immediately sat up in bed, trembling all over, so Jungle Jim could place his famous listening device on my chest and back. That took quite a while. He repeatedly frowned, shook his head carefully, and finally said, with a straight face: "I'm really sorry, Hansrudi, but you only have one hour to live. Can I grant you one last wish?" "Yes, Jim," I said. "My last wish is that you get out of my room as quickly as possible!" Laughing and waving, he ran away and soon afterward sent a messenger with malaria tablets to my room.

    Word got around quickly that I was ill. Daniel was soon the next visitor in front of my bed. He wanted to know if he could use my Land Rover to take the day's bread to the camps, orphanages, and the hospital, as his truck was broken. Of course, he was allowed to, so I could continue to devote myself entirely to shivering. Soon after "Speedy Gonzales" entered the room, a likable much respected young doctor from Colombia. He looked into my feverish eyes, mumbled something in his colorful special dialect, a mixture of Spanish, English, and German, looked at my medication and disappeared again. Shortly thereafter, Agbo knocked and reported that two articulated trucks with wheat from Oturkpo had arrived, asking whether the freight should be brought to store seven or better still to store 18. As soon as that was settled and I snuggled up in my blankets again, Lucy Ugoyi, one of the kpoff-kpoff women came up to my bed. She brought me oranges and said, "When I found out that you were ill Hansrudi, I immediately asked around." That's how she found out where I lived and hurried over. Because the only chair in the room was occupied, Lucy, uncomplicated as she was, sat down next to me on the bed and looked at me with concern. Suddenly I felt a little less cold, being ill took a back seat, and I even started dreaming. For the first time I noticed how pretty this young war widow with the blue headscarf was. Especially when she laughed and flashed her perfect snow-white teeth. My goodness, the fever attacks were getting more and more dramatic with my first day of illness in this distant, war-torn country.

Lucy had barely left when there was another knock. Now Felicia and Grace, two other kpoff-kpoff ladies, came into the sickroom with worried expressions. They also brought oranges, asked how I was, wished me a speedy recovery, and sat down – somewhat hesitantly – on the edge of the bed. We chatted about their kpoff-kpoff production, the raw materials they needed their children, and much more. The conversation ended abruptly when a very friendly English doctor, George Hobbs, entered. He had brought along Patience Opara, the black nurse from the Nigerian Red Cross. However, her eyes darkened as soon as she saw the two Igbo women sitting on my bed. With a grim look on her face, Patience immediately shooed the two away. Girlfriends, even if they were supposed to be friends, had no place in my sickroom. She would have been amazed had I told her that these two women were my business partners in kpoff-kpoff production. When Felicia and Grace fled my room, George stuck a thermometer in my mouth. Indeed, Hansrudi had a high fever today. Who was to blame malaria or my visitors? What a day! No chance of restful rest. In between, our good house boy Seppli brewed a black tea for me and put a few biscuits out as well. The next visitor to my hospital room, also an American, was the new area coordinator, Allan Whear. He only stayed until blonde Alison Begbie walked in, a very experienced, personable Australian nurse. She had come to Enugu from the Awgu Bush Clinic to prepare for her journey home to Melbourne. To distract me, Alison proudly told me about her climb of Kilimanjaro in Tanzania last year and checked my pulse at the same time. I don't know what the trigger was, malaria, the strong tea, or maybe even Alison. Suddenly I suffered a profuse sweat; so blatantly that I thought I was sitting in the sauna in Zurich-Seebach. While our Seppli changed the sheets Alison toweled me dry again. I lay down exhausted and was finally able to fall asleep.

The next visitors trundled in after work and woke me up. It was our four car mechanics who wanted to know how I was doing. Although I felt a little better, I was bathed in sweat again, exhausted and longing for rest. So, I was secretly very happy that the four Swiss colleagues quickly said goodbye. But I felt a warmth inside me that had nothing to do with my fever. The certainty that so many people cared for me, visited me, and made me happy touched me deeply. Doctors, nurses, kpoff-kpoff women and workmates had come to cure, cheer, entertain, and bring me gifts. Who would have thought? I could not have been better cared for in any Swiss hospital than here in Biafra. Both things probably helped me to get back on my feet quickly: the medication and the caring people around me. Still a little weak, but extremely grateful, I returned to my work the next morning, but malaria forced me to bed two more times. Both times the miraculous was repeated. Doctors and friends looked after me and quickly got me well again.

In mid-July, we had a distinguished visitor. Our supreme boss, Mr. Naville, President of the ICRC in Geneva, landed at the otherwise closed Enugu airfield. He was visibly pleased with the cleanliness, order, and control system in the warehouses. I took the unique opportunity and handed him a list of urgently needed items. Next, Mr. Naville took a look at the Swiss mechanics' vehicle repair shop, where Mario Kropf was in charge. The men had a lot to repair. The many bad roads and paths took a toll on our Land Rovers and trucks. The work was done in an empty Niger Motors facility. We also refuelled our vehicles there. One of the mechanics, Peter Amacher, was also from the Bernese Oberland. He came from Brienzwiler. We met again years later in Bangladesh and became friends. The team at the Swiss Bush Clinic in Ihe also received a visit from Mr. Naville. So, in the afternoon, we Swiss accompanied our top boss from Geneva to the small waiting plane. Before leaving, he thanked us all for our important work in war-ravaged Biafra and for what we had done so far.

Ihe, where the Swiss team's bush clinic was stationed, was about 30 kilometers from Enugu, in the direction of Awka. This bush clinic was slightly elevated on a small hill. Up to 200 patients lay on simple straw mats. Dr. Ruckstuhl from Kloten, near Zurich, was the team boss, his wife worked as a nurse. Madeleine was part of the Swiss team as were Magdalena and Gertrude, with whom I had visited the cattle ranch. A few local employees completed the team. They all had their hands full with so many sick, malnourished people. Such a medical team also required an administrator who, in addition to completing the paperwork, was responsible for maintenance, warehouse management, and food distribution. In Ihe, Peter Künzi from Biel carried this responsibility. This team had its own truck at its disposal, which simplified the organization considerably. So, on certain days, Peter, with a nurse and helpers, drove the truck, fully loaded with rice, beans, dried cod, and more to the surrounding villages. The team was always greeted with the same picture when they drove into a particular village. On the village square, two to three thousand people sat in rows on the ground and patiently waited for the food to be poured into the containers they had brought with them. First however, the skinny stockfish had to be chopped into pieces about 10 centimeters long with an axe. A tedious job because the fish were almost as hard as wood. Next door, the food they had brought with them was cooked in halved barrels over a wood fire. Only then could the distribution of food to the seated begin. To get food, they had to be able to produce a corresponding ticket. Unfortunately, those who didn't have a ticket went away empty-handed. It was doctors who issued such cards, and exclusively to those people who urgently needed help. The food also had to be eaten on the spot under supervision. This procedure had become necessary because it had been learned that the food of the weaker, more needy people had been taken away by the stronger ones. Only when everyone had eaten were they allowed to get up again. So, nobody could be served twice. Only thanks to such strict rules was a fair distribution of food guaranteed. The Igbo chiefs were always responsible for the smooth running. The nurse usually found sick people among these needy people. These were picked up on the truck and taken to the clinic. It was always the children who were hit the hardest by the famine. The sight of thin limbs, swollen belly, sad suffering, pleading eyes was hard to bear. You never get used to that.

The English medical team in Uturu was housed in a former mission school. Brother James, an Irishman and like all missionaries a very kind man, drove me in his car from Uturu to the former Red Cross Hospital in Okigwe one Sunday morning. A year earlier, Nigerian soldiers had shot dead four white members of the Red Cross during a military attack. Among them was an elderly English couple who were buried next to a church in Okigwe. I put flowers on their grave a few times.

The front was still near Okigwe and Uturu. When I slept in Uturu, I heard explosions and booming machine gun fire. This battle noise regularly prevented me from falling asleep. So, I sat down at the window and followed the tracers in the sky, bringing death and destruction in the darkness. I wondered anxiously how long this terrible war would last; how many more innocent people would starve to death. It was no different for my colleagues. This war, which claimed more and more disabled, starving, and dying people, motivated all of us to work faster and longer. But ideas for cheering up were always very welcome. One day the Swiss car mechanics decided to restore the Enugu Sports Club's rather neglected swimming pool, which had been closed for a long time. There was still enough chlorine, and surprisingly the filter system also worked without any problems. We all looked forward to the opening day but did not expect any surprise. No sooner had I passed the entrance gate when I was grabbed and mercilessly thrown, in a high arc into the water, in clothes and shoes. Whether it was a doctor or an English professor, everyone was tossed fully clothed into the swimming pool. Nobody got angry, on the contrary, everyone joined in the fun and laughed and helped throw the next victim into the water. From then on, the swimming pool offered everyone a welcome and refreshing change from their otherwise rather monotonous free time.

Jungle Jim and I started jogging as a hobby. Twice a week we started running – always before dinner – and ran two laps of 2.5 kilometers each. For the locals, it was something utterly alien to see two pale faces running in gym shorts. But they quickly got used to this strange behavior. The hilly route we chose also led through a roadblock. As we once again approached this checkpoint at a brisk pace, the Nigerian soldier standing guard confronted us at the point with a rifle. He probably thought we were on the run. But we didn't want to be stopped, duped him by waving at him with a laugh and simply ignoring his gun. Jungle Jim had pointed meaningfully to the Red Cross emblem on his shirt, and we jogged past his puzzled face. During the next round and thus our second passage, he understood. Now he was laughing too, waving his rifle at us shouting, "Go, go!"

One Sunday, Andy Okoro, head of the Nigerian Red Cross, organized a football match for the benefit of war orphans. An army team played against a police team at the Enugu football stadium. Countless soldiers, police officers, locals, and we Red Cross people made the pilgrimage to the stadium to cheer on the players. There was a great atmosphere that made us forget the war for a while. A military band played deafeningly loud Nigerian folk music throughout the match. The charity match ended fairly in a draw: 3-3.

Every now and then we would go out in Enugu after dinner to relax and quench our thirst. I always joined our car mechanics. There were still a few restaurants in town where you could buy bottled beer. That's where we were drawn to. We always found it interesting to watch and talk to the other local guests, all of whom were younger. Mostly Nigerian music was played from records or cassettes. It sounded exotic to our ears, but also light and lively. Now and then, in the absence of female guests, two or more young men would dance to these Nigerian tunes. They seemed to fall into a trance, suppressed war and suffering for a short time, and certainly also dream of a peaceful life.

One night, when we arrived at the Day Spring restaurant for a beer, we found bleeding, shocked people in front of the building. At the same time, two dark green Land Rovers roared up and stopped right next to us, their brakes squealing. About a dozen heavily armed MPs jumped out, some stormed in, others sealed the entrance and began questioning people. What happened? A policeman explained to us: "Someone threw a bomb into the restaurant, which immediately exploded." For us, this was the signal to take a right turn, drive back home and get the after-work beer out of the fridge, even though beer in a Biafran "pub" somehow tasted better.

Two or three weeks later, our thirst irresistibly lured us towards a pub. We boldly set off, and ventured into another restaurant, cautiously looking around. We strategically sat down at a table that offered some protection to the side of the counter and we ordered the longed-for beer. The young Igbo landlady was happy to have guests and personally served us. We liked it there! It didn't stop with this one beer, because this beer was really tasty, and the music was good too. After the third beer, the four of us started to brag. When a colleague had to go to the toilet, he immediately and excitedly ran back in a flash, without closing the door to the toilet. Pale and with wide-open eyes, he hissed at us: "Pay now and get out of here! There's a bomb in the toilet!" One of them hastily paid the surprised landlady and alerted her about the bomb. We all got up at the same time and hastily left the bar. However, I couldn't resist taking a quick look into the toilet room. Sure enough, there, under the sink, was a flat plastic sack with a round object sticking out of it. Disturbingly, insulated wires seemed attached to it. This brief glance was enough: whether it was a real bomb or just a nasty joke, we drove straight to the police to report this object. For a long time, we had absolutely no desire to visit the inn.

I experienced another episode while walking in Enugu city center one day. Suddenly three military police officers armed with automatic guns came toward me. I recognized one of them immediately, his name was Victor. He beamed at me and greeted me happily. "Where are you going?" I asked him. He laughed mischievously: "We're hunting women all day today!" I thought I had misheard: "And you need submachine guns for that?" I replied, amazed. "Of course, it's much faster that way," says Victor proudly. "We don't have to haggle for long, the women always agree to come along immediately. All we have to do is raise our weapons slightly!" Now that was enough for me. I said reprovingly, "And I always thought you were a decent soldier. I'm disappointed. What are you doing with these women?" Victor laughed again and happily explained to me: "We take these women to the hospital to donate blood. The doctors don't always have enough blood to treat our wounded soldiers." Quite relieved and now also laughing, I said goodbye to these three successful woman hunters.

I also liked to use my non-working Sundays for short visits to our medical teams in the bush. A good opportunity to deepen personal contacts as well as to discuss problems and the current situation, and I always drove back to Enugu with a list of urgently needed goods. So I was able to combine one of my favorite leisure activities with something useful. Such journeys could be quite dangerous at times. I was driving on a lonely bush road on a Sunday like this when my passenger Daniel suddenly shouted in panic, "STOP!" Now I too saw and heard the two small planes diving in our direction! We threw ourselves out of the car, dived into the ditch, and held our breath. Meanwhile, the two pilots steered their machines low over us, then immediately pulled them up again. Nothing happened! But my heart had raced with fear. I then assumed that it was Swedish mercenary pilots who flew for Biafra and only attacked Nigerian targets. Maybe they spotted the big red crosses on our Land Rover, or maybe we just weren't a worthwhile target. Only now, after the shock had subsided, did I notice that we were not only lying in the ditch but also in high grass, where snakes like to be. We left the uncomfortable place quickly and quietly and drove meekly to the next checkpoint. There, too, the two low-flying aircraft had caused a stir.

Another incident happened when I was traveling alone between Udi and Awka. I was driving up the narrow, sloping road lined with tall grass when a soldier came into view at the checkpoint there. He was kicking a person lying on the ground with his boots. I accelerated, and immediately sounded the horn, and it was deafening. The guy stopped! "What a lousy guy!" I said to myself – in the widest Grindelwalder dialect. I pulled over, jumped out of the Land Rover, and ran towards him angrily. I didn't care about his rifle slung over his shoulder. I yelled at him about what he was thinking, punching down a defenceless woman. The "hero" was speechless, and looked down in embarrassment, while the woman, writhing on the floor in pain, wept. Now I suddenly heard someone laughing behind my back. I turned around immediately. A second gunman was standing on the raised curb in front of the small checkpoint shack, grinning. He was oddly delighted that his comrade had received a verbal beating from me, and the explosive situation was defused. Now I helped the poor woman to her feet, led her to my Land Rover, and told her to get in. At the same time, she made me understand in sparse English that the two guys had also taken money from her: two Nigerian pounds. So, I went back to the two guys and categorically and firmly demanded the return of the money directly into the hand of the woman, which also shamed the two. These two checkpoint highwaymen mistreated the poor woman because they hoped to get even more money from her. I did not accept such behavior at any time and from anyone. I wanted to know from the two men in uniform where their officer was stationed, and what his name was. So, I drove straight on to the village after that and reported the incident to the lieutenant in question. He was visibly embarrassed about the crime I described, especially when the woman showed him her injuries. He expressly apologized and promised to investigate the incident the same day and hold the two soldiers accountable. I took the woman to Awka, where she was treated in the Red Cross clinic. One team member advised me to look the other way in such dangerous situations. But a Grindelwalder cannot do that, especially not when he is a Red Cross delegate and proudly wears the ICRC badge on his chest.

If we had been able to reach the medical field teams by telephone, we would have been spared many dangerous journeys. But the entire local telephone network was paralyzed and radio contact with the teams in this confusing combat area was not permitted. However, there was radio contact between the capital Lagos and Enugu, as well as between Enugu and the Oturkpo train station, 170 kilometers away. Aid that had arrived by train had to be loaded onto trucks and transported to Enugu because the Biafrans had blown up several railway bridges on their retreat. A young Dutchman, Jan van der Kolk, was in charge of the reloading in Oturkpo. Every evening we discussed the current situation over the radio. In order to bring the relief supplies delivered by train from Lagos to Oturpo to Enugu, we had to use additional civilian trucks. We had a contract with the entrepreneur Alhaji Nasidi in Oturpo, and the cooperation was good.

One day Mr Nasidi came to my office and reported that a few days ago he had nearly been killed by a corrupt sergeant at a roadblock 60 kilometers from Enugu. The man had asked him for seven

Nigerian pounds (around 85 Swiss francs) plus a crate of beer, which he had with him in the cabin. He had no choice but to meet these conditions. But the non-commissioned officer would not let the poor man continue and sent him the 100 or so kilometers back to Oturpo. This was obviously a serious case of corruption against the Red Cross. So, I immediately contacted our head of transport, Mario Kropf, who in turn drove straight to the head of the military police in Enugu, an old warhorse he knew well. He had the sergeant arrested immediately and taken to Enugu. The man was demoted and sent to the front. This set an example that such corrupt machinations would entail draconian penalties.

A black telephone stood ready to hand on my desk. However, it never bothered me while working as the line was dead. As already mentioned, this always gave me a good reason to visit the teams, especially at the weekend. We also made do with quickly written letters that we gave to the drivers, doctors, or nurses for the field teams. But the answers were often a long time coming. Time was hardly ever on our side. Over time, I knew the many remote side roads and winding roads almost by heart. Despite the white Land Rover and large red crosses painted on it, I always felt a slight uneasiness in certain "difficult" areas. In a war so close to the front – especially on a rainy day – no Red Cross person can rely on the RC emblems. Attacking soldiers instinctively fire immediately. It was no different in the Biafra war when RC delegates were shot. I was always aware that something unexpected could happen at any time: an ambush by Biafran soldiers, crossfire, Biafran planes, or drunk soldiers at the next roadblock. There were endless possibilities for incidents of this kind. At the roadblocks, soldiers often asked to be taken to the next village or the one after that. Without exception, these requests were always refused. The Red Cross must never transport soldiers and must always remain strictly neutral and independent. That was the case then and it is no different today.

One day, two experienced American nurses, Madie and Barbara, asked me if I could drive them on a discovery tour. Of course, I said yes straight away. The two women did not want to travel alone to new territory recently conquered by the Nigerians. Although they had heard that fighting was still going on in some places, the civilian population there urgently needed help. So, Madie and Barbara decided to explore the situation themselves. I didn't know exactly which area it was. It was always difficult to orientate oneself in this hilly, green bush region and to find one's way, especially on side roads or bush paths, even if you already knew them. With Madie and Barbara, on the other hand, I was breaking completely new ground. We didn't have a compass, so it was easy to lose general direction and get lost. In a war zone, that was dangerous. Signposts and place-name signs had long since been removed, and we had no local road maps available. In unfamiliar, confusing areas, you had to be careful, otherwise, you could drive through a weakly manned front line and arrive at the other side of the front, drive over a landmine, taken prisoner or even get shot. During my time in this region this fortunately never happened to anybody among us.

Another even greater danger, however, were possible landmines. Those invisible death traps terrified me the most. This exploratory trip with Madie and Barbara had it all. I remember very well how we struggled to find the right turn, carefully ask our way to a specific spot we assumed were the quarters of the local military commander. To make matters worse, most of the locals we encountered didn't speak English. I knew all too well I should have taken Daniel with me. But my little Land Rover only had room for three people in the cabin and the hold was stuffed to the brim with blankets, clothes, and a few sacks of corn-soy flour (CSM) as first aid for the starving local population. Now and then we would hear gunfire, and look at each other questioningly, "Shall we go on? Or should we perhaps turn back?" We agreed without saying a word: "Turning back is not an option." In this area, which was still unfamiliar to us, an unknown but certainly large number of suffering people were waiting for help. If we capitulated, those poor people would continue to be completely at the mercy of their terrible fate. So, we drove on, grimly determined. Although "drive" is the wrong word. Rather, we cautiously felt our way forward; from one village to the next. Finally, we met some soldiers who described the way to the military quarters. A little later, at a checkpoint, we were told: "Get out and leave the Land Rover behind." One of the soldiers standing guard there led us along a winding path through the bush. This seemed adventurous to me, and I had a queasy feeling. Suddenly we stood in front of a simple house that was well camouflaged by thick bushes. Only now did we see two guards standing in the bushes. Our companion announced us in the house and we were allowed to enter. A higher officer told us to take a seat in the almost dark room. A single small window provided some light. The officer seemed pleased to be able to greet us foreigners. After we had explained to him the reason for our coming, he stated that the situation here was not completely under control. Therefore, he could not guarantee our safety. If we still wanted to continue, he could provide an escort. We gave him two replies: "Yes, we want to continue. No, we are not allowed to be accompanied by soldiers." We also explained to him why we could not accept his noble gesture. With an army escort, we would implicate Red Cross people with the military, and we absolutely had to always remain neutral. The officer understood that and drew us a small sketch of the dirt roads and villages in the vicinity. When we said goodbye, he asked us to move exclusively within this sketch. In this way, he guaranteed us a kind of safe conduct. At least I hoped so, but I had good reason to believe it because the Nigerian officers treated us Red Cross people courteously everywhere. They showed themselves helpful and also grateful because we took care of the needy civilian population. Thanks to this drawing, we found our way around quickly on the onward journey.

Turning off at the right place went smoothly. Within a short time, we came across several villages. From time-to-time gunfire could be heard quite close by, but we no longer let ourselves be unsettled or distracted, as the helpful officer had assured us of safe conduct within this area. It was as we had feared: there were refugees everywhere in the villages. Many children had swollen legs, bloated bellies, and sometimes swollen eyes, like after a bee sting. The adults seemed to be in better shape. We had been told that parents would eat first and then the children would have what was left over. Was that perhaps the real reason for the unusually high infant mortality rate in the Biafra war? I secretly asked myself that from time to time. I had observed something disturbing several times in places where we had organised first food distribution: there were women carrying fruit and vegetables on their heads on their way to the market. On their backs, they carried a small child who was obviously starving. However, this was by no means the rule, especially not in the remote, isolated villages. There was also a lack of responsible Igbo chiefs who organised and called for mutual help in the most difficult times. Not all Igbo chiefs were strong leaders who could take their responsibility seriously with a strong common-sense leadership.

On this first day of exploration, in an area still unknown to us, the help we brought with us did not go far. The few clothes, blankets, and CSM food were quickly distributed. It pained us that we couldn't have taken more with us for this reconnaissance. Upon our return, Madie and Barbara immediately checked in with our RC coordinator. Their wish was to be able to transport relief supplies, especially food, to the new area as quickly as possible. The Nigerians were making a slow and tenacious advance. For its part, the ICRC had set itself the goal of returning to the recently conquered villages as quickly as possible, to be able to quickly alleviate the suffering of the civilian population there.

In the autumn a new British team arrived in Enugu that would be based at Awka. This small town on the road to Onitsha on the Niger lay in ruins. Akwa was probably the most hotly contested places in Biafra at the time. The occupying forces had changed several times. Awka was still a frontline territory, with the Federals the occupying power. Because of the large number of refugees in the area, it was imperative to station a medical team there. Finding a suitable building in this small town was difficult because most of the houses had been destroyed. After a thorough search, the people from the Nigerian Red Cross finally found a damaged but still habitable house and were permitted to use it. The British team was able to move in. However, the necessary furniture was missing. Again, I was responsible for that. So, I went with Daniel to Enugu to buy suitable used furniture. That worked quite well. One of our trucks became a furniture moving van, which – with Daniel as driver – transported the valuable freight to Awka. Our head of transport, Mario Kropf, and I followed in the Land Rover. After unloading at Awka, Daniel drove the truck back to Enugu empty while Mario and I helped set up the British team who were already there. We were so busy with this work that we forgot the time. When we looked at the clock again, it was already too late to be back in Enugu before nightfall. Since we were forbidden to drive at night, to be on the safe side, we always had our narrow, foldable camp beds with us in our luggage. This also included a tiny can opener and tin cans as emergency rations. So, a cold dinner was taken care of because we didn't want to be a burden to the English team. They didn't have it much better. At least they could settle down on the ground floor where the windowpanes were still intact, with only a little dripping from the ceiling.

Mario and I went to the upper floor and unfolded our barely 2.5 kg heavy camp beds. This floor was unfurnished and there were no doors at all to the large balcony. In addition, all the windowpanes were missing and there was a large hole in the western brick wall; apparently from a grenade hit. The entire first floor was therefore excellently ventilated on all sides, almost like an open-air arena. Unfortunately, the weather didn't cooperate, and a storm was building. We could see lightning flashing in the night sky. But that's not all. Suddenly there was a live machine gun fire very close by. Tracers floated through the air and then slowly descended and disappeared. In the midst of these two scenarios, sleep was out of the question. So, we stood for a while on the edge of the open balcony, looking, listening, and marvelling at this flashing and thundering spectacle. The thunder and lightning and the noisy salvos of machine guns with their tracer tracks seemed to be fighting each other for supremacy. A strong wind scared us two spectators away quickly to seek shelter behind an inner wall. But there it was already dripping a little from the ceiling. So, we looked elsewhere for shelter from the wind and water. On top of that, we hadn't brought any flashlights. We had simply forgotten in Enugu. Thanks to regular flashes of lightning, we located a dry spot for our night's camp. At least that's what we thought. The wind began to drive the pouring rain horizontally through the open balcony and the pane less window frames, into the house. At the same time, a fierce battle seemed to be going on outside, below the main road about 200 meters away. We heard screams, the rattle of machine guns, and the explosion of hand grenades. All this mixed with lightning, thunder, pouring rain, and wind. We experienced here what we have often been told: Biafran soldiers preferred to attack during thunderstorms. We fervently hoped that the defending Federals on the front line could hold their ground. Otherwise, only the Red Cross flag could help all of us in the house.

We finally lay down on our narrow-gauge beds, although sleep was out of the question. The still flashing lightning bolts with the instant crack of thunder made it clear that the storm was passing directly over us. The bitter, deadly struggle between Federals and Biafrans also continued. The ugly loud sounds of gun shots, explosions and screams continued to echo through our uncomfortable, cold, and increasingly wet "bedroom." The ceiling seemed to be leaking more and more, and the drops of water seemed to be falling faster and faster. If only we had at least an umbrella! Again and again, we pushed the camp beds to a supposedly not dripping spot. In vain, after a while, it dripped down on us there too. Soon our clothes were soaked, and we got wet to the skin. The storm had meanwhile moved on but had given way to continuous rain which in turn found more leaks in the roof to deprive us of the sleep we needed. The battle for Awka seemed to weaken for a short time. We breathed a sigh of relief: "At least that!" But then the gunshots and detonations flared up again from a different direction. The Biafrans hadn't given up and were looking elsewhere for a breakthrough. We were now tired, very tired, even apathetic. We longed for a dry bed, a non-drip ceiling – and even more so for peace in the country. We couldn't get any sleep during what was for us an endless long night. The fighting on the road below finally died down just before dawn, the front had held. At first light, Mario and I stood up in shock. We didn't have to wash our faces; they had already been sprayed with rainwater during the night. There was no breakfast, at 6 o'clock the two of us drove off, the battle events of that night deeply internalized in us. On the short way down to the street, we suddenly noticed bleached human bones. Here, scattered among the bushes, were skulls, skeletons, limb bones, and scraps of clothing. All sad witnesses to earlier heavy fighting for the city of Awka. The punctured main street below was now bustling with comings and goings: military vehicles were parked or driving about, and soldiers were busy cleaning up. Below the road was the fighting trench of the previous night. We slowly drove past in our land rover, but only 100 meters further on we couldn't believe our eyes. We caught our breath and I stopped. It was unbelievable - a military truck with an open loading area and half-height barriers on the sides was parked at the side of the road. Quite a number of dead soldiers lay on the ground - they had fallen in the night. It was not clear whether they were Biafrans or Nigerians, everyone wore similar gym shorts. What we could see, however, were bloody bullet and shrapnel wounds. This direct look at the horrors of war shook Mario and me deeply. During that terrible stormy night and hours of bloody battle, these soldiers had paid with their lives like countless others in the course of this wretched civil war. The ugly face of war was showing itself somewhere other than the faces of the population threatened by starvation and the refugees. We met war victims every day, they were the focus of everything we thought and did in our operations on behalf of the ICRC. But here we saw dead soldiers. This fact made us quiet. A feeling of great powerlessness had captured us, but suddenly, Mario and I were seized with rage and fury! Before our eyes, two soldiers had begun to load the fallen soldiers onto a truck. They did this without any human reverence and respect for the dead. One grabbed the feet, the other the hands of a dead soldier, then they began to swing and heave the corpse in a high arc, over the side railing, and hit the unseen truck bed with an ugly sound. An extremely uncomfortable, even horrible feeling shot through me like I was feeling the pain of hitting the truck bed for the dead. These two rude fellows were loading "goods" and not dead soldier; it didn't matter whether they were fallen comrades or enemies. I shouted in a sharp voice to the two soldiers to load up the dead slowly and gracefully. They paused and looked up at me questioningly, not seeming to understand. When I repeated my request, which was more like an order, using sign language, they just grinned in embarrassment. They obviously had no idea what problem I had with their "clean-up work." War was war and deadening. Human behavior had never been asked for or had been lost altogether over time. We two Red Cross men fled from this event and drove back to Enugu by the shortest route. Under the long-awaited shower, in fresh, dry clothes, the chef served us a hearty breakfast, spirits returned, and a lot of work awaited us. Meaningful work helped us get over what we just experienced. However, there was no shortage of other adventures.

The journey from Enugu to Umuahia and back was one of a kind. The city of Umuahia had become Biafra's second capital after the fall of Enugu. In May 1969, three months before our trip there, Umuahia had been conquered by Nigerian troops. The hospital there had been empty ever since. Some of our Red Cross doctors wanted to visit this hospital on a Sunday. They had in mind to restore this hospital and put it back into operation. Unfortunately, Umuahia was difficult to reach from Enugu due to the turmoil of war. For the last section of the 140 kilometers by car, there was only a narrow, makeshift emergency road near the front. To make matters worse, just before Umuahia, a narrow corridor led right through the middle of enemy Biafran territory. All signposts had been removed at the beginning of the war.

Such a trip was entirely to my liking, so I offered my services as a driver to our boss and the doctors. They immediately agreed. All we knew at the time was that the hastily constructed road was open and passable with a four-wheel drive. So, everything was fine for us, we could confidently start this adventure! On a Sunday morning at five thirty am, six ICRC people left Enugu in a flagged Red Cross Safari Land Rover. I knew the first 100 kilometers to Uturu well. We enjoyed this Sunday drive and made good progress on the winding asphalt road, although regular roadblocks stopped us every four to six kilometers. Armed Nigerian soldiers guarded a rope stretched across the road between two barrels. During the day these soldiers were mostly friendly and let us pass after a look at the passengers in the vehicle. But at night it was extremely important to know the right password. Without a password, it became difficult and even more dangerous.

In Uturu, we went to the Irish mission station with Brother John, whom we knew well. He gave us a warm welcome, but immediately frowned when he heard that we were going to Umuahia. He warned and admonished us: "The narrow, hastily constructed, bad emergency road leads through frontline territory. You have to drive very carefully on the way because the front is very close at times. The situation can change quickly." I reassured him by referring to my experiences in similar situations. After an invigorating black tea, we left Brother John in good spirits and soon turned behind Uturu onto the bumpy emergency road. This hardly deserved the name little road, as it was an unstable dirt track. With a four-wheel drive, the journey went over sticks, stones, and clay. My passengers were well shaken up, even though I was driving slowly. As we drove slightly down a muddy slope, parallel to a creek below, the sky suddenly became overcast, and it immediately began to rain. The vehicle quickly began to slide on the slippery clay. We descended dangerously, sliding towards the creek bed several meters below and breathed a sigh of relief when we reached a flatter, wooded area. But suddenly shots were fired into the gloomy surroundings on our right-hand side. I stopped immediately. We peered tensely in all directions and pricked up our ears. Trees and bushes blocked our view so we couldn't see far. When the shooting stopped, we crept on at a walking pace, stopping briefly at every bend from then on, to be on the safe side. When we finally reached the edge of the forest, the village of Ahaba was already in front of us. The army had set up an emergency hospital here because many of the wounded would not have survived the transport over this road. When I asked an officer who crossed our path, he told us that Umuahia was 20 minutes away. He continued to warn that we would have to travel a dangerously long, narrow frontline corridor. We took note of that, thanked him, and drove on in good spirits. Arriving at this bottleneck, we were presented with a worrying picture: trenches lined the road to the left and right. Here the battlefront ran on both sides of the street. So, we drove as if on a salver through the said corridor. Luckily there was a lull in the fighting. Soldiers even waved from the trenches when they saw the Red Cross flag flying. But it was a macabre and terrifying route to drive because the Nigerian soldiers had not buried their Biafran enemies who had died in battle. Instead, as a deterrent, they had tied them up in uniform along the road, fastened onto trees or poles. Mostly only the skull and parts of the skeleton in a torn uniform flapping in the wind could be seen. We were all shocked and speechless. I accelerated again to get us out of this terrifying corridor as quickly as possible; knowing full well that we would encounter these disturbing facts a second time on the way back.

When we reached Umuahia, the sun was shining again. We all immediately noticed the scenic beauty of this embattled city perched on a plateau. We could see far over the lower lying, peaceful-looking green country that was still under Biafran control. Seen from this perspective, it seemed inconceivable that people were starving there day after day, especially children. The front ran in a semicircle around the city. The Nigerians were up on the ridge, the Biafrans in the bush below. When we went to the local commander, suddenly the noise of shooting could be heard. The war didn't seem particularly frightening to the few civilians in the city. There were small market stalls on almost every street corner where people could buy cigarettes, chewing gum, or vegetables and fruit. However, most of the houses appeared uninhabited, many were damaged, had numerous bullet holes and windows with missing panes. Climbing and creeping plants grew up the walls of the houses. Soldiers with rifles appeared to be patrolling. When we pulled up in front of the officers' mess and climbed out, we were immediately greeted by a friendly captain. He led us into a spacious room and told us to sit down at a long table. "You must be hungry and thirsty after the long journey from Enugu," he stated. When we nodded eagerly, an NCO immediately brought ice-cold bottles of beer and mineral water. Barely ten minutes later, soldiers placed plates, cutlery, serviettes, and to our complete surprise, two large pots of delicious goulash on the table in front of us. We really didn't expect such a VIP reception. Apparently, our trip had been radioed from Ahaba. We thanked our attentive host several times during the meal. For a short time, we thought we were in peaceful times. But then we were startled when gunshots rang out very close by. We looked at the captain with concern. These were his soldiers who have their sights set on the Biafrans down in the bush. Now we also heard isolated shots from afar. The Biafrans were shooting back. "We are in the blind spot and therefore safe," the captain reassured us. "It only gets dangerous if you stick your heads over the edge of the hill." And on that day the war was back for us too. We had lost our appetite now, so we put the knife and fork away, realizing that we were sitting at the forefront of a year-long, bitter civil war because, in 1966, Colonel Ojukwu and his comrades-in-arms had proclaimed the East Central State province the Republic of Biafra.

An elderly man walking in front of our vehicle guided us to the nearby empty and dilapidated hospital. The many one-story buildings, connected by covered walkways, remained intact. But some brick walls were damaged by bullets. Dirt and disorder reigned in every room. Looters had rampaged here, stealing furniture and equipment. Even a partial reopening was out of the question at this point. The front ran meters behind the hospital. During our tour, the uninterrupted eerie noise of shooting echoed in the rooms. The doctors didn't want to give up so easily, so they took a closer look at the few rusty devices that were still there. I finally had to urge them to leave. The overcast skies and the long drive home worried me a bit. At 3 p.m., the storm clouds were already gathering, so we left the embattled Umuhahia. When we drove through the long neck of the bottle again, everyone deliberately looked straight ahead to avoid the uniformed skeletons. I just honked the horn a few times to salute the soldiers in the trenches, who in turn waved back. Shortly before the village of Ussoli, the feared heavy thunderstorm suddenly set in. I stopped in the village square, where there was a large military tent, to let the storm pass. Then we heard music, got out quickly, and ran into the tent in the thunderstorm. The big tent was packed with soldiers and officers sitting at tables, drinking beer. A band played wistful Nigerian tunes on exotic instruments. We had just driven along the corridor of dead but standing soldiers, and now we found ourselves amazed in a festive military tent, while a thunderstorm drummed heavily onto the roof while Nigerian music was played. We were on a real rollercoaster of perceptions and feelings. Some officers and soldiers jumped up from their seats when they saw us Red Cross people and asked us to take their seats. As soon as we sat down, we were each given a bottle of beer. Blonde Monika became the focus of general interest. She didn't care, she just smiled mischievously. We told an officer who had sat down with us the reason for our trip today. We were not allowed to pay for the beer. "You are our welcome guests here," we were told. When the storm subsided, we drove on quickly. It urged us home.

After Ahaba we turned again into the spooky forest in the direction of Uturu, where there had been shooting in the morning. The thunderstorm had made the narrow, uneven emergency road very muddy. I put the four-wheel drive back on. The narrow path made it impossible to avoid the waterholes. The only option was to step on the gas pedal and go through with it. But at a particularly long, sodden spot in the forest, the Land Rover got stuck in the mud. All forward and backward attempts were useless. John, a young English doctor got out to check. He immediately sank up to his knees in the wet mud. Everyone laughed as he climbed back in muddy pants. But we stopped laughing thoroughly when we realized our situation. We men had no choice: we took off our shirts, trousers and shoes and sank into the mud in our under pants. We first tried to push away the reddish mud in front of each wheel with our hands. The doctors in underpants were busy hauling away watery mud in front of their wheel and I struggled on the fourth wheel. But the mud ran right back. A prize-worthy situation that Monika enjoyed from the passenger seat. Too bad nobody brought a camera. That would have made an image for eternity.

We found some sticks nearby, which we put in the mud in front of the wheels. Wasted hope, that didn't help either, the Land Rover remained stuck. We couldn't even tear our hair! Our muddy fingers wouldn't allow it. Our frustrated faces kept getting longer. It had definitely been much more comfortable in the military hut with beer and music. It was a hopeless situation. Without help, we were threatened with spending the night in the forest. Then shock drove through our limbs: shots were fired on the left side, dangerously close. The four of us, still in our muddy underwear, ducked behind the vehicle. Only then did we see a dugout between the trees about 200 meters away, and also recognized a camouflage-colored tent. That was obviously where the front ran. When the firing finally died down a little, an idea hit me like lightning, which I immediately shared with my fellow sufferers: "The soldiers crouching there must have shovels with them!" As the driver, I was responsible for my fellow passengers. It was clear that I had to get us away from here as quickly as possible. So, I told the Australian Fred Zerfas, one of the doctors, to take the Red Cross flag off the fender, hold it up and wave it back and forth. He did so with vehemence, while I shouted as loudly as I could: "We are Red Cross and need shovels!" Shortly thereafter, it sounded back: "We have shovels, come and get them!" As I ran in my underpants, Fred Zerfas shouted "Good luck, mate!" But halfway there the shooting intensified. I threw myself on the reddish, wet forest floor and crawled on my stomach as fast as I could. Then, breathing heavily, I reached the ditch and jumped in, loud laughter greeted me. Armed soldiers pointed at me, laughing. When I asked why they were laughing, one said: "We have never seen such a dirty white man." I looked down at myself and now had to laugh as well. I was only wearing my muddy underpants and was covered in reddish mud. I wasn't even embarrassed among these soldiers, too many adventurous episodes had already happened that day. An officer brought two shovels and handed them to me, saying it was not necessary to bring them back, a soldier would get them later. I was just about to say goodbye when the shooting started again. Quickly I sat down on the wet trench floor, watched the soldiers above me firing at the enemy, then heard shots being fired from the other side. There were several dull impacts, which probably went into tree trunks. When the duel eventually died down, the officer came around the corner of the trench requesting me to run back quickly, he had ordered a ceasefire. I didn't have to be told twice. I grabbed the shovels, waved thanks to the warriors, climbed out of the trench, and ran fast like a sprinter through the water-soaked ground, back to the Land Rover where my worried mates were desperately waiting. Two of the doctors immediately shovelled away the mud in front of the front wheels like mad. But shovelling didn't help either. The mud ran back faster than it was shovelled away. We had to give up reluctantly, realizing that we would not be able to get out of this mud without more help. With mixed feelings, we prepared ourselves to maybe even have to spend the night here. Now we had to wait and hope that other crazy people would dare to drive along the front line on this muddy emergency road. We knew that dusk would soon set in. The dirt on our bodies had dried in the meantime, we men put our pants and shirts back on, to cover our dirty bodies and look more civilized. Monika smiled to thank us.

Now and then, there was more shooting in the forest. We tried to bridge the waiting time with gallows humor. Suddenly we pricked up our ears and thought we heard the sound of an engine. The mood rose immediately, there was hope again! Then we saw, what we had hoped for, a dark green military Land Rover, approaching slowly from the next bend, followed by a second one, both full of soldiers. Our vehicle was blocking the way, so they had to stop. A lieutenant, non-commissioned officers, and soldiers got out and looked critically at our vehicle in the mud hole. We didn't have to explain anything. The lieutenant immediately ordered the soldiers to look for two thin fallen trees in the area. After a few minutes, they came back with two skinny logs, and placed them under the front and rear bumper. On command, the soldiers heaved our heavy Land Rover out of the mud like a toy and carried it a dozen meters forward onto solid ground. We watched in amazement, thanked our rescuers profusely, and gave them our emergency ration package, the so-called C-rations, as a farewell gift. We drove on with a sigh of relief, but our odyssey was far from over. A light rain had set in again and it was beginning to get dark as we drove out of the forest. Now the slippery clay slope had to be overcome. This time it went slightly up. The afternoon's thunderstorm had dug a deep, meter-wide deep ditch in the slope and again we were stuck. I suggested building a low jump, like a snow jump we boys had built many years ago in Switzerland during winter. With enough run-up speed, I would certainly be able to hop over it with the Land Rover. My doubtful comrades were imagining our vehicle laying in the swollen creek below the emergency road if our attempt failed. Already laying in the swollen creek below the emergency road. I was in good spirits and persuaded my fellow passengers to try it. We had no other choice but to move forward at this point. With our bare hands, we now dug large lumps out of the clay slope under my guidance, built a clay jump with them in front of the cross ditch, and reinforced the whole thing with our shoes. A final inspection of the clay jump was positive. I then ordered the other five to get to safety above the lane. I now slowly drove a good 200 meters backward, swallowed three times, then raced faster and faster while shifting up the gears towards the jump, flew elegantly over the ditch at full throttle, and stopped. Cheers of bravo rang out. Everyone quickly got back in, and the journey continued. Very relieved and confident that we finally had all the hardships behind us, we happily chugged on. But far from it. A few minutes later, three military trucks with soldiers came toward us. Passing here on the slope was impossible. No problem for the soldiers, however. Within a few minutes, they dug an alternative spot into the slope for us, so that we could continue our journey with a sigh of relief. The last 20 minutes to the mission in Uturu passed without further surprises, but we drove on in silence. In the meantime, darkness had fallen. Brother John had been very worried about our long absence. So, we first had to tell him in detail all of what had happened. After that, we washed off some dried mud. A quick bite and black tea restored us. We still had the last 100 kilometers to go home. We could easily do that now we thought. But the three doctors had seen enough today, they preferred to spend the night in Uturu. But our boss Allan, Monika, and I felt the urge to continue this final journey. We really wanted to go home, there was a lot of work waiting for us the next day. So, the three of us said goodbye to the doctors and Brother John. Our big boss, Allen Whear, gave me permission for this 100 kilometers night drive home to Enugu. But on the way home, we thought several times that it would have been safer if we had also stayed at the mission station. We were repeatedly made aware of how dangerous driving at night was and why, with few exceptions, it was forbidden. Only special permits – in this case, the one given by Allen Whear – made it possible to drive a car after dark. Already on the way to our vehicle, we caught our breath again. Powerful fireworks could be seen in the night sky from the direction of Umuhahia. Tracer trains flew incessantly, silently, and in long arcs through the night sky, from left to right and back. Another nightly artillery duel. The war never sleeps. We felt uneasy and thoughtfully drove away. Brother John had given us the password valid for the night for the roadblocks. This drive at night unsettled us, it was scary. Whenever we slowly approached one of these roadblocks, two or three scared soldiers would jump up, guns raised and scream: "STOP! PASSWORD!" The glare of our Land Rover's headlights clearly made them very nervous. I immediately shouted the password and "Red Cross" out the side window. That calmed the warriors down a bit. Then one of them slowly walked up to the vehicle with a gun pointed at us, looked in suspiciously while Monika smiled at him, asked a few questions, and then let us drive on. So far, so good. We didn't know at the time that this password was only valid for a certain section of the route. None of the soldiers told us that a different password was used at one of the next barriers. The men probably didn't know that themselves. So, it happened three times that I called the wrong password out of the window. The soldiers were always in a state of excitement and yelled in panic: "GET OUT ALL and HANDS UP!" We barely dared to breathe as we walked slowly, arms raised toward the soldiers aiming at us in the Land Rover headlights, we shouted again, "RED CROSS!" loudly and clearly. But they were too nervous and suspicious to believe us. The procedure was always the same: the gun barrels were pushed into our backs, and they herded us to a nearby dugout. It's an extremely uncomfortable scary feeling to feel a soldier's gun barrel in your back. A soldier only needed to stumble on uneven ground in the dark or be drunk and we were history! We knew that the Biafrans regularly attacked such roadblock teams at night. One more reason for the insecure soldiers to drink palm wine to calm them down. So, we always found the same picture in every dugout we had been taken to, a sleepy, unfriendly sergeant who was annoyed that we were rousing him from his sleep. He gruffly asked for our IDs and wanted to know why we were still out in the middle of the night. In order to defuse the tense situation a little, we let blonde Monika answer each time. With her charm and an irresistible smile, she explained the reasons to the non-commissioned officer, mentioned our Red Cross work, and didn't forget to praise his important work here. It worked wonderfully every time, the ice was broken. So, we got the password for the next roadblock and said goodbye with a friendly handshake. We approached Enugu excruciatingly slowly. The tension that had lasted since the morning was now making itself felt on the home stretch. All three of us were getting more and more tired by the minute. We longed, or so it seemed to us, more than ever for our bed. Then at last, already at the witching hour, we reached and passed the last roadblock at the Nine Miles Corner. Moments later, far below, we saw the twinkling lights of Enugu. Now we could breathe deeply for the first time, and the tension eased. The policeman who was on guard in front of our house couldn't help but be amazed when we arrived long after midnight. We didn't linger long on explanations. Finally, we men could take a shower and get rid of the remaining dried red mud. Totally exhausted, I went to bed and half asleep, mumbled a short prayer of thanks. What an exciting 20-hour day we had put behind us! Full of dangers, surprises, and events. We were very lucky this Sunday to be able to return home unscathed. We had no more desire to continue driving at night. At 6 a.m. the alarm clock rattled again. A hearty breakfast got me going and gave me strength again. As always, I set out with the heavy bunch of keys to unlock the many doors of the large warehouses. Over 110 workers and some truck drivers were waiting for me. Normal everyday life was back. From my second trip to Umuahia, which luckily was less dramatic, I brought an orphan boy back to Enugu. On the way back, just before the infamous bottleneck, an officer stepped onto the road when he saw the white ICRC Land Rover coming. He stopped me and asked if I might help. "A few days ago, my soldiers picked up an orphan boy coming through the front lines. He's still here. We feed him and take care of him. But, of course, he can't stay here, his father died in the war and his mother died of yellow fever. The boy still has a grandmother, but she lives on the other side of the front." I agreed to take the boy with me. Soldiers brought the 12-year-old, shy, insecure orphan named Eze to my car. The officer told him he could now go to Enugu with me. I would arrange for him to be placed in an orphanage. Eze nodded imperceptibly, trying to smile a little. I asked him to get in. The officer thanked me warmly, obviously glad that he could hand over responsibility. Eze didn't speak English and I felt really sorry for him. So, I stopped with him at the Irish Mission in Uturu for tea and biscuits with Brother Francis, to cheer him up. Brother Francis coaxed Eze: "You will be in good hands at the orphanage and will make many new friends," he said soothingly. Once in Enugu, I drove straight to the orphanage and spoke to the lovely director Florence. She immediately agreed to take Eze in. For my part, I promised Eze that I would visit him soon. I had a tailor make two pairs of pants and two shirts for Eze out of white, empty wheat sacks of amazing quality. They fit him perfectly. From then on, whenever I visited the orphanage, he would come running, shake my hand, smile, and say softly, "Thank you!" A few weeks later I drove with Barbara and Jungle Jim to a village between Awka and Onitsha. We wanted to get an idea of the food distribution that had started a few days earlier with the help of the Nigerian Red Cross. We also came through a narrow, densely overgrown hilly passage near Awka. Here the Biafrans had ambushed a Nigerian military convoy months before and shot everyone. Several destroyed, burned, or shot-up military vehicles lay in the bush next to the narrow, uphill road. A macabre, oppressive reminder of what happened. When we arrived in the village, we met the local camp commandant, a very personable, courteous man. During the past few days, there had been a strong influx of new refugees. This Nigerian officer, a first lieutenant, helped them wherever he could. Almost like a father, he cared for these Igbo refugees, who had escaped the misery in ever-shrinking Biafra by tortuous, secret paths. This warm-hearted man invited us three Red Cross people to his house for lunch. He had a delicious curry rice dish served with chicken, unfortunately, it was more than just a bit too spicy for us. Our taste buds burned like hell. We tried to extinguish the fire first with water, then with beer. That only seemed to make the problem worse. Dr. Jungle Jim and I suddenly started sweating profusely. Great fun for everyone around the table. Two orphans, Patricia and a little boy called Nhwafor, also lived in this officer's house. He had temporarily taken in both children as refugees three weeks ago, provided them with clothes, and also shared food with them. He was pleased when I suggested asking for a place for Nhwafor at the Enugu Orphanage. Ten-year-old Patricia decided to stay there because she wanted to return to her uncle in her village after the war.

The next time I drove towards Onitsha, I picked Nhwafor up and took him to Florence Okoro's orphanage, where he was warmly welcomed. He also got his wheat sack shirts and pants from me. Now I had two protégés in the orphanage, my "stepfather pride" increased.

They were even allowed to attend the then-only school in Enugu, together with the other orphans. I was particularly taken with the orphanages. It made me very happy and gave me deep satisfaction to be able to help with the daily deliveries of bread, the kpoff-kpoffs, and other food and clothing. The children always ran towards me with howls of joy, laughing and – expectantly waiting – squeezed my hands, because I always brought them something sweet. Before I left, I got a song or two sung as a grateful thank you. With these orphans, I drew new strength, cheerful courage, and confidence for the strenuous, psychologically stressful work. I very much enjoyed working there. The sight of the many exhausted sufferers, the hungry and dying, who reached a distribution camp after arduous walks on bush paths near the front, spurred me on to do more, to work longer, to react even faster in order to be able to make important decisions. Thanks to my short and medium wave radio, I was able to take part in world events in the evenings. Of course, Biafra was in the news every day at the time. I couldn't believe my ears when Radio Enugu mentioned my name one night, praising the continued support of the local orphanages. For me and our employees that was good for the soul. That's how working really made sense. I put my heart and soul into it, the work made me blossom. The experience that the ICRC officials already entrusted me with such a responsible task on my first assignment overwhelmed and encouraged me: I had found my calling with the Red Cross. Forever!

In August we heard on our private shortwave radios that the ICRC had to withdraw from Nigeria. The Nigerians had decided to continue the relief effort alone. For the time being, these were probably just rumours. But more rumours made the rounds from there. It was clear to all of us that if it came to that, most of us would probably have to return home. Even at this thought, I was overcome by a slight melancholy. It would be a pity because I liked the varied work. Every day was full of challenges with unique experiences and events, knowing that I could help suffering, innocent people. But it was still several weeks before it really happened. There were more than enough experiences and events to come. One day I had a very special experience late in the afternoon on the way back from Okigwe to Enugu. The evening sun was already illuminating the wooded hills near Awgu, letting the many treetops shine in a magnificent, green-blue sea of colour. Then suddenly there was a bang. Unexpectedly, I heard heavy gunfire nearby. It seemed to be right in front of me from the bushes on both sides of the road. I've hardly ever brought my Land Rover to a standstill so quickly. The brakes were still squeaking, and already I had opened the door and dived, literally flew into the green ditch. The eerily close banging of shots continued, seemingly wanting no end. Now I heard the rapidly approaching engine noise of an airplane, ventured a look at the sky, and saw a small airplane disappear into the treetops above me. I exhaled. They didn't have their sights on me. They shot at the enemy plane. Shock and terror were still deep in my limbs. I was shaking and barely able to move. Then soldiers stepped onto the street, waved, came up to me, and asked if everything was okay apart from a graze on my hand, grass stains on my shirt, and fairly battered ego, I had nothing to complain about. I drove on relieved but kept glancing suspiciously at the sky. My interest in green nature had dropped to zero. Almost every day there were bigger and smaller experiences that stuck with me. Driving once or twice a week to the many distant medical teams close to the front was the only regular way to pick up their orders in time. The telephone system in the war zone was dead and radio communication not allowed. We had to operate as though we were living in the previous century.

*****

In Enugu there were a few empty office buildings guarded by police officers. Ministries had their offices there when Enugu was still the capital of the independent Republic of Biafra. A police officer I knew took me on one of his patrols through these abandoned offices. I couldn't stop being amazed. Virtually every musty-smelling, open-plan office I looked into was in a huge mess. All the drawers had been ripped out, their contents full of files strewn knee-deep in the room. In one of these offices, there were even new Biafran passports lying around among other papers. Cupboards, chairs, desks, and telephones piled on top of each other everywhere, even in the corridors. A sad discouraging chaos, as evidenced by what lay in front of me. The Biafran Republic, at the administrative and paper level: after the bureaucrats had left their rooms and buildings in great haste, the conquerors came and soon transformed the administrative order of Biafra into this total mess. It felt eerie in here, I thought I could still physically feel the brute force, the desire to destroy, the wanton creation of chaos even now, years later. I urged the policeman to let me leave and go outside into the fresh air as quickly as possible.

In mid-August, I was informed that my contract had been extended until the end of September. That meant a little relief for me in the short term. Nevertheless, it was already noticeable that change was in the air. At the end of August, at the behest of the ICRC in Lagos, we were able to stop buying relief goods from northern contractors locally, which made our work significantly easier. From then on, all deliveries of food were brought directly from Lagos with large articulated lorries. Now there was time to deal with things that had been postponed and left behind. But time just flew by for me. At least that's how it seemed. I was already packing my suitcase when, towards the end of September, I received the message that my contract had been extended until the end of November. That suited me perfectly. At the end of October, our coordinator then applied for a further contract extension for four months from December. For a long time, the answer did not come. These days were characterized by uncertainty paired with anxious waiting. Then I heard that the Nigerian Red Cross was about to take over the ICRC's relief effort. A corresponding agreement had already been signed. But what did "next" mean? I just assumed that I probably wouldn't be needed any longer. Weeks ago, I had planned ahead. My assistant Abo Okonkwo was appointed as my successor, I consciously deployed him, and gradually gave him more responsibility. For me, the most important point of all was: On the day the Nigerian Red Cross (NRC) took over the warehouses and transports, there had to be a manager who had everything under control. This was the only way I could rightly end my mission in Biafra. I wanted to return to Switzerland, knowing that I had done my utmost to ensure that the sick and those suffering from hunger continued to receive help. But even in these uncertain days, I still hoped for my contract extension. When there was still no notification on November 20, I had to make the decision myself. That's how I determined November 26th as departure day while still hoping to be able to postpone this into the next year. But on the day before my departure, I got the certainty that I had to start the return journey. The message came over the radio that my contract would not be extended. So, it was true, that the NRC took over the relief effort. At least Monika and the car mechanics could stay as specialists. And of course, nothing has changed for the medical teams in the field at the moment. So now it was decided, my departure was final. It's a pity, there wasn't much time left to really say goodbye to the many staff and the many acquaintances. And of course, I drove to the orphanage to say goodbye to Eze, Nwafhor, and Florence Okoro. Before leaving, I went to warehouse one for the last time, shook hands with all the employees with a sad heart, and thanked everyone for the work they had done during a difficult time, combined with the wish for peace in the Igbo country and reconciliation with their Nigerian brothers.

On November 26, 1969, shortly before noon, I drove with the American Dr. Stewart Weyand away from Enugu. He had worked there as a doctor and medical consultant for three months and was returning to the USA. We stopped on Milliken Hill, looked down one last time at Enugu, the place and country that had brought a new dimension and inspiration to my life, and I hoped an interesting future too. I stayed in Lagos for six days, reported to the ICRC headquarters, answered many questions, and did the necessary "final bureaucracy." Then I was free, so went to a beach to swim and watched the hustle and bustle of the city. Above all, however, I didn't want to return straight back home to Switzerland. I wanted to soften the gap between the chaos of war and the peace of home. I was drawn to South and East Africa. My uncle Christen Roth lived in Southern Rhodesia (now Zimbabwe). I wanted to know how he had lived since 1938; 31 years after his immigration. If the second World War hadn't broken out, my parents would have also immigrated to South Africa with us children. So, I took advantage of the moment to see what we were denied back then. So before I returned to Switzerland, I took an exciting journey from Lagos, and via Brazzaville to South Africa, Southern Rhodesia, Malawi, Tanzania, and Kilimanjaro, Kenya.

CHAPTER TWO

From Nigeria to South- and East Africa: 1969-1970

On December 3, 1969, I boarded a southbound Trans World Airline plane at the airport in Lagos, Nigeria. At an altitude of 10,000 meters, the plane flew over the huge Niger Delta. I was able to look down on war-torn Biafra one last time. It was almost unbelievable what, I had experienced, learned and achieved down there in such a short time. In my mind, I relived those impressive weeks and months on this flight.

It was already dark when we descended over the city of Brazzaville and the broad Congo River and landed at Kinshasa Airport. Just one hour later I was on the onward flight to Johannesburg, where we landed in the night during a heavy rainstorm. In the city centre I found a simple hotel room and fell asleep immediately. Hours later, a hearty breakfast quickly got me back on my feet. The first thing on my agenda was a walk through the city. Here in Johannesburg, in 1938, my immigrant uncle and "Götti" (godfather) Christen Roth, got his first job as a supervisor in a gold mine. But I didn't like the city of Johannesburg. The many skyscrapers looked nearly the same, and the lack of greenery in the city centre, the serious-looking people, everything seemed somehow unnatural to me. In Biafra I had seen people laughing. There was life in them, often even happiness; even when they were suffering, sorrowful, or grieving. But here in Johannesburg I saw no laughter, no happiness on the streets. The apartheid policy, the strict racial segregation, seemed to me the reason for this. There were even different counters in the post office: one was marked "Whites only" and the other "Non-Whites." Blacks were treated as second-class citizens in every area of life here. This shook me deeply and I was glad to be able to fly on to Cape Town. I immediately liked this city between the sea and the Table Mountain towering behind it. A friendly taxi driver took me to a cheap but clean hotel where I felt comfortable. I stayed in Cape Town for a whole week, rode in a gondola up Table Mountain, where I enjoyed a great view. The next day I drove along the coast in an excursion bus, visited beautifully situated wineries, combined with real passes in the mountainous hinterland. I also stood at the Cape of Good Hope, first circumnavigated by Bartolomeo Diaz almost 500 years ago. But even in Cape Town, strict racial segregation was evident everywhere, on the city bus, the counters and toilets in train stations, "Whites only" or "Non-Whites" was written everywhere. Even the railway wagons were segregated by race. For me, this was unimaginably unworthy.

When I went up Table Mountain for the second time, I met a young German in the gondola. He had just arrived in Cape Town

TO THE HORIZON AND BEYOND

after a three month visit to his uncle in southwest Africa. He enthusiastically told me about his wonderful time on the farm there. Never had he seen such unique colours as when the afternoon sun enchanted the high-contrast hilly landscape with the mountains in the background in a magnificent, slowly changing spectrum of colours. "I could never get enough of it," he enthused, smiling, eyes shining. "I kept discovering other colour variants. Time stood still for me every time." I would have preferred my next flight to be southwest Africa. But my onward journey went in a different direction.

On December 11th I flew along the Indian Ocean with a stopover in Port Elizabeth and on to Durban. Many modern hotels stood here on the long beach. But I didn't come here to swim. In the evening I looked at the large harbor with its many cranes and lights, which were reflected in the water in different colours.

I flew back to Johannesburg the very next day. Just before landing there, I looked down at huge yellow sand pyramids; the output of the nearly 3,000-meter-deep gold mines. A fellow passenger explained to me that the ground near Johannesburg was crisscrossed with an unmanageable system of shafts, corridors, and tunnels. "Countless black workers toil down there," this man told me. "It's supposed to be incredibly hot in these tunnels. No worker can work there for more than nine months. Then others must come in and replace them." He continued: "These hard-working people have no rights, only duties." This cheap labour not only came from South Africa, but also from Mozambique, Southern Rhodesia, and Malawi. So here, in these hot mines, my uncle worked as a supervisor during the second World War. After working in Johannesburg, he moved to Mozambique, where deep in bush he managed a sawmill for 25 years. Now I was to visit him and his family in Southern Rhodesia. I was only six years-old when he visited us in Grindelwald to say goodbye in 1938. I hadn't seen him since then.

On the same day I flew on an Air Rhodesia propeller plane and landed about two hours later in Salisbury, the capital of Southern Rhodesia. Today the city is called Harare and the country Zimbabwe. Christen Roth was waiting for me at the airport, together with his German wife, his 11-year-old son Bernhard and younger daughter Yvonne. I recognized my uncle immediately, even after 31 years. He had teary eyes as we hugged. He was extremely happy to see his nephew, who was about to turn 38, after such a long time. For years he has lived on a small hobby farm, 30 kilometers outside of Salisbury and had long been a Southern Rhodesian citizen.

In the weeks that followed, I took part in the life of my uncle and his family and enjoyed it with all my heart. It was here in southern Africa that I celebrated Christmas abroad for the first time. Because it was pleasantly warm, I didn't feel the festive mood until Christmas Day; candles, decorations, gifts, the shared singing of "Silent Night, Holy Night," before the excellent feast, this all made us feel very happy.

We then made a flying visit to the famous Victoria Falls on the border between Southern and Northern Rhodesia - today's Zambia. Already in the plane we could - 100 kilometers before the falls - see the long chasm in the earth, from which the sun-illuminated clouds of spray rose high into the air. At a width of almost 1,700 meters, every second, millions of litres of water from the Zambezi River tumbled down into the narrow, deep gorge with eerie thunder and roar. A 130-meter-high bridge spanned the gorge, and we tourists walked to the white centre line of it that marked the border between Southern and Northern Rhodesia. We paused for a while in front of that simple yet so significant line. Then I took a step – just one step – across that white line and all hell broke loose! Two Zambian border guards at the end of the bridge about 100 meters away yelled something and came galloping, with their rifles swinging wildly, stopping right in front of me, their rifles aimed at the asphalt at my feet. Of course, I had long since stepped back behind the boundary line. Now the two red faced border warriors gave me a loud, menacing sermon. What was I thinking of, stepping over the white line without permission? They would have arrested me immediately if I hadn't already retreated.

The two uniformed screamers obviously enjoyed showing off their tried and tested two-man show in front of the tourists, but as a Biafra veteran, they had not intimidated me. They calmed down again after I said, "I am sorry," while thinking, "I can now say, I've been to Zambia!"

After a month full of experiences and memories, on January 12, 1970, I said goodbye to my uncle and his family at Salisbury airport and flew on towards east Africa. The flight would end in Blantyre, the capital of Malawi - the former Nyasaland.

During the leisurely check-in, the hostess asked me the reason for my trip, and we started chatting. When I mentioned my work in Biafra, she pricked up her ears and called over her colleagues. Everyone wanted to know how it had been there and marvelled at my stories. It seemed impossible to them that I had survived this mission unscathed. Biafra was in the news every hour those days. The Federals had pushed the Biafrans further and further into a corner, the end of the war seemed near. I was overcome with sadness. I would have loved to still be there. Meanwhile, it was time to board the Comet plane, all passengers were directed to the right. As I was also about to go in that direction, a charming hostess stopped me, pointed to the left, lifted a curtain and said with a smile: "You can choose a seat here in 1st class because you have worked for the Red Cross in Biafra. The captain ordered it that way." What a big surprise! So, I chose a seat that seemed particularly good and soon realized I was the only passenger. Suddenly the African flight captain looked in, welcomed me, and wished me a good flight. As soon as we reached the right altitude, "my hostess" came and offered snacks and drinks. She spoiled me during this flight; even with a fine meal on porcelain dishes. I felt like a real VIP.

As we flew over the almost 600-kilometer-long Lake Nyassa, a memory from my school days in Grindelwald unexpectedly surfaced. With forefinger on the map of Africa, in amazement, I had traced over this large Lake Nyasa and pondered what it would be like to see it for real. Now I wasn't dreaming anymore, I was sitting in this plane looking down on Lake Nyasa. That childhood dream had come true!

However, later, I found out that I had been in a flying time bomb. Comet jet planes were known to suddenly break apart in mid-air due to material fatigue. "Hansrudi," I told to myself, "You've been lucky once again."

When approaching Dar-es-Salam, we flew low over the island of Zanzibar, also known as the Spice Island (cloves, cinnamon, nutmeg and more). Zanzibar belongs to Tanzania, the former Tanganijka. We landed safely in Dar-es Salaam. A bit tipsy from all the drinks on the plane, I swayed in the sweltering heat as I got off the plane, and quickly found a problem waiting for me. The Tanzanian customs officer refused me an entry visa when he saw the stamps of South Africa and Southern Rhodesia in my passport. Tourists visiting these countries are not welcome in Tanzania, he told me in a stern voice. But I had a key to open the Tanzania door, pulled out my Red Cross identity card and presented it together with my job reference from my assignment in Biafra. The tide turned immediately for me! The customs officer excitedly called over colleagues and showed them my papers, "No problem, sir!" Suddenly, my visa was issued, and the stamp was in my passport! But that was not all. Next, a smiling police officer stood in front of me, showed great interest in Biafra and invited me into his office for a chat. Then, by phone, he got me a cheap hotel room in the city and gave me information for the onward journey in Tanzania. After that, when I went to a counter to buy a bus ticket to go into town, the cashier gave me a free ticket and said: "I heard you were in Biafra. You go for free." Biafra had become a magic word in Africa.

The next day I exchanged traveller's checks in town and bought a plane ticket to Moshi, which is near Mount Kilimanjaro. Our Australian nurse Allison Begbie, had told me enough about this magical mountain to make it interesting for me too. When I got off the Fokker plane at the airfield in Moshi, I stopped and admired the majestic Kilimanjaro with its white shimmering peak for a while and was happy to be so close to it. But not close enough: I wanted to go to the top!

For two shillings I travelled in a decrepit, rickety bus to Marangu, the starting point of my first African mountain tour. I found accommodation in the Marangu Hotel, which was 1,500 m above sea level. I was lucky and was assigned to a group that was supposed to start marching the next day. Everything was well organized here. All equipment could be rented, including warm clothes, socks, hats, gloves, sunglasses and of course mountain boots. Furthermore, each participant was assigned a personal porter. Meals and accommodation in three different huts were also organized. The whole mountain tour lasted five days and cost "all inclusive" equivalent of 300 Swiss francs.

The next morning, our group of 15 tourists, with four guides, set off at a leisurely pace to Bismarck hut at 3,000 meters. There were also 25 porters with us, some of whom had already marched off. Our only luggage was a camera and a long walking stick. The slow pace let us acclimatize well, and the group chatted with each other. Almost all of my colleagues were from the USA. At almost 38 years old, I was the oldest. Eleven were members of the Kennedy Peace Corps, aged about 20 to 25, seven of them were women. After a six-month assignment as school teachers in Liberia, West Africa, they wanted to climb Kilimanjaro as the crowning glory.

On that first day it started raining halfway. When we arrived at the Bismarck hut, on the edge of a forest, we were already quite soaked. The hut offered sleeping bunks for around 50 people. Our clothes dried quickly by the warm fire and our supervisors cooked us a good dinner.

After a hearty breakfast the next morning, we set off again at 9 a.m. At first, our path led through an increasingly clear rainforest.

Again, light rain trickled from the low clouds. Soon we were marching through open heath land with plants I didn't know. The blue sky came out, and in the background between hills, the white cap of Kilimanjaro greeted us. It still seemed far away, but just looking at it spurred us on.

Our hike to the Peters hut, at almost 4,000 m, was also easy to master. Some of the American women had never climbed a mountain but remained unconcerned and cheerful. I felt comfortable with these young, like-minded people. The mood became lighter by the hour. The initial group soon became a team with a common goal. Everyone was happy with their daily performance. The guides looked after us hikers and treated us to drinks along the way. We were amazed at what the porters carried with them. They also served us a delicious dinner with meat, vegetables, salad, pudding or fruit salad and tea. In front of the Peters hut we were rewarded with a fantastic view far over the green Tanzanian lowlands. Former mountaineers had written all sorts of sayings on the wall inside the hut: "You better turn back here, or Killer Manjaro will get you!" or: "Once, but never again!"

That evening, when we stepped outside the hut, countless stars twinkled in the sky. In the depths, the lights of Moshi shone and behind us, high above the hut, the bright cap of Kilimanjaro shimmered. We hoped we would all be up there the day after. But now it was time for the bunks and to slip into the sleeping bag. The brook rushing down behind the hut splashed us a cheerful lullaby.

The next morning, we started again at 9 o'clock, but took it easy; because the Kibo hut, at almost 5,000 m, was only four hours away. Two hours later we already reached a wide saddle that spread out next to Kilimanjaro and its subsidiary peak Mowenzi. Here began a long and dusty, gently sloping plateau. Suddenly, Anne, one of the Americans, called for help. One of her contact lenses had fallen into the brown trail dust. Eight of us knelt around the spot and gingerly searched for the colourless piece of plastic. After a while, someone shouted "Here!" and pulled the escapee out of the dust. Anne sighed with relief and poured water over it. We all watched in amazement as she pushed the small lens back into her eye. Her great gratitude made us all happy. That was teamwork and as if on command, we all knocked the fine dust out of our trousers and on we went.

The last ascent to the Kibo hut, although not steep, gave us a bit of trouble because of the thin air, but soon after we were standing next to the hut, looking up at the mountain which appeared frighteningly high. Zigzag lines could be seen on the steep, snow-covered slope. In the morning, at two o'clock, we would try to scramble up there. There was already some snow behind the hut, which encouraged a snowball fight before becoming quickly out of breath. Suddenly, only one of the teachers, Judy Hallgren, and I were standing in the snow. We had mostly marched together since the second day, joking and sharing our experiences in Liberia and Biafra. Judy stood there in the snow, wrapped up in a jacket, scarf, hat and gloves and looked with uncertainty towards the mountain. It was her first mountain tour, and the planned ascent scared her a little. I took her in my arms, gave her a kiss on both cheeks and promised to help her with the climb. She beamed and immediately thanked me with a kiss on my cheek.

Fog slowly crept around the Kibo hut and robbed us of our view.

It got noticeably colder. After dinner we all got pills to swallow against the altitude headaches that plagued some. At 7 p.m. we went to bed, with a wake up planned at 1 a.m. Most got hardly any sleep. I was also plagued by the headache, the pills barely helped. It was a relief to get up at the planned time for a small breakfast with hot tea. We set off with our headlamps donned, and then slowly trotted in single file behind the guide. Nobody spoke a word, only the monotonous crunching of the many shoes could be heard.

The headlamps illuminated the narrow, dark path for us. The first heavy breathing and isolated sighs became audible. Finally, the guide stopped briefly to allow us to rest. After a few minutes it started again. But we had to stop more and more to give our hard-working lungs a "time out." We didn't feel like talking anymore, panting was the order of the day. Some were probably wondering what they were doing here in this African scree. But no one gave up, everyone struggled bravely and resolutely, higher and higher.

Finally, we no longer needed the headlamps, and it gave us a boost to see the Kibo hut far below us. On the zigzag path, we slowly fought our way higher and higher. Judy walked ahead of me as agreed. I didn't take my eyes off her, but she didn't need my help at all, it was rather the other way around. I was gasping for air, not her. The little path up became more and more slippery and seemed to consist only of small stones and black sand. We took five steps up, two steps back, heart pounding and lungs screaming for more air. The guides kept encouraging us as they watched our upward struggle.

Our tour guide climbed Kilimanjaro for the 120th time that day.

He stood above us on the path, at around 5,500 m above sea level, lit a cigarette, drew the smoke into his lungs with relish and polluted the scarce air for us beginners. We were amazed but panted on. The edge of the crater didn't seem far, but more and more we had to stop and catch our breath.

The first of us finally reached the rim of the crater - Gilmans Point at 18,635 feet or 5,680 m above sea level. A few minutes later the last of us arrived. Laughing and out of breath, we congratulated each other and shared congratulatory kisses at the summit. The sun was shining, and an overwhelming view rewarded us for the day's hardship. We were amazed at how much glistening glacial ice lay in the huge crater. Porters and guides poured tea and distributed canned fruit salad. A guide then asked if anyone was interested in walking the crater rim to the main summit at 5,895m. That meant another two hours of ascent. I would have liked to try, but nobody else showed any interest and I preferred to stay with the team to enjoy the descent together. Everyone quickly scribbled their names in the Gilmans Point summit book, then the tour guide said it was time to go.

High-spirited and without "zigzagging" we now scurried down the notorious scree slope which was covered with light snow. After just thirty minutes, everyone reached the Kibo hut, where lunch was served to us. Afterwards we marched on to the Peters hut, where we spent the night. Everyone slept like logs.

On the morning of the fifth and last day we set off early, it was about 20 kilometers to Marangu, mostly a slightly downhill trek. But for many, this turned out to be the toughest part of the whole tour. Sore muscles, weak knees, sore feet and other ailments tormented us. A comforting surprise awaited us in the Bismarck hut: All participants received a wreath of straw roses on their tired heads from their personal bearer. We had made it; Kilimanjaro had been climbed! After we had been served sweets and tea, we walked the last nine kilometers refreshed.

But they were really long kilometers that didn't want to end. As we walked through small villages, the heat was also getting to us. The locals eyed us, seeming to enjoy our waddling walk. Tired and sweaty, we finally reached the long-awaited hotel in Marangu. A warm bath and the "four o'clock tea" awakened our spirits again. We proudly accepted our certificates for the successful ascent. Most of the participants said goodbye, but I stayed until the next morning.

After a restful night's sleep, I travelled back to Moshi in the same battered, decrepit bus and boarded an East African Airline flight around noon. After a somewhat turbulent one-hour flight, I landed at Nairobi Airport and took a bus to the capital of Kenya, which seemed European to me with its many high-rise buildings and magnificent flower gardens. I noticed that in addition to black people, there were also many white and Indian people in the city. In many shop windows I saw elaborate wood carvings and the travel agencies outbid each other with tempting photo safaris. But I was drawn home to Switzerland. Suddenly I felt really homesick for the first time. I could hardly wait for the six-hour night flight home on a Swissair Coronado.

On January 19, 1970, at 08:15 the plane landed, and I returned to Swiss soil at the Zurich-Kloten airport. When I boarded the train to Oerlikon, I was shaking miserably in my thin African clothing and my thoughts rushed back to West Africa. I let memories pass me by, relived a whole series of unique encounters with Biafrans stricken by war, hunger and misery. My thoughts lingered with those who have nothing and yet brave a difficult life with humour and laughter.

I truly owed them all for the most exciting and satisfying time of my life. It felt good to know I had contributed a little to making life slightly easier for these war victims. I finally knew where my path led, where I felt "centered." And I was looking forward to my future with all my heart.

My parents, friends and acquaintances were of course very happy to see me safe and sound. I was a little proud to have managed to work abroad, even if only for a short time. "The next chance for a new assignment will definitely come," I secretly said to myself.

When I arrived back in Switzerland, I saw many things with different eyes. Being in the middle of the Biafra war had changed my perspective significantly within a few months. My country people, and life itself, seemed unusual and different, even strange. At least that's how it seemed to me. In Biafra I had often seen people laugh despite the war, misery and hunger. The Biafrans were frugal, delighted in trifles, were not in a hurry. Life there was more relaxed, more informal, even more natural than in my home country. What a rollercoaster of impressions and feelings for me: being in Africa for the first time as a down-to-earth Swiss and experiencing this attitude to life despite the civil war and misery! Then, after a number of months, back in Switzerland, the complete opposite: in the shops, a land of milk and honey with fully stocked food shelves, always several types and brands of each article; all colourful, perfectly packaged and inviting to buy. Despite all this, there was rush and stress in the air. Nowhere in everyday life was there even a pinch of happiness paired with a smile to be felt and certainly not to be seen. Involuntarily, my thoughts wandered back to Biafra and its survival strategy, of which hilarity and laughter were an important part. It probably had to be in order to somehow survive the insanity of war.

My first "official act" was a trip to Geneva for the obligatory final meeting at the ICRC, the so-called debriefing. The big highlight: I was put on the list for possible further assignments abroad. Back in Zurich, I immediately contacted the temporary work agency Manpower. In order to be quickly available for the ICRC at any time, I did not look for a permanent position. Temporary work was suitable for me at the time. Manpower immediately gave me temporary jobs; as a warehouse clerk and later I worked as dispatcher in a transport company for a while. Sometimes I also worked the night shift on Friday or Saturday as taxi driver. Finding work was still easy at the time. The switch to simple jobs was no problem for me at all. I always enjoyed working for a different company and getting to know other employees and colleagues. In addition, it was in my nature to quickly familiarize myself with a new job, learn new things and move on to the next temporary employment.

The days and weeks passed quickly as the home routine returned. But I never lost sight of my goal of going abroad again. The inner fire not only smouldered, it burned.

CHAPTER THREE

Anatolia – The Asian Part of Turkey, 1970-1971

At the end of March 1970, ten weeks after my return from Africa, there was still a lot of snow in the Swiss mountains, and I had a great time joining my friends on ski tours at weekends. We either went by car to central Switzerland or opted for the mountains in the east. Early in the morning we drove to a starting point, strapped special skin furs underneath the skis, and leisurely began ski-walking upwards. The skin furs prevented the skis from sliding backward. The ascent with like-minded friends in the cold, fresh air, first through snow-covered fir forests, then past alpine huts towards a high peak, was just as wonderful as the summit. Resting there, we ate our food, occasionally with a glass of white wine, and enjoyed the great views. The subsequent skiing descent through virgin powder snow was always the "icing on the cake," our well-deserved reward for the hours of ascent. One such weekend ski tour remains unforgettable.

We took the train to Bergün below the Albula Pass on a Saturday morning. From there, with skis and backpacks on our shoulders, we marched through the Tuor valley until we reached the first snow. There we mounted our skin furs underneath the skis and moved up to the beautifully situated Kesch hut. For supper we had sausages with bread, and a glass of wine and the hut warden served us a nutritious vegetable soup. We lay down early and got up at 5 a.m. It was still dark and bitterly cold, but a glorious starry sky promised a great day. When we left shortly before 6 a.m., the first rays of sunshine hit the striking 3,418-meter-high peak of Piz Kesch, our destination. We could see across the long zigzag ascent route that would take us close to the summit. While slowly ascending steep slopes in zigzag lines, countless other distant mountains came into view. It was like an overwhelming, all-white winter panorama of mountain peaks stretching high up into the cold blue sky. The higher we went, the further we could see. Sometimes we stopped in our single file, absorbing the views gratefully and enjoying this magnificent greatness in its freezing atmosphere. An enlarged photo of these distant views still reminds me of those unforgettable hours of cold sunshine on that early Sunday morning. We left our skis behind the summit and fought our way in stiff ski boots through deep snow up the very steep ascent to the Piz Kesch peak. The girls were rewarded with a cold summit kiss. Now we let our happiness, high spirits, and joy of life run free and sang the mountain vagabond song with smiling faces:

> *"Magnificent mountains,*
> *sunny heights,*
> *we are mountain vagabonds,*
> *yes, we are ... yes we are!"*

A bottle of cold white wine made the rounds as a summit drink. That gave us the right impetus for the long descent, accompanied by cheers and yodels through the deep powdery snow slopes back down to the Tuor valley. Tired, content and grateful we marched back to Bergün station for the journey home. The memories of this greatest of weekend tours will never be forgotten.

The following Wednesday evening we all met again for our gymnastics lesson and a netball game in a Zurich school house. Saturday afternoons I often sat in the sauna in Zurich-Oerlikon or ran a few laps on the long, softly springy sawdust track in the hilly forest near the zoo. Days and weeks passed far too quickly, home routines had returned. But I never lost sight of my goal to go abroad again. The inner embers continued to smolder. Unfortunately, I had brought home an annoying vice from Biafra. The sometimes life-threatening situations near the front stupidly tempted me to smoke again. I was unable to stop, every attempt was in vain, although I started jogging again. I didn't puff much, but it still took quite a while before the opportunity to break this addiction came. In 1970, the New Ski Club Zurich held its traditional Easter ski camp in its own Schwarzenberg clubhouse in the Flumser mountains. My girlfriend Helen Piguet and I signed up as members. This long Easter weekend turned into a starting point of a new chapter in my life. From Good Friday onwards, thanks to good weather, every morning we strapped our skin furs under the skis and slowly aspired towards the surrounding heights. The view from the summits stretched far and wide, over to the Churfirsten mountains, the Alvier, and the towering Gonzen landmark above Sargans, or west to the steep cone of the Spitzmeilen.

In the afternoon we enjoyed ourselves at a cheerful ski school near the clubhouse. The club's many amateur cooks took care of tasty meals and others happily did the washing, wiping, and cleaning up. A friendly, relaxed, and cheerful atmosphere filled the clubhouse, we beamed, laughed, and felt happy to be there. Here I got into conversation with Willy Fritz, an architect and head of a department at the well-known Durisol company. He told me about his current project, building schoolhouses in Turkey. The year before, a massive earthquake in Anatolia had destroyed countless villages and claimed many lives. After consultations with other countries and the Turkish government, the Swiss Red Cross, Caritas, the workers' relief organization, *Enfants du Monde*, and the organization of Protestant churches jointly decided to pool the collected money, and build new schoolhouses, prefabricated in Switzerland. All parts would be sent by rail to the affected province of Kütahya in Anatolia, the Asian part of Turkey. These schools, also called pavilions, could also be used as village centers. The required raw material was to be supplied by various Swiss companies. Willy Fritz was now looking for a clerk and logistician for this project, initially to coordinate the loading of the building materials into Swiss rail freight wagons and shipped to Turkey, with subsequent deployment to the affected villages in the earthquake areas. After I told him about my Red Cross work in Biafra, he invited me to his office in Dietikon for an interview. I was successful and was employed by Durisol as the man in charge of coordinating this program. I also got to know Mr. Karl Ketterer, a highly respected, proactive member of the Swiss Parliament in Berne. Mr. Ketterer not only recommended this entire aid campaign but also coordinated it with the aid organizations, the Turkish authorities, and Durisol AG. As a former CEO of Migros-Turk for five years in Istanbul, he knew the conditions in Turkey very well. He even travelled to Kütahya immediately after the earthquake and strongly recommended building new schoolhouses because so many were either destroyed or badly damaged. The companies Durisol, Alusuisse, and Zehnder Winterthur then jointly developed a high-quality element construction process that was surprisingly inexpensive and could be delivered quickly. These buildings would also be able to withstand earthquakes. The total sum of 2.25 million Swiss francs was enough for an astonishing number of 31 school buildings.

My new job as a clerk at Durisol AG in Dietikon in the Limmat Valley began three weeks after Easter. Suddenly, I was sitting alone in a modern office and studying all relevant documents, correspondence, and reports, and making phone calls to orient myself to ten different factories around Switzerland, which manufactured different parts of these schoolhouses. My boss, Willy Fritz, was very helpful in making contacts, introduced me to National Councilor Ketterer in Zurich, and also showed me the large Durisol main factory in Villmergen. I would not only coordinate the dispatch of materials but later be responsible for storage and material issues in Turkey. So, my next assignment abroad was programmed faster than I had dreamed or hoped for. All thanks to my great love for snow skiing. The material for the 31 school buildings was manufactured by companies in various Swiss regions. Wall elements, beams and roof trusses around Zurich, ceiling and wall panels as well as concrete iron in Aargau, anodized wall and roof sheet metal in Visp, insulation mats in French-speaking western Switzerland, and other school accessories in Glarus. All these companies ordered freight railcars at a coordinated time and rolled independently to the border station of Buchs in eastern Switzerland. All rail wagons were then put together there to form a special freight train which, after about three weeks of travel through Austria, Yugoslavia, Bulgaria, and on a train ferry across the Bosporus, finally reached the Turkish earthquake region in Anatolia. The Turkish government sent two civil engineers to Switzerland to familiarize themselves with the construction of these school buildings. They later were supposed to take over the supervision of construction in the far-flung villages. National Councilor Ketterer arranged the construction of a prototype school building on the premises of the company Zehnder Element Constructions in the town of Winterthur near Zurich. Wooden elements were erected for one classroom. The whole exercise lasted barely two hours. Mr. Ketterer and Willy Fritz informed the people from the press about the whole project, the transport and construction in Anatolia, as well as the concept of the developed element construction process. The two Turkish engineers were also present. I was surprised because both engineers didn't seem to be interested at all, they didn't even ask any questions during this simple construction. I wondered how they would be able to lead this program in Kütahya province. Too bad, my camera stayed at home, the photos would have helped me later in Turkey.

The first freight train loaded with building material also included an electric forklift donated by the Migros company. This would help me to store the material properly in Kütahya. Now it was time for me to report my departure at the Zurich town hall and to the district command. The Swiss army should know that if war broke out, they would have to fight without Hansrudi. Once again I said goodbye to my parents and friends. Karl Ketterer and Willy Fritz gave me final tips and promised to come to Kütahya for the opening of the first school building. In good spirits, I flew to Istanbul with Swissair. There I boarded a Turkish Airline plane and flew to Izmir at the Turkish Aegean Sea. Izmir used to be called Smyrna and is one of the oldest cities in the world. But I was not there as a tourist, so I found a cheap hotel room near the train station and bought a ticket for the trip in the morning to Kütahya. The long train left on time at 8 a.m. Before it left I had bought a sandwich at a kiosk. It was a leisurely, almost eight-hour, winding train journey through hilly Anatolian landscapes. The train was pulled by a black diesel locomotive adorned with a red crescent in the front, through lonely valleys dotted with tunnels. Then we crossed long monotonous plains. The train regularly stopped at stations, to let local travelers get on and off. I had never heard any of the station names, not even towns like Turgutlu, Sahlili, Usak, or Afyon. But this journey was an uplifting experience for me. I was again abroad, which I had dreamed of. At each station stood a black-uniformed station master holding a nostalgic red signal, ready to wave the driver on. Now and then I was able to converse in German with fellow travelers who had worked in Germany. Sometimes I dozed off or wondered why the drive was taking so long. What would I expect in Kütahya? Then finally, the conductor called out the next station: "Kütahya!" I was wide awake immediately, looked out of the window, and saw a small town with mountains behind it. I immediately liked that. Great round antique towers came into view on a high hill above the town, apparently ruins of an ancient fortress from bygone times.

With a whistling crunch, my train stopped in Kütahya. I grabbed my suitcase, got out with a pounding heart, and walked a few steps towards the ward. Suddenly a young man stood in front of me and asked in English whether I was Mr. Brawand. Then he introduced himself as Osman Ismail, welcomed me, and said he had been sent by the governor to pick me up. He immediately drove me to the large, blue and white-colored administration building decorated with red and white shutters. There I was welcomed by the governor and his deputy. They assured me of their full support in the work. A man brought me a domed glass of spiced hot tea and I burned my fingers on it. Then Osman drove me to my new accommodation in the guest house of the large, state-owned sugar factory on the outskirts of Kütahya. The porter showed us the way to the huge park-like area. The two-story white guest house in the large compound, surrounded by trees, bushes, and family houses, made a good impression. The manager introduced me to a simple, clean room, with a toilet and shower on the ground floor; my new home in Anatolia. He then took me to the factory's restaurant, which was located by a stream. As an official guest of the Turkish government, I would enjoy my free meals here including accommodation, as had been agreed in the contract. Kütahya is the small capital of the province with the same name. The city had around 50,000 inhabitants in 1970, is 970 meters above sea level, and lies at the foot of the Azem Zagi, an 1800 meter high mountain. Kütahya is famous for its ceramics and has a faience factory that is around 500 years old. I didn't have time yet for the surroundings and the local handicrafts, plenty of work awaited me. A large part of the material for the 31 school buildings had already arrived before my arrival. Unfortunately, the Kütahya station master had decreed that these building materials must be unloaded within four hours. The Turkish workers had contented themselves with storing it all over the place on a meadow in the sugar factory area. To make matters worse, a violent storm set in shortly afterward and hit the wooden elements in particular. Other material from Switzerland was already in a large warehouse made available by the Turkish government. But this too was a shambles, without any consideration or planning. Everything had been piled up side-by-side. It took me and two workers almost two full days to create order, space, and overview, as well as take a provisional inventory. Luckily, the Migros forklift arrived safely, and I was able to move the heaviest boxes and pallets with it. But the worst thing was that the building authorities had already transported ten trucks of material to villages, without knowing which particular items or quantities they were. No schoolhouse foundations had been built either. There were hardly any storage facilities in these villages, everything was laid in the open, exposed to rain, theft, or damage. I urgently needed a translator, however, the building authority could not provide me with a suitable man. Luckily, the son of the sugar factory's electrical engineer was home during his semester break. His name was Tamer Yöntem, he spoke good English and studied electronics in the capital Ankara. He became my first interpreter. Tamer happily accompanied me and the driver in our jeep, when we visited the villages that had already received material. Two empty trucks accompanied us to bring this rained-on material back to Kütahya. What idleness from the building authority and their strategists. This provincial office, responsible for construction in the province of Kütahya, was called

Bayandirlik in Turkish. From now on I will only refer to the building authority as Bayandirlik. During the months that followed, I had to fight out several issues with this particular director, wasting my time, often without achieving anything. He let me know he was the boss and didn't want interference from a random Swiss guy. The problem was also interpreters. Other than Tamer, some had trouble with the translation because of their poor German. Instead of presenting my questions or information as straight forward and simple as possible, they let out a torrent of Turkish, which was answered just as awkwardly by the director I was talking to and in the end, received an answer to a question I hadn't even asked. Different standards are obviously applied here, and it was difficult to get used to them. On my first trip to several nearby villages, my first driver Hamid - I always called him Genghis Khan because of his long mustache - drove much too slowly. Even on tar-sealed roads, he was never faster than 40 kilometers an hour. He refused to drive faster. When I questioned him about his timidity, he said that the vice governor had told him to always drive very carefully and slowly so that nothing happened to the Swiss and he didn't get scared. Laughing, I was able to allay Ghengis Khan's concerns and told him how we sometimes escaped a fire of bullets in Biafra by zigzagging away. He now wanted to demonstrate his driving skills. Despite bad tires, he didn't shy away from performing tricks at really breakneck speeds. I asked him to immediately stop this show. The next morning I also asked the vice governor to allow my Hamid a free ride. He agreed with a smile, I had relieved him of responsibility with this request.

More Swiss freight wagons with building materials were now

arriving regularly. With some Bayandirlik workers assisting, I enjoyed unloading the elements and boxes with the forklift and storing them properly, in the large warehouse, where beet sugar was usually stored. It became fuller and fuller.

Time was pressing to start building the first schoolhouse. But first some foundations had to be built. The internationally experienced but already retired Swiss civil engineer, Carlo Hubacher from Gandria, had recently arrived in Kütahya for this purpose. He was already around 70, a true personality and great character full of humour and mischief. He told me lots of fascinating stories from his many years as a site manager at home and abroad. One of his stories concerned Kemal Atatürk, a very successful army general, famous as the revolutionary founder of modern Turkey. The Grand National Assembly proclaimed the country a Turkish republic in 1923, and elected Kemal President. He was bestowed the title Ataturk, Father of the Turks, in recognition of his outstanding service. He gained great political power and determined the development and future of the country. He remained President until he died in 1938. Carlo Hubacher told me more than once that Kemal Atatürk, during a state visit to Germany, bought a large double bed with an iron frame and decorations, and had it shipped to Turkey. But the whole cargo ended up in a Turkish port. While Kemal Atatürk was the most powerful and important man in the country, Turkish customs remained almost impregnable. Only after a 12-month Turkish paper war, did the customs authorities finally give in and handed over Kemal Ataturk's bed set. But the beautiful bed set was already totally rusted! The fame and reverence among the Turkish people for their Ataturk have never faded. In many houses, even out in the most remote villages, I saw his picture on the kitchen or living room walls. His picture hangs high on the wall above a desk in every Turkish office, watching over the legions of bureaucrats and tea brewers.

Unfortunately, Carlo Hubacher only stayed three weeks. He gave me lots of very valuable tips and information when we drove to villages where school foundations were under construction. He explained and showed me the basic construction of such a foundation: first the rubble bed, then a concrete layer, then the insulation panels with vapor barriers. After that came the reinforcement of iron mesh with the cement coating on top, framed by the reinforced concrete wall of the foundation. Carlo got annoyed every time he looked at a foundation site. It was seldom of any use if he had to instruct the contractor and the workers to fish all the dirt out of the framework and to tamp the concrete carefully. In two villages the foundation wasn't even laid exactly according to plan. It was also very important to concrete the steel hinges in one straight line, to be connected later with wall elements. Once, the concrete didn't seem hard enough: two sly contractors tried to save on cement. A push in Bayandirlik to use experienced craftsmen was a waste of time. At least I learned from Carlo what was important here since he only stayed for a short time. Above all, contractors had only one goal in mind: to build the foundation as quickly as possible, then immediately apply to be paid by Bayandirlik and tackle the next foundation as quickly as possible. When Carlo left, only four foundations were under construction and none were yet finished. From then on I spoke with a firmer voice as the responsible Swiss Delegate in charge. The Bayandirlik also sent people to oversee the construction of these foundations, but I didn't trust them either because I saw that they didn't complain about obvious shortcomings. They just shrugged when I pointed it out. Swiss people with their sense of responsibility, have a hard time in Anatolia because of the ever-present *"Inshallah"* (God willing) mentality. The two Turkish civil engineers, who were sent to Switzerland to become familiar with the construction of the 31 schoolhouses were to lead the whole program in the 22 different villages, while I was responsible for the storage and ongoing delivery of the components. I was also the link between Durisol AG, Mr. Ketterer, and the Turkish authorities. The first of these two engineers worked at a government construction site in Kütahya. When I reminded him about his responsibility to take over, he denied any responsibility claiming he had no time for this. Even the Bayandirlik director played deaf and the governor said he wasn't responsible either. Now I wrote letters to both engineers, reminding them of the corresponding written and signed agreement with Mr Ketterer in Switzerland. But in Turkey, letters seem to silently disappear in some drawer or folder. A paper war can last forever, only coming to a standstill when one party throws in the towel. This was the beginning of my never-ending struggle against the very slow grinding wheels of the Turkish bureaucracy, which kept throwing sand into my work. There was nothing more to do now but drive over 300 kilometers to the capital Ankara and ask the second engineer in the Ministry of Construction to come to Kütahya and take over the construction management. So, I took the bus with my young interpreter Tamer to Ankara. At least the Turkish bus transport system is excellently organized and cheap, around two Swiss francs per 100 kilometers.

In Eskisehir, 90 kilometers away, we changed to the Ankara bus. On the way, the bus regularly stopped at 24-hour restaurants known in English as roadhouses. Warm dishes were displayed behind glass cases, I only had to point to this or that dish and a steaming, tasty meal was served on my plate dirt cheap. Twenty minutes later the bus drove on. In Ankara, I checked into a clean hotel while Tamer went to his dormitory. The next morning we reported at the Ministry of Construction but had to wait a long time at the reception. A man guided us to our engineer. He was enthroned behind a massive desk, in a snow-white shirt with tie, wearing a dark suit, showing off with a perfectly combed hairdo and a black moustache. He was on the phone while some fellows with documents waited patiently for a stamped signature. The engineer, whose name escapes me, finally welcomed us with a gracious smile asked us to sit down, and ordered tea. He was obviously an important man, probably a departmental head. He seemed very proud to show us his importance "live." I could not imagine that this fine gentleman was willing to leave his bureaucratic throne and deal with contractors in the Kütahya mountain villages, maybe even get dirty there. He let me know immediately this Kütahya program was certainly not his responsibility. He had used the weeks in Switzerland as a welcome free holiday. Now I demanded to speak to his superior, mentioning that according to the contract at least one of the two engineers who were in Switzerland had to take over the construction management. He seemed offended but phoned his boss on a higher floor. Half an hour later we were welcomed by this man in a very friendly manner, were immediately served tea, as the man listened to the situation, which he of course already knew from the engineer over the phone. He tried to make me believe that the whole thing was based on a misunderstanding with Switzerland – clearly an attempt to get rid of us. Now I demanded to speak to the Minister personally since he had signed the contract. But of course, he wasn't in Ankara at the moment. I would have to make an appointment at least one week in advance. Apart from expenses, loss of time, frustration, drinking tea, and more experiences with the Turkish bureaucracy, we had achieved nothing. At least the situation was clear now. Before returning to Kütahya, I quickly drove to the Swiss embassy and informed the friendly Ambassador about the current status of the school building project, which he already knew. I didn't want to bother him to contact the Minister of Construction, that would only become yet another waste of time. This schoolhouse program in Kütahya needed a determined "quick fix" man who liked to spit into his hands, and not an autocratic magistrate sitting on his bureaucratic career ladder. That afternoon in Ankara, I seriously considered taking over the construction management myself, being the only person familiar with the whole project. I sent telegrams with a proposal that I take over the project to Mr. Ketterer and the Swiss Red Cross, who had shortly before, taken over my employment from Durisol AG because of the delays. So, out of the blue, I had suddenly become a happily smiling Red Cross delegate again. Wow, great! The answer came immediately. The Swiss Red Cross directors and Mr. Ketterer agreed to my proposal, congratulated my courage, and promised help if necessary. Now I had the green light. To feel safer, I immediately sent a quick prayer to heaven. It was clear to me that I was now completely on my own, couldn't or wasn't allowed to ask anyone, and even make the Turks believe that I was an experienced engineer myself. After all, thanks to my trust in God, I was able to count on my common sense, and during my first three months in Kütahya, I did not allow myself even one single day off. The railway wagons that regularly arrived from home had to be carefully unloaded immediately and stored clearly arranged in the large warehouse, which was soon overflowing. Floor tiles, linoleum rolls, insulation mats, and the window glass had also arrived in the meantime. But I had to waste a lot of valuable time drinking tea and "waiting for Godot" in the Kütahya town offices, in Bayandirlik, and the Ministry of Education, time that I later tried to make up with overtime. But the joy and determination to face this great challenge left little time for negative thoughts. This was certainly to become an exciting unforgettable chapter in my life. It was now high time to choose one of the 22 villages to build "my" first schoolhouse. I chose Büyüksaka, which means "big sparrow" in English, and was only 20 kilometers away. Two schools had been allocated to this village, one for three grades and the other for two. In the meantime, the foundation had been completed here, and we could start. I was fully aware that this first school was to be the most important one of all. Nothing at all must go wrong if I didn't want to lose my "civil engineering face." But first, very important homework had to be done - where else but in the familiar seclusion of my warehouse. On a Friday of course; the working week in Turkey was from Saturday to Thursday.

First, I laid out the different types of wall panels according to the plan, then roof trusses and beams, and the fully equipped toolbox in the middle of the hall. That would keep me busy enough for tomorrow. Outside the sun was shining. I sweated, sighed, and scratched through my hair. Then I marked everything, checked all with a tape measure, tried to decipher the construction plan, wrote notes, and finally treated myself to a cup of tea from the thermos. Every beginning is difficult, especially for a trained baker-pastry chef, who decidedly tried to build schoolhouses instead of crème slices. Sometimes doubts crept into my brain when I didn't understand the plan details. What had I gotten myself into? There was only one thing, I was talking to myself and I convinced myself that I could do that as a citizen of Grindelwald. I sang with confidence my favourite verse from the Grindelwald song, where it says: "Let us walk forward for the good things in life." And here I had the best opportunity to do something good for the education and future of countless students. My self-confidence returned, and suddenly I was looking forward to tomorrow when construction of the first school would begin. The Bayandirlik had already informed the contractor Ibrahim that construction would be under my direction. On Saturday morning I was already sitting in the sugar factory restaurant at 7 a.m., allowing myself a hearty breakfast for the day's "baptism of fire." It could be a long day. Luckily the sun was shining again. At 8.15 the fully loaded truck drove off, followed by my new interpreter Ferid with our driver Ahmed, and me. Ibrahim and his workers were already waiting at the construction site on a large meadow near the village of Büyüksaka. Now many male villagers also came along. The women stayed in the background, as is strict Islamic custom. I was pleased to see the men help unload the truck while I directed where to lay down the components. Now I stood on a box, gave a short speech, informed the people about the background of this construction program, about the spontaneous willingness of the Swiss population to donate enough money to build many school houses in 22 villages, and two of those new schools were for their village Büyüksaka and its children. I added that the building material was very expensive and while it had arrived undamaged over the 2,500-kilometer-long route to Kütahya, they had to be careful with it because there was no replacement for any damaged parts. I also told Ibrahim's workers that I was going to show them how to use the prefabricated elements. But they would have to get used to the idea of later building the other schoolhouses mostly on their own if they could prove their abilities. It was therefore important that they followed my instructions exactly to ensure a successful build. The whole thing was continuously translated by Ferid into Turkish. In the end, everyone applauded enthusiastically. Now we could finally begin a corner. The first two heavy wooden corner elements were placed on steel hinges anchored in the concrete and connected with thick screws. Further on different kinds of elements were added until the end wall stood with both corners. This was of course much slower than described here. Instructions constantly had to be translated into Turkish, while I put on a poker face, pretending to be 'Mister Know It All,' when I seemingly confidently studied the blueprint, because all eyes were on me the "engineer." Maybe I could have become an actor after all!

Now the reinforced roof trusses, which looked like a long flat triangle, had to be placed and screwed onto the still wobbly wall elements, a relatively easy task. The whole thing was slowly taking shape. I drew hope, even dared a shy, somewhat tense smile when a villager handed me a glass of hot tea. I quickly had to put the glass on the concrete floor immediately, as I had burned my fingers again.

Everyone laughed as I blew my fingers and made a face. Now it was the turn of other elements for the front and rear long walls, some of which had window frames but still no panes of glass. And the sloping roof trusses were continuously connected to one another with roof battens. It was time for a lunch break, we school builders had to eat something and unpacked the food we had brought with us. My breakfast waiter Ismail had packed tender mutton, tomatoes, onions, and a delicious flatbread. Very close by was one of those antique wells that I saw as biblical, with a long, sloping wooden pole as a lever. A girl slowly pulled down the pole with a rope, while at the same time a bucket filled with water came up from the deep well. The girl now secured the rope to a post. Then she filled a clay jug with the fresh water from the bucket and came over to pour us some. It was absolutely clear, cool water, a drink from 1001 Arabian Nights for me! These wells fascinated me, looking at them, time seemed to stand still. I could imagine how it had been hundreds, even thousands of years ago, here in the Middle East, where Jesus Christ lived, but also Mohammed, the prophet of Islam.

On the large meadow next to our building site there were other wonders to be seen. Farming families drove up with long two-axle ox carts, laid out their ears of grain on large cloths, and began to beat the ears of corn with their swinging flails. Again, time stood still, I was amazed, I seemed to be dreaming. Because right behind it, a whole flock of snow-white geese waddled around and plucked grass. If you got too close to them, a loud protesting chatter would start. Donkeys also ran around eating grass. Later, I saw whole packs of donkey's in other villages and once tried to be a rider. When the farmers had finally threshed their stalks of grain enough, they shook out the almost empty ears again and stacked them aside as straw. They seemed to know when enough wind was blowing. With a wide wooden shovel on a long handle, the farmer threw the grain lying on the cloth into the air, the wind blew away the chaff and the grain fell back onto the cloth. I was an astonished witness to this millenary tradition. But then it was time to return to the present. Meanwhile, during recess, many school children had rushed out of their ancient, ramshackle, badly damaged schoolhouse to take a closer look at the construction of their new school. We got back to work, and the experiences from the morning helped a bit. When work ended at 5 p.m., the walls and roof beams were still standing tight and aligned in their place, just as we had cobbled them together with trust in God and the help of Allah. Time to breathe a sigh of relief, my reputation as a site manager had remained intact. Hopefully, no wind would blow all this splendor down again in the night, so we would continue the next morning; a Sunday. My day was far from over. After dinner, I returned to the warehouse to go through the Sunday work schedule and get the supplies ready. For the first schoolhouse, I always had to be one day ahead in knowledge of the Turkish workers.

On Sunday morning Ismail again put a packed lunch on my breakfast table. Thank God the unfinished skeleton of the schoolhouse was still standing securely on the foundation when we reached Büyüksaka. Two other contractors and a Bayandirlik engineer had come at my request to become familiar with the construction. On this second day, we actually managed to assemble all the wall elements and roof beams. My heart beat faster when I looked at our work from a distance. The entire length of the three classrooms stood dead straight, the sloping roof truss beams also revealed the final shape. The inner walls, roof battens and wooden grids for the Durisol ceiling panels, the wall insulation, the window glass, the doors, and of course the roof and corrugated iron cladding were still missing. My lonely "school homework " in the warehouse had paid off so far. But I would not praise the day before the evening; difficult, delicate work still lay ahead. This worried me because the workers on the assembly team were not professional carpenters, as agreed in the contract - all were simple workers or handymen. Although they were willing to work, they had to be constantly monitored. How was I supposed to manage, when new teams were building in different villages? My protests to the governor and the Bayindirlik director were of no use. They only replied with a tired smile. I had to scratch my hair or black beard, which grew longer and longer. Three brothers also worked in Ibrahim's group, their names were Ali, Ahmed, and Ismail. All three, good-natured and willing, they had to be constantly monitored, otherwise they quickly messed up. Later on, there was a lot of trouble in the village of Keçiller because of their bungling. We had to spend hours dismantling the roof trying to repair the damage. The villagers of Büyüksaka were very hospitable. There was always someone with tea and delicious melons to refresh us. Usually, a lot of people crowded around the construction site, watching and commenting on the construction of their new school. If people stood in our way, I tried to hire them for help. Every few hours the monotonous, melancholy chant of the Muezzin to pray could be heard from the minaret. These impressive, strange melodies have always gripped me, especially at night, when the full moon bathed the landscape and the village in a magical, shimmering light. Then I felt I was living in a fairy-tale from the Arabian Nights.

Because the aluminium sheet assembly was rather delicate and had to be carried out very precisely, Alusuisse delegated an experienced specialist to Kütahya. I telegraphed to Berne that he must come as soon as possible. In the meantime, we continued to work on the interior design. Our aluminum teacher finally arrived, by bus from Istanbul, a day's journey. On the return journey from East Asia, he made a three-day stop here to train us beginners. His name was Ferdi Wyssmann, an amiable. patient professional. Once again I was able to speak Swiss German, a pleasant change. I was finally allowed to talk to someone, to tell them about all the difficulties, handicaps, and wasted time by trying to master the program daily on my own. Ferdi suggested training only the most capable and reliable workers from Ibrahim's group. The three brothers were out of the question. Of the remaining four workers, at most Yussuf could be considered, there was no other choice. When Yussuf found out about it, he beamed like a cockchafer on the maiden flight. Ferdi now showed Yussuf and me exactly how to professionally assemble the green anodised outer wall panels, for Yussuf of course via the interpreter. The most important thing is a tape measure. First, you measure the exact position, width, and length of the wall element beams. Then the piece of sheet metal is pressed and measured because now the wooden beams are covered up. This is the only way to be sure that the nails sink into the beam. Without precise measurement control, the nail will miss the wood, resulting in an ugly hole in the sheet metal. Yussuf slowly seemed to get the hang of it. I also tried my luck with this technique, after all, I would teach the other teams. The next day, Ferdi, Yussuf, and I climbed onto the roof to learn how to mount the corrugated roof sheeting. Interpreter Ferid also had to climb up. So the Swiss Ferdi explained to Ferid in English what he should say to Yussuf in Turkish. And Ferdi instructed me in Swiss German. So we four roofers were trilingual up here. The roof assembly was the same as that of the outer walls, but here screws had to be used. Measure again and again exactly, punch a hole in the high wave of the sheet metal with the tip, and turn a long screw into the roof batten underneath. You had to be very precise so that the sheet metal ends formed a straight longitudinal line at the bottom. After a few lengths of wall and roof mounting, we looked at it from a distance. I was pleasantly surprised and pleased at how well the neutral-looking green aluminium looked to the eye. A real adrenaline rush for my battered senses. I thanked Ferdi for his valuable help. The following day was to be his last day and he still wanted to show how to put on the corner and ridge sheets. Why do you think I told this sheet metal story in such detail? There are several reasons for this. Mainly because sheet metal assembly became a problem at several schools. And the following story should serve as an example of the unbelievable obstacles, surprises and setbacks I was regularly confronted with. As we went back to work happily the next morning, our sheet metal apprentice Yussuf was missing. We waited in vain. When Ibrahim came at half past eight, we asked where Yussef was. Ibrahim was surprised that we didn't know. Yussuf had left to begin his compulsory two-year military service that morning?!? We didn't think we heard properly, we were dumbfounded. A good reason to scratch my hair again. Nobody had told us anything beforehand. The day before, I let Yussuf know that he could also clad the other schools that Ibrahim would build with sheet metal, and Yussuf had acknowledged it with a grinning nod. So Ferdi wasted two full days with this strange guy. Now I quickly chose Mohamed (not the Prophet) for the sheet metal work. He got a quick lesson on Ferdi's last day. From then on nothing surprised me anymore in Anatolia. You could hardly rely on others. The total lack of communication also cost me not just hours, but days, even weeks, in the coming months. Nobody had a mobile phone back then only a few villages had a house phone. Finding a phone in the village was a waste of time. To whom should I call then? To the governor or to Bayandirlik by a translator? There was only one thing left for me to do: drive around, for hours, for days, from construction site to construction site, on potted, winding asphalt or bumpy dirt roads, over muddy country lanes, through winding centuries-old villages, with astonished children, cackling geese or passing a donkey with his long penis hanging down. Wide streams, swampy meadows, stony paths, and narrow forest tracks were rarely insurmountable obstacles to our driver Ahmed who took shortcuts to gain time. Despite this, these incredible trips were my best hours in Anatolia. Individual mountains such as the majestic Murat in the background rises to well over 2,000 meters. Some villages are about 1500 meters high. The trips up there were always a very special experience. Past gorges, through open fir forests, the narrow mountain roads winding their way up, to enjoy beautiful views. The lonely, hilly, and peaceful mountainous landscapes, the elegant white minarets, which look from far like space rockets ready to launch, all calmed me down. I was happy to be able to experience such sceneries in this foreign country. Like a deserved compensation for all the difficulties, obstacles, and hassles of dealing with the never-ending bureaucracy and the lack of professional workers. On these long journeys to the far-flung villages, as a nature lover, I saw so many beautiful things that made me quickly forget these problems. In order to train other contractor teams as quickly as possible, I managed to set up foundations in two other nearby villages in Kiraspinar, which means cherry stone, and means Two Hills in Ikizhöyük. Both places got a two-classroom school, plus a complete plastic shower cubicle for the teacher. One of these new entrepreneurs was called Ahmed, he quickly understood what was important and controlled his workers well. The other contractor was called Mehmet. His hair, moustache and eyes were all black, even his clothes. So from day one, I called him Robin Hood, the "Avenger of the Disinherited." He was proud of his new name and tried not to anger me too much after I read him the riot act about his team's sloppy work. But all the teams had problems with sheet metal assembly. In the beginning, I had to spend a lot of time, swear words, and threats on the construction sites. Mere admonitions were useless. Unfortunately, I wasn't always able to monitor assembly in all the villages. At times, up to four entrepreneurs were working on various widely scattered construction sites. I could not quarter myself and had to confine myself to daily inspection trips. Before leaving, I had to check the loading of the building material that had been provided the night before in the warehouse and - as already mentioned - I often had to go to the authorities because this or that didn't work out. My timetable was constantly getting mixed up. Sometimes I felt like I was a member of the fire brigade, constantly on the move to put out fires. But it wouldn't be right to always complain. The villagers have always been very hospitable to me, showing their gratitude. Now and then I was invited for lunch by the Mukhtar, the mayor of the community. You sit around a table with other men in a simple farmhouse and enjoy the simple Turkish dishes. I choose white cheese, yoghurt, leek, spinach and egg dishes as my favorites. In the beginning, it struck me as quite strange that there were no plates, every man scoops with his spoon directly from the filled bowls on the table. Chairs and benches were available but not everywhere because sometimes the table is only about 20 centimeters high so that you have to sit cross-legged on the floor. It didn't bother the Turks, but I couldn't sit it in this uncomfortable position for more than five minutes. When I groaned and ate the soup with a pained expression, the Turks laughed and gave me a pillow or two for help. Wherever I have gone, in the poorest farmhouse as well as in the city apartment, the guest is truly a king and treated accordingly. If the family has no money of its own, they don't hesitate for a moment to borrow something from the neighbour to be able to serve food to the guest. But I have seldom encountered a female being in a Turkish house, at most, a woman might scurry, scurry, to quickly bring in a meal, set it down, and immediately disappear again without taking a look at the guest. The women have to stay in the background, they are taboo. You do meet women on the street, but they are mostly heavily veiled. The eyes and a bit of the nose, that's all you see. If I was walking through a village and a veiled figure came towards me, then their eyes would be covered with a hand in a hurry, so that the stranger would not have the opportunity to look into a Turkish women's eyes. As a result, I never knew whether I had met a young girl or an older woman. But sometimes I had to smile when a tiny gap in their fingers opened up and a curious glance fell on me, the tall, bearded stranger. I would have loved to take pictures of these veiled Turkish village women, but I was never allowed to do so. All persuasion failed miserably. It was always "*yok.*" I heard the word *yok* every day from morning to night. It means "no" or "not." A true *yok* spirit seems to permeate the land. Sometimes the Turks just throw their heads up or close their eyes for a moment. This also means *yok*. I've seen Turks, who were even too lazy to close their eyes, their eyes just looked upwards for a second without moving their heads, even that meant *yok*. If something doesn't suit them, if they're too lazy to get something or don't want to be disturbed, they immediately say *yok*. Another word kept ringing in my ears: "*yaren,*" meaning, tomorrow. They will do this or that tomorrow, not today. Over time, it got on my nerves when people kept saying "*yok, yaren*" to me! I got into the habit of saying, "*Yok, yaren! Bugün!*" - "Not tomorrow, but today!" In Switzerland, I explained to the Turks, it was not customary to postpone all work until the next day. They only smiled, as they were content with themselves and the world. Every day, as I drove through the villages and towns, I saw hundreds of Turks sitting around. At any time of the day, I would find them, arguing, chatting, or impassive, just staring at nowhere. They wait without a goal, without any kind of work spirit, this has always remained a mystery to me. It sometimes seemed to me as if they were just vegetating and waiting for death. Since Ataturk's rule, progress and development have been highly praised. In the countless isolated villages of Anatolia, however, there was no sign of progress. Here, future and present are synonymous with the past. As nice as it was for me to know that a hundred, two hundred, or even more years ago it looked the same as it did then, it still hurts to see how listless, quiet, and serious most people lived through the day. Two examples speak for themselves: At the end of March 1969, a year after the terrible earthquake struck the barren, mountainous region, countless houses were still in ruins, just as they had been when they collapsed. A few meters away the men sat around and waited until evening came. Not a stone, not a beam was removed. Everything was left to fate. Certainly, it was not like that in all villages. In some villages, probably thanks to an active village elder or dominant Mukhtar, it had been shown that men were willing to help with the reconstruction. On the way between Ören and Aslehanlar, which was made immediately muddy by the slightest rain and could only be passed with a four-wheel drive, there was one particular deep, muddy spot only 200 meters outside of Ören. Because of this obstacle, I was unable to send any material for building the school in Aslehanlar for three months. Everything had to be laboriously transported from Ören by horse and cart. To repair the bad, muddy road, ten men would have had to work two days at most. There was certainly no lack of material. Millions of stones were lying around everywhere. When I once again saw dozens of men squatting around in front of a village inn, I went up to them with the interpreter and asked why they wouldn't repair the road, as it is in their interest, they would all benefit from it, and use the road even when it rains. That's not our job, some replied, the road construction department is responsible for it. Even good persuasion didn't help. They just shrugged.

I had no choice but to give up my good advice and move on. It was now October and noticeably cooler. Far too few schools had been built up to now, my timetable was falling more and more behind. The Turkish bureaucracy could not be accelerated. But the work did not slow mentality. Winter was soon to come. Because I didn't want to catch a cold in the daily draft in the jeep, which didn't close properly, I went on a shopping spree in Kütahya with a long list. I bought two warm sweaters, a thick scarf, gloves, a lined leather jacket and an elegant half-length leather coat. A knitted hat and a Turkish roof cap were also a must. I increasingly looked more and more like a Turk.

The sugar factory, my home, was now in full swing thanks to the sugar beet harvest which began in mid-September. Trucks, tractors with trailers, and horse-drawn carriages rolled through the entrance non-stop. They all had to first weigh themselves on the long scales on the large square in front of the factory building. The sugar beets were then emptied into a long shaft, where workers sprayed the beets with high-pressure water. From there, the beets were transported underground on a conveyor belt to what is known as the beet bunker. The next station was the cutting machine, where the goods were chopped up into finger-thick slices before they were placed in a large cooking vessel to be softened before the subsequent steaming process. I was allowed to see the factory with the electrician Hayri Yöntem, two or three times from the inside. A delicious sweet taste floated throughout the large, multi-story facility, amidst the treadmills, drive belts, ducts, stairways and huge steam boilers. The many horse-drawn vehicles were often accompanied by a dog. But some of the farmers' dogs preferred to stay in the compound, they didn't want to go home anymore. Over time, a whole pack of stray dogs formed, which had found a new home there and roamed through the huge area together. They were even officially fed because it happened that farmers came back to collect their lost dog. But after the end of the sugar beet harvest, the remaining dogs were all shot.

Hot springs sprang from the ground everywhere in the earthquake zone of Anatolia. In many villages, the spring water had been used to build baths. On my way home in the evening, when it was already dark, I occasionally visited one of these warm mineral baths. Admission was dirt cheap, converted into Swiss currency, no more than ten cents. About every two weeks I also went to a Turkish sweat bath in Kütahya in the evening. The first time I almost lost my hearing and sight when I was lying on a large heated stone slab in the middle of the bathhouse. All around, a few Turks were sitting in their bathing niches and laughingly watched as the masseur, a burly man weighing eighty kilograms, turned me onto my stomach and stood on my back. He walked around on my back like a victor, suddenly jerked my arms up in the air, it almost took my breath away. Then he worked mercilessly on the legs, pulling, hitting, tapping and almost twisting them until I no longer knew which was the left or the right leg. The toes and fingers were roughly loosened and stretched. Then he grabbed my hair and jerked my head up several times. The tormented limbs complained with loud creaks. Completely exhausted and panting heavily, when I thought I was relieved, an onlooker warned me about the cold water, but a bucket of hot water fell on me first. After four more alternating buckets of cold and hot water, I was lathered all over my body with soap then hosed down again, accompanied by the gloating laughter of the Turks. My nuisance now held a small rag in his hand. With this he scrubbed my tormented body and proudly pointed to the black welts that he got out of the reddish skin and pores. That was rather embarrassing, since I thought I was clean. I threw him an annoyed look and silently wondered what it was, what he had against me, was he harassing me for so long for the amusement of the Turks? But when I got up, I felt wonderfully relieved, light, like a new-born. I left the bathroom like an Arabian desert sheikh who has just survived a hot battle. From then on I was happy to return regularly to my torturer, in order to surrender to his drastic methods, with the feeling that I was doing something good for my health and fitness.

* * * * *

One day Ibrahim, who's team had built the first school in Büyüksaka, informed me that there would be a festival, the Friday after next, in his village east of Kütahya. This would be an important day for the whole village. He invited me and Ferid as his guests. It was to be the day of the traditional circumcision of boys. Of course, I didn't want to miss out on this, we gratefully accepted the invitation. The deputy governor kindly provided us with the jeep and driver Ahmed, because there was no work in Islamic countries on Fridays.

We left early on a cloudless autumn day and reached the mountain village, hidden behind many hills, at nine o'clock. Ibrahim gave us a warm welcome and the ceremony had already begun. Two musicians, a wooden trumpet player and a drummer played Turkish folk tunes on the narrow village street, already quite familiar to my Swiss ears. These strange, wistful melodies fitted perfectly into this village, the people, the animals, and the surrounding barren landscape, just as an alphorn and yodelling match the mountainous landscapes in Switzerland. A boy, approximately 7-years-old with a serious looking face, was dancing all alone to these foreign melodies, wearing long white trousers with a shirt and a round white cap on his head. Some villagers and children watched. This boy was one of the seven, four-to seven-year-old boys that had been selected for circumcision that day. I would witness an ancient Islamic tradition being carried out. After a while the musicians moved on to another house, where the next circumcision candidate, also dressed in white, began to dance. When all seven boys had performed their dance ritual, Ibrahim invited us to a chai. His simple house was already full of people, waiting for the important event. The circumciser, a grey-haired man of about 50, was already there. We greeted each other and he willingly answered my questions which Ferid put to him. This man wasn't a doctor, more like an experienced barber or trained specialist who was called to a village on a Friday to carry out these "operations." Ibrahim's little son had now been brought in. He seemed scared, poor boy. I was glad that I was born in Grindelwald and not in this area. The "wandering doctor" now took the four required utensils from his small gray suitcase. A long green plastic grandmother's knitting needle, a small pair of old flat-nose pliers, a scary looking folded straight razor, and a small spray bottle of disinfectant solution. Ibrahim now placed his defenceless little son on an ancient wooden stool and held him by the arms from behind. Everyone crowded closer. Someone took off the boy's trousers and underpants and another shone a flashlight on the exposed penis. The circumciser knelt and sprayed the disinfectant solution. Then he slowly and carefully inserted the knitting needle into the urethra, holding the needle between the pinky and ring finger of his left hand. His remaining three fingers were suddenly holding the small flat-nosed pliers. With this he carefully grasped the small foreskin and pulled it slightly forward, holding it there. The unfortunate little boy began to cry, trying to fight back when the man grabbed the opened razor blade with his right hand, but the father wouldn't let him go. Now the small foreskin was loosened with practiced quick cuts and got stuck on the flat-nosed pliers. The little patient screamed like crazy, the wound was bleeding profusely, it was sprayed, thickly bandaged and the knitting needle pulled out at the end. Ibrahim comforted his crying son and carried him into the next room, laying him on a bed there. After a while, when the shock and burning pain had subsided a little, we were allowed to visit to congratulate him and generously lay banknotes into his white dance hat, laying on the bed. The "circumciser" now carried out his last official act. He impaled the severed foreskin on a large safety pin and stuck it through a small piece of cardboard. Then he wrote the date, the names of the boy, his father and the village on the cardboard, and placed all into an old square tin with a lid. When I asked through Ferid, what would happen to this foreskin, he replied with a smile: "The boy will receive it back when he gets married!" This was my first circumcision procedure as an eye witness. I went through two more such tortures in the same village. It was the same cruel show every time, the boy's fear, his shock of being held by his father on the stool, the shock at the sight of the razor, then the merciless procedure; the sudden cruel pain of cutting his sensitive, intimate parts, before everyone's eyes. I had seen enough, that's how it was practised in Islamic countries since countless years. There seems to be no hesitation using such antiquated methods on helpless children. However, I also felt a little proud of the fact that I, as a foreigner, had been invited and able to witness it all.

But that festive day in this remote mountain village was far from over. Now the celebration began, after the circumciser had "freed" the seven boys and taken care of the booty in his tin can. He too celebrated happily. We were served a select lunch at Ibrahim's house. Lots of deliciously prepared lamb dishes, all kinds of vegetables, egg dishes, crispy flatbread and yoghurt: an Anatolian feast. However, the men sat cross-legged around the low table, this too is a tradition, and of course, unfamiliar to me. I needed two pillows, and sat with my back to the wall. This feast also included a drink called *raki*, (much like the German, *schnaps*) at the end. The small glass had to be emptied in one gulp, so that refills could be poured immediately. But I didn't take part in this ritual for long, preferring instead to drink spiced Turkish tea. Finally, Ibrahim motioned for us to follow him to the next event. We walked to the big village square. There was a larger house there and we entered a huge room. More than fifty men from the village must have been sitting there on chairs and benches. They seemed tipsy and in high spirits. Only now did I see that most of them were holding a bottle of beer. They all talked, drank, laughed and sang. Of course, I didn't understand a word and didn't feel comfortable in this society of tipsy men. After a while someone gave a loud command and it became immediately quiet.

Everyone started counting out loud together: one, two, three… and I was puzzled to see that many men were suddenly holding a revolver or a pistol and pointing it up to the high, white ceiling. The counting went on and – probably at ten – the gunslingers pulled the trigger, hooting with a cracking bang. Fine white sand and dust now trickled down onto those present, accompanied by loud growls and laughter. I got up quickly and left into safety outside in the warm afternoon sun. Here, at the edge of the village square some men were dancing, swinging their arms in all directions, turning elegantly and elatedly to the monotonous music of the two musicians. They encouraged me to participate. Why not? There was no harm in trying. But first I tried to memorize these strange dance steps. Then I stepped forward and tried. Apparently I must have looked funny as an Anatolian folk dancer, because the children present immediately started to laugh. A few men waved and nodded encouragingly, telling me to keep kicking. But for me, at most, swinging my arms worked to some extent. I could also turned if necessary, but my two left legs kept getting in each other's way. I still enjoyed it and strained my ears to follow the melodies better. Meanwhile, more and more people streamed together, watching me with interest. It wasn't every day that a foreigner was clumsily dancing around in their village square. At least I got a laughing applause at the end.

With the oncoming twilight, this unique day slowly came to an end. But Ibrahim only let us go after a simple and delicious dinner. The three of us guests thanked him for his heartfelt hospitality, for allowing us to spend this unforgettable day with him. Lost in thought, we slowly drove back to Kütahya in the magical light of the full moon. I had trouble falling asleep, the experiences in this foreign country kept me awake.

Nestled between a wooded high hill and a slightly flatter one, over which the narrow dirt road led, lay the remote village of Keçiller, which means male goats in German. This somewhat sleepy, lonely place was repeatedly, at least once a week, rudely disturbed by light tremors. But a big earthquake in the previous year so houses collapse and the old school. The stones laid between traditional half-timbered houses had fallen off from the wooden beams down on the residents, causing injuries and death. Keçiller looked like a forgotten village from a bygone century. At times a plastic bucket or battery radio's betrayed the antique village appearance. The ruins of the collapsed schoolhouse had been cleared away, to make room for two new Swiss school buildings. The construction of the foundation had also begun. The amiable young teacher gave lessons outside on the meadow behind the building site. The black-uniformed students sat shivering, huddled together at the old-fashioned, undamaged desks in front of a split, faded blackboard. Time was pressing to build a two-and-three-room school before winter. Supervision during construction could be problematic due to the long distance from Kütahya. Ibrahim was the builder here, with the three brothers who had to be watched over to avoid mischief when Ibrahim wasn't around. The descent to Keçiller took almost two-and a-half hours, with a direct ascent that was bumpy but usually a little longer because we stopped by other construction sites whenever possible. It could happen that we sat in the jeep for six to eight hours a day and got out of it like we were exhausted. Sometimes driving to villages we stayed hungry for hours if we did not bring a packed lunch. Once, during an endless drive without food, we finally found a tea house in a village. The owner only had eggs and flatbread in stock. First the three of us Ferid, the driver and I, ordered three fried eggs each with onions, garlic and bread, along with tea. With eating came appetite. We ordered more: three more serves, this time with two eggs. But I asked for more flat bread, I was so starved on this chilly afternoon. We had eaten close to 20 eggs, plenty of flatbread and emptied a large pot of tea. This gave us enough courage to make our way for the first time through a narrow, gloomy valley to a village surrounded by forest, where the stone bed for the foundation had only just been laid. As already mentioned, the telephone had not yet been "invented" in these very remote, lonely Anatolian hills. It felt like time had not passed. I was happy to be able to feel this sense of an ancient time, out in this remote mountain area, as though it was still the Middle Ages when a day really was a whole day, and life was governed by nature and the seasons. Not like today in modern life, where the working day consists only of fleeting hours into which, one wants to squeeze in everything possible. On our long drives through the hilly hinterland we often met farmers on horseback. They all looked somehow the same, moustached, stubbly, older, a rod in hand so that the shaggy donkey wouldn't fall asleep during the lonely ride. The riders were in rough, dusty shoes, baggy trousers, wore old-fashioned smocks with an indefinable neckerchief, and on their heads they wore either a sturdy cap or a worn-out hat, which were certainly in fashion during Atatürk's time.

Here in the wild Anatolian west, such lonely riders sometimes reminded me of the legendary Buffalo Bill. However, I never saw a colt in a holster. The tough, frugal donkeys often had to carry their master for hours in the same monotonous trot over mountains, through valleys, hill and dale to his destination and then back home again. The donkey has been a cheap means of transport since time immemorial. It feeds on the barren grass and, as a thank you, fertilizes the thin layer of humus where it stands. I had taken a liking to the young donkeys. I would sometimes tease the little guys and cuddle them. I stopped once at a large meadow in a village. Countless donkeys, probably around fifty, were grazing here. Their "E-R, E-R" screams, which I had become familiar with, rang out again and again on this meadow. Individual donkeys immediately became restless and galloped off. Perhaps their beloved one was calling. They longed for a quick sweetheart hour. I saw some donkey stallions there in the meadow with their taut penises hanging down. One jumped on his beloved to produce offspring. It was time for me to move on and get back to work.

I remember another village, I think it was called Aslehanlar, where the school was held outdoors. There, too, school children dressed in black and crowded ancient school desks. They watched the teacher write on the long-faded blackboard leaning against a stone wall, bathed in the afternoon sun. The teacher also wore black clothes and had a moustache, like so many Turks. I took the opportunity to photograph this unforgettable image. At the same time, the new three-class school was being built less than 20 meters away. The inhabitants of the village of Aslehanlar were different from the villages I had known, especially the women. They didn't cover their faces, nor did they run into the house when I came near. Their clothes were brightly colored and much was knitted. Knitting seemed to be their favorite pastime, as they kept glimpsing the making of the new school. Once, I came a little closer to them with the interpreter Ferid. Proud and smiling, the women showed me their colorful knitting. I was finally able to exchange a few words with women in a Turkish village and took the opportunity to help an old woman spool yarn. They thanked me with a laugh. And the men, who in Anatolia, persistently tried to hide their wives under their clothes and in the house, took no offense here at all. I carefully asked about the reason for this openness and difference. It was said that their ancestors had settled here many generations ago. At that time, they had arrived from a neighbouring Turkish country, Bulgaria. So that explained the difference. They confidently maintained the traditional culture of their forefathers through all the generations. Unfortunately, it did not occur to me at the time to ask which religion they belonged to. Here, in this village, I finally wanted to try riding a donkey. When a man got off his four-legged friend next to me, I grabbed the opportunity and asked him using sign language if I could also have a go. The man laughed, gave me a welcoming wave and said, "*Hosh Geldenis*," (welcome!) It was now or never! Because I'm tall, I quickly sat on the strong, saddleless gray animal. But as soon as I made myself comfortable, the guy eloped with me. I was just able to grab onto the shaggy mane in a flash, otherwise I would have been thrown off from behind. I heard the eyewitnesses laugh out loud as my donkey galloped down the narrow village lane, with me swaying to and from, throwing up its thick buttocks again and again to throw off my heavy weight. But I held on, trying desperately with my legs to get the fast runner to stop. I heard people running after me, laughing, at last another sensation in the village without the earth shaking. Two men in the alley rushed to safety, but afterwards called out some advice in

Turkish. They probably wanted to tell me where the brake pedal was. The village well came into view and my racing donkey made a beeline for it. Maybe he wanted to throw me in. Suddenly, right in front of the village well, the donkey slowed down and came to a gentle, non-jerking stop. A tenth of a second later I was back on solid ground and immediately jumped to the side so he couldn't kick me. By now this donkey was already slurping water from the well, the fast ride had made him thirsty. I didn't have to worry about Turkish mockery. Nevertheless, I was allowed to keep my head high, as the donkey didn't throw me off at my first rodeo show.

When the second school in Büyüksaka was finished, the provincial school director decided to hold a small official opening ceremony. The students decorated the new school building with flowers, drawings and flags. I contributed a Swiss flag. The villagers brought food and soft drinks. The school director and the Mukhtar, the mayor, gave short speeches and thanked the Swiss population for this generous help in times of need. My contribution was also thanked warmly, and the Mukhtar presented me with a small souvenir as a token of gratitude. He went on to say that the municipality intended to erect a protective stone wall around the schools as soon as possible and plant trees. The students sang some songs with joy and pride. My thoughts involuntarily wandered back to Grindelwald. With the same joie de vivre, we pupils also sang at events back then. In the meantime, the construction of the school building in Keçiller had begun. Because the three brothers Ali, Ahmed and Ismail worked here, I supervised the work for two days. I told the team leader Ibrahim not to start the sheet metal assembly without my presence. But then our jeep had to go to the repair shop for three days without being replaced. I worked in the warehouse instead. I had suspicions about what was happening on the remote construction sites. When I arrived in Keçiller at noon on the fourth day, I was extremely annoyed. Ibrahim was absent! The workers had installed almost the entire roof all by themselves, but how. It looked catastrophic. The sheet metal had been screwed to the roof battens at an increasingly slanted angle. The metal ends at the bottom of the overhang therefore did not form a straight longitudinal line, it looked like steps that were getting bigger and bigger. Interpreter Ferid didn't need to translate, they understood my Swiss-German tirade well, I could tell from the embarrassment shining on Ali's, Ahmed's and Ismail's faces. All sheet metal had to be removed and I saw that they had not screwed in the screws as they had been shown in Büyüksaka, but simply hammered them into the roof battens and partially damaged them. The only option left was to dismantle, not only the corrugated iron, but also the roof battens and then nail them back on at an angle so that the same holes in the metal could be used again. A tedious, annoying job–the whole afternoon I knelt, measured, nailed, and screwed. At the end of the day the roof was fixed and looked normal. At dusk we drove off again. Our driver Kemal drove at a brisk pace on the narrow dirt road through a forest. After a curve, suddenly a huge full moon appeared in the dark sky over the opposite hill. A very impressive, gorgeous image of nature. The journey now led along a small river. The driver hit the gas again. That was our undoing. Suddenly, a rabbit hopped across the narrow gravel road. The driver swerved, over-revved, and we flew over the embankment into the river, which fortunately had little water. We landed with a crash, raced along the flat stream bed to the other bank and only came to a standstill at the top of a small hill. We looked at each other stupidly and in disbelief, surprised at how quickly it had happened. When we realized that we were unharmed and the engine was still running, we grinned in embarrassment. But my heart was pounding. Only the locked toolbox and two shovels had fallen off the dock leveller into the water. Kemal immediately took off his shoes, rolled up his trousers, and cautiously stepped into the cold, sluggishly flowing water lit by the full moon, to search for and fish out the lost tools. Then, thanks to four-wheel drive, he found a safe way back through the water and back up the gently sloping hill to the road. We had been very lucky because we landed in the water at the only safe spot. Certainly several guardian angels had been waiting for us. We could hardly have counted on quick help in this remote place at that time. The guilty rabbit was probably on his way to say good night to the fox. Thoughtful but grateful, we slowly rattled home in the moonlight.

Birds are abundantly represented in Anatolia. In late autumn, when the time came for them to gather and fly to warmer countries, I sometimes saw thousands and thousands of migratory birds huddled together in a field or sitting in trees. At the beginning of November, near Haydarlar, we unexpectedly startled a huge flock of quail. They flew away, squawking loudly, and the sky darkened for a few seconds. Often, we could observe large flocks of birds high up in the sky. Like a dark cloud, drawing wide circles, they floated slowly, silently. When the sunlight suddenly refracted their shiny plumage as they flew in a different direction, the cloud became silvery bright.

I also met herons strutting leisurely along creeks. And foxes seemed to feel at home here in the woods. Hardly a day went by when several of these bushy fellows didn't scurry across the street in front of us in the twilight. At night we sometimes only saw two small lights from afar, fox eyes, which were illuminated by the headlights. Now and then hares would also hop around between the countless stones and bushes in the landscape, linger a little behind a stone and the next moment straighten up with ears pricked up to make sure that the huge noisy animal, our jeep, was not coming to get him. Between Keçiller and Dumlupinar, a rarely used, narrow, bumpy pass road led far up through a huge, magnificent dark fir forest. Up there, bears lived, almost 2,000 meters above sea level. Unfortunately, no matter how much we looked around, we never got to see any of these beautiful, furry animals. In the villages, we encountered herds of geese every day, blocking our jeep's path in groups of 10 to 20 animals. Loudly chattering in protest, their heads swaying like ears of corn in the wind, they scolded us, then waddled a little faster to clear the way.

Even more remote than Keçiller was the village of Saraycik. Ferid said, this translates to "lonely castle." The dusty route from Keçiller to Saraycik, was sometimes muddy in bad weather. It took about half an hour and led in tight curves over a ridge. Saraycik was also allocated two schools, but their construction was associated with many problems. I tried to build the schools in Saraycik at the same time as in Keçiller, because the two villages were not far apart. The Saraycik Mukhtar was responsible for bringing sand and stones for the foundations by an agreed date. More than two weeks later, despite repeated reminders, there was neither sand nor stones on the pitch. I had no choice but to announce to the assembled villagers that I was sorry, but school houses could not be built in Sarayçik for the time being because the Mukhtar had not taken care of the sand and stones. The assembly group would now work in other villages first. A great wailing began, and I was assailed from all sides. The next morning, at 8 a.m., the Sarayçik Mukhtar was already standing in front of the warehouse in the sugar factory. He insisted eagerly that I could rest assured; by twelve o'clock that afternoon all the sand and stones would be on site. I let myself be softened, thinking of the many children who otherwise had to continue studying in their half-ruined, damp schoolhouse. They had long since earned their two new schoolhouses. Due to his sizeable belly, I referred to the contractor for the foundation as 'the Fatty.' Unfortunately, he was unreliable and indifferent. Carlo Hubacher had already warned me about his botched work. A solid, properly poured foundation was the be-all and end-all for a schoolhouse. Carlo Hubacher went to a lot of trouble and explained the entire work process to Fatty, including string tensioning, iron laying, formwork, concreting, and tamping. However, we had no influence on the choice of contractors. This was decided by Mr. Lütfi, the difficult director of the Kütahya provincial building authority; on the basis of the offers received. While construction was going on in Keçiller, Fatty, started work on the foundations in Sarayçik. This enabled me to visit both construction sites on the same day. I constantly had to admonish Fatty to work more carefully with his team. On the very day when the concrete was to be poured, our jeep had to go back to the workshop for repairs. When we arrived in Sarayçik in the afternoon of the next day, Fatty came to the jeep and proudly announced that the foundations were ready. As usual, when the three of us arrived at a building site, the villagers, mostly men and children, flocked to witness our visit. This time they got their money's worth as spectators. When I inspected the foundations, I couldn't believe my eyes at first. It was hopeless Fatty just couldn't do it. He had obviously skimped on the cement, which was uneven and friable rather than solid. The angle irons were cast in a slight wavy line, five centimeters higher in the middle than at the corners. Fatty had messed up incredibly, it was completely impossible to build on such a "foundation." Now I started to swear, loud and clear, but not in English, but plainly in my Grindelwald dialect. First, I pointed out each botched detail while looking at Fatty. I was sure that he understood my Grindelwald German. Continuing to curse, I pointed to the worthless concrete, then again to the disastrously placed angle irons, but was suddenly stopped by a roar of rage from Fatty who shouted something and ran away. Ferid immediately grabbed my arm and called out: "Sir! Quick! To the car and away from here. This guy wants to shoot you!" We immediately ran to the nearby jeep and luckily, Fatty's car was parked further away. He must have hidden a gun there. Our driver Kemal was already in the jeep, we hopped in and drove screaming, out of the village, leaving a cloud of dust behind us. This was the start of a long "live" chase towards Keçiller. We had quite a lead and Kemal proved to be a skilled rally driver through the tight hairpin bends up to the ridge. But Fatty was chasing us, we could see a big cloud of dust behind us. He certainly wanted to send me to the eternal hunting grounds. Behind the pass, driving suddenly became dangerous, a big truck came towards us and Kemal had to drive back a few meters. At any moment Fatty could appear and take revenge because I had exposed him in front of the whole village and obviously insulted him in Grindelwald German. Waiting, gulping, with my heart pounding–until the truck finally drove by. It had felt like Russian roulette. Breathing a sigh of relief, we raced off again, throwing up dust and stones, hoping that the truck would now also block Fatty. At breakneck speed we went down to Keçiller. We drove past our construction site there. People looked at us in amazement as we rattled through the village, throwing up dust and honking our horn, and immediately tackling the next hill. Then we disappeared into a long stretch of forest. In the next village we turned onto a dirt road, camouflaged by bushes, and waited at a safe distance for Fatty's cloud of dust. He came and drove through the village towards Kütahya. We breathed a sigh of relief, he hadn't seen us. After half an hour we drove on and reached the sugar factory. At night I didn't leave my window open. "You never know," I thought. Surely Fatty's anger had evaporated, but hot bloods like that are capable of shooting down a person in anger, only to then throw themselves over him crying the next second, bitterly regretting their deed. The fact that Fatty had followed me, reminded me to be careful. Since I knew that he was often at the building office, in the morning, I sent Ferid over there the next day to check the situation. He came back laughing and said everything was fine again, he'd met Fatty and talked to him. His inner life was back to normal for the time being and he did not intend to shoot anyone. Fatty thought I had called him insulting names in front of the villagers, that is, I had besmirched his honor. So he hadn't really understood my native dialect after all. Three days later I happened to meet Fatty again. We shook hands with a smile, smoked a peace pipe together and Ferid photographed the peaceful scene. A few weeks later in Bezirgan, through Fatty's fault, the foundations were again badly built. The building authorities were now fed up: the fat man was relieved of his position as an independent building contractor for our school buildings. He was replaced by an inspector from the building authority, who was not much more reliable. Most of the time he was away from the site, and it so happened that the foundations at Bezirgan turned out to be as poor as some other places. The fresh concrete was too thin and mixed with too little cement. The concrete layer was unusable and had to be picked away again. The director of the building department now had the strange idea of blaming Fatty, who had long since been relieved of his post. One evening Fatty came to my guest house with Ferid and asked for help. Now he must have been glad that he didn't shoot me in Sarayçik. Big tears rolled down his cheeks, he grieved deeply about the false accusations from the building authority. I was angry about these unjust measures, as this time, Fatty was innocent. I wrote a report, explaining that for these new mistakes in Bezirgan, the fault lay exclusively with the building authority, and it was not correct to demand money from the wrong man for mistakes he had not made. The next day I gave this report to the Director of the Building Department, with a copy to the Deputy Governor. As a result, a huge months-long paper war broke out between these two offices. Nothing happened in Bezirgan for a whole three months, work there stopped. Finally, I personally intervened with the governor that it was irresponsible to keep the students waiting so long because of this unnecessary bureaucratic struggle. The governor finally put his foot down, the foundation was completed in an acceptable manner and Fatty didn't have to pay. The daily recurring problems with unskilled workers, the incredibly sluggish bureaucracy, as well as our chronically late evening return from the construction sites sapped my strength. After countless seven-day weeks, I now rested every Friday, the Turkish Sunday. When the Friday weather was nice, I hiked up to the hills and mountains that tower over Kütahya. Or I would borrow an old bicycle from the sugar factory and pedal back and forth on country lanes through the area. These solitary excursions were like a soothing balm.

Every now and then, early on a Friday morning, Ferid and I would take the bus to Eskishehir, 90 kilometers away, and in the afternoon we would watch a home game of FC Eskishehir. They played in the top Turkish football league. Top teams from Istanbul each brought many loud fans to the stadium: the background noise was indescribably loud every time. And I also shouted and screamed as loud as I could, welcoming an outlet to free myself from all the accumulated frustrations.

There were new delays in the interior fit-out of the schools. Each of the countless Durisol ceiling panels had to be painstakingly screwed into the ceiling beams by hand with ten screws. This was much too slow, we urgently needed a mobile generator to do this work electrically. Getting a generator from the building authority in Kütahya was hopeless. Lütfi, the director only had a weary smile and said, shaking his head, "*Yok.*" So, we drove back to the capital Ankara, determined to find a generator there and I was definitely not going to accept a *yok*. The somewhat older Ahmed drove and Ferid came along as an interpreter. It was clear that for this application to the Ministry of Construction, we had to exercise patience, waste time and sip loads of hot spiced tea. At half past ten we reported to the porter and a man took us to the office of the head of department, who had ignominiously let me down the last time. Now the next round began. He seemed quite surprised to see me again unexpectedly and probably sensed trouble. I declined the obligatory tea and immediately let the cat out of the bag. The engineer immediately shared the fact that he was not responsible for equipment. He should at least give me a written recommendation for the responsible man, I replied. But he didn't want to do that, instead he sent me to some other office they would help me further. Of course they couldn't, they passed Ferid and me on to another floor. There we were warmly welcomed, we could hardly refuse the tea, and as we drank watched the boss talking into two telephones at the same time. Two officials with documents were already waiting impatiently in front of the massive desk for a signature and stamp. In this office, the picture of the ubiquitous Kemal Atatürk hung on the wall next to the red and white Turkish flag.

The boss watched graciously as we carefully slurped the spiced tea from the hot glass. I would much rather have a glass of cool water from the draw well in Keçiller or Büyüksaka and breathe in the fresh country air. This man couldn't help us either, he sent us to another warm room with best wishes, announcing us by telephone. But we had to wait outside because the bureaucrat had a visitor. When we were allowed to enter, we were put off until the afternoon. With my patience still intact, we took a few deep breaths and went out to eat. I didn't want to return to Kütahya without a generator. I was determined to snatch the much-needed generator from these Turkish bureaucrats if need be. They should get to know me! At 2 p.m. we reported back to the same office. I refused the tea and put pressure on this boss. This seemed to displease him, he quickly recommended me to another floor, where they would certainly help further. Again we sat in a feudal office, watched the repeated paper and telephone work for a while. Surely this was another dead end? But wait, what was that? Outside in the corridor I thought I could clearly hear a long, continuous neighing, it sounded like laughter. Oh, of course, now I knew what it was. It could only be the notorious Turkish official, who galloped through the spacious corridors, reminding everybody in each office to put on the bureaucratic brakes. Ferid and I were just two of his numerous, patiently waiting, tea-sipping victims. We spent that whole afternoon waiting, twiddling our thumbs and yawning, sitting in front of desks while friendly, smiling, promising officials had only one thing in mind: to get rid of us quickly and pass us on as soon as our tea glasses were empty. When we left the ministry after closing time, I first had to walk around for half an hour to calm down. In the evening I called the Swiss ambassador, told him about today's idle time and my plans for the next morning. He invited me to dinner next evening if I was still in Ankara. When work started the next morning, I wanted to go back to "our" engineer and give him an ultimatum. It was said, he was at an important meeting. So wait and see again, drink tea, twiddle your thumbs while Kemal Atatürk sternly looked down from the wall at us.

More and more document carriers entered the office wanting signatures. Some waited, others gave up and left because the high lord was not sitting on his throne. We had no choice but to accept the time wasting, sip tea or occasionally visit a toilet. Then I requested Ferid to strictly translate every sentence, every word, on an ongoing basis when I was going to talk to the engineer, as this would be the only way to get a generator. Because I wouldn't mince my words anymore. Ferid promised to translate exactly, but it didn't sound convincing. Finally, after about 1 ½ hours of waiting, the engineer came in and hesitated when he saw us. I let him put signatures and stamps on the many documents, so that the waiting paper carriers could leave. Then I allowed him just one phone call. When he tried to dial a number for the second time, I immediately stood up, put my hand over the phone harshly and said, "Stop! Enough! Now it's my turn, I won't let you fool me any longer! You were sent to Switzerland to learn about the schoolhouse program in Kütahya province but refused to go to Kütahya and lead this important school building program. And now instead of pulling out all the stops to help us get a generator, you're letting me run from pillar to post for days without success here at the Ministry of Construction!" I felt Ferid translated every sentence truthfully, because the fine "gentleman" seemed surprised and went pale but responded again with meaningless excuses. I simply cut him off and said: "I'm giving you an ultimatum! By 3:00 p.m. this afternoon, I will receive a certified letter from you that I can pick up a portable mobile generator for our bilateral schoolhouse program from your ministry's warehouse in Ankara with a receipt. This generator will be used under my responsibility to speed up the assembly of the ceiling panels for the 31 Swiss school buildings currently under construction, so that countless children can finally go to school again!" Now I had really talked myself into action, and Ferid came under pressure to translate quickly. He seemed quite embarrassed, his face flushed. But I went one better and finally said to the now quiet engineer: "How you get this writing is up to you. But I am telling you here and now, if I do not receive this paper this afternoon, I will make a beeline for the Minister's office, and there I will make a big fuss about your wrongdoing and misbehaviour, leaving no details out. In addition, a corresponding telegram will be sent to the Swiss Red Cross, the project initiator National Councillor Karl Ketterer, with a copy to the Swiss Ambassador in Ankara!" Then I got up, said goodbye, and walked straight out of the office with Ferid who breathed a sigh of relief. For him, translating my harsh words to a senior bureaucrat had been difficult and embarrassing. But I felt comfortable and relaxed and went to a well-deserved lunch with the loyal Ferid. At about two-thirty we returned expectantly to our engineer. He greeted us with a frosty expression. Then he let the cat out of the bag. We should immediately go to the Minister's office, he was already waiting for us. 'Aha,' something had happened during the lunch break. An officer showed us upstairs to the impressive reception office of the Turkish construction minister. The handsome grey-haired man with a prominent nose stood up as soon as we entered, gave us a friendly welcome and of course tea was brought straight away. He first inquired about the current status of the school buildings and possible problems. I oriented him comprehensively, not skimping on the many practical difficulties that kept slowing down the whole program. I pointed out, amongst other things, that unskilled workers had been used, not professionals, contrary to the contract. The Minister already knew that because he had received corresponding letters from Switzerland and promised to get in touch with Kütahya. Then he finally said that he had already approved the generator I had requested. I could pick up the voucher in the course of this afternoon. We said goodbye with many thanks. The trip to Ankara was worth it – only just. We picked up the voucher later from the taciturn engineer. Unfortunately, the equipment magazine was already closed when we got there. In the evening I was the guest of the Swiss ambassador and his charming wife. An excellent dinner and the interesting conversation made up for all the hardships in the ministry. The next morning we picked up the new generator from the equipment depot, had its handling and maintenance explained to us in detail, with the condition that we handed the device over to the Kütahya building authority at the end.

Cheerfully we drove the 350 kilometers back to Kütahya. Word quickly got around that we now had a generator available, every contractor wanted it first. A roster brought some order. Despite this, the generator sometimes inexplicably disappeared from the site overnight. We feared it had been stolen. Then I caught Mehmet "Robin Hood" red-handed with the generator on his construction site. He had "stolen" it from another construction site on the way home the night before in order to speed up the construction of his schoolhouse. They were just rascals, these contractors, never at a loss to use tricks to gain advantages. Mehmet "Robin Hood" was the worst. Still, I couldn't really be angry with him because he did a good job with his men. But he masterfully understood how to get the workers away from his school building site and quickly deploy them to one of his private building sites. For example, when I went to Kiraspinar or Sadikiri, I met no one. The wooden skeleton stood there lonely and abandoned.

When I finally met "Robin Hood" and wanted to know where his workers were, he said with a laugh: "*Yok, Yaren*! Tomorrow, they'll be back tomorrow!" But I didn't believe him, because *Yaren* means tomorrow, but in Anatolia that is even more vague than maybe. And with maybe nobody can build schoolhouses. Now I took action and brought Ibrahim's men to Sadikiri by jeep. But the intelligence service in Anatolia works quickly even without a telephone. "Robin Hood" knew a few hours later that Ibrahim's group was working on "his" schoolhouse. He immediately came to Sadikiri with two workers and chased Ibrahim's people away from the site, which of course again resulted in a great deal of palaver. But I made it clear to "Robin Hood" that I would no longer tolerate his tricks: he may lose his contract with the authorities, if he does not change his tricky behaviour. He understood and worked correctly from then on.

I had long since gotten into the habit of taking my cassette tape with me. If I was satisfied with the work, and there were indeed many workers who obeyed the instructions and worked reliably, I let rustic country music ring out at full volume. Suddenly all village people came running, the workers put their tools aside for a moment, listened with pricked ears and bright eyes to the strange melodies from distant Switzerland. The yodelling songs always generated the most enthusiasm. Sometimes they asked me if these were the Muezzins for prayer in my country. The work then proceeded with renewed vigour and in good spirits, and I was assured that they were already looking forward to my next visit. The next time I was greeted again, full of joy: "*Hosh Geldinis*!" (Welcome to you!) To me, it always sounded like a magic word from the heart, letting me feel a little safe in this strange and foreign country.

I don't know how many sheep there are in Turkey. There must be legions. Everywhere you go you come across flocks of sheep struggling to find their scanty fodder. The flocks are always accompanied by shepherds. In winter they wear long sheepskins to protect them from the cold. Donkeys loaded with sacks of provisions can also be seen, accompanying the herd over hill and dale, through fields and forests. The big beige dogs that protect the herd from wolves always made me happy. They were so very different from the over bred dogs in Switzerland. There was so much wild in them, but they showed respect for people. They bark loudly and dangerously, but rarely bare their teeth or consider attacking a human. I was most impressed by these powerful shepherd dogs when the lambs were born. While the ewe gave birth to her lamb, the herd slowly moved on. Immediately the dog came and sat next to the ewe and the new-born, standing guard to protect both from possible predators. As soon as the lamb had suckled for the first time and was able to walk, the dog slowly led the two back to the herd. We stopped sometimes and approached this impressive miracle of birth out in the wilderness. The dog sitting guard let us come closer without growling.

These dogs seem to take particular pleasure in competing with a vehicle on a rocky mountain road or on a swampy cart path. It's as if they're trying to drive invaders out of their territory. It often happened that our jeep was slower on muddy dirt roads than the dog running alongside. The dog then gave up the race and trotted, offended, back to his herd. Unfortunately, dogs often fell victim to their play instinct when they dared to approach a car too quickly and too closely. Every week I saw one of these caring fellows stretched out in a ditch, now prey for certain species of birds that feasted on the dog carcasses.

In Keçiller and three other villages, the earthquake had also destroyed the mosque. The men in the village used the school, which was still under construction, as a temporary house of prayer. I felt proud when I discreetly observed the men in the still unfinished school building during their prayers. The school served here first as a house of God, a house of Allah. In some other villages the building material that had arrived was lacking storage room and was simply piled up in the mosque. More than once I was able to watch with a smile as the men in the mosque performed their prayers accompanied by many bows between sheets of aluminium, roof battens, wall elements and other items, while the monotonous prayer song of the Muezzin was almost swallowed up by the insulating mats. In the eyes of these devout Mohammedans I was an unbeliever, a sinner so to speak, but I remained a welcome guest in their simple mosques, only having to take off my shoes.

November had already rolled around in the country. With it came the cold and the frost. For weeks, Mount Murat showed its cold winter dress in the background. It shone at us virginally white, while we drove through the hilly landscapes to work. But we didn't have much time on construction sites, dusk fell early, and it was usually already nightfall when we got ready to drive home. We didn't have a heater in the jeep and the ice-cold draft blew through cracks and crevices. We had to wrap up and disguise ourselves more and more. To cheer ourselves up during such chilly bumpy rides, we liked to sing songs or tell jokes to each other. These paths and dirt roads belonged to us alone, only crazy people were not at home at this time. All the same, the three of us who returned home were not all alone. Again and again, golden animal eyes shone at us, they mostly came from foxes or rabbits that were surprised by the car headlights. More than once, however, there were several animals that ducked behind trees when the headlights shone into the forest. Then our singing stopped immediately and the driver carefully pressed the gas pedal to get away from this inhospitable spot. We wanted nothing to do with wolves. A breakdown or an accident could be dangerous in winter at night in such isolation.

On a very cold November morning we drove up a narrow pass road in the fog. Shortly before the top of the pass the sun broke through, we suddenly drove through an enchanted fairy-tale landscape. The fog had covered the trees, bushes and shrubs with icing sugar. Ice crystals had formed. Big trees looked like they had white hair. At the top of the pass there was a small hut, it looked like a white sugar house, which reminded me of the witch's house from Hansel and Gretel. I knocked on the frost-crystal door, but no one came out. The old witch was probably still asleep. It was bitingly cold up in this white, sun-drenched dream landscape. We froze, got red ears, ran around waving our arms, and our breath produced "smoke." For a long time, we marvelled at this white wonderland with its countless frozen creations glistening in the cold sunlight. The thin fog slowly cleared and a great view opened up to us on the valley side. The driver pointed to a small village far below, which was called Kiraspinar. There, next to the village, I discovered a small greenish spot that could only be the schoolhouse that we had built there. I was filled with joy and pride because our work was visible from so far away. I felt such surprising moments as a gift from the God. This compensated me a thousand times over for many hardships and worries in this interesting foreign country.

TO THE HORIZON AND BEYOND

Of course, on my daily trips, I kept talking to Ferid and the driver. Sometimes I heard things that almost made me smile pityingly. But it also happened that I was filled with admiration for the Turks. Whenever we talked about Islam, the conversation tended to get interesting. I was always amazed at how deeply and genuinely many Turks believe in Allah. Driver Halil, for example, used the waiting time to visit the mosque and pray. He stayed there for at least half an hour. If our stay was brief, he would spread his prayer rug by the side of the schoolhouse, kneel and bow innumerable times, stretch out his arms, and murmur his prayers in a low voice. No one paid any attention to him except me, who sometimes stole a glance at the praying man.

* * * * *

The end of the year was approaching faster and faster, but frost and an icy wind slowed down the construction program. The thickly hooded workers tried to warm themselves up at an open wood fire. But firewood was scarce in Anatolia. A forester risked a lot if he caught wood trespassers and wanted to report them. Many foresters had already paid with their lives for this. On our trips to the remote villages, we sometimes only met the abandoned construction site. The workers had gone home because of the extreme cold, I couldn't blame them. We three masked people in the windy jeep, frozen like dogs, were happy when we found a tea room in a village to warm up. There, in the middle of the room, the village barber often opened his shop. He didn't need much, at most a worm-eaten wobbly chair, a small chest of drawers, two pairs of scissors, a proper shaving brush, a mighty razor and a hand mirror, a small basin, and a broom with a shovel. After the shave, the moustached-face gardener offered cologne and some fat for the hair. I usually had my hair cut in a tea room like this, while sipping tea and resting. Finally, he trimmed my beard, so that people would recognize me again, as it was too long. How should things continue in this cold season? I definitely didn't want to spend Christmas there. My application for vacation was approved in Berne. The construction work continued on a reduced scale during my absence. Ferid and a building authority engineer supervised the whole thing. Early in the morning, on December 20th, I boarded the bus from Kütahya, to Istanbul, then flew to Zurich the next day. When I presented my Swiss passport and my Turkish residence papers at the airport customs in Istanbul, the customs officer disappeared with them. Then he came back and said that because I worked in Turkey, I had to pay customs or taxes and gave the amount in Turkish currency, the equivalent of around US$ 200. I said there must be a misunderstanding, because as a guest of the Turkish government and site manager for dozens of school buildings in the Kütahya earthquake region, financed by the Swiss people, I was tax-free. That didn't interest the customs officer; it doesn't matter, I definitely have to pay, otherwise I'm not allowed to leave the country. But I wasn't willing to back down, first of all I didn't have much Turkish money with me, credit cards were unknown at the time, my Swissair plane was waiting outside, and I had some experience with Turkish bureaucracy, although not necessarily with customs officials. Customs had no right to fleece me for this reconstruction work anyway. I repeated my arguments, a little louder this time other passengers took notice and stopped to listen. When the officer still didn't understand, I asked to speak to the boss. But it took a while until he showed up. I was running out of time. For the third time I explained the current situation, this time to the customs chief. I was now surrounded by curiously listening passengers who had been checked at other counters. The boss also refused me the green light. Now I was fully charged at the right moment to play the trump card. "Sir," I began in a loud voice, "I declare for the last time that, as a guest of the Turkish government, I am the head of an earthquake reconstruction program and therefore do not owe any taxes. This can be seen in the submitted papers. If you still refuse me to leave the country, then I demand that you now use the telephone number on this business card, it is the direct number to the Minister in the Ministry of Construction in Ankara." The customs chief was silent. He seemed to be thinking. Maybe he was embarrassed because so many viewers were staring at him waiting for his decision. Suddenly he instructed his officer to stamp my passport and hand it over to me with the papers. Then he said, face stiff, "You can go!" He turned on his heel and disappeared. Some viewers shouted, "Bravo!" I quickly grabbed my travel bag and was the last to run through the gate and down onto the waiting bus. That wasn't the last of my Turkish adventures. I faced more to come upon my return.

In Zurich I hurried to my apartment in Oerlikon suburb, slept in my own bed once again, and called my friends. Oerlikon lay under a blanket of fog, the sidewalks and shops were full of people. Christmas was just around the corner. Only then did I feel the busy Christmas atmosphere, and quickly went on a shopping spree to get used to the familiar world of home again. I was happy to spend

Christmas and the holidays with my parents in Interlaken. My mother cooked a feast for Christmas Eve, and for dessert, just like when I was a child, there was *nidla*, (whipped cream). During these days I slept a lot, to recover from the strenuous Turkish months. From New Year on I took the train to Grindelwald every day and let off steam on the wonderful ski slopes between Kleine Scheidegg and Maennlichen. A sandwich with coffee was enough for lunch. Then I drove back down the deep powder snow-covered slopes to the next chair lift, which took me back up to the start. Even sudden snowfall couldn't slow down my exuberant joie de vivre. I just put on the snow goggles and slowly wagged down the slopes. The next day I chose the other side of the valley and went skiing on First and the Oberjoch. In the restaurant on First, I met my old school mate Bohren Hans. He was sitting at the table with an elderly gentleman. Hans asked me: "Do you know him?" I looked at him, but didn't recognize him. "That's Thönen Fritz," said Hans. What a surprise! Thönen Fritz had been our respected French teacher in secondary school. He had married the daughter of our revered Grindelwald pastor, Martin Nil, who had baptized and confirmed me. I hesitated a bit, suddenly talking to my revered and respected teacher. We shook hands warmly. He was happy when I told him about my interesting life so far. Before I took the train back to Interlaken, I quickly stopped by my best friend from school, Ringgenberg Max. We were both trained as bakers, were both truck drivers in the army in an anti-aircraft unit, and hatched cheeky rascals pranks during school days. Max worked in his parent's bakery in order to one day take over the popular business in Grindelwald. The vacation days passed quickly. I spent the last two days before returning to Anatolia at the Swiss Red Cross in Berne and discussed the whole schoolhouse program with the popular international project manager Ms. Zuyderhoff. She continued to assure me of her full support and was happy with what I had done so far achieved under very difficult conditions. In Zurich, before leaving, I met National Councilor Mr. Ketterer. He wanted to come to Kutahya himself soon to take a look. With renewed enthusiasm, I flew back to Istanbul. There I was able to stay in the house of Hedi Köse and her husband. Hedi, a native of Eastern Switzerland, was my sister Greti's long time friend and married to a lovely Turkish jeweller. The next day I did not board the direct bus to Kütahya, I wanted to travel a different route to see other areas. First the trip went along the Sea of Marmara to the Dardanelles. The European peninsula of Gallipoli now came into view and we were sailing along the Straits of Canakkale. I got out in the port city of Canakkale. It was bitterly cold again. I moved into a simple room in a pension next to the bus stop. I didn't realize how cold it really was that night until I got up the next morning. On the dresser was a shallow bowl, filled with water the night before, for washing. But nothing came of it, when I wanted to dip the washcloth in the bowl in the semi-darkness, all the water was frozen rock-hard, it was ice! I quickly rubbed my palms on the ice until they became damp, washing my face. This arctic cat wash awakened the spirits faster than an espresso. Shortly before six, I sat trembling on the bus, ready to leave. An old woman came in with hot tea. Thank God! I thawed my ice-cold fingers on the hot tea glass. My gaze wandered to the other side of the road and across the 1.5 kilometer wide strait, over to hilly Gallipoli on the Dardanelles peninsula. During the first World War, one of the bloodiest, most brutal battles had raged over there. British, French, Australian, New Zealand, Canadian and Indian troops landed at Gallipoli in 1915 to block passage to the Black Sea. They fought against the Turkish army under the command of General Mustafa Kemal, later President Kemal Atatürk. Memories of our history teacher Dr. Sägesser emerged, who vividly brought this bitter, bloody battle for Gallipoli closer to us. The allied army finally had to give up the hopeless fight and was shipped to the western front. The coastal cliffs, hills and valleys of Gallipoli are drenched in the blood of a quarter of a million Allied and Turkish soldiers.

After the old woman had collected her tea glasses again, the bus drove off. A boy acted as conductor and sold the tickets. He also regularly walked the bus with a bottle of cologne; those who wanted held out their hands, got a few splashes, rubbed their faces with them and enjoyed the fresh smell. This service was common practice on all buses back then. No bus drove through the countryside without music. On every bus ride I had to listen to the saddest and most sentimental love songs blaring for hours on the loudspeakers, but nobody cried. The passengers seemed to be dreaming of great love and longing, but to my ears it sounded, unfortunately, like ever-repeating songs of misery, a musical perpetuum mobile. Swiss country music would have appealed to me more. One of the first stops was the famous Troy. I didn't want to get out in this cold weather. I rubbed the misted window with my handkerchief to keep an eye out for the wooden Trojan horse that had led the Greeks to victory over the Trojans over 3,000 years before. It had probably long since been burned as firewood. In Bergama, south of Troy, I got out to continue in the other direction. But first I took a taxi high up to the famous Pergamon Amphitheatre. This theater, clinging to a long, incredibly steep slope, could seat 10,000 people. The views of the ancient town of Bergama far below were breath-taking despite the bitter cold. In the afternoon I continued on a local bus. They had it all, these smaller buses off the main roads. They were mostly of advanced age, full of dents and scratches that were simply painted over with different colours. Bent bumpers testified to past battles against rivals. I stopped looking at the tread of the tires, otherwise I probably would never have got on. Of course, such veteran buses produced a lot of black smoke when they started, or when they struggled up a rocky pass road like hard workers while a sad Laila yodelled her heart-rending love songs from the scratchy loudspeaker. Finally, after another change, I reached the small town of Gediz, here, again in the Kütahya province we also wanted to build two schools. Only 180 kilometers to Kütahya, it was long after dark when I got there. Back home! The next morning I reported back to everyone. Not much had been built during my absence, the workers preferred to sit at home in a warm room. A driver, Ferit and I went on scouting trips to the villages again. On the second day, between Keçiller and Saraycık, the driver suddenly stopped and pointed to the edge of the forest about 200 meters away. There stood a whole pack of gray wolves between the trees. They looked over at us, and didn't move. Too bad, with binoculars I could have taken a closer look at these dangerous animals. We were glad to be in the jeep and not on a hike in the woods. Our trips sometimes took us near a railway line. Every now and then we were lucky enough to come across a train, which was always pulled by a really nostalgic looking steam engine. Time stood still for me immediately, I became the little boy again, who used to play with his own steam engine train on the floor of my room. But this was a real, steam-belching Choo-Choo-Loki, pulling six or seven old passenger or freight cars across the countryside. Once we saw from a hill such a steam train driving through the valley, leaving the long nostalgic chain of white steam clouds behind. From up here it looked like a little toy train on its slow journey through curves, tunnels, and over bridges to a stop at a small train station in the next village. When I walked back to the guest house one evening after dinner in the snow flurry, a white-brown cat meowed desperately at the front door. As soon as I opened the door, she scurried in, followed me to my room and made herself comfortable on a small carpet. I let her do it, she must have been cold and needed some warmth. A little later, when I came out of the bathroom unsuspectingly, I saw the mess. While I was taking a long shower, my cat had become a mother of five on the small rug and was now licking her tiny children. What should I do? Kicking it out was impossible. Outside in the corridor I found newspapers and prepared an emergency bed with an old T-shirt at the bottom of the closet. In the morning the house boy brought a box with litter and a vessel to drink water. The cat family spent a whole week in the closet, and I brought treats from the restaurant. The houseboy finally found someone who would take in the large family and "relieve" me. This winter was tough, biting cold and fog alternated with snowfall. New foundations could not be built, so we concentrated on the creating the interiors of the schools. One day I "lost" Ferid, my reliable interpreter, was needed elsewhere. Two weeks later a replacement appeared, his name was Ali, but unfortunately he spoke only bad German.

This created new problems because Ali too often misunderstood me and consequently didn't translate correctly. The answer of the respective interlocutor sometimes showed that he had understood the complete opposite. I had no one else available than this Ali, who had been learning some German in Hamburg for a while. A few weeks later, the limited cooperation improved somewhat, and he taught himself what was important in construction. To gain time, I sent him alone to individual construction sites in a second vehicle. Until I found out that he had abused my trust in him. In these villages he had behaved as if he were the builder and demanded gifts of turkeys from the Mukhtar. This was the only way that the new school building would be built in the foreseeable future. Various witnesses in one village confirmed to me that Ali had already received two turkeys. But Ali claimed to me that he had bought these turkeys on the way. I ended working with Ali and again had to travel for weeks without an interpreter. At least I understood a bit of Turkish: counting, days of the week, activity words and other frequently used words. When that wasn't enough, I used sign language and my index finger to point out flaws in the schoolhouse framework. The extreme cold finally abated and the foundation work got going again. Swiss railway freight wagons still arrived from Switzerland with building materials and later were delivered to the construction sites by truck as required.

Bad tyres without tread were the order of the day. I once explained to one of the truck drivers that he would have his driver's license revoked immediately if he had such tyres in Switzerland. Abdullah, father of seven, just shrugged his shoulders and said these tyres should last at least another year. Another driver had been in custody for over three months at the time. In November of previous year, when he was transporting material for our school buildings, he took a man with him who had waved for a lift, and made him sit on the wooden elements at the back. An accident happened - obviously due to increased speed on a bad road - and the man fell down and died. Since I wanted to visit our driver, I also made the acquaintance of a Turkish prison, where to my astonishment I met two other old acquaintances: a forester and a postman. The warden looked like a comfortable fatherly friend in his old-fashioned uniform, like a police sergeant from a bygone era - only the sabre was missing. I was allowed to talk to my three acquaintances over tea and coffee in his dilapidated office. The postman translated our conversation. More than three hundred prisoners were housed in this old, winding, and dilapidated prison. Only a few, who were particularly dangerous, had a solitary cell. The others slept in large rooms with about fifty beds. They were treated decently and were often allowed to "walk around" in the small prison yard. Incidentally, they did not wear prison clothing, but their own clothes. My three "friends" thanked me warmly for the visit and asked me to come back very soon.

In spring the white storks came back. In some of the lower-lying villages there was a tall mast with a small wooden platform on top where a pair of storks hatched their eggs. It was always a happy day for the villagers when a pair of storks began to nest. I encountered more and more storks strutting along the lowlands and streams in search of food. During a bus trip towards Afyon, I once counted 114 storks in the fields in one hour.

The official opening of a school, in the presence of visitors from

TO THE HORIZON AND BEYOND

Switzerland and the Turkish authorities, was approaching. A tour and opening ceremony was to take place in Dumlupinar, some 70 kilometers away, where three schools were under construction. Dumlupinar is a historical place. The last decisive battle against a Greek army was fought here at the end of August 1922. It ended with the victory of the Turks, commanded by General Kemal Atatürk. The long advance of the Greeks was stopped here. An impressive memorial outside of Dumlupinar commemorates this historic battle. When the first of three foundations was built in Dumlupinar, a larger village, in March, I had wall elements and roof trusses transported there. The Mukhtar had assured me that all material would be stored nearby until construction began. Nevertheless, two days later everything was still unprotected outside in the rain, and the Mukhtar was absent. The following day I preached to him that this material had survived the long journey from Switzerland to here undamaged. It is irresponsible to the donors and students that this precious material is wilfully exposed to the rain. These are not just any goods, they are gifts of charity from thousands of donors. He promised to get the material out that same day, although he said it would be difficult to find people to move it. When I offered him to go to the village inns myself and give a fiery speech to the men sitting around there, he declined. He seemed embarrassed to trouble a stranger. When I came back two days later, the material was still in the dirt. Only heavy artillery helped here. This time I didn't go to Mister Mukhtar, he was supposed to come to me. I sent Tamer, the young temporary interpreter, to say that all building materials would be returned to Kutahya the next day. Fifteen minutes later Tamer came back with this strange village mufti. "*Bey Mukhtar*," I said, "you have exactly one hour to move this wet in-the-dirt material into a shelter, if not, it will be picked up tomorrow morning!" This tangible threat finally worked wonders. A short time later some men came along and silently, like elves, began to carry the wooden elements and the roof wood into a shed. The contract for the three Dumlupinar schoolhouses went to Kemal, a fairly reliable builder, whom I respected as his people did a satisfactory job. However, things went wrong with the first school in Dumlupinar. The workers had trouble putting the wall elements together because they had been in the rain for days and the wood had swollen. The director of the building authority advised them to plane two centimeters off the element posts. When I inspected the building the next day, the walls were shaking like loose shutters in a wind storm. All that remained was to take the walls apart again and add the planed wood with thin battens. These and other problems repeated themselves often in some form. Because the construction sites were sometimes up to 200 kilometers apart, we needed far too much time to get there and often arrived too late to prevent mistakes or botched work in time. Such mistakes often took much time to restore. Nevertheless, the more schools were built, fewer mistakes happened, and the skills slowly caught on. Dumlupinar school house's number two and three were built in record time thanks to Kemal's good control. Nothing stood in the way of the official inauguration in mid-May. The Swiss delegation with National Councilor Ketterer, Durisol engineer Willy Fritz and representatives of the Swiss media arrived in time by bus from Istanbul. Even Helene Piguet came to see me again and the Minister of Construction also came from Ankara.

The next day all the Swiss guests went to Dumlupinar with the minister, the governor and the school director. Flags of Turkey, Switzerland and the Red Cross were attached to the school buildings. The guests took a tour of the classrooms and asked many questions. Speeches were given, the school children sang songs and even a sheep was slaughtered for the dedication. The guests seemed impressed. In the following two days, the new schools in Calköy, Aslanapa and other villages were also inaugurated. After months of difficulties, shedding drops of sweat, I was able to breathe a sigh of relief and be happy. But we had to hurry, in some villages the construction hadn't even started yet, the Turkish bureaucracy and the distances didn't allow for a faster pace. Mr. Ketterer sent me newspaper clippings from Switzerland with photos of the school building inauguration in mid-May, the interesting reports were definitely positive. Sometimes at a school inauguration I would receive a small gift as recognition. In one village, shortly after the start of construction, the Mukhtar asked me for a passport photo. At the ceremonial inauguration, I was presented with a large porcelain wall plate with a deceptively similar painted passport photo on it, framed by Islamic ornaments. But in a small, remote village whose complicated name I have unfortunately forgotten, the Mukhtar surprised me with an honour that surpassed anything experienced before. First there was a traditional meal. Ferid and I sat with other men around the low, richly laid lunch table. Everyone sat cross-legged on the carpet, only I had three pillows pushed under me as usual. Everyone used a wooden spoon to scoop directly from bowls and large plates. Such a rich selection of traditional country dishes and the warm atmosphere in this simple house appealed to me more than a tasteful meal in a fine restaurant. Finally, the Mukhtar got up, gave a little after-lunch speech and on behalf of the residents thanked us for the beautiful new school building. The students couldn't wait to go back to school. It was also decided today to award me with a special honour as a sign of thanks and appreciation to call the next prayer from the minaret. At first I thought Ferit hadn't translated correctly. The Mukhtar repeated what was said, but I thought they were joking. However, the other men gave me nods of confirmation. "I can't do that, I'm not a Muslim," I said. "We know that," the Mukhtar replied, "that's why we're giving you this very special honour." I shook my head again, "I can't speak Turkish at all and I only know the call to prayer, "*Allahu akbar*" (God is greatest). "That's enough," the Mukhtar replied, "You are the Muezzin here today. You just sing in your language and ask us to pray." I had to admit defeat, but swallowed hard and felt my heart pounding, it was a real dilemma. In just under three hours, at 5 p.m, my airy, solo singing lesson was to take place. I still had enough time to think about what on earth I a layman, could present from the top of the elegant and slender minaret. To boost my mental self-confidence, I drank a few glasses of tea and asked Ferid a series of questions to keep my nervousness in check. The guy was meanly laughing up his sleeve, obviously looking forward to the show. The moment of truth was slowly approaching, more and more men gathered in front of the mosque. No one wanted to miss the maiden chant of an unbelieving Muezzin. Even the women lined up with their children between the houses or looked over walls. Shortly before five and feeling emotional, I watched as the men lined up several rows deep in front of the mosque and the minaret.

They obviously wanted to pray outside and not inside the mosque. Perhaps as a precaution to catch him should that honorary prayer caller get dizzy up there and fall off. I gave Ferid my camera and asked him to pull the trigger while I sang. At 4.56 p.m. the time had come, Ferid said with an ambiguous smile: "Good luck to you!" Then, I suddenly stood all alone at the bottom inside of the minaret tower and was shocked when I looked up and saw how far up the narrow, steep, stone spiral staircase led. Time seemed to stand still as I slowly climbed the first few steps with my heart pounding. I was able to secure myself using the wall rope with one hand. I was in no hurry. I hadn't felt so lonely and abandoned in a long time. I wasn't actually nervous, rather uneasy because of the silence in this semi-darkness. I stopped halfway, looked up at the small bright exit above me, and tried to concentrate. When I finally reached the top on the narrow winding staircase, holding myself tight to the wall rope, I waited a few more seconds before stepping out onto the narrow, airy minaret terrace. The afternoon sun shone in my face. My trepidation was gone, the magnificent view over the village, and the fields overwhelmed me. Only now did I notice that all the villagers were looking up at me expectantly. The men stood lined up at the foot of the minaret and waited for my calls to prayer. I made a cup over my mouth with my hands and chanted the Arabic words five times as loudly as I could: "*ALLAHU AKBAR, ALLAHU AKBAR, ALLAHU AKBAR, ALLAHU AKBAR, "ALLAHU AKBAR!*"

Immediately the men began their prayers, bowing, kneeling, bending forward, standing again… and slowly, as loud as I could, I continued singing the first and last verses of the Grindelwald song in the Grindelwald dialect, including the chorus:

> "Close to the glaciers in Grindelwald,
> It's good to live here,
> We've never been homesick,
> Go where the earth takes
> you to the moon
> to the sun if you want,
> You do not find of form and
> figure a more beautiful valley than Grindelwald.
> Haalio, oh haaliohaalio...
> Close to the glaciers in Grindelwald,
> Comes death, it is Gods will.
> We also want to be buried here in the graveyard by the church.
> Oh don't lament at our grave because the only place is the kingdom of heaven where we like it even more than here in beautiful Grindelwald.
> Haalio, oh haaliohaalio..."

I couldn't have been such a bad Muezzin, as the men at the foot of the minaret had continued to pray in faith, they deserved an encore. My hands formed a funnel again as I sang the following verse in French:

> "La-haut sur la montagne l'etait un vieux Chalet.
> Mur blanc, toit de bardeaux,
> devant la porte un vieux bouleau,
> La-haut sur la montagnel'était un vieux chalet...
> Q and Jean vint au chalet,
> pleura de tout son coer sur les debris de son bonheur..."

["High up a mountain there was an old Chalet,
with a white wall and shingle roof.
In front of the door there stood an old birch,
when John went to the chalet,
he cried with all his heart,
on to the debris of his good nature.
High up a mountain there was an old Chalet..."]

Enough of praying, I thought, and began the final chord: "*ALLAHU AKBAR, ALLAHU AKBAR, ALLAHU AKBAR, ALLAHU AKBAR, ALLAHU AKBAR.*" "My" believers stopped praying, the prayer caller from Grindelwald had his honourable duty completed. One last time I looked out over the village from a lofty height into the wide, peaceful landscape, an impressive, unforgettable moment and highlight in my life. Relaxed, I slowly descended the narrow steps and was greeted warmly by the men. They thanked me for this extraordinary hour of prayer and Ferid said he took two pictures of me. I was happiest when the teacher came with a few children to sing a beautiful farewell song to thank me again.

* * * * *

A short time later, the annual four-weeks fasting period, Ramadan, began. The starting date moves by about 11 days every year. I was amazed at the control and discipline with which the Mohammedans observed the imposed fasting and washing regulations. Eating, drinking and smoking were forbidden from sunrise to sunset. Not even the smallest sip of water was allowed, otherwise, it was said the Ramadan would be ruined. But this depends if you did it intentionally or by mistake. By mistake it does not count and you can continue the rest of the day as normal. If you do it intentionally then it would be best to seek forgiveness from Allah. Our assembly workers also strictly adhered to Ramadan. They worked undeterred until sunset. No tea was served in the offices either. When I unpacked my packed lunch on the construction site, I could read on the faces of the workers and villagers what they were thinking of me at that moment: it's really a shame that this unbeliever, this Swiss, has sinned so badly! He will never go to heaven. In the second week of Ramadan I said to myself as a non-believer I can do that too. The restaurant in the sugar factory opened one hour before sunrise during Ramadan. I sat there early in the morning, filled my stomach with a hearty breakfast and drank a lot of tea and water. I didn't take a packed lunch with me. The first day of fasting became difficult in the afternoon, I was plagued by thirst. But I bravely held out until sunset. It was easier on the second and third day. I managed to fast for a whole week. Ferid, driver Ahmed and the workers paid tribute to me. In the late afternoon, when the sun was slowly going down, we bought bread, cheese and onions in some village on the way home and eagerly looked at the time, because the empty stomachs were growling so loud that they almost drowned out the engine. When the time had finally come that the sun was no longer to be seen far and wide, we headed for the next well. Our driver Ahmed seemed to know all wells in Anatolia, including the remote ones. Suddenly, he left the field path either to the left or to the right, drove over hill and dale into the wasteland, and just as suddenly, as if by magic, a hidden well or spring lay before us. There we sat down peacefully and refreshed ourselves with the well-deserved simple meal. Sometimes the romantic ringing of bells from a flock of sheep grazing nearby could be heard across the wide, lonely landscape. And when the moon rose behind a chain of hills, the cool wind caressed our ears and the first stars twinkled. In these moments I looked forward to my life and was happy. That's how it must have been here, thousands of years ago, I thought. All worries and problems were forgotten and gone. Only when we had to think about leaving and Ahmed started the engine did we slowly find our way back from timeless dreams of the past.

My fast lasted six days, then I threw in the towel. I needed my strength and senses for the long working days.

* * * * *

Lent and Ramadan: A comparison: Lent is a religious aspect in the religion Christianity and Ramadan is the sacred aspect of the religion Islam. From Ash Wednesday to Easter many Christians observe Lent. It is known that some fasting Muslims, in a show of solidarity, also to the poor.

* * * * *

The fasting Turks longed for the end of Ramadan, which is celebrated with the three-day Eid-ul-Fitr, when Allah rewards people for their long fasts. Friends and relatives come together for community prayer. Cows are slaughtered and the meat distributed among the poor. The greeting during the Ramadan festival is called *Eid*

Mubarak, people wish one another a blessed *Eid* feast, just as we wish one another a Merry Christmas. Nobody works during this big festival. For this reason I decided to go on a four-day trip. On the first day I went alone to Ankara by bus and from there flew by plane to Simav on the Black Sea. The next morning I drove along the Black Sea coast in shared *dolmus* taxis and minibuses. At most, they drove to the next town, where I changed to another dolmus taxi or small bus. Everywhere people greeted each other with "*Eid Mubarak*" at the big celebrations. The people were dressed for this holiday, and on the way I saw people in the villages on their way to the mosque. Most of the time there was at least one German-speaking Turk on the bus, so I could talk, get my bearings, ask questions. I rarely saw any sandy beaches just stones, but the steep slopes from the road up to the Pontic mountain range seemed very fertile. There were huge hazelnut, apricot and tea plantations here. Unfortunately there was no sun, the sea looked really dark and hazy, the sky was overcast. It didn't matter to me, I was happy to drive through this unknown region with strangers, to get an idea of what it looks like here, and to know where the hazelnuts that I love to eat grew. In the afternoon I reached the larger city of Trabzon and stayed the night here. I would have gladly gone 200 kilometers further to Batumi on the Russian border. But unfortunately there wasn't enough time. The next day I took a bus up into the Pontic mountains. The narrow winding and steep road led over the spectacular 2,000 meter high Zigana Pass. The magnificent mountain panorama changed constantly in the many hairpin bends. I got an uneasy feeling a few times when I saw deep down in a valley or in a gorge, the fallen wrecks of buses or trucks lying there in a creek.

TO THE HORIZON AND BEYOND

At such moments I thought I was sitting defencelessly in a sardine can. That day's destination was Erzurum, the largest city in Eastern Anatolia about 300 kilometers from the Iran border. I hardly had time for a small city tour. The next morning at 6 a.m., I was already back on the bus that was supposed to take me to Ankara, almost 1,000 kilometers away. The more than 15 (!) hour drive led via Erzincan and Sivas to the Turkish capital. The whole long day I was exposed to the rasping loudspeaker, which blared out one plaintive, wistful love song after another and acoustically tormented my Swiss ears. I didn't understand the words, but I could guess the meaning from the sad, pleading voices. As in every bus, a young conductor regularly came down the aisle with cologne to wet the hands of the passengers. At each stop, hawkers sold tea and snacks, and a meal stop was turned on every few hours. There was also "free music" on the loudspeakers in the "roadhouse." I couldn't hear it anymore, the deliciously seasoned lamb with vegetables tasted too good. It was long past nine p.m. when we reached the bus station in Ankara, apathetic and tired. I quickly found a room there and soon fell asleep. The next afternoon I reached Kütahya, my fast, very long "musical" trip was over. In the room I put one of my Swiss cassettes on to drive the Turkish love songs out of my head.

Now the last leg of my mission in Turkey began: the remaining interior work such as flooring and painting. Laying tiles and linoleum required know-how that I didn't have at the time. I had long ago asked Carlo Hubacher in Gandria to send me the necessary information. His insightful details and recommendations helped me clear this important hurdle as well. But the Turkish official whinnied loudly and audibly again and threw clubs at our feet when the work was being implemented. Again, I had to deal with the building department and the governor to negotiate an agreement, or an acceptable compromise. To be on the safe side, I wrote a confirmation of such agreements on the same day, as I had done before, and handed them in at the offices against a receipt. I had long since become a self-assuring bureaucrat. "Our" 31 schoolhouses now adorned the 22 villages. That was a great satisfaction for us and a reason to be happy every time we drove up to a school. Despite all resistance, difficulties, relapses and obstacles, the beautiful green schoolhouses stood their ground. Schooling had started in more than half of them.

My mission in Turkey mission had brought me a lot of new experiences, motivation, self-confidence, joie de vivre, assertiveness and the will to set off for new shores and tasks. Summer had long since arrived when the Vice Governor invited me to a final dinner. Directors of the school and building authorities, as well as other people were present. After-dinner speeches were held, and I couldn't help but thank them for the long cooperation and hospitality.

Before my return flight to Switzerland, I again embarked on an extended tour of Turkey on buses. The lamenting love songs while driving couldn't harm me anymore, it was summer time, the sun was shining, I felt happy. The long journey took me to Kayseri, Konya, Adana, Pamukkale, Malatya, Elazig and beyond Bingöl, where days earlier a severe earthquake had claimed hundreds of lives. The many rescue workers tried their best to find buried people. I was shocked to see how such an earthquake could bring down seemingly solid concrete buildings, causing so much pain, despair and tragedy. Two days later I stayed in a newer, three-storey guesthouse at a place between Elazig and Malatya. My room was on the third floor. In the middle of the night I was rudely awakened from sleep, my bed seemed to be moving, unfamiliar noises in the house woke me completely. It sounded like a groan, creaking or crunching. I finally found the light switch. My shirt on the wall hook was shaking. It must have been an earthquake. Then it shook more, the groaning became a cracking noise, and the light went out. In the wooden house, the interlocking wooden beams and posts probably came under great pressure, but "resisted" the movements coming from below and created this eerie wooden noise. When the light went out an oppressive feeling crept over me in the darkness in this strange house. The fear went away. I didn't dare go down the stairwell without a light on but heard voices. Then the door opened, the owner shone a flashlight in and asked me to come downstairs with him. A few meters away from the house, a few guests were already sitting at a long table in their pyjamas. A kerosene lantern burned on the table and flickered in the frightened faces. Only when the owner brought glasses and poured tea did people thaw a bit and start talking. I only understood a few words. At first light we saw that there was hardly any damage except roof tiles lay shattered on the ground, and here and there cracks yawned in the walls. It had been the cracking, squeaking noise of the beams and posts that had so frightened us in the dark. I should quickly get away from here I thought and got on the first local bus towards Malatya. From then on, I only slept if possible in ground-floor rooms, so I could jump out of the window in the dark if I had to. Ferid had once told me that he had been with his wife at a dance event in Kütahya when a violent earthquake suddenly struck. Those present tried to flee as quickly as possible, but were, falling over one another because the floor was constantly moving slightly, accompanied by the creaking noise of the shaking building and the terrified screams of the people. They were lucky, the building held up.

My extensive tour of Turkey continued to the impressive snow-white terraces of Pamukkale, which had formed from limestone deposits from the local mineral springs. Since ancient times Pamukkale had been famous for these springs. From afar I thought I saw a snowy landscape. I rented a room with a warm, mineral spring pool in front of my room. The ancient town of Hierapolis is also located near these mineral springs. Numerous stone sarcophagi still lay around. The next stop was the bizarre volcanic landscape near Kayseri, with countless slender rock cones and dwellings. There are even huge subterranean "cities" carved deep into the soft rock in ancient times to provide refuge and protection for tens of thousands of people from enemy conquerors.

I also paid a visit to the famous ruined city of Ephesus, located 70 kilometers south of Izmir near the Aegean coast. The long round trip through this large country impressed me with the variety of strange landscapes, with the simple people and the great cultural heritage of past millennia. Once again I returned to Kütahya to get my things deposited there and to say goodbye to friends and acquaintances. One last time I said "*AllahaIsmarladik*!" (Goodbye) and the friends' reply was always, "*Güla güla!*" which sounded like "Bye-bye." Even the little five-year-old Güler, the youngest sister of my first interpreter and friend Tamer, waved goodbye to me with a smile and called: "*Gülagüla,* uncle." A little sad, a little proud, and above all grateful, I boarded the bus to Istanbul.

In that short year I had experienced and seen so much in that lonely province. I had also learned to assert myself in difficult situations and at the same time enjoy the positive and the strange. I finally found time to see some of Istanbul's sights. Mrs. Köse, my sister's friend, took me through the huge ancient Topkapi Palace with all its great art treasures, known as the crown jewel of the Ottoman Empire. I have never been so impressed by a museum. We also visited the famous Sultan Ahmed Mosque, the most impressive Muslim house of worship in Istanbul, better known as the Blue Mosque because of its many blue tiles. And just opposite is another great mosque, the Hagia Sofia, which now serves as a museum. The next day we spent hours wandering Istanbul's huge covered bazaar. I was amazed as there seemed to be nothing you couldn't buy. Mainly leather, brass and pottery, of course lots of jewelry and carpets. The traders tried to lure us in for tea – no thanks my Turkish tea time was long gone. The many oriental smells in this teeming bazaar also stimulated my senses. On the penultimate day in Istanbul, charming Hedi showed me the famous Golden Horn, a long bay on the Bosphorus with an impressive view over the water, the Galata Bridge and parts of the city. Hedi Köse brought me to the airport on the last day. She and her husband had been generous, gracious hosts to me. This time the Turkish custom did not try to fleece me. During the flight to Zurich, I reviewed my exciting mission in Turkey. It was done, the target was met, 31 Swiss schools were standing in 22 Anatolian villages. Countless students went back to school after a severe earthquake. For me, this task was also learning time, a school of life, so to speak. Along with the school houses my self-confidence had grown as well. I had tapped into my dormant potential, so maybe I would get more opportunities to go abroad? The Swiss Red Cross in Berne expressed their gratitude for what was achieved under difficult circumstances. Ms. Zuyderhoff, the head of the SRC relief campaign, and Mr. Jaques, gave me good references and hoped that I would work on a future relief campaign. But now I was back on the streets, looking for a new job in Zurich and celebrating the reunion with my friends. Manpower soon found me a new job, this time at Battery Oerlikon as a warehouse clerk, with regulated working hours and simple, easy work. Just right to adjust and finding myself again in the progressive modern times of my home land. My thoughts kept returning to Anatolia, to the common people and children in the remote villages, the animals, the landscapes and the many unique experiences. In August I saw a promising job ad from an agency in a newspaper. A man from Texas was looking for an English-speaking student as a chauffeur for a tour of Europe for six weeks. I immediately applied to the agency, including my references and was hired ten days later by Mr. King this Texan man. I was prepaid a flight ticket Zurich – Stuttgart in Southern Germany, because Mr King had ordered a brand new upper class Mercedes in the Mercedes factory in Stuttgart-Untertuerkheim. When I arrived there I took the opportunity in the morning to join a fascinating tour through the Mercedes factory. In the afternoon at the reception I was introduced to the white haired stocky Mr. King and his slightly younger Partner Mrs. Farell. Soon after I was handed over the brand new beige Mercedes by a Mechanic. The car smelled wonderfully of paint and leather. After I had stowed the luggage in the trunk, I opened the rear doors for Mr. King and his partner and slowly drove off. Our long European journey had begun. On this first day we only went as far as Baden-Baden and stayed there for two nights. Mr. King gave me a list of places they wanted to visit in Europe, I could choose all the routes myself. Of course I didn't want to sleep in the same expensive hotels like my two passengers. I was paid my Hotel bills plus 100 US$ per day salary. For me these six weeks driving leisurely through Western Europe were for me also very pleasant paid holidays. Our next stop was in Basel at the Rhine river, were I had lived in my younger years and became a baker and pastry cook 18 years earlier. Of course I knew my way around in Basel and was able to show my passengers many sights. Next stop in Switzerland was Interlaken where my parents now lived. We stayed three nights there, and I could stay every night with my beloved parents. There was so much to see for tourists here in this world famous wonderland, even the weather cooperated. My Texans were enthusiastic about our three-pass trip over Grimsel, Furka and the Susten, and other excursions. Next stop was Lucerne where my sister lives with her family. My passengers made an excursion there by cableway onto Mount Pilatus were they enjoyed fantastic views all around central Switzerland. Mr. King often invited me to join them for lunch or dinner. However, Mr. King was a bit grumpy and moody at times, but his partner quickly calmed him down with her charm and humor. Mr. King had owned a candy factory in Fort Worth near Dallas. Now he finally wanted to discover Europe with his partner, and I was the third in the group, but I didn't feel like the fifth wheel on the wagon. Mr. King gradually became more approachable he seemed to really enjoy the constantly changing landscapes. In Vaduz we admired the stately palace from the outside, the beautiful seat of the Liechtenstein prince family. Little did I know then that a few years later I would meet in Africa the youngest prince Nicolas and later on his famous mother Princess Gina of Liechtenstein.

Our journey continued to Austria through Vorarlberg and Tyrol to Kitzbühel, where we stayed for a few days. We made detours to Berchtesgaden, up to Hitler's former eagle's nest and to Salzburg and Passau. Mr. King had bought in Texas two tickets for the famous Passion Play in Oberammergau, 90 kilometers south of Munich. They were sold out, but the farmer I stayed with got me a ticket too. This famous play lasts all day and only takes place every ten years. They are all lay actors from the village of Oberammergau. I didn't know that I would be back there again 30 years later with my future wife for us to enjoy this unique play, the story of the life of Jesus. The next time the play is due to be performed is in 2030. The weather was kind to us as we continued our journey. This highly interesting Tour d'Europe came to an end with stops in Munich, Nuremberg, Strasbourg, Nancy, Luxembourg, Reims and Paris. In the Ville Lumière I said goodbye to Mr. King and Mrs. Farrel. They flew on to Moscow and their Mercedes was shipped to Texas. They paid for my flight home to Zurich, but I bought a train ticket to Calais with the money, took the ferry to Dover and spent a few days exploring London. Then I took a ferry to Ostend and drove a few days through Belgium, Holland and via Germany back to Zurich. My wanderlust had been filled for the time being, and I got back to Manpower looking again for temporary jobs, but always hoping another Red Cross mission would occur.

CHAPTER FOUR

Bangladesh, 1971-1973: Life Changes

SPOTLIGHT ON BANGLADESH

The Bangladesh war came about in 1947 when the British-Indian Empire was divided and gained independence. This resulted in two states: on the one hand, the predominantly secular India (church and state strictly separated), on the other hand, Muslim Pakistan, consisting of East and West Pakistan. Separated by India, East and West Pakistan were geographically distant. Since West Pakistan claimed leadership of both parts of the country, conflicts with East Pakistan soon arose due to cultural, economic, and political differences. The East Pakistani's (Bengalis), who make up half of the total population, were significantly underrepresented in the state leadership – especially in the army leadership. The situation first came to a head in 1948 when Muhammad Ali Jinnah, the first Governor-General of Pakistan, decided to establish "Urdu, and

Bangladesh [2]

only Urdu" as the state language in both parts of Pakistan. East Pakistan fought back with the "Bengali Language Movement" and was finally able to get two official languages, Urdu and Bengali (later called Bangla), enshrined in Pakistan's constitution in 1956. Despite this, East Pakistan's massive economic and political disadvantages persisted. The tropical cyclone (also known as the Bhola cyclone) that swept across East Pakistan on November 12, 1970, caused irreconcilable differences between the two parts of the country, which shortly afterwards led to the Bangladesh war. The catastrophic effects of this devastating natural disaster, primarily affected East Pakistan and the Indian state of West Bengal. Between three and 500,000 people died. This destruction caused by the cyclone lead to even greater discontent in East Pakistan, leading the opposition East Pakistan Awami League to victory in Pakistan's national elections in December 1970 and March 1971. The military

---

[2] Source: https://commons.wikimedia.org/wiki/File:Pakistan_Ost-_und_West_1971.svg

central government in West Pakistan saw this as a threat to its supremacy on the one hand and to Pakistan's unity on the other. So, it refused to recognize the victory of the Awami League and hand over the affairs of state. This in turn strengthened East Pakistan's already existing efforts to break away. When the military government of West Pakistan suspended the Constituent Assembly in March 1971, the Awami League called for civil disobedience. The resulting general strike led to the collapse of public order throughout East Pakistan. On March 25, 1971, West Pakistani military and government chief Yahya Khan broke off all negotiations with the Awami League. He immediately ordered the Pakistani units stationed in East Pakistan to arrest Mujibur Rahman, the leader of the Awami League, which they did. The rest of the leaders of the Awami League, which was in exile in India, then proclaimed the independent state of "Bangladesh" on the same day. However, the existence of this state depended exclusively on the military success of the guerrilla movement. This resistance army, called the Mukti Bahini, engaged in guerrilla warfare against the West Pakistanis; knowing that they could count on India's support. Not only did India train East Pakistan's guerrillas, but it also closed the borders for supplies to West Pakistan. When the flow of East Pakistan refugees finally swelled to up to 10 million people, India also decided to intervene directly. From June 1971, Indian paramilitaries (Border Security Force) penetrated deeper into East Pakistani territory to support the guerrillas. This led to a further escalation of the conflict. The fact that India got so involved in this war had to do with its great strategic self-interest: India wanted an independent Bangladesh; because this would – in view of possible further wars with Pakistan – eliminate the previous difficult two-front situation in the east and west of India. In East Pakistan this war ended on December 16, 1971, with the capitulation of the West Pakistani units in East Pakistan on December 17 with an armistice with India. The Pakistani military government in West Pakistan had to resign as a result of the defeat, as did Prime Minister Nurul Amin, who had been installed two weeks earlier. During the nine-month war, the Pakistani army, and its local collaborators - the Razakars and Al Badr - killed three million people. Rapes of Bengali women and forced prostitution were reported. The number of women raped is estimated at up to 200,000. In addition, ten million people, mostly Hindus, were displaced across the border into India. The first victims of the purges were politicians and supporters of the Awami League, as well as Bengali security and police forces. Some escaped with their weapons and launched a guerrilla war against the initially overwhelmingly superior West Pakistani army. The overwhelming majority of the victims of detention, torture, rape and killings were defenceless, ordinary citizens caught unexpectedly and unprepared by the violence.[3]

FLYING TO NEW SHORES IN 1971

When I received the long-awaited phone call from Berne, Henriette Zuyderhoff, head of the Swiss Red Cross foreign aid programs asked me if I was still interested in another assignment abroad. "We currently still lack a materials manager in a medical team," she explained to me; a deployment in East Pakistan is planned. Of

---

3   Source: Wikipedia

course, I was interested and said yes immediately. I could hardly believe it: Another chance was here! The next night I could barely sleep for excitement. Information was needed. So, in the days that followed I studied the atlas and read the news about the constantly changing events on the Indian subcontinent. I saw parallels to my mission in Biafra. The unimaginable suffering of the population, victims of a most cruel political and religious power struggle.

Once again this affected me from the great distance of safe, peaceful Switzerland. The departure date of the medical team had not yet been determined. The requirement for this was the military development on site. I packed my belongings full of enthusiasm and travelled to Berne for meetings and vaccinations. The departure from Basel with a DC 6 was finally set for December 16, 1971. The team consisted of two doctors, four nurses, (including a male nurse), an administrator and me as the materials manager. We met each other the evening before departure in a hotel near Basel train station. Team leader was Dr. Roman Fischer, a very experienced surgeon from Wetzikon, who had been on previous missions and Dr. Andreas Hof from Uster. The nurses: Magdalena Betsche from Basel, Erna Russi from Fiesch, Therese Meyer from Eschenz, and David Keller from Aadorf. The administrator was Daniel Oswald from Reinach, the Red Cross radio operator was Kurt Tanner from Kirchlindach and myself, from Zurich, responsible for the large amount of material and for any other work that needed to be done.

The following morning at 6 am we met downstairs at the big breakfast table to have our first meal together. We enjoyed the steaming milk coffee and the fresh, crispy *gipfeli* (croissants). We would probably have to do without such "summits" for a long time.

Soon after, we were sitting in a minibus that took us to Blotzheim, Basel's Airport on French soil, where some members of the press were waiting for us. The large, silvery DC 6, bearing the Red Cross emblems, was already loaded and ready to go. Only the rearmost part of the plane had seating for us team members and the two Balair hostesses who were flying with us. In this way, as much space as possible was created for the extensive material. This was now stacked up to the ceiling in the passenger compartment and secured with rope nets and bolts. Even a large DC 6 reserve engine had been loaded and anchored. In addition, someone had even donated a big Christmas tree, well tied up and secured at the very top under a blanket. The two pilots assigned to us, Kurt Herzog, Balair's chief pilot, and Captain Rupert Vogel from Basel, both very experienced veterans and popular flight captains. Soon it was 9 a.m. and our DC 6 took off. We hovered in a long curve over the wide landscape of Upper Alsace slowly gaining altitude, flying over the city of Basel. As we flew along the Rhine in the direction of Lake Constance I recognized the town of Liestal on the lower right. In the distance the snow-capped chain of the Alps greeted us. At that minute, I realized, this winter I wouldn't go skiing, but a new and exciting future had just begun. "What will it bring?" I wondered.

It was going to be a long, very long flight. A DC 6 didn't fly particularly fast, not even very high. According to the announcement from the cockpit, the speed was around 450 kilometers per hour. We had to land regularly to refuel. There was plenty of time to look at the landscapes slowly passing by below, and get to know each other better. The longer we were in the air, the more we got the travel bug. During lunch we were already flying over the Mediterranean Sea. A warm, exciting travel atmosphere had spread. As the hours went by, those of us who were curious climbed over boxes, suitcases and bypassed the reserve engine to the cockpit with the two pilots, Herzog and Vogel, who explained to us how to fly. But the countless instruments, control lamps, buttons and levers were and remained a closed book for us. We admired the two accomplished men doing it all so well and in a relaxed manner as they chatted with us. "Flying is easier than driving," Captain Vogel assured us. "I'm not so sure about that," I replied. Meanwhile we were already over the Lebanese mountains and flew over the border to Syria. I took a nap and only woke up when the plane touched down with a gentle lurch on the Damascus airstrip. It was time for the plane, and us, to refuel.

It was already getting dark when we were served an invigorating oriental chai tea in the airport restaurant. We were surprised to see two mighty, beautifully decorated Christmas trees in the hall, a surprising image at Damascus airport. Our team leader Dr. Fischer spoke enthusiastically about this ancient city of Damascus, which stood on an oasis of 30 square kilometers, where one could buy beautiful oriental treasures at the market. An hour and a half later we climbed into the air again and saw thousands of lights in Damascus glittering and sparkling below us. Dinner was now due, and with it, our charming hostesses served us real Syrian muscatel wine. Meanwhile we flew in the dark over the endless deserts of Saudi Arabia towards the Persian Gulf. We soon switched off the reading lights and tried to get some sleep under the lulling monotonous noise of the engines. A few hours later we landed again, this time in Dubai. Sleep deprived, we marched to the airport building to get some exercise. Dubai airport was still rather small at that time. Apart from a lonely bar selling a bottle of Johnny Walker Whiskey duty free for $2.50 and a few small souvenir shops, there was little to see and so, we were all soon back on the plane, ready for the onward flight, but the start was delayed. Our DC 6 finally took off at dawn. We snoozed on the way to Bombay, across the Arabian Sea. Only the breakfast coffee on board - with a view of the morning sun rising on the distant horizon - woke our spirits again. Captain Herzog reported that Bombay could not be flown directly for safety reasons. This is due to the war between India and Pakistan. So, we took a two-hour detour. We had already filled up on additional fuel in Dubai; at the expense of some material boxes that had to be unloaded for this. Finally, in the distance, the Indian subcontinent came into view. My heart rejoiced, the place I had so longed for was already before my eyes! Memories suddenly flashed in my mind: how many times had I, as a student in geography class, my favourite subject, put my index finger over the map of India and started daydreaming. Hard to believe, but these dreams had now come true!

We flew along the coast and finally landed in Bombay after a long six hours of dozing. With tired legs and weary expressions, we strolled to the airport building. It quickly became clear that we were now in a war zone. At the entrance we met the first armed Indian soldiers. They sat on the steps, ancient bolt-action rifles in their hands. These antique guns must have been used at the Khyber Pass during the colonial era. All the windows in the airport were covered with paper to black out the light. We were all fatigued by the lack of sleep and such a long sitting. We longed for a bed. But an hour later the journey began again. The next stop was the Indian capital New Delhi. Again, it was dark when we landed there. The journey from Basel to the Indian capital took around 28 hours. Full of anticipation, we now took taxis to the Hotel Ashoka, which was surrounded by tall trees and stood in the middle of the foreign embassy quarter. Tired and worn out from sitting for hours, we went straight to bed after dinner.

Well rested, we met for breakfast the next morning in the dining room, where the Swiss ambassador joined us shortly afterwards. He updated us on the current situation in East Pakistan, now a separate country called Bangladesh. To prevent further bloodshed, the West Pakistan army in East Pakistan had surrendered to the Indian forces on December 16, 1971 - the day we left Basel. A ceasefire agreement was signed between West Pakistan and India the following day. As a result, the West Pakistan military government had to resign. It quickly became clear that the onward flight would be delayed. Captain Herzog waited in vain for permission to land in Dhaka. Not surprising, since the new state of Bangladesh was only two days old. However, we knew what to do but we first needed Indian rupees. Our treasurer, Daniel Oswald, got them from a nearby bank and gave us some pocket money. So well prepared, we set off on a city tour of New Delhi in a small bus. First, we visited a colourful, ancient mosque with a huge minaret. I immediately thought of my calling for prayer, when on assignment in Anatolia. A visit to the famous tomb of Mahatma Gandhi - a large, black, rectangular marble slab - was also a must. This simple but all the more impressive tomb was very tastefully decorated with yellow-red marigold flowers. Pandit Nehru, India's first prime minister, had also found his final resting place next to Mahatma Gandhi's grave.

The onward flight to Calcutta was scheduled for the next morning. At seven a.m. sharp, our DC 6 took off again. A long-serving veteran, this plane had served as a Red Cross airliner for years and had flown countless dangerous relief missions to trapped Biafra. Our Captain Vogel was also in the cockpit back then. It was December 19th and we were rested again and happy for the journey to continue. We had been spoiled by the weather, but that day we had a bit of bad luck. Haze prevented a clear view of the long chain of the Himalayas. "If the weather was clear, we would clearly see Mount Everest," Captain Vogel assured us. A short time later he reported to us over the loudspeaker that we would not be flying to Calcutta but directly to Dhaka (previously Dacca) in order to request permission to land at the airfield. That was exciting and adventurous. But a quarter of an hour later this plan was abandoned. It was said that the airstrip in Dhaka was still closed after a bombing by the Indian Air Force. So, we turned a bit to the right, in the direction of Calcutta, this huge city we had all heard and read so much about. My thirst for adventure increased with my excitement for new challenges. Towards noon we flew over the city of Calcutta, over which a haze hovered. During the landing approach we could see how fertile this area was. In between buildings, ponds glittered everywhere in the sunlight. A wonderful, impressive arrival!

In unusual heat and high humidity, we quickly unloaded as much material as possible. Shortly thereafter, our DC 6 took off without us and flew on towards Dhaka. The pilots wanted to inspect the condition of the runway there, so we hiked again into the airport building. There the Basel doctor and Red Cross delegate Dr. Spirgy welcomed us. Together with him we drove to Calcutta in a small bus and were amazed at the city. It was pure vibrant life. I've never seen so many people walking around. Calcutta seemed to me a great human anthill. Battered buses, taxis, trucks, cars, rickshaws, coolies (carriers), pedestrians, beggars, street vendors, dogs and sacred cows all crisscrossed and fought for space. We made slow progress in the throng of traffic. No problem for us, we couldn't get enough of the sights: construction workers were doing gymnastics on a dizzying height through fragile bamboo scaffolding. Antediluvian buses packed with passengers blocked the roads. Whole crowds of people were hanging on the buses, some fare dodgers were sitting on the roof. Double-decker buses also fought their way through the crowd. A thick, stinking mist of exhaust fumes polluted the air, irritated our noses and eyes, and the non-stop honking of horns all around us hurt our ears. I observed a picturesque street corner: there was an Indian man at his stand, twisting sugar cane stalks through a press, catching the sweet juice in glasses and selling them to waiting customers. Next to the customers stood a cow, which apathetically chewed the squeezed stalks and then, in gratitude, dropped a sacred cow patty on the asphalt, which splattered far and wide.

After an impressive first hour of live Calcutta, we reached our hotel; not just any hotel, but the famous Oberoi, a nostalgic-looking colonial building surrounded by green-painted arbours and a shady courtyard. Outside of the hotel I saw a stately, elderly, colourfully dressed Indian with a turban. He wore a well-groomed beard, a giant moustache and white gloves. "That must be a *Maharaja*," I thought. I was certain: "Only a *Maharaja* dresses like that to distinguish himself from the lower castes. He was probably waiting here for his uniformed Rolls Royce chauffeur to take his wife, the *Maharani*, for a drive. "How lucky," I thought to see a *Maharajah* in person! Elated, I got out of the bus and walked up to him. He gave me a friendly smile while I beamed "Good morning, Sir!" My *Maharaja* bowed slightly and said invitingly, "Welcome Sir to Hotel Oberoi!" Then he called a porter to carry our luggage to the hotel. That was my first and only encounter with an Indian *Maharaja*, who unfortunately turned out to be the "Welcome Officer" of the Hotel Oberoi.

After a cold buffet in the dining room, we set off on our first exploration on foot. The white shirts and embroidered Red Cross emblems made us stand out like sore thumbs. People stopped and stared at us. Immediately, beggars' hands reached out to us, eyes fixed on us with suffering expressions of hope, saying *Sahib* a few times in a pleading voice requesting *baksheesh*. It was exasperating: if we ignored them, they would run after us. If we gave a beggar a coin, others immediately ran towards us. There were old men with long hair, mothers with babies in their arms, little ragged rascals, but also an alarming number of disabled people queuing for alms. We had stocked up with enough spare change to be able to give something to at least the poorest of these poor.

Crossing a street became an adventure, we had to be careful with this noisy, undisciplined left-hand traffic. At an intersection, in the midst of pure chaos, a traffic cop with white arm warmers tried to calmly bring some order to the swarming traffic. The constant honking didn't seem to disturb him, he probably didn't hear it anymore. We ourselves quickly learned to find our way in this confusing hustle and bustle. We followed the example of the locals and as newcomers, were much less relaxed. The zigzag course through this endless colourful crowd was no less adventurous. We took it as a sporting task to find faster and quicker ways of slipping through the crowds. Here and there a long smouldering cord hung down the walls of the building; a service to the customer, so to speak, because smokers could light a cigarette in passing. Many strange scents, surprised, confused and even overwhelmed the nose at first. That took some getting used to. Our eyes got used to the goods on display in the shop windows faster. We kept stopping to look at them. Our young colleagues Erna, Magdalena and Therese couldn't get enough of the beautiful silk sari fabrics, some even interwoven with gold threads. Their pocket money was already put aside in spirit in order to buy one later. We were especially happy at the sight of the beautiful Indian women in their colourful saris, which brought out their brown skin colour even better.

That afternoon our emotions were up and down. On the one hand, we were amazed and happy with laughter. But on the other hand, the frightening poverty, which was only too visible to the public, hit us much more deeply. That got us thinking and contemplative. These impressions were like the anticipation of what awaited us as Red Cross people. After breakfast the next morning we were informed that the landing permit in Dhaka was still pending. So, the whole team walked to a nearby restaurant called Amber for lunch. The food tasted so good that we were drawn back there several times. After each meal, paying the bill was always a lot of fun: Daniel, our reliable treasurer, always took the bill. Then he wrinkled his forehead deeply, checked off item after item with concentration, asked questions to the waiter and added up the bill twice for the follow-up check. Only then did Daniel carefully open his black treasure case, take out the required rupees, added a tip and handed over the sum. The waiter bowed deeply and thanked him with a polite smile. We also thanked our Daniel mischievously for the generous "invitation."

The multi-day wait for the onward flight was not what we wanted at all and gradually we became impatient. We wanted to work, not stroll through Calcutta, and see the sights like tourists. According to the calendar, it was December 22nd, so Christmas was just around the corner; a side issue for us at that moment. The large Basel fir tree that we flew with us, our Christmas tree, was standing prominently next to the hotel swimming pool. Our colleagues Erna, Magdalena and Therese decorated it with coloured balls, gold, and silver tinsel. Only the candles were missing, these would have melted quickly in the oppressively hot sun of Calcutta. But Christmas tree or not, we were not in a festive mood. We wanted to get to work in Bangladesh. On December 23rd we capitulated and started preparations for Christmas Eve. Two of us rushed to the old town to buy fine wire, to make candlesticks. Our nurses got jewellery and locked themselves in Magdalena's room on the afternoon of December 24th. "No access for unauthorized persons" was the strict rule. For their part, the Balair crew had invited us to a small Christmas party to be held in one of the meeting rooms. Magdalena, Erna and Therese dressed up for the party and appeared in beautiful Indian saris, their hair braided with matching ribbons. When we all entered the meeting room, the candles on the Christmas tree that had recently stood by the swimming pool were already burning. Appetizers were also waiting for us. Captain

Herzog welcomed us with a warm "Merry Christmas." The representatives of the ICRC were also present. The mood was cordial. But the talks revolved almost exclusively around "how long do we have to stay here in Calcutta?" "The Bangladeshi's are making all of us wait too long." "There's still little that functions in Bangladesh," Dr Fischer said once more. To distract from this ongoing theme, he unexpectedly intoned "Silent Night, Holy Night" and, wonder of wonders, everyone joined in the melody. Christmas had finally arrived and we all felt how solemn it suddenly had become in the candle-lit room. After two other well-known Christmas carols, we team members said goodbye with a "Merry Christmas!" But that was just the beginning of the evening. We now celebrated our own team Christmas in Magdalena's room, which the three women had also decorated for Christmas. This Christmas tree was small and plain, but festive with white candles and angel hair. To our delight, Magdalena had brought home-baked Christmas biscuits from Switzerland, which we began to nibble on and team boss Fischer read the Christmas message in candlelight like a father. Christmas carols followed, first sung by us, and also played from a tape. After also feasting on pineapples, oranges, bananas, nuts, and tea, we boarded two taxis in front of the hotel at 11:30pm, which took us to St. Thomas' Church for midnight Catholic mass. It was only with difficulty that we found space in the packed church, which was decorated for Christmas. I was surprised to meet so many Indian Christians there in Calcutta. A young, likeable pastor announced the Christmas message, and the solemn organ music brought us closer to God and loved ones at home. On 26th December 1971 we met the famous Swiss Toni Hagen in the hotel. Originally working in Nepal as a geologist he had made a name for himself with many years of important development programs in Nepal. Now he had become the UN chief delegate for Bangladesh leading a very urgent major nutrition program.

In the afternoon, Captain Herzog surprised us with the long-awaited message: "Tomorrow we can continue flying!" On the morning of December 27, three Indian Red Cross jeeps took us to the airport. Now it happened in quick succession: the take-off took place at 12 o'clock sharp and at 12.30 pm we were already flying over Jessore, the first town in Bangladesh. The vast landscape lay perfectly flat below us. Countless rivers and watercourses meandered through wide-open plains. Along the waters there were many trees and bushes, in the shade of which individual houses, sometimes a village, could be seen. The soil looked fertile, green rice fields of all possible sizes and shades were planted everywhere. Rice was obviously the staple food in this most densely populated country on earth. There was nothing to indicate that war had recently raged between Indian and West Pakistani troops down there. Only once did I see a ruined bridge on a narrow river. A little later our destination appeared on the horizon: Dhaka. Slowly descending, we circled Bangladesh's capital in a wide arc. The huge city below us looked like an island in an endless green plain. The houses in the old town were crowded together. More modern blocks of flats also became visible during our descent, with a striking number of large palm trees towering between the buildings. The landing approach took us just past the large Intercontinental Hotel, which had been declared a neutral zone during the war. When the DC 6 touched down on the newly repaired runway, the wheels kicked up a lot of dust. Machine gun positions, anti-aircraft guns and bunkers could still be seen everywhere. Soldiers and officers stood by and watched the taxiing of our plane. It is quite possible that this was the first arrival of a foreign aircraft in the young state of Bangladesh. As soon as we set foot on Bangladesh soil, we were warmly received by ICRC Chief Delegate Laurent Marti and all material was immediately loaded onto two Red Cross trucks. Meanwhile, we filled out forms at customs clearance. Our personal details were laboriously entered into a large list by two customs officers. On the 11th day since the founding of Bangladesh, it really looked like improvisation, but everything went smoothly. ICRC vehicles then took us to the Intercontinental Hotel in barely fifteen minutes. Thousands of three-wheeler cycle rickshaws and noisy baby taxis, also three-wheelers, enlivened the streets in Dhaka. There were also smoking buses and trucks. On the sidewalks, in front of small shops, there were many people who were obviously happy to be Bangladeshi and no longer East Pakistani. Many laughed and waved, often shouting "*Joy Bangla*" (Happy Bangladesh) when they saw us in the Red Cross vehicle. Everything looked peaceful and somehow unreal; two weeks earlier a state of war had prevailed, and terrible atrocities were the order of the day.

We checked into our hotel rooms, ate something in the restaurant, then drove together to the nearby Holy Family Hospital. We brought letters from Switzerland for Sister Bernarda, from a Swiss religious establishment in Menzingen. She was very pleased to greet such a large number of her country people. Our doctors asked her many questions about the hospital and the current situation. A local doctor then led us through the Christian-run hospital in Dhaka, which made a good impression on us. There was an option to let our team work here. All of our material had already been stored there.

The next morning, we looked at the densely populated city together. Here we encountered no more sacred cows. In the old town we were surrounded and questioned by young people. Everyone wanted to be photographed, laughing, throwing their hands up and shouting "*Joy Bangla*!" Again and again, someone shouted "*Joy Bangla*" and a growing crowd answered with the same refrain. The people were obviously happy to be rid of the exploitative and patronizing yoke of West Pakistan. In the old town, we were particularly amazed at the incredibly dense, tangle of countless electrical cables and thin telephone wires above our heads. Everything seemed to be going somewhere. A federally qualified electrician from Switzerland would have run away screaming from such chaos! Here, too, colourful, rickety, dented and smoke-emitting buses drove slowly through the narrow streets of the old town in search of passengers, blocking the way for rickshaws and baby taxis and blowing their poisonous exhaust gases in people's faces. Many shops were closed because, we heard, their owners had fled or been killed in the war. As we stepped out of the old town, we were unexpectedly standing directly on a main thoroughfare. We literally caught our breath. Rickshaw after rickshaw, as close together as the eye could see, with a passenger or two in the raised seat behind the struggling driver. Once I counted 36 rickshaws moving in a row, one behind the other. The passengers came from all walks of life. The simple Bangladeshi used this ride as well as women in colorful saris, students or noble gentlemen with ties and briefcases. Sometimes whole families sat on a rickshaw, pressed close together or on each other's laps, while the emaciated, sweating and tired looking driver struggled to move his too heavy rickshaw forward. These Bengali rickshaws not only transported people, but also goods of all kinds and quantities. It's amazing what these rickshaw coolies were able to carry: cardboard boxes, crates, heavy baskets of vegetables, fruit, or meat straight from the slaughterhouse, large dripping ice cream sticks, barrels, cement bags, bolts of cloth, window glass, water pumps and televisions, to name just a modest selection. Almost all rickshaws were beautifully painted with flowers, people, landscapes, and fantasy images. Although the traffic on the streets there was also violent, it was considerably less noisy chaos than in Calcutta. In addition, the sacred cows that are ubiquitous in Calcutta were missing here. When we returned to the hotel, we were told that we would be flying onto the port city of Chittagong the next day. Our team would be deployed there in the Medical College Hospital. It was originally planned that we would work not far from Dhaka, in the hospital of Mitsapur. But since this hospital was not yet in operation again, we would have lost too much time with the repairs. So off to Chittagong! I immediately liked this name because of its exotic sound. I couldn't wait to get there. Our material was already loaded onto two trucks in the evening, so that we could set off at 5 a.m. the next morning without breakfast. Daniel Oswald and I personally piloted the two trucks to the airfield and carefully reversed them backwards to the loading hatch of the DC 6. Since there were no workers to be found at this early hour, we hoisted the heavy crates of material into the passenger compartment ourselves and stacked everything there and pulled the net ropes over it. Hooray! Finally, we were allowed to work, despite a growling, empty stomach.

At 7 o'clock sharp we taxied to the start and, to the relief of all of us, were given the go-ahead. When Captain Vogel let our heavy bird soar into the misty morning air with roaring engines, we knew: "Here we go! Chittagong, here we come!"

Rivers, streams and rice fields appeared below us again, glittering in the light of the rising sun. After about an hour, we landed at Patenga Airfield near Chittagong where the Karnaphuli flows into the Bay of Bengal. Chittagong city and port are just a few kilometers upstream. Numerous Indian soldiers, watching us curiously, were standing at the airfield. The Geneva Red Cross League, which operates here, had sent two trucks to bring our material to Chittagong. As soon as the last crate was unloaded and the hatch closed, Captain Herzog waved goodbye from the open cockpit window and taxied to the start without us to fly back to Calcutta. Except for me, all team members now boarded a Red Cross VW bus that would take them to the Hotel Agrabad in Chittagong. But I sat down on the load of the second truck so as not to lose sight of the precious material entrusted to me. The bumpy ride started, past large trees, and along the wide river. There was a lot to see: there was a wrecked, broken-up freighter stranded in the middle of the river; only the superstructure was still sticking out of the water. My eyes met other ships that were still afloat but completely burned out. A little later we passed a small bridge that had been obviously blown up by the Mukti Bahini, the freedom fighters. All of these were witnesses to the war that had just ended. The city soon came into view. A steel arch, painted green and slightly rusted, spanned the street with, "Welcome to Chittagong" written on it. The young people in the street laughed when they saw me perched high on the crates. They waved at me and cheered, "*Joy Bangla!*"

The Geneva-based Red Cross League, which had become the International Federation of Red Cross and Red Crescent Societies (IFRCS), had its office in Chittagong in the Al Karim House, an older block of flats in a beautiful, park-like neighbourhood. Robert Koch from the German Red Cross, head of the IFRCS in Chittagong, made a room available for our extensive material. I liked the port city of Chittagong right away. Even in the city centre there were wooded green hills. In between were small valleys with sprawling trees and bushes. The green hilly landscape stretches far into the hinterland and everywhere there were tall palm trees laden with green coconuts. Although it was still closed due to the war, we were able to settle into the stately Hotel Agrabad. Director Günther, a German, made this possible. He had hired some people to take care of us. The restaurant, however, remained closed. The next day our doctors Fisher and Hof went to the Medical College Hospital to look around. That's where the team would work. But the start of work was delayed because the talks with the hospital management and the authorities took more time than hoped. A striking number of shops were closed in this port city, as evidenced by the drawn down shutters. We were told that many of the shop owners were West Pakistanis who fled when Indian troops entered Chittagong. In the run-up to this, however, the West Pakistani military had raged here, arresting many local owners, shooting them, and burying them in mass graves. To get an idea of the current situation, we drove through the city and looked around. We passed a quarter that consisted almost entirely of ruins. The soldiers had first set the houses on fire and then either shot or stabbed the unfortunate people who rushed out. In many cases, women and children were abused and raped beforehand. Eyewitnesses told us that blood literally flowed in the gutter. The dead were buried on the spot between the houses, or they were thrown into the sewage system. I later came back several times and spoke to survivors of these unimaginable massacres. What I heard and was credibly shown was difficult to cope with. That uniformed soldiers could commit such atrocities against innocent people and their own fellow citizens was, and remains, incomprehensible to me. Locals took me to several earth-covered mass graves in Chittagong that were starting to grow some grass again. Torn pieces of colored clothing, leg bones, skeletons, and skulls, some with tufts of hair and dried skin on them, were lying around. I had to press the handkerchief over my nose because a dull, sickly sweet smell of decay still hung over these places of horror.

In order not to wait idle after our arrival at the end of December, we pooled our pocket money and hired a chauffeur-driven minibus for a day trip to Cox's Bazaar, 100 kilometers away. Because a bridge had been blown up during the war, we crossed the Karnaphuli by ferry and an hour later paid a short visit to an American mission station with a small hospital, where war wounded patients were lying. The doctors and nurses there selflessly and energetically not only cared for the sick and injured in the hospital, but also helped the poor population in the large hilly catchment area, the Chittagong Hill Tracts, where the native tribes live. The narrow, potholed road to Cox's Bazar was not without danger because of rural traffic. Our driver kept honking his horn at the many rickshaws, baby taxis, buses and trucks. This was the only way he could make himself noticed, intimidate the smaller vehicles and force them aside. More than once he passed turning rickshaws, taking our breath away. We finally asked him to slow down and use the horn more sparingly. That worked instantly; because a driver without a horn feels defenceless in Bangladesh, drives more slowly, and takes fewer risks. Finally, we could breathe a sigh of relief and relax, no longer needing to stare anxiously at the road ahead.

Cox's Bazaar is located in the southernmost tip of the country on the Bay of Bengal, only around 20 kilometers from the Burmese border. The town of Cox's Bazaar has always been a popular tourist spot, famous for over 100 kilometers of sandy beaches. An English captain named Cox gave this place its name. The British government sent him here in 1798 to settle Buddhist immigrants from Burma.

First, we visited the airfield near the beach, which was badly damaged by the Indian Air Force. The airfield building was in ruins and several deep bomb craters gaped in the runway and an unexploded bomb still lay unguarded in the grass next to it. The beach is completely flat. We could have walked barefoot on the fine gray sandy beach almost all the way back to Chittagong. But we didn't think about returning for the time being and climbed the weather radar station on a hill instead. From there we had a magnificent view over the small town to the horizon of the Bay of Bengal. This radar station rose to fame in 1969 after capturing images of the devastating cyclone and its centre, the Big Eye. This terrible hurricane claimed up to 500,000 lives, especially in the Ganges estuary (see start of this chapter).

Back in Chittagong on January 1st we visited the Catholic orphanage in the old town, directly opposite the cathedral. Sister

Maud, the dainty director, led us through the well-kept garden to the delightfully clean premises. Babies lay in their cribs in a large room, looked after by a young nun. We were also introduced to the teacher, Sister Carmel Rebeiro, in a classroom, who was giving arithmetic lessons to her twenty or so 10-to-12-year-old students. They spontaneously tuned into a melodious Bengali song in honour of us guests. In another room about twenty children of kindergarten age were sitting and playing. Sister Maud reported that soon a dozen five to seven-year-old orphans would travel to Switzerland to be adopted by Swiss parents. The experienced sister Bernadette would accompany the children, look after them and take enough time until they felt at home with their Swiss adoptive parents. The Bangladesh war had orphaned countless children. We were deeply impressed by the devotion and love with which these selfless Catholic sisters gave the many orphans a safe home, security, and education.

January 10 1972 was a day of celebration for Bangladeshis: Sheik Mujibur Rahman (the founding father of Bangladesh) returned to Dhaka aboard a British Air Force Hercules transport. The West Pakistani government had finally released him from prison – after great international pressure.

Thousands of cheering Bangladeshis welcomed their great idol at the airfield and enthusiastically shouted *"Mujib zindabad!"* (Long live Mujib!) and *"Joy Bangla!"* They had received their leader back and celebrated frenetically. A few days later the provisional government was formed, whose first very popular Prime Minister was Sheik Mujibur Rahman.

Our medical team was finally able to start its work. Our doctors, nurses and attendants began to take action at the Medical College Hospital in Chittagong. I unpacked the corps material, supported by two local drivers from the Red Cross League. The resulting mountain of wrapping paper and newspaper was carefully folded, since practically everything was reused and nothing usable was thrown away. Later, paper bags were to be glued from the paper. With the work came a good, happy atmosphere. We were finally able to do what we had come to do: help the war-disabled population. Dr. Fisher, Dr. Hof, Magdalena, Erna, Therese, and David were immediately in their medical element. They were given a part of the building with 50 beds in the Medical College Hospital. Many patients with gunshot wounds lay here, some of them also suffering from dangerous infections. From time to time I could smell when David Keller changed bandages, the disgusting smell of pus spread immediately.

Our popular Dr. Roman Fischer operated daily, supported by Erna, Magdalena, or Therese. Chandragona is located 40 kilometers east of Chittagong, directly at the Karnaphuli river. There is the Christian Chandragona Hospital, which was run by an English missionary team with a Dr. Flowers and under the direction of Dr. Brian Whitty. This hospital was founded in 1910 by the British Baptist Mission, which continues to this day. In January 1972, patients with war injuries were also lying here. Dr. Fischer took a look at them, discussed the situation with Dr. Witty and then with the Swiss Red Cross in Berne. Soon Dr. Fischer also operated in Chandragona on certain days, assisted by our nursing professionals. Dressed appropriately, I was allowed to watch operations a few times while Dr. Fischer humorously explained his delicate work to me. The hospital also had its own leprosy station on its premises. There I saw for the first time what this terrible infectious disease does, how it mutilates fingers, toes, noses, or forms large blisters on the skin. This visit affected me deeply; not least because of how these unfortunate human beings were forced to vegetate, away from any social contact.

The hospital in Chandragona was in the catchment area of many indigenous tribes who live in the green, wooded hills of the Hill Tracts, speak their own languages clinging to their independent, frugal way of life. The Hill Tracts borders with India and Burma now called Myanmar. The largest water reservoir in Bangladesh, Lake Kaptai, is also located there. Together we team members undertook a trip to the dam near Kaptai. There we rented a motorboat with a skipper taking us to Rangamati, the main town of the Hill Tracts region, on the long, branched, and fairly shallow lake. The trip on this large, wide, remote lake with its many small islands remains unforgettable. We docked at one of the trees and bush covered islands to chat with tribesmen and women who lived in simple bamboo-weave huts. The women wore beautiful, hand-woven reddish cloths and smoked a local tobacco grass out of a thick bamboo tube, which seemed to be very relaxing. Many of these tribal people lost their land and homes in 1962 when the Kaptai Dam and power plant were completed, and the water began to back up. Some unfortunate tribes had no choice but move to higher land including the newly formed islands. In the end, the lake covered a water surface of 11,000 square kilometers, which corresponds to a quarter of the area of Switzerland. However, the remaining area on land was not enough to continue to be home to all the residents. It is estimated that around 40,000 of these people were forced to cross the Indian and Burmese borders to settle there. Tensions in this remote, disputed tri-state region of Bangladesh-India-Myanmar have never subsided. At that time the scenically very beautiful Hill Tracts soon became a restricted area. The situation in the now-pacified Bangladesh settled down faster than expected in early 1972. The use of our medical team in Chittagong and Chandragona was needed less and less. After consultation with the Swiss Red Cross in Berne, it was decided to terminate our mission there and hand over all material to the two hospitals. The team should return to Switzerland as soon as possible. Too bad for me, I would have loved to stay there longer, I liked Chittagong. So now I tried my luck with the League of Red Cross Societies in Bangladesh and applied there with the consent of the Swiss Red Cross. Shortly before my Swiss colleagues flew back to Switzerland, my wish came true: I became a delegate of the International Red Cross League. My joy was great. For the final time, I sat with my Swiss colleagues around the big table in the Gate of London, our favourite Chinese restaurant in Chittagong, enjoying our beloved dishes that only cost a fraction of the prices in Switzerland. Dr. Fischer thanked everyone for the good cooperation and great patience during this all-too-short assignment. The next day, I chauffeured the team to Patenga Airfield. But the plane of Bangladesh Biman was a delayed for a long time and everyone was slowly getting hungry. So, Dr. Fischer requested me to quickly drive back to Chittagong and get eight batches of chicken tikka, a team favourite. A task I was happy to do. But to my great chagrin I came back late to find the team had left in the meantime. That hurt, I would have loved to say goodbye to my colleagues who had all become friends. The comfort was that we did not lose sight of each other and met later in Switzerland from time to time. But I didn't know that then, so I stood, at the airfield, sad, lost and alone with my eight chicken tikka snacks. My new Red Cross League colleagues in the Alkarim office later enjoyed these delicacies and were happy for the gift. For me this was a good debut with a new team. I continued to be employed by the Swiss Red Cross, but from now on I worked on behalf of the League of Red Cross Societies based in Geneva. Every national Red Cross and Red Crescent Society in the world is a member of the International Red Cross League and can turn to Geneva for assistance in case of an emergency of various kinds including a refugee crisis. The league, for its part, then asks all its members for support after examining the respective call for help in a country. The Red Cross League in Geneva is the umbrella organization for all national Red Cross/Red Crescent Societies. Most Red Cross League delegates are employed by their national Red Cross but work in a League mission.

To my great regret I could no longer work in Chittagong and was assigned a new task in the capital Dhaka. There I worked in one of the large Red Cross *godowns*, which was very busy day in and day out. A warehouse in Bangladesh is commonly called *godown* - no one called them a store or warehouse. We were pushed to the limit to provide the most urgent supplies for the needy population in the greater Dhaka area. It was here in these warehouses that I met Ture Andersson, a lovely Swede of the same age from Linköping. He had previously worked for years as a technical consultant in Kaptai on the Karnaphuli River behind Chittagong. We liked each other straight away, eventually became lifelong friends, and visited each other in Sweden and Switzerland. But then we spent every day counting bales of wool blankets, sacks of rice, sugar, flour, and countless other relief items from all over the world that were in urgent need. With humour and full of enthusiasm we hurried through the narrow corridors between the high mountains of stacked goods, supervised the many sweating, dusty workers, ordered trucks, and wrote delivery notes. In between we drank water or ate bananas and sandwiches we had brought with us. I quickly got used to the mixture of countless smells in the different halls. Every new delivery that arrived smelt different. Smells from North America, Japan, Europe, South America, and Australia collided creating a new unique odour.

Our boss, Sven Lampell, was also Swedish, a tall, handsome man in his early fifties, a former commander and colonel in the Swedish Air Force. He had served as an officer in the UN peacekeeping force in the Congo and had for years served as the highly esteemed, world-experienced chief delegate of the Red Cross League on missions in crisis areas. For our own protection, like most foreigners, we stayed in the Intercontinental Hotel, which was still guarded; because the situation in Bangladesh was still a bit uncertain, on some nights we heard isolated shootings. We also heard that the Mukti Bahini (Resistance Army) took bloody revenge on non-Bengali war collaborators. Many of these non-Bengali citizens – so-called Bihari – had worked with the West Pakistan Army and their own language was their undoing. They were instantly recognized as Bihari when speaking in Bangla. Photos surfaced showing uniformed Mukti Bahini mercenaries with Bihari collaborators, hand-cuffed and laid down on the ground in a sport stadium in front of many passive spectators. In revenge these former freedom fighters rammed rifle mounted bayonets into the chest of the terrorised, screaming unfortunate Bihari victims. Images like that burned deep inside me.

Thanks to my humanitarian work for the civilian population, the horrific images of stabbed Biharis receded into the background after a while and there was more than enough work for us! Ture Andersson and I were almost the same age, only 42 days apart. We had a lot to talk about, even though we had only been running the *godowns* for a few weeks, delivering large quantities of relief supplies to the neediest people in the greater Dhaka area. We were amazed at the huge selection of wool blankets stored in the *godowns*. Some were ordinary and thin but, we also found others that were brightly-coloured and picturesquely patterned of astonishingly good quality. Blankets were in high demand and in short supply, especially during the Bengal winter. We had to take good care of them, because wool blankets were unaffordable, especially for the poorest.

Four new motorboats, a welcome donation from the Swedish Red Cross, had also been stored in the *godown* and we waited for direction as to which area they were most needed. They were worth their weight in gold in this land of a thousand rivers and waterways. One morning three trucks loaded with rice were waiting in front of a *godown,* ready to leave, when I came out with the delivery note. There I saw a young fellow who had climbed onto one of the trucks and was tampering with a sack- and filling a large can with rice. "Come down now," I called out. The fellow was startled and scared when I reached out my arms to help him down. As I grabbed his arms, a stream of urine suddenly spattered over me soaking my head, upper body, and shirt in urine. There was no gloating as I washed it off at the sink. From December to the end of February, when a chilly breeze blows through the thin, bamboo-woven walls of a traditional house, it was uncomfortably cold at night for the people of Bangladesh. The blankets we delivered were wrapped and tightly tied in bales so as not to tempt the truck drivers along the way. In addition, we were very careful that nothing disappeared in the *godown*; because we didn't want to let these valuable Red Cross goods, coming from many countries, be stolen. Occasionally I would escort a truck loaded with groceries to destinations in Dhaka. I wanted to see where our relief supplies were going to. We also delivered relief supplies to the heavily guarded Bihari camp in the suburb of Mohamedpur. Bihari's had an unfortunate past behind them, and now they were fighting for their lives. Most of the population of Bangladesh professes Islam. With only one percent of the population, the Bihari were one of the few minorities in the country. They originally came from the Indian state of Bihar. However, the religious conflicts during the partition of British India in 1947 caused the Bihari to move to what was then East Pakistan. As I have described elsewhere, they sided with the West Pakistanis during the Bangladesh war and now had to pay for it bitterly.

Our "big Boss," Sven Lampell rarely came to visit us in the warehouse because he had more important things to do, and he also knew that he could rely on us. He confidently led this broad-based, complex relief operation, negotiating with authorities, coordinating the entire Red Cross mission with all those involved, such as the ICRC in Geneva, the UN and many other international organizations and non-Government organisations - commonly referred to as NGOs. But Sven also took the time to visit the Red Cross delegates in the provinces. However, one of his most important assignments was working with the Bangladesh Red Cross. This young organization needed to be motivated, supported, promoted, and also expanded. The Red Cross League itself only stayed in the country for a certain amount of time, appropriate to the problems. So, it was urgent to strengthen the Red Cross Society of Bangladesh, preparing it for its independent tasks and to introduce its many staff and volunteers to future challenging mission. It was also important to insure the great "Red Cross Spirit" became second nature to them. We all valued our Sven Lampell very much. He always knew what to do when problems arose. He, in turn, appreciated and counted on us to use our own common sense and act accordingly. On Valentine's Day - an hour before lunchtime - Ture asked me to meet Sven Lampell in the hotel. He wanted to discuss something with me. A bit surprised I went, with Ture warning me to be back by 12 o'clock sharp. It seemed to me that he was up to something. When I returned at 12 o'clock, I caught my breath: In the large office, all the *godown* employees were crowded together singing in unison, "Happy 40th Birthday dear Rudi Brawand!" A garland of flowers was placed around my neck and a large cake greeted me on the table with the inscription: "Happy 40th Birthday, dear Boss." The whole room was decorated. Flower garlands, coloured ribbons and colourful balloons hung on walls and ceilings. In a corner, three local musicians began playing Bengali folk tunes, while some flower-bedecked young women in colourful saris performed traditional dances. I stood there smiling deeply amazed, surprised, and moved to tears. Everyone in our warehouse team was able to put workload and stress aside for a few minutes. What a great surprise for me to be celebrated in this exotic way in a newly founded country on the Bay of Bengal, which nevertheless had a history of more than a thousand years. We all enjoyed the birthday celebration, and I will never forget it.

The newly independent state of Bangladesh (land of the Bengalis) remained in its infancy for quite a while. The veteran officials from West Pakistan who had been running the bureaucratic machinery had fled, leaving their less experienced Bengali colleagues unprepared. This slowed down the development of the newly formed state, and unfortunately encouraged corruption. Many young, inexperienced officials suddenly found themselves in senior positions and could not resist taking advantage of them. The countless West Pakistanis who fled to save their lives, whether officials or businesspeople, had to leave behind all their possessions such as houses, large villas and companies. For cunning native Bengalis these abandoned buildings became gold mines. With tricky bureaucratic machinations, they grabbed abandoned buildings or lots of land became new home and landowners overnight; thanks, of course to appropriately forged documents issued by corrupt officials. And it happened under the guise of "nationalization." I later had to intercede personally and fight to prevent a Swiss trading company from losing its valuable land and buildings in such a disgraceful way. Ture and I were staying at that time - like most foreigners - in the still guarded Intercontinental Hotel in Dhaka. The situation at night was still somewhat dangerous, occasionally I heard gunfire. As previously mentioned, during the war, the Red Cross had, in 1971, declared the Intercontinental Hotel a neutral zone. On the orders of the West Pakistani army commander, journalists were not allowed to leave the hotel to prevent them from reporting on the terrible massacres. However, a few foreign journalists hid in the city and were able to inform the world anyway.

In February 1972, the hotel lobby was bustling with activity, packed with journalists, photographers, businesspeople, diplomats, and members of international organizations. I often overheard the current situation being discussed. I also learned a lot during breakfast in the restaurant, Americans in particular spoke loudly and clearly without consideration. A few times I sat at the breakfast table with the famous Swiss Toni Hagen. As mentioned earlier, he was the UN chief delegate here in Bangladesh for the major international food aid program. I told him about my previous job. At the next breakfast he asked me if I would be interested in working at the UN in the UNDP (United Nations Development Program). I told him I would consider the opportunity. It was clear to me that this would be a long-term, well-paid work in developing countries. At first glance, a tempting alternative, but did I want that? Starting a new career in Africa and Asia? Work in a developing country for two or three years, then get transferred to another country and probably with office work mainly involved. Although faraway places had always lured me, and continued to, my roots still remained deep in my native Swiss soil. I needed my beautiful homeland, the familiar dialects, the many friends there, the mountains and skiing. I needed time for all this; more time than just three weeks of vacation. With the Swiss Red Cross, that had worked perfectly up until now. After every assignment abroad, I immediately found work in Switzerland again, where I was able to cultivate "my roots," until my wanderlust returned. My decision was therefore made quickly: I remained loyal to the Red Cross, renounced a career move and financial security. The work in a Red Cross mission was more intensive and demanding, always associated with many imponderables. But that's what made this job for me interesting. I really appreciated being able to tackle challenges independently. This is where my real strengths lay. A major development program that inevitably involved a lot of bureaucracy was not the right choice for me. That's what my gut feeling told me and that settled everything. That I had to think about this completely unexpectedly was quite good. This questioning of my current job, my professional and private future, strengthened me for my daily life in the local project. Even though the days were so filled with work that we were all pushed to the limit, I was now more aware of how much I liked this way of working. I didn't want any other job; everything was fine for me.

At that time, Dhaka Airport was almost in the middle of the city and could be reached from the Intercontinental Hotel in just a few minutes. Fully loaded cargo planes with aid supplies from all over the world landed there day and night. Sven Lampell appointed me as their recipient. So as soon as a plane with donations for the Red Cross League landed, the phone on my bedside table in room 817 rang at any time of the night. It rudely tore me out of my dreams several times a week and robbed me of my sleep. "Please come to the airport immediately. A cargo plane with goods for the Red Cross has just landed. Please organize trucks and labourers as well. Unloading must be done quickly." "Okay, I'm coming!" I answered drowsily and slammed the receiver back on the cradle. Occasionally, when those late-night calls were too frequent, I'd also yell angrily, "No, not again!" Nonetheless, I leapt out of bed again and again. I had perfected the procedure: first, a few hasty sips of black tea from the thermos bottle that had been filled the night before as a precaution, at the same time mobilizing a few trucks and workers by telephone via a Bengali liaison man; then a lightning-fast cat washing at the sink, into the pants and a Red Cross shirt and finally slipping into sandals. Off in the lift and down to the reception, where the concierge always greeted me with a friendly "Good morning, sir. How are you?" That felt good, made me cheerful and relieved stress for a short time. Quickly I ran to my Land Rover and drove through almost empty night-time streets in a few minutes to the airport, which actually didn't deserve the name, as it was more like an outdated military airfield. As a rule, these night operations ran smoothly. When I arrived, I immediately reported to the right office, where the captain of the aircraft that had arrived was waiting for me with the delivery papers. Among others, the Japanese Red Cross in Tokyo sent 20 tons of relief supplies. Blankets, tents, medicines, baby food and sacks of rice were waiting to be loaded onto the trucks. Afterwards, I immediately guided these precious donations to our warehouse, to which I always carried the keys. When everything was done, I returned to the hotel – still at night. I didn't get any sleep, but I was glad to have breakfast served to my room and used the time to write letters to my loved ones in Switzerland. From time to time my time was wasted when I arrived at the airport, to find out that the plane had brought relief goods for another aid organisation. Nevertheless, I was proud to be right in the middle of the wheels of this highly complex international aid operation to help the people in urgent need.

Regularly at the end of the month, Sven Lampell summoned the field delegates from the provinces to Dhaka for reporting, to explain problems, strive for improvements, and provide new instructions. On the eve of my first of these meetings, we RC delegates were invited to a party at Sven's house. Many of us only knew our colleagues by voice from radio contacts with each other. At this party I got to know the people behind every voice. We were an interesting, fascinating RC organisation, coming from many different countries, united by the English language and even more so by our common, highly motivating task of the international service and spirit of the Red Cross. This spirit immediately contributed to a very good mood and friendly atmosphere. When our boss Sven, the very sovereign "Chairman," opened the meeting at 9 a.m. the next morning, more than 20 international and national Red Cross representatives sat around a long table with their written reporting documents. There were Bangladeshis, Norwegians, Swedes, Danes, Germans, Finns, Austrians, French, Dutch, Americans, Canadians, Australians and Swiss. Each delegate read out their detailed monthly report, which was then up for discussion. At this table, many problems would be solved every month, and the organization improved and adapted to the constantly changing circumstances. This significantly accelerated the distribution of many relief supplies. I loved listening to the diversity of accents of the English-speaking delegates at these meetings. I quickly recognized the nationality of a speaker: whether German, Scandinavian, French, Italian, Dutch or Swiss, they all had a typical accent when speaking the English language; including myself. After living in countries where

English is the official language for 40 years now, I still do. Once, an older Australian lady noticed my accent. "You have a pretty strong accent," she stated and asked: "Are you from South Africa?" "No," I replied with a smile, "I'm from Switzerland!"

One evening I received a call at the hotel from Carmel Rebeiro, the nun from the orphanage in Chittagong. She'd arrived in Dhaka the previous day on the Red Cross plane and wanted to visit with me, she said. I was very happy about that. "Welcome Sister," I said, and arranged to meet her in the hotel lobby on Friday, my only day off. On Friday afternoon I suddenly heard a soft knock on the door to my room. So, I went to open it and unexpectedly found myself face to face with three young and charming nuns in religious attire. Carmel Rebeiro had simply asked at the reception for my room number, and here they were. Carmel beamed at me and asked: "May we come in?" A little overwhelmed, I invited the three ladies in and immediately apologized because I only had one chair available. "No problem!" The three of them sat down on my large double bed, laughing, as if that were the most natural thing in the world for them. It made it all the more difficult for me to cope with the situation, I felt somehow embarrassed, having three smiling young nuns sitting on my double bed, but saved myself by ordering drinks and snacks for my charming visitors. All three had come to Dhaka from Chittagong on the Balair DC6 to attend a nursing class in Dhaka. Carmel Rebeiro, who seemed to like me a lot, thanked me warmly because – a few weeks earlier in Chittagong – I had pleaded with Captain Rupert Vogel to let the nuns fly with him if necessary. He was surprised but smiled, happy to agree, thinking it was a very good idea, as he had never flown nuns before. And so, my three visitors were able to enjoy a free flight amid relief supplies. After a refreshing teatime with lively conversations, I accompanied my three visitors to the hotel lobby, where we said goodbye. All four of us hoped to see each other again soon in Chittagong. A few days later, Sven Lampell actually delegated me back to the port city, where the handling of large quantities of relief supplies was needed. The team there urgently needed reinforcement. Like a little boy, I was happy to go back to Chittagong. Although I had not yet lost my heart in Chittagong, I felt comfortable and somehow at home in this romantic city with the green hills and magnificent palm trees. In addition, the nightly work assignments at the airport in Dhaka had worn me out a bit. In Chittagong, I hoped I would be able to sleep undisturbed again. I was thoroughly mistaken. Travelling overland from Dhaka to Chittagong back then involved time-consuming obstacles. Four times along the way, one had to queue at one of the major rivers, hoping to get a seat on the next car ferry, which was crowded with trucks, buses, cars, pedestrians, beggars, and hawkers. But I didn't have to drive, I could fly. The German Red Cross provided the Red Cross League in Bangladesh with a helicopter complete with a pilot and mechanic. This allowed the delegates to fly to provinces in need within a few hours, to discuss the situation on the spot with the local Red Cross Chairman and then immediately start the appropriate emergency aid. This German helicopter was worth the money and saved countless lives at the time. Sven Lampell arranged for me and my few belongings to be seated next to Rainer the pilot in the helicopter flying to Chittagong. Karl Heinz, the German mechanic with his heavy toolbox, sat in the back with another passenger. It was a deeply impressive experience for me to fly at low altitude for the first time over this flat landscape, which is crisscrossed by countless watercourses. The many bodies of water were reflected in the backlight of the morning sun like flashing, fiery dots. A seemingly endless area of green paddy fields spread out before our eyes. Arranged like a chessboard, their coloured tones constantly changed, depending on the sunlight, clouds, and wind. Green colours blended with blue sky on the distant hazy horizon. Sometimes water glistened between the stalks. Villages and hamlets lay hidden between the streams under clumps of trees. Children ran out of the houses and excitedly waved at us. A boat was tied up at almost every house; it was the only way the farmers could go about their work in the rice fields. It was on this helicopter flight that I now realized how dependent the people here were on the waterways. The scenes I saw from this low altitude were unique: Sometimes an engine driven wooden trawler came into view or the white, brown, and patched sails of loaded sampans moving a slow a zigzag upstream on the Meghna (Ganges) through the glittering waters towards their destination. Sometimes all I could see in the distance was the billowing sail shining out of the green sea of rice plants. Beside each of the farmhouses, crouching in the shade of trees and bushes, was a square pond. These ponds were created because excavation was needed to create a flood-proof clay platform on which to build the house. The resulting ponds were used by these farmers for fish farming, which benefited the family's diet. Most of Bangladesh is alluvial plain, a vast delta of fertile soil. The great rivers Ganges and Brahmaputra have been carrying this earth down from the Himalayas since primeval times, depositing it here during the annual floods and thus fertilizing this seemingly endless plain, which is broken through by innumerable watercourses. Suddenly the picture changed! Now some hills came into view on the left side, the border area to the Indian state of Assam. The vast expanse of water of the Bay of Bengal glittered to the right. Far below we were approaching a long, crowded, diesel-hauled passenger train that, from my bird's-eye view, it looked like a toy train set. Countless passengers were sitting or even standing on top of the carriages, some seemed to wave at us. Then we flew over the first suburbs of Chittagong, followed by an industrial area with jute factories. Shortly after, the waterfront district at the Karnaphuli River emerged. Rainer wanted to show us the extent of the destruction caused by the Indian Air Force. It was a depressing picture that presented itself to us: what used to be large warehouses had been razed to the ground and burned out. Cargo ships lay half-sunk in the harbour, their damaged, scorched superstructure and masts sticking out of the brackish water. I quickly snapped some photos. Then Rainer steered his helicopter towards the landing site; on the flat roof of the four-storey Alkarim building, headquarters of the Int. Red Cross League. Gently hovering, Rainer set the machine down on the concrete roof, which was painted with a large H and a Red cross. This was the gentle end of my first helicopter flight.

Two floors below, Robert Koch, the head of the RC league in Chittagong and his deputy Werner Janz, gave me a warm welcome. Robert was a tall, blond from Germany, Werner came from Graz in Styria , Austria, where he had studied medicine. So, the three of us were able to converse in German, which was not only a pleasure but also a relief. Now I also got to know the local clerks, accountant

Marshal de Souza and the secretary Mavis McDermott, both locals in Chittagong. I was then assigned a bare room with a slab floor. In addition to an old iron bed with a mattress that was too soft, there was also a small chest of drawers and a lonely chair in the large, white washed room. What was clearly missing in this bed chamber, I was to learn painfully during the first night when a horde of Bengali mosquitoes attacked me - tapping me like a blood donor – lacking was a mosquito net. Again and again, I got up in a rage to address the beasts waiting on the walls, swinging a towel to kill them. When the last bloodsuckers stuck to the walls or lay dead in their own blood on the floor, I finally found some sleep. Werner Janz apologized in the morning and immediately arranged for a wooden frame with a mosquito net to be mounted on the bed.

After breakfast, Robert Koch and Werner Janz drove me to the Red Cross *godowns* between the railway station and Karnaphuli river port. These large buildings, some of which had two floors, belonged to the international Swiss trading company Volkart Brothers. A great manor-house, standing on a hill between trees, was also part of it. The war and the potential danger that the new government could nationalize such a property had persuaded the Volkart Brothers to rent their buildings free of charge to the League of Red Cross Societies as a precaution. There was a lot of important work going on there. Over 60 local staff including 15 drivers for 12 white-painted trucks with Red Cross emblems. Ten field officers also worked there - they were all young men who spoke perfect English. They were members of a Catholic minority, so-called Anglo-Indians, who have lived in India and Pakistan for centuries. Almost all had Portuguese names like Pereira, Rodrigues,

Gonsalves, d'Silva, Dias, Gomes, and others. This huge *godown*, plus the additionally rented ones, was actually the most important League of Red Cross transhipment point in that young country. All Red Cross relief goods arriving by ships in large quantities had to be forwarded as quickly as possible to all other provinces in Bangladesh. The Volkart *godown* became my workplace from then on. Werner Janz introduced me to the foremen, showed me through the spacious, mostly-full *godowns*, explained the bookkeeping, the security system and the day and night surveillance. Recently arrived goods had to be forwarded as fast as possible to make room for new supplies. New deliveries arrived by ship from overseas every week and had to be unloaded immediately in port. I liked such a restless business; planning, organizing, and making decisions was easy for me. Werner Janz stayed just two days to help familiarize me, then I was on my own and responsible for the *godowns* with all the activities that went with it. Of course, all work had to be coordinated with our boss Robert Koch. An office with an antechamber on the first floor was assigned to me. The secretary there was Jessie Paul, a young, shy, and very reliable Anglo-Indian. When I arrived every morning into the anteroom, she insisted on getting up straight away with a serious expression and greeting me with "Good Morning, Mr. Brawand." I had to get used to the fact that someone stood up because of me to belt out the morning greeting. Here I met a growing work pressure, the ever larger and more complicated orders, the daily struggle against time and the dramatic lack of space with calming humour and common sense. When even that wasn't enough, we tried to do magic and toiled into the night. Nevertheless: I actually felt comfortable in this rush, knowing that when the supplies for the starving Bangladeshis arrived by ship, the fastest possible transhipment was vital. We didn't actually need a boss in the form of a person giving order. Those rigorous working days didn't feel like working. Rather, for all of us in this large team, it was carrying out an assignment on a challenging and very important life saving mission. I quickly learned that millions of people living in distant provinces up north were depending on our supplies. This knowledge allowed us to work considerably longer hours without getting noticeably tired - at first. But you had to be careful: the workers and drivers had their families plus relatives who were waiting for the wages of the only breadwinner. So, these men were under almost unbearable pressure to perform. Every day they laboured here amidst these many precious commodities in the *godown* halls and rooms. This aroused many desires and they tried to steal whenever there was an opportunity. As great as I understood it, thefts had to be punished just as severely. Anyone caught stealing was fired without any "ifs or buts." Drastic deterrence was the only way to nip in the bud the urge to steal. My vehicle was a classic, dark green 1964 Chevrolet, decorated with the Red Cross flag and emblems. This magnificent "sled by auto" also belonged to the inventory of the Volkart Brothers. At first, I drove myself; but Sven Lampell soon demanded that we delegates stop driving ourselves; to risk an accident was just too great. Should an accident occur, road users and witnesses could ignite anger among the pedestrians, which could endanger the driver. Ali, a slightly older Bihari, therefore, became my personal chauffeur. He was well assimilated before the war and spoke the Bengali language correctly. Both were guarantees that Ali was the right driver for me. In the evenings – on private trips – special caution was called for at the wheel. Our boss kept pointing this out.

My room in the Alkarim building was soon needed for other purposes. That was fine with me, so I moved back to the Agrabad Hotel with my small suitcase, where I was better off. Because the few hotel guests only occupied the second floor, the other seven floors were still empty, I had the opportunity to do some sport again. Before 6 a.m. every morning I was running silently up the carpet-covered steps from the second floor to the roof terrace on the eighth floor, doing some gymnastics, and enjoying the magnificent panoramic view over the waking Chittagong, then jogging contentedly back down to take a shower and have breakfast. My condition improved quickly and soon I was running up the stairs twice.

The Karnaphuli river port of Chittagong was the lifeline for the young Bangladesh in 1972. Cargo ships from all over the world arrived there with essential food for the population. More than 10 million refugees had fled to India's West Bengal during the dangerous 1971 war while it was still East Pakistan. But East Pakistan had become Bangladesh, and these refugees were beginning returning home to their now peaceful homeland. However, cargo ships were still on their way to India with relief supplies, especially to Calcutta. These ships were now suddenly diverted to Chittagong, and we got bogged down in more and more work. Our problem was how to forward these freights in the fastest possible way to the Bangladesh provinces, some of which were far away up north. New urgent orders were received daily by radio from the coordination office in Dhaka. We ordered more and more empty railway freight wagons, but we could never get enough of them. We organized sampans, which are slowly pushed upstream by their large sails in a zigzag course, transporting our live saving Red Cross goods towards their destination. Two Balair DC6 Red Cross planes, each loaded with 12 tons of food, landed two times a day. Our trucks always had to be loaded in time at the Volkart *godown*, so they were ready and waiting at Patenga Airport when the planes landed. A long-term sampan transport program was then launched in March from Chittagong's port. The not very large sampan ships had sails, a loading capacity of between 20 to over 100 tons. We loaded these mainly with rice, wheat, soya flour and wool blankets. Thanks to the countless rivers and watercourses, the skippers were able to reach practically every district up north. We also supplied the coastal areas, but there we had a problem because shipping was heavily dependent on tides and the weather gods. Sometimes it took days before the sampans could finally leave. Again and again, they had to seek shelter on the shore or river because of strong winds. It also happened that we sent sampans in a convoy. Such a convoy was always accompanied by two of our loyal field officers, so that the skippers would not even consider the idea of selling any goods on the way. Since we never had enough trucks of our own, we brought in the local, reliable, and honest contractor Mr. Rahman. He could always organize extra trucks and workers as needed and was very helpful. More ships with Red Cross cargo kept arriving, additional *godowns* were hired, more workers employed. Our tasks became more and more extensive, complex, and time-consuming, because the warehouse accounting and reports also had to be strictly kept up to date. Our working week actually started on Saturday morning and ended late Thursday afternoon. However, more and more extra shifts had to be arranged in order to cope with the growing tasks. One evening, just before midnight, the workers were sweating and busy filling a newly rented *godown* with 100 kg sacks of sugar brought by a German cargo ship. When I got there, they complained that the storage room was almost full and there wasn't enough space left to offload the last truck. "You have to stack the sacks all the way up to the ceiling," I advised them. "That is impossible," they said, these sacks are too heavy for that. "Okay, I'll show you how to make it possible," I said. First, I made the workers build a steep staircase with the heavy sacks of sugar. Then, at the truck bridge, I loaded one of those mighty 100kg sacks on my back and slowly, hunched over and panting but determined, climbed slowly up the sugar bag staircase. There I laid down the heavy load under the ceiling. The workers were amazed, looked at each other - and a loud palaver began. I didn't understand anything, but it was obvious their ambition was awakened, "What the boss can do, we can do too!" Suddenly the workers began to sing in a choir. It sounded like a refreshing encouragement at this late hour: "*Ayvallaah, Ayvallaah, Ayvallaah,*" they sang, and the first worker put the next 100 kg of sugar on his back, struggled to breathe, but climbed slowly up the high steps of the sugar bag ladder, uplifted by the non-stop *Ayvallah* cheerings, and put the sack below the ceiling. We all applauded happily, singing and accompanying the remaining quintals of enthusiastic *Ayvallahs* to the top. Each *Ayvallah* strengthened its bearer, helping him carry the heavy burden aloft. This acrobatic show at the witching hour made everyone happy. That had been real teamwork. But now it was high time for everyone to go to sleep.

HANSRUDI BRAWAND

* * * *

The Bangladesh Red Cross set out to register the neediest mothers and children across the country and established over eleven hundred so-called milk feeding centres. The children's food – powdered milk and soybean flour – supplied by the Red Cross League was distributed there. In our Chittagong province, there were more than 50 such centres spread far and wide. Two of our trucks delivered to these places daily. Two hard-to-reach centers Hill Tracts and in Teknaf, located on the southernmost sandy tip of Bangladesh, were also supplied with baby food on a daily basis. A German freighter had brought other treasures including 5,000 pieces of white quality men's underwear and sleeveless white vests. This ship surprised us with a very welcome gift - three large MAN semi-trailers. A large crane lifted these heavy vehicles out of the deep hold of the ship and carefully placed them on the pier. I almost couldn't believe it! My heart beat faster when I examined the three MAN semi-trailers donated by the German Red Cross. Each of these trucks could load 20 tons. That almost doubled our red Cross transport capacity. But articulated trucks are more difficult to steer, especially while reversing. In order to ensure that the selected drivers were able to handle these heavy vehicles safely through the dangerous rickshaw, baby taxi and pedestrian traffic, I made them drive around the winding port area to become familiar with long vehicles.

We had urged Sven Lampell to send an additional delegate to Chittagong. One day he finally arrived. Pedro Sturzenegger quickly turned out to be an affable, experienced Swiss from South America. Pedro was exactly the right man for us and immediately took over some of my previous tasks. Now I didn't have to rush like a fireman in action, driving to the port, the airport, railway station, and the scattered extra *godowns*. Now I could devote myself to deferred tasks. But not for long. Another German freighter, the *MS Bärenfels*, which had been diverted en route, arrived, and gave us a 1,700-ton load of urgently needed flour. This amount exceeded our transport capacity by far. This created a lot of pressure because the cargo had to be unloaded quickly. However, we were only able to free a few trucks from other tasks. The anxious question now was what to do. Here it became evident how good the cooperation between the various missions was. Our boss Robert Koch alerted Sven Lampell in Dhaka, who immediately contacted the large UN mission. The UN had recently received new trucks for its major relief effort, which had arrived in Chittagong by ship. Surprisingly, the UN made 20 of these trucks available to us at short notice. We exhaled audibly. But we had to take care of the drivers ourselves. Robert Koch gave me exactly three hours to find 40 truck drivers, 40 passengers, 100 workers and other support staff for temporary day and night shifts. I swallowed hard three times. Had I misheard, or was it a joke? Robert smiled, but he meant it. I immediately went on full alert but doubted finding over 180 people in 180 minutes, quickly called all the foremen and field officers who were there to the office. It might be possible, some said, after I had described this quick-fix exercise to them; but three hours was really extremely short. Immediately everyone swarmed to the places where job seekers could be found. It wasn't long before the first applicants stormed in. Now everything ran like clockwork: Siddiki, the chief foreman, spoke to them, took the workers aside and sent the drivers to me on the first floor, where the secretary Jessie Paul acted as an interpreter and took all personal details. Fortunately, the drivers all had a truck licence, some even had certificates. It all took time, and the seconds and minutes just flew by. I hardly dared to look at the clock. Of course, there was no time for a driving test. When the first 20 drivers were hired and the antechamber was still full of applicants, I ordered a pot of delicious Isfahani black tea to keep me alert. Soon after, Siddiki came into the office with a beaming face and reported that the required 100 workers and 40 passengers had been hired, their personal details had been taken, and he only had to choose for each truck a passenger. The queue finally got shorter. When I had decided on the 40 drivers, three were still standing outside in the anteroom. I hired them as reserve drivers at the same time. With a sigh of relief, I dared to look at the clock: Unbelievable, we had made it in 2 ¾ hours! But that was no reason to sit back and relax. The unloading of the ship's cargo had to begin immediately. Siddiki divided all the newly employed into day or night shifts. We had previously rented additional empty *godowns* and hired several night watchmen known as *Choggidars*, who could produce certificates. We had also bought the heaviest padlocks on the market and put screws into the gate hinges that couldn't be loosened with ordinary screwdrivers. *Choggidars* in Bangladesh were everywhere, even in front of private houses. Thickly masked, with hats and scarves, armed with a flashlight, they could be seen everywhere after 6 p.m. until 6 a.m. Standing, sitting or even lying in-front of buildings and private houses as guards, blinking patiently and sleepily into the morning.

I had meticulously organized the transport from the ship to the *godowns*, because there was always the risk that a whole truckload would disappear en route, that is, getting unloaded somewhere else; without us noticing it. This danger existed especially for the many temporary drivers and passengers. Each loaded truck was therefore sent on its way in the port with a pre-printed delivery note. The delivery note stated the date, exact departure time, truck number, name of driver and passenger, plus the number of bags and name of *godown*. When the truck arrived at the designated *godown*, the foreman there wrote down the arrival time and the number of bags offloaded on the same delivery note. The goods received were noted in the *godown* book. The passengers, in turn, were only allowed to make a maximum of two trips with the same driver. One of us delegates was always on the move between the port and the *godown*, for constant monitoring. During this time, I slept between one and four hours at the most, on a narrow Red Cross camp bed in the *godown* office. The 1,700 tons of flour from the German Red Cross was in our *godowns* in exactly 80 hours. Exhausted and battered, Werner, Pedro and I crawled out of this par force performance. We had granted our otherwise always available humour a short-term vacation during these days and nights. All other activities, such as the daily deliveries to the airport, the railway and river port, as well as supplies to the 50 milk centres, radio communication with Dhaka and the bureaucracy continued to run normally. The performance of our employees, who completed their extremely important work on time without being checked, made me particularly happy and filled me with pride. We could rely on our local employees, even if they had to take responsibility for themselves.

Meanwhile, the 5,000 pieces of valuable underwear were still in the *godown*. We awaited the instructions from Dhaka where they were most needed. But, oh dear, one morning foreman Siddiki came into the office and reported breathlessly that all the boxes with the German underpants and singlets had disappeared. In fact, the storing place was empty. I informed my colleagues about this brazen theft. It was immediately clear to us: there could only be an insider behind it. Suspicion immediately fell on the young, local field officers. We agreed: only one of these trusted fellows would be capable of concocting such a serious theft and outwitting security. This underwear fetched a lot of money on the black market. So, I interviewed each and every one of these field officers, who I liked and who had always been reliable. No one seemed or wanted to have any idea of this theft. Still, my suspicions didn't go away. I was pretty sure at least one of them was involved. So, I gave them 24 hours to figure out who it might have been. I waited in vain, nobody answered, so I let another day pass. All remained silent on that front. So, I called all twelve to come to the office next morning. It couldn't be tolerated for someone to steal these valuable items and get away with it. "I now give each of you exactly seven days' to ensure that the 5,000 pieces of underwear appear again and are placed back in their place in the *godown*!" I said plainly. "If that doesn't happen, I'm sorry, I'll have to dismiss you all without notice and without a report card!" They realized that the situation was now very serious for them and left the office dejected. Three days later, Siddiki came into the office and reported that the boxes with the underwear were back, in the old place. It was true, nothing seemed to be missing. So, the serious threat had worked. Still, I had a bad feeling because I now definitely knew we had one or more thieves among us; obviously among the 12 trusted field officers. And that was extremely worrying. I now instructed Siddiki to deal with the problem. A few days later he was able to give me the name of the man who apparently had organised the theft. The other field officers also had a great interest in the case being cleared up. I had the offending field officer come in with Siddiki and let him know that we knew about the theft. He didn't say a word, seemed shocked and fell unconscious on the ground so suddenly that we couldn't catch him as he fell. He regained consciousness quickly and sat down on the chair provided. Dejected, and pale in the face, he admitted the theft. He had acted alone and also described how he had managed to make everything look like a normal delivery by truck without anyone noticing. I nevertheless felt sorry for this thief in his misery sitting on the chair in front of us. But in this case I had the police come and take him away. We showed zero tolerance for petty theft amongst ordinary workers, so the same had to apply to a field officer if he became a thief as well.

A few weeks later, Siddiki and I had to appear and testify at a court hearing in the old reddish "High Court" building with the sea waybills and *godown* book as witnesses. Our former employee was then unconditionally sentenced to two years in prison. This was a harsh judgement. It was however not the only time I appeared in this High Court.

Even though the hard-working days with all their imponderables completely absorbed my thoughts and actions, I still enjoyed the colourful, pulsating life anew when walking through the streets of Chittagong. Countless colourful, bell ringing, empty and laden rickshaws, hurrying yellow-black baby taxis, single-axle handcarts with empty barrels piled high, battered, smoking buses and overloaded trucks getting in each other's way, honking their horns again and again, while whole legions of pedestrians tried to get past each other, on the uneven sidewalks. I admired the rickshaw drivers who had to pedal harder here in hilly Chittagong than anywhere else. If the road got too steep and the passengers too heavy in a the drivers would dismount and laboriously push their three-wheeler rickshaw on foot. Despite long hours of work and waiting and constant exposure to the weather, these frugal, willowy men earned little. Most of them did not even own the rickshaw, so they paid rent for their company vehicle and, as often the only earners, had to support a family and all of their relatives. Rickshaw drivers don't just transport people in Bangladesh. There's almost nothing they don't ship somewhere cheap; from goods to small animals, there is room for everything on a rickshaw. I was no less fascinated by the fast-moving porters. With their hands close to their shoulders, supported by their necks, they held a wooden stick from which a basket filled with all sorts of goods hung by strings on the left and right. Often these hard-working, gaunt porters came straight from the slaughterhouse carrying heavy cuts of meat to market. Big crows would perch on tottering baskets of meat, pecking their thick beaks into the fresh meat. The panting porters didn't even frighten away these cheeky stowaway birds. As much as I felt at home in Chittagong, its nature and people it fascinated me, but when it came to hygiene I was and remained a Swiss.

On April 10, 1972, my life took a decisive turn. I had arrived in the *godown* office as usual at 6:30 a.m. to prepare the work for the day ahead. There was a lot to organize: the two Balair DC 6 planes would land twice that day to load relief supplies. Our trucks, loaded to the brim, had to be ready at the airport in good time, along with sufficiently strong and nimble workers. Furthermore, an Indian freighter with supplies for us was expected in the port during the day. Sampans with goods for North Bangladesh also had to be loaded and as usual another two trucks were supposed to supply some of the more than 50 milk-feeding centres. In short: a busy day with the usual race against time was to be expected. At 9 a.m. the phone rang. I answered, more or less prepared for a problem. But a strange, friendly and euphonious female voice said, "Good morning," and asked for a certain director I didn't know. It turned out she had dialled the wrong number, immediately apologized and was about to say goodbye when a voice inside me called "STOP!" Because her amiable, sympathetic-sounding voice had immediately electrified me. I managed to engage the unknown interlocutor in a conversation. I introduced myself, cautiously asked for her name. But she hesitated at first, saying only that she was calling on behalf of Glaxo pharmaceutical laboratories, where she worked as a switchboard operator and receptionist. The longer I heard her voice, the more I wished to get to know this woman. At last, she introduced herself: "My name is Ann Gomes." She was certainly, like our field officers, an excellent English-speaking Anglo Indian (British-Indian descendant). When she was about to end the conversation, I took my last chance and bravely invited her to dinner at the Chinese restaurant Gate of London. That is impossible, she told me curtly and dismissively. But I didn't give up: "Perhaps tomorrow or the evening after?" "I'm sorry, that is impossible, I'm not going out with a stranger," was the clear answer.

"That is a pity," I regretted this decision. "Nevertheless, I will be in the Gate of London at 6 p.m. tonight and would feel honoured if you, as my guest, would also come." My dark beard is a distinguishing feature. There was a short silence, now all I could hear was: "I'm sorry, I have to go now, thanks." I took a deep breath to collect myself after this unexpected "out of the blue" conversation. Although there was still unfinished business waiting in front of me on the desk, my thoughts kept drifting off in a very unusual way. The melodious, kind voice of that Ann Gomes still rang in my ears and made me dream. But not for long, because Siddiki ran breathlessly into my office and brought me back to earth. "One of our drivers had an accident with his truck!" he reported excitedly. He had crashed into another truck. "Fortunately, there was only material damage," he reassured himself and me in equal parts.

The day's eventful working day went by in no time, only my concentration left something to be desired. Thoughts kept coming back to that morning phone call. "Will she come to the Gate of London after all?" I kept asking myself. It's a pity that I didn't have a white daisy to give me an answer by plucking the petals: "She's coming, she's not coming, she comes...!" Five minutes before 6 p.m. I sat down at the Gate of London expectantly and hopeful at the first table by the glass door entrance. There weren't any other guests yet, and my heart started to pound a little. At five past six I was still sitting alone in the restaurant, now I ordered an orange juice. It was ten past six, then quarter past six. Too bad, Ann Gomes had kept her word. Apparently, it really was impossible for her to meet a stranger. At 18 minutes past 6 p.m. I looked at my watch one last time, peeped through the glass door - and caught my breath. A young, very pretty woman in a simple yellow brownish dress was slowly approaching the stairs. I was sure: "She just has to be Ann Gomes!" Immediately I jumped up, opened the door with a smile and said, "Good evening, welcome!" She smiled too, we shook hands and I asked her to choose a table. After we sat down, before we started talking, we looked at each other again. I noticed immediately that Ann was a smart lady who radiated a lot of self-confidence. Her voice, which I had liked so much on the phone, now receded into the background, I admired her beauty all the more, her attractive brown skin and I especially liked her dark, shining eyes. I forgot everything else. My whole self focused only on Ann and I fell in love with this beautiful woman!

I let Ann choose the dishes from the menu, as a gentleman should. The waitress handed us a jug of spicy Chinese tea in advance. A delicious chicken soup was served as a starter. The main courses were fried rice, with large portions of fried prawns and chicken, and selected vegetables. We took our time with dinner and had a lot to tell each other. I forgot the time. Cautiously asked her why she had nevertheless decided to accept my invitation. Ann hesitated a little before answering. "My work colleague and friend Nita urged me this morning to come here," she finally admitted. Nita said that since this man is a Red Cross delegate, she had nothing to fear. Still, Ann decided against it. Only when her eldest sister Susie, with whom she was staying, also encouraged her to accept my invitation, did Ann suddenly change her mind at this last minute, quickly dressed up for the occasion and hopped on a rickshaw. The Gate of London was less than two kilometers away and now she had arrived.

At 8:30 p.m., Ann said she now must go home. I suggested driving her home, to which she agreed. She guided my Chevrolet car with the flapping Red Cross flag in front, towards the Jamalkhan church where she lived close by with her sister. "Stop, this is where I live!" Ann suddenly said, and I stopped in front of a garden gate. Now I said a smiling good night to Ann, thanked her for this very special evening and walked up the two flights of stairs to gallantly open the gate for her. But it was already locked. I had brought Ann home too late. The gate was locked about 9 p.m. with a key, she explained to me. Spontaneously I grabbed the surprised willowy Ann by the hips, playfully lifted her over the wooden gate and carefully lowered her to the ground behind it. She was amazed but relieved, thanked me, turned around, walked the few steps to the house and knocked, waited until someone opened and waved again. I drove home very slowly. No doubt I was in love, in love with a very beautiful, lovely woman. The popular North German singer Maria Klodt came to mind. In 1967 I was sitting with friends in one of her concerts in Zurich when she sang our favourite song: "A day as beautiful as today, a day like this should never go away." I felt the same now. Refreshed, energized and full of energy - I could have uprooted trees.

I was back at work early the next morning. At half past nine I sent my reliable Bihari driver Ali to the nearest pharmacy on foot to buy a Palmolive soap, and a bottle of perfume. He should bring both back in a suitable box. Unfortunately, a flower shop was not nearby. So, armed with the office scissors, I went down into the yard and cut off some flower branches from a deep red-blooming hibiscus bush. From this I made my first Bengal bouquet. Then I wrote a few lines to Ann and sent Ali to the Glaxo Laboratories reception with the gift box and flowers. He had clear instructions to deliver both personally to Ann Gomes. Ali came back smiling - with a thank you note. She had made big eyes, he reported. Our everyday problems, the time and work pressure, none of that could harm me anymore. The *godown* office suddenly seemed to be full of violins; five to six hours of sleep was enough to recharge my batteries.

A few days later I invited Ann to dinner again, at the Gate of London of course. This time she didn't hesitate accepting my invitation. We were now looking forward to getting to know each other better, were curious, had a lot to ask and to tell. We came from very different worlds: a tall European mountain man and a radiantly beautiful woman from Bengal. Both no longer young, but maybe made for each other, at least I hoped so. Ann was a devout Catholic and attended church every Sunday. She seemed disappointed that I was Protestant and rarely went to church. That's when I realized: the way to Ann's heart led safely through the church and faith in God. Ann had been baptized with the names Ann Martha Cecilia. Unfortunately, her parents Paulinus and Janet Gomes were no longer alive. They had raised eleven children, seven girls and four boys. All bore Christian names: Elizabeth, Helena, Stella, Elsie, Susie, Blanchie and the boys: Leo, Aldrick, Cyril, and Francis. Four of the siblings were no longer alive. Ann had worked at Glaxo Laboratories for eleven years. A small company bus picked her up every day and brought her home after work. Ann lived in a big house at the bottom of a hill. During the previous year's War of Independence, she, her sister Susie and neighbours could hear local prisoners being tortured up on the hill house. Ann told me that the whole family and neighbours had heard the cries of pain from people in distress over and over again, filled with fear and anxiety. These months of war had been a very difficult and dangerous time for people throughout Chittagong. As a young, attractive woman, Ann was particularly at risk. She had therefore found secure shelter for a few months in the Catholic convent next to the large cathedral. Ann knew this place very well. As a girl, she had also attended the Catholic school in the convent, opposite of the Cathedral. Ann's parents and four of her deceased siblings also rest in the Cathedral cemetery. English was mostly spoken at school and at home. The Catholic Anglo-Indians in Bangladesh grow up bilingual, speaking English and Bangla. But many of them, including Ann, never learned the Bangla script. English was her mother-tongue. We started seeing each other more often at one of the many Chinese restaurants for dinner. We came from two completely different worlds, so there was much to speak of. In conversation and exchange of ideas, we slowly explored each other's background. Affection, esteem with respect and love was growing, and we looked forward more to the next happy get-together. Of course, Ann's many relatives knew about our growing relationship. Some weeks later, one evening Ann invited me into the house and introduced me to her sister Susie, who was a widow, and her children. It seemed to me that Susie was looking at me with benevolence. That was good for me, I was relieved and inspired. I can't imagine what a negative attitude on the part of Ann's closest relatives would have done. From now on I got to know more and more people of Ann's relatives, some of whom were also neighbours or at least lived in the same quarters.

Due to my long working days, I had little time to chat with them in depth. So, I just tried to make a good impression. However, not only was I pressed for time because of work, but my current contract with the Red Cross expired end of June and there was no guarantee that it would be renewed. The Red Cross had a habit of extending the contract during the last few days. But the relationship with Ann required time, much more time. Would I get that amount of time with Ann? Or did I have to leave Bangladesh before I had fully won her over? My decision had been made already, Ann was a very intelligent, confident and kind woman with strong beliefs, and was respected and admired by people. I wanted to marry Ann! But I couldn't and wasn't allowed to ask her the "big question" after such a short time. Now and then I tried indirectly to receive an indication of what Ann's answer might be if I were to ask her. Germans have practice of discretely and indirectly 'talking' through the gift of flowers. The response to such a gift might indicate the receivers feelings. I tried this technique a number of times - without success.

* * * * *

Our regular meetings never interfered with my long working days. On the contrary, I felt spurred on, inspired, and excited. It all happened in April, the busiest month of the year so far. Cargo handling in the *godowns* had intensified as more and more aid-loaded ships diverted to Chittagong docked in the port. The chronic lack of space got worse and worse, the pressure on me as a warehouse manager increased every day. I urgently needed to find solutions to get more, much more storage capacity. There was only one way left for us, we had to increase the turnover of goods to create new storage space. In other words, that meant loading even more sampans and railroad freight cars. However, this was not possible without additional staff. For weeks everyone had been toiling away in shift work with extra hours. Another German freighter arrived and brought 49 used vehicles, all of which had previously been serviced and repaired in Germany. There were also some ambulances and vans. Unfortunately, these vehicles, very valuable to Bangladesh, were moored on the ship's open deck, exposed to the salty sea air day and night. So, the vehicles arrived pretty rusty and had to be laboriously de-rusted before we could forward them to Dhaka. A few other Swiss had found shelter in the Hotel Agrabad, my current accommodation. They were delegates of the ICRC and responsible for the more than 2,000 interned West Pakistanis in the Dogra and the Bihari camps which we supplied with food. These ICRC people were mainly young lawyers who earned their spurs in the international arena. They not only checked the medical and food aid there, but they also made sure that the detention conditions complied with international humanitarian law, that the detainees were not subjected to torture or humiliation and that they were adequately fed. They also had to be able to contact their families. The middle-aged Swiss Dr. Hans Meyenberg from Zofingen, where he had a medical practice, was one of these ICRC men. I got along with him particularly well. We eventually became friends and later visited each other in Switzerland from time to time. Here in Chittagong, he became my confidant and I shared with him my relationship with Ann one evening at the hotel. He seemed dismayed, and immediately and urgently advised me against committing myself here in this foreign country. The chances of a harmonious marriage would be small, but the risk would be all the greater because of the great contrasts. He meant well and wanted to protect me from making a hasty decision, but he accepted my invitation that we go out for dinner with Ann. A few evenings later the three of us sat at a dinner table in the Gate of London. Hans Meyenberg had ample opportunity to talk to Ann and get to know her. The next day, a little embarrassed, he came to me and apologized. He was truly sorry for having so vehemently advised me against marrying Ann before he had even met her. In short: Ann in her own way made a great impression on him. His hasty concerns had all vanished. He could only congratulate me and wish us both all the best. I was very pleased to hear this from an experienced, well-established Swiss. It seemed to me that the time had come to ask Ann the big question. First, however, I wanted to find out about the customs and traditions of the local Catholic community. Sister Berneadette, director of the orphanage in the convent, seemed to me to be the right person. Since the visits in January with Dr. Fischer, when she showed us around the orphanage, I saw her as someone I trusted. So, I went to see her and ask to give me an insight into the customs in this country. She was happy to do that. "Here it is customary to ask the father for his daughter's hand," Sister Bernadette explained to me, adding that, as a rule, the parents had decided long in advance who would marry whom. This clarity didn't help me much because neither of Ann's parents were still alive. But Sister Bernadette knew Ann of course because she had gone to school in the convent. Since then, Ann had become an impeccable, upright, self-confident lady. Sister Bernadette said she had always been in a friendly contact with her father, Paulinus. A few years ago, he once told her that Ann was his favourite daughter because from an early age, she was always the most active in helping out in the big family and was also useful to the neighbours. He was sure that Ann would go far one day, even if she hadn't made a commitment yet. All of this made me happy. The very next day, at lunchtime, I drove to Jamalkhan Road and knocked on Ann's door, a little shaky with excitement. I wanted to speak to her oldest sister Susie, while Ann was not home. Susie, small in stature, opened the door with a smile, was pleased to see me, and offered me tea in the anteroom; I had brought some Bengali sweets with me. I plucked up courage and told Susie the whole, albeit short love story between Ann and me, trying to put myself in a good light and telling her about my work, background, and plans. I assured Susie that my love for Ann was genuine, that I would like to marry her, take care of her and be a good and faithful husband. In this way, I asked Susie for her much younger sister's hand. She seemed surprised and a little overwhelmed, to hear such a declaration of love from me. After thinking for a while, Susie replied, "I can't say much about this. Ann is at an age and will decide for herself what she wants." In the evening she would tell Ann about my visit and the conversation. Then Susie added: "Ann is the good spirit for everyone here in our house." All the children in the neighbourhood love her. Ann takes them regularly to Almas Cinema when they show children movies. Back at work, I was struggling to concentrate during the afternoon. The challenges that were increasing daily, required quick decisions, but were now mixed with the rosy future of my private life. During the course of the next few days important things would be decided for me. There seemed to be nothing in my head other than the anxious question: what will Ann say if I ask her? I knew Susie would tell her about our conversation tonight. Knowing this made me wonder and restless.

I gave Ann three days to think; then we sat again at a quiet corner in the Gate of London for dinner. Ann looked happy and beaming, and lovely in her blue dress. It was clear to me: she suspected that I wanted to ask her something. Finally, over dessert, my heart pounding, I laid my hand on hers, smiled and looked into her beautiful eyes and asked shyly, "Ann, will you marry me?" She smiled but said nothing while I gulped and thought I could hear the seconds ticking. "You know," she finally replied, "this all comes as a great surprise to me. We've only known each other for a short time. Yes, I'm in love, but I still don't know enough about you. Sometimes I seem to dream, or float, and try to find the ground under my feet again. My home is here in Chittagong with Susie and the other sisters and brothers, as well as all the children and their parents in the neighbourhood. Our Catholic minority has a strong sense of belonging. But I also would like to see more of the world. That's why I had applied for the position as flight attendant at PIA (Pakistan International Airlines) two years ago. Unfortunately, tensions between West and East Pakistan were increasing during this period, so I preferred to remain here in Chittagong with my loved ones." After this speech, which was unusually long for her, she took a deep breath and continued: "Hansrudi, I would like to know so much more about you, your background, your relatives, your job, and your plans for the future." I could start with that immediately! I was only too happy to tell Ann about my life so far and even more about what I wanted so much for the future. It turned out to be a long evening, during which we got a great deal closer to each other. A few evenings later we sat again across from each other again; this time in a small restaurant behind the Medical College Hospital. Ann was in particularly good spirits today, full of humour and in the mood for a laugh. That was good for my soul. I encouraged Ann to tell me more about her late parents, whom she adored. Ann told me of her father's later years when he became blind in both eyes because of a cataract and could not afford an expensive operation. Ann consulted her trusted ophthalmologist Dr. Zaffar and begged him to perform the urgent surgery. She offered to bear the costs but could only pay in installments; 50 Pakistan rupees a month from her salary. To Ann's delight Dr. Zaffar agreed, operated on both eyes successfully and saved her father from his blindness. When it became clear that Paulinus could see again, it was an unparalleled day of joy and happiness for the whole family, friends, and neighbours. Out of gratitude her father signed over a piece of land to Ann. Just this story alone made me once again clearly aware of why Ann was the lady and love of my life. Now I took hold of Ann's hand again, she seemed to have an inkling of my question. My heart was pumping for the second time when I asked her: "Ann, will you marry me?" Now she smiled, squeezed my hand, and said: "Yes, Hansrudi, I am going to marry you!" I was speechless for a moment. Her long-awaited words echoed in me. I would have loved to stand up and hug Ann with a kiss. But unfortunately, I wasn't allowed to do that. Islamic customs prevailed here, as we were not alone in the restaurant. But we were allowed to hold hands and look into each other's eyes with our happiness. Only on the drive home did we find our language again, the words just gushed out of us. We were in no hurry to get home. We both enjoyed the most exciting and happy ride home, except that I took all sorts of detours through the city and along the river. Amazingly, Ann found the garden gate unlocked when I kissed her good night. What a pity, I had been looking forward to lifting my sweetheart once more over the gate.

From that day onwards, time for us was now of the essence. We had to decide quickly because we wanted to get married here in Chittagong before the possibility of my contract ending. The engagement party was to take place on the evening of May 6th. We planned to celebrate it in the Volkart bungalow. I sent a cleaning crew and some workers to Sarson Road where the large two-storey bungalow stood on a small hill at the front of the huge property. Cleaning so many rooms, including seven bedrooms, kitchen, dining and living rooms, and a wide balcony that wraps around two corners of the house, required a lot of work. The magnificent property covered 17,000 square meters. A wide variety of old shade-giving trees, coconut palms, hibiscus, other exotic and rose bushes were cleverly distributed. There was even a fishpond in a hollow. A few small houses were reflected in it, where normally the domestic employees were housed. It was a real mansion, a wonderfully green dream residence, but unfortunately totally neglected. In times of war and long after, the interest in well-kept residences was rather low. After three days of hard work, the Volkart property awoke to new splendour. Only the residents were missing. Sven Lampell came to Chittagong by helicopter for a surprise visit at the end of April. He was shown the *godowns*, the vehicle parks, the

Alkarim building and the port. Werner, Pedro and I were happy to discuss the many upcoming tasks with him and to look for solutions to the ongoing problems. Sven was very satisfied and praised us for our commitment. It was good for the three of us to hear from a qualified source that we were doing a good job with the many employees we had. To round off the visit, we invited Sven to dinner. This was an opportunity for me to introduce him to Ann which made him very happy. Before his return flight, we proudly showed our boss the freshly cleaned and decorated Volkart bungalow the next morning. Sven couldn't help but be amazed and immediately became enthusiastic: "I would like to live here with my family, retire and write my memoirs." He spoke to us from the heart. We too could very well imagine life here as pensioners in this peaceful oasis. But for the time being, this kind of daydreaming had no place with me. Rather, I had to take care of my wardrobe in a very pragmatic way. While it was good enough for the Red Cross man, it was too ordinary for the groom-to-be. In short: I urgently needed "decent new clothes." Ann knew how to go about this. We quickly bought shirts, ties and matching shoes from shops in the New Market. In a fabric shop we bought a dark quality fabric that we took to the tailor around the corner. He measured me with a practiced hand and promised: "You can try the suit on the day after tomorrow." We had our Chittagong engagement rings made by a goldsmith. Two days later, Ann was amazed when I presented myself to her in my new robe. She clapped her hands and shouted smiling, "Wow, you look great!"

"How does a foreigner marry a woman Bangladesh?" This question inevitably came to my mind. I didn't want to ask Ann that as well, I had to find out for myself. But who could have the right answer ready? Once again, I turned to Sister Bernadette of the Catholic Orphanage for help. If anyone could help me, it was her. It was as hoped. She knew a High Court judge in Chittagong, gave me his name and direct phone number. On May 3rd, a Wednesday, three days before our engagement party, I called him, introduced myself as a foreigner and asked for information about the planned marriage. "Then you'd better come to me in the courthouse," said a friendly voice. "I still have an appointment available for next Saturday, May 6th. Please come to my office at 12 o'clock with your bride and the identity papers, and we can discuss the matter." I thanked him warmly and promised to be there on time together with Ann. "It's going like clockwork," I said happily. Ann protested, "We can't go to that judge, our engagement party is on Saturday!" I reassured her: "Don't be worried, our party is in the evening." I had already thought everything through and said to Ann: "You come to me with your ID on Saturday at 11 o'clock to the *godown*, so we can go up to the High Court in time. The meeting there won't last long, and afterwards we'll pick up our engagement rings from the goldsmith." Ann allowed herself to be persuaded and agreed to this approach. My alarm went off very early on that Saturday. A long day was ahead, work didn't stop even on my engagement day. But I had of course no idea how very memorable this 6th of May was going to be for us; full of surprises, embarrassments, but also happiness.

As agreed, Pedro Sturzenegger relieved me in the office shortly before 11 a.m. Soon after, Ann and I made our way to our meeting with the judge. From the New Market we climbed up a steep, bush-lined zigzagged footpath up Fairy Hill where the impressive, reddish High Court building stood. When we arrived, we asked a member of staff for the judge's office. He led us around the building on a gravel path, pointed to a tall, double wing door, opened it, and said the man we were looking for was in here. Then he opened a second door, asked us to walk in and quickly closed the door behind us. Only now did I feel Ann's hand in mine - but at the same time we both froze into two pillars of salt! This was not an office at all, but a very large courtroom full of people with a trial in full swing. The hearing was immediately interrupted. At least 50 people were present, sitting in their chairs with their backs to us. Now all turned around and staring at us intruders. Police officers were also present - because of two accused men tied to iron bars with thick ropes on the right-hand wall. Law enforcement officers, both prisoners, all the other people and the high court judge with his assistants were all staring at us intruders. We instantly had become the centre of attraction in that large courtroom. We were feeling extremely embarrassed and wished to sink into the ground. Now the high court judge from a distance called out with a loud voice: "Who are you? What do you want here?" Still holding Ann's hand, I now replied: "Sir, I am very sorry, we seem to have entered through a wrong door. My name is Rudi Brawand, I phoned you this week, to discuss our planned marriage and was told to see you today at this time. Now people began chatting loud even laughing at us, but the judge requested us to come forward. Hand in hand with Ann, we rushed forward. From both sides of the aisle people kept on staring, whispering, and laughing at us. When we finally arrived in front of the judge like two watered poodles, he looked at us over his glasses, which had slipped down his nose. His previously frowned brows had smoothed out. A barely perceptible smile began to play around the corners of his mouth. He seemed to be thinking while he let us both stew in the whispering behind us. After an embarrassing "forever," the judge suddenly stretched out his right arm, pointed to someone in our back, and commanded, "Mr Rahman, please take these people to my office and discuss the matter with them!" Immediately a man stood up and asked us to follow him. I hastily but politely thanked the judge, and then escaped through a side door with Ann, feeling suddenly relieved. Mr Rahman, who was obviously a lawyer, first welcomed us into the judge's spacious office, sat down behind the heavy desk and asked me about our problem. I was very happy to be able to present the somewhat tricky situation to an expert. Mr. Rahman listened, looked at our IDs, then wordlessly pulled a law book from the bookshelf and leafed through it for a while. "No problem," he finally said, smiled and took an official document from the desk drawer. "You two can get married right here and now if you want." To reinforce his words, he tapped his right forefinger on the said document, which on the letterhead read GOVERNMENT OF PAKISTAN in large letters. However, the word PAKISTAN had been over stamped and replaced with BANGLADESH. Hardly surprising since this country, which at only 142 days young, had significantly more serious problems to solve than having new marriage certificates printed. Completely surprised, I looked questioningly at Ann. She frowned, shook her head very firmly and said clearly: "No!" But I really wanted to marry her right away, I didn't know yet if my contract would actually be extended at the end of the month! And already we had our first disagreement! I tried one last time and asked Ann in a pleading voice, "Why not?" "It's going too fast for me, just like that, without preparation and anticipation," she explained. She added, "We're not even dressed appropriately for a civil wedding!" Unfortunately, I had to agree with her. Now Mr Rahman, who had followed our dispute with interest, spoke up. "I'll make you a suggestion." Trying to find a middle ground, he said, "I'll give you two hours to get changed and maybe eat something. In the meantime, I'll write the marriage certificate here, which you'll come to sign later. You may bring a witness with you, but it is not absolutely necessary." Again, we considered and consulted. Ann was really struggling to make up her mind. She was unexpectedly under great pressure and needed time to think; Above all, she worried: What would all her people say? Tonight, while our engagement party was supposed to take place first. I looked calmly at Ann; all kinds of thoughts must have gone through her mind. "Let your heart decide, Ann!" I said now, grabbing her hand squeezing it. She looked at me thoughtfully, suddenly smiled and pulled herself together. "Okay, Hansrudi, let us do it!" she decided with a firm voice. My joy and relief were overwhelming. Mr Rahman smiled to himself, and we promised to be back in two hours. We hastily said goodbye. "But please don't come back through the courtroom anymore!" he called after us, laughing. This time I took Ann home in the most direct way and now we were both pretty hungry. Susie, who was able to adjust to the unexpected situation quickly, served us some rice with vegetables in no time. Then I went to Hotel Agrabad to change. To my relief, I met Paul Santschi from the ICRC at the reception. I relayed our marriage plans to him, and he immediately agreed to act as best man. Now all I had to do was throw myself into my engagement robe and then we could start. We picked up Ann, who had dressed wonderfully and festively in this short time. We two men beamed at this beautiful woman and as though in a race, drove with her elatedly to the courthouse. Lawyer Rahman had kept his word. The marriage certificate was filled out - and how! At the top were Ann's and her parents' names, dates of birth, address. Among other things, it said, Ann Martha Cecilia Gomes loves Hansrudi Brawand, son of Fritz, from Grindelwald Switzerland. So, she decided to marry him. Paul Santschi enjoyed being there, even if his signature was not required. Of course, we also had to pay a fee. Ann and I signed the certificate, Mr Rahman and Paul Santschi congratulated us and I was allowed to kiss Ann, my wife. Everything was perfect and wonderful. I looked at the marriage certificate again - and my eyes caught on a detail: Something was not quite right. It was written here Ann married Hansrudi. It was not mentioned that Hansrudi also married Ann. I immediately pointed this out to Mr Rahmann. He just laughed and asked: "Yes, do you also want such a certificate, Mr. Brawand?" "Of course," I confirmed, nodding my head. "But one with the opposite words, please. I want to marry my beloved Ann too!" Mr Rahman understood that but had to tell me that it was already too late for today. "I won't be able to write this document until the day after tomorrow. You can both come and sign them here on Monday afternoon and take them with you for an additional fee." We laughed whole-heartedly. Our current situation was really extraordinary: Ann had married me that day and I married her two days later. We were already 50 percent husband and wife, but still not engaged! That celebration took place that evening in the big bungalow on Sarson Road.

First, we went to the shop where we had ordered our engagement rings. When we arrived in the bungalow, the drinks were ready in the large, festively decorated lounge. Ann's relatives had done a good job. Shortly after 7 p.m. we welcomed the first guests. I met many of Ann's relatives here for the first time. They were all curious to finally meet the tall man from Switzerland. I laughed when one of the guys came up with a tray of beer glasses filled to the brim with straws stuck in them. I quickly turned him around to go back to the kitchen and remove the straws. Besides Paul Santschi, Werner, Pedro, Sidikki and also Jessie Paul came to the party. But apart from our best man, Paul, nobody knew that we had in the afternoon been married civilly in the High Court. Instead, everyone was enjoying the engagement party and I was a bit frightened to come out with the truth. First, I had to drink up some courage before I dared to show my colours. After the second glass of red wine, as the party really got going with the buzz of voices and happy laughter, Ann tugged at my sleeve and whispered that it was time to enlighten the guests. So, we both stood up, I banged my glass with a spoon and started: "Ann and I would like to give you all a warm welcome. We both feel honoured you all came to our engagement party." Looking at Ann, I continued, "For both of us, this truly is a very special, almost unbelievable day." I had to gather myself for a moment and take a deep breath, before I could continue: "Don't be alarmed please, because tonight we're not only celebrating our happy engagement; this afternoon we have been to the Fairy Hill, High Court, and celebrated our civil marriage there, we now are happily standing in front of you as husband and wife. I gave Ann a loving kiss! Instantly the big room became dead quiet. Ann's relatives were visibly shocked, staring at us in disbelief. Some frowned and someone shouted "What?!" Almost all were devout Catholics who had never experienced anything like this. But I reacted quickly. To bridge the awkward silence, I called out to the crowd of guests, laughing: "Please don't be shocked and sad! Look at both of us, our future together as husband and wife has already begun! Today is our absolute happy day. We are inviting all of you to a proper wedding dinner at Hotel Agrabad next Saturday evening!" With that, this difficult hurdle was cleared. Everybody spontaneously clapped, smiled, and got excited. They all came to congratulate us. We now exchanged our engagement rings, as our makeshift wedding bands and the party continued. A catering family took care of the physical well-being of our hungry guests with Bangladesh delicacies. After the dinner, Ann and I said goodbye and drove to the Agrabad Hotel. Hotel manager Günter spontaneously invited us to have a drink at the bar after I introduced him to my wife. Then I took Ann to my beautiful room on the second floor. Here we spent our happy wedding night, which was also our first night together. The annoying alarm clock rattled us back to reality early in the morning. We both had to go back to work, newly married or not. Our honeymoon would have to wait. There was a large bouquet of flowers on my office table in the *godown*. Word had spread like wildfire that I was now married. Everyone wanted to shake my hand and say congratulations. Everyone was happy, all seemed proud that I had married one of theirs; a "Chittagonian girl." I was still walking around as if on clouds. In between, I pinched myself to feel that yesterday was a wonderful fact and not just a long-cherished pipe dream. Full of enthusiasm, with new energy and fresh impetus, I set to work. Again, and again my eyes lovingly grazed the photo of Ann on the desk. A few days later, Ann came to me with a sad face. She had spoken to her Priest at her Jamalkhan Church about our church wedding. However, because I was a Protestant, the Priest refused to marry us. The Catholic laws were very strict in this country; at that time marriage between a Catholic and non-Catholic was not allowed. This verdict really disappointed Ann and angered her against such strict and unjust rules. Ann was so much looking forward to our church wedding, which for her was without question a must and a fulfilment! So, we looked for an at least acceptable solution to Ann's dilemma. Ann found this at the Church Council, which had been founded by Europeans living in Chittagong. Here we had our marriage registered by the secretary Mr. Smith on June 4th; only a small consolation, but at least that. For a very long time, the turbulent years that followed in other Islamic countries made it impossible for us to be married in church. It wasn't until 21 years later, in September 1993, that we were properly married by Irish Priest and friend, Tom Gayne, at Our Lady of Mercy Catholic Church in Girrawheen, Western Australia.

A few days after our memorable civil flash marriage in the High Court, I received an urgent summons to the Alkarim Building. There I was told that our boss Sven Lampell in Dhaka wanted to speak to me on the Red Cross radio. So, I immediately got in touch with Sven, assuming there was important Red Cross news to discuss. But first Sven whole heartedly congratulated me on my marriage. After a short personal conversation, Sven then got down to the real reason for his contact. "I want you and your wife to move into the Volkart bungalow as soon as possible! I wish you both happiness and blessings and I am already looking forward to my next trip to Chittagong to meet you both." He said all that in a very assertive "boss" tone. I was speechless for a while and had to get my act together before I could thank Sven, in a rather stammering manner, for this good news. In the evening I surprised Ann with this unique message. We didn't have to think twice about "obeying." Like little children we looked forward to our first address together: 15, Sarson Road, Chittagong. And what an address! A fully furnished house was waiting for us, equipped with beds, tables, chairs, and kitchen linen plus lots of kitchen utensils and crockery. Before we moved in two days later, we made a complete inventory of the furniture and all the household effects. We really didn't have to buy anything else. However, it quickly became clear to us that we alone would not be able to maintain and care for this building and the huge surrounding area - it was much too large for us. We urgently needed to look for staff, a task for Ann. So, she hired a cook at our expense, then a cleaning lady and finally a part-time gardener. The steep plot behind and above the large house had to be carefully tended; the lawn around the house in particular had to be cut short to keep the dangerous cobras as far away as possible. Here we felt like a kind of property manager who had to ensure that this stately property was able to survive the difficult post-war period. Our official wedding celebration then took place as planned a Saturday evening. We invited more than 40 people to a dinner at the Hotel Agrabad. When we left our bungalow at 7 p.m. – this time dressed as a wedding couple. A pleasant surprise awaited us. While we had been busy getting dressed, Ann's relatives, along with the chauffeur, had secretly decorated the green Chevrolet with white ribbons and flowers. My car had been turned into a magnificent wedding carriage. We proudly allowed ourselves to be chauffeured through the Chittagong streets in it. People stopped, waved happily at us, rickshaw drivers rang their bells and baby taxis honked their horns. As the first guests, my three Swiss colleagues from the ICRC welcomed us at the hotel and took pictures of us. They were delighted to greet their compatriot Hansrudi and his lovely wife Ann in her beautiful white wedding dress. They also brought us a telegram of congratulations from their boss in Dhaka, which read:

> *Congratulations to Hansrudi and Ann! You represent our extremely successful, memorable intensive aid campaign in the most beautiful way. All the best and be happy!*
>
> *Laurent Marti*

Hotel manager Günther, who was also invited with his wife, handed us another telegram. This came from Switzerland from my parents:

> *To Annie and Hansrudi - We wish you the best of luck and God's blessings on your wedding day. We look forward to your return home.*
>
> *Aetti and Muetti*

Again and again, I admired Ann who looked so beautiful in her long white wedding dress. But I saw also a small glimmer of sadness in her eyes because the priest had refused to marry us in church. I could empathize with her and squeezed her hand again and again. Despite this quiet melancholy, it was a beautiful evening. Along with the ICRC and RC League delegates and some *godown* staff, Ann's relatives came to celebrate with us and to bring us their happy congratulations. The long, festively decorated tables were admired from all sides, and the excellent dinner was praised. Since nobody wanted to make a toast, I took it upon myself to welcome our guests. I briefly told something about my background and my Red Cross work here in this beautiful City of Chittagong. We also caused laughter about our surprising, lightning-fast marriage. Despite the slight bitterness that resonated because of my "wrong" religious affiliation, our wedding made us optimistic and left us with fond memories.

Cheerfully we resumed our daily duties next morning. Work at the *godown* didn't get any less, the opposite was the case. More and more cargo ships arrived with relief supplies from all over the world. We filled all the *godown* rooms to the ceiling. However, the greatest challenge was still the forwarding of these relief goods on as quickly as possible using every conceivable means of transport, because the Red Cross *godowns* in the provinces urgently needed more supplies. It was a race against a looming shortage of food. We struggled daily with limited transport capacities. We were often overcome by sheer desperation: the sampans sailed only slowly upstream, the airplanes had limited payloads and we could never get enough rail wagons. Free time was getting scarcer. Ann was more and more surprised when I went back to work after dinner. It was precisely during these particularly hectic days that the hard-working Pedro Sturzenegger, who was transferred to the province of Kulna as an emergency, left us. Fortunately, Ron Feist, his replacement, arrived shortly afterwards. Ron was an energetic Canadian from Calgary who did his first overseas assignment with us. He quickly got used to the hustle and bustle of the *godown* and was soon irreplaceable. Both Balair's DC 6 continued to land twice a day in Chittagong to load relief supplies and fly them to Dhaka, Ishurdi and North Bangladesh. But those 50 tons a day were simply, still short to meet the required demands. Eventually the Red Cross League began chartering a US Hercules-130 transport aircraft able to carry 20 tons. This made it much easier for us to get supplies to the provinces, but it also presented us with new problems. This Hercules flew five times a day from Chittagong, i.e., every two hours, which corresponded to a daily capacity of 100 tons. It forced us to load 60 tons of rice or flour onto three articulated trucks the night before. Under no circumstances should we have this expensive Hercules and both DC 6's, not working. All three planes always had absolute priority. If a semi-trailer driver was missing from time to time, I hopped into the cab myself and drove the heavy vehicle with ten workers sitting on the load through the chaotic city traffic to the airport. I really enjoyed driving a heavy vehicle every so often. When I was young, I had transported heating oil across Switzerland, but here it was lifesaving relief supplies. The Hercules 130 had a full-width hatch with a loading ramp under the upwardly angled tail. The 12-meter-long loading space was "studded" with countless small rolls on the floor. Large plywood boards were placed on top before the sacks to be transported were professionally stacked on top. Finally, the 20 tons load got secured by the loadmaster with ropes, nets, and bolts and then the hatch was closed. The loadmaster gave the captain the green light to start via the on-board telephone. At the point of arrival, the hatch was opened, and the loading ramp extended. Now the loadmaster removed all bolts, ropes, and the net before signalling the ok to the cockpit. The captain accelerated briefly so that the entire load on the floor rollers slid through the open hatch and over the ramp onto the cement floor in a matter of seconds. Not a single sack slipped during this manoeuvre! I had seen this incredible interaction with my own eyes when I was once allowed to fly at the captain's invitation. For this flight I took a seat on the bench seat at the rear wall of the cockpit. An unforgettable experience awaited me! Huge cumulus clouds were in the sky. The captain circled these mighty formations, looking for a way through white glowing or shadowy crests and valleys of clouds in the uppermost layer. It looked as if we were sailing through a floating fairy-tale landscape made of cotton wool. Sometimes I thought I was flying slalom in a majestic winter landscape. My long-ago Aletsch Glacier ski tour popped up in my memory; maybe because glacier goggles were now sitting on my nose and the contrasts were even stronger. After a while the captain got up, went to the coffee machine on the side wall and served me a real Italian cappuccino with biscuits. I was completely happy, my senses cheered. This fairy-tale flight made up for countless sweaty overtime hours. The two pilots thoroughly enjoyed their seemingly easy craft. They chatted, cracked jokes, one smoked a cigar and the other puffed his pipe. We finally got out of the "cloudy mountains."

Far below, the endless alluvial plain became visible. The co-pilot now showed me our destination, the Ishurdi airfield near the Ganges and the border with India. I could only see the runway as a tiny light line, which quickly grew larger during a long descent turn. Now I also saw the missing section of the long bridge over the Ganges, the result of bombing during the war. During the landing approach, the pilots fiddled with various levers and buttons, but continued to talk calmly about private matters. In the meantime, I was staring spellbound and a little tense at the increasingly fast approaching runway. The two experts continued chatting casually shortly before and during the soft landing. "Please stop the time so we can find out how long we need to unload!" the captain said to me. He may also have wanted to show me how quickly and efficiently they operated while we taxied to the airport building. As soon as the machine came to a stop, I went straight to the back of the hold. The large hatch was already open, the loading ramp was extended, and the loadmaster was about to loosen the rope nets and pull out the bolts. Then he reported "Ready to go," to the front of the cockpit. Immediately the four engines roared, the plane moved forward, and the 20-tonne cargo rolled – as if by magic – through the tail hatch and out over the ramp onto the cement floor. Two local Red Cross men waved a thank-you from outside, the hatch closed, and we taxied back to the start. All this took just under seven minutes time in Ishurdi. It only took a little longer after the fifth and last offloading there, because the bay had to be reloaded for the next day. My return flight was no less beautiful, again the Hercules curved elegantly through the snow-white cloudy landscape in the direction of Chittagong. Through a hole in the clouds, I saw the grey waters of a great river. It was the Brahmaputra, locally called Jamuna. In Chittagong, the Hercules took on another 20 tons of flour for Ishurdi. But after this unique flight, I drove back to the *godown* with sparkling eyes and went about my work, much buoyed.

In the yard of the Volkart *godown* stood a few tall, sprawling trees, home to a noisy rookery of crows. The big birds fought every day. The constant loud lamentation and croaking often got on my nerves and disturbed me when I was working on the first floor. Some of these black troublemakers even had the nerve to land on the windowsill and watch me through the window. They seemed to croak when I made a mistake. So, I started plotting revenge. I wanted to teach these noisy and cheeky neighbours a lesson. In a shed I found a rectangular steel plate, drilled a hole in each corner, pulled string through it and connected it with a thicker string, which I attached to a beam above my office window. I sprinkled bird seeds under the steel plate, which was now hovering just above ground. My crow trap was ready. I sent Sunny, the office boy, to observe in the yard and asked him to alert me as soon as a crow ate any of the grain underneath the heavy plate. It took a while for Sunny to call me. I quickly grabbed the office scissors that had been laid out, went to the window, and cut the cord. The slab fell to the ground, but the crow had already flown away. Three more times I tried to satisfy my "lust for revenge." However, the crows were always faster and these cunning birds did not touch the grains under the plate after that; 1- 0 for the clever Bengal crows. I threw in the towel, henceforth respecting their sovereignty. But word of my "invention" got around quickly. At the next monthly meeting in Dhaka, delegates from other regions teased me, laughingly inquiring about the hit rate of my crow trap. What is that familiar saying? "Whoever has the damage does not have to worry about the ridicule."

* * * * *

On the eve of this monthly meeting, we had our traditional happy party at Sven's house. For the first time I didn't come alone. There was a big hello as I proudly introduced everyone to Ann as my wife. She received a very warm welcome from my colleagues. In honour of Ann, we were the first to start dancing.

The next day, during a break at the Intercontinental Hotel, I took the elevator up to the third floor and knocked on a door. At that time, the provisional "Embassy of Switzerland" was housed here. My goal was to apply for a Swiss passport for Ann. Mr. Meneghetti, the secretary, invited me in. I immediately handed him over our marriage documents. First, he smiled happily, then he looked at me, started to laugh and called to his wife in the next room: "Come here, darling, you absolutely have to read this!" Mrs. Meneghetti also laughed happily when she had read the documents. It was slowly becoming embarrassing and, last but not least, uncomfortable. What was the matter with our papers? Finally, Mr. Meneghetti posed, still smiling firmly: "Excuse me, Mr. Brawand, but we have never seen such funny marriage certificates. They are written in such a refreshingly open-hearted way." There are even words like "falling in love" and "Son of Fritz of Grindelwald." I hadn't even noticed the extremely flowery writing of our wedding documents; our flash marriage had overwhelmed me so much. Only two facts counted for me: they were on official paper, stamped, signed and therefore legally valid. Secretary Meneghetti promised to send the two documents to Berne by the next diplomatic post. "As soon as we get an answer, I'll call you in Chittagong." Just three weeks later, Mr. Meneghetti called to announce the good news. "It's okay, Mr. Brawand, your wife can come to the embassy so we can issue her with a Swiss passport." At the end of July, during our next stay in Dhaka, Ann was soon holding her new red passport in amazement. Now she was the proud holder of passports from three countries: Pakistan, Bangladesh and now Switzerland. Ann was beaming when we moved into the Volkart bungalow. There was so much space and peace for the two of us. Even before the maid started working for us, Ann took up the fight against dirt and dust. The bungalow had been tidied up by a cleaning crew before our so-called engagement party, but Ann wasn't happy with the result. When I returned home in the evening, I was amazed to find Ann sweeping, dusting, cleaning toilets and windows. She couldn't stand dirt and dust. It was a "red rag" for her and remained so. She also set the same strict standards for herself. She always looked fresh, well-groomed and had a flair for beautiful dresses. That has remained the case to this day.

After cleaning, Ann eagerly began to make the most important rooms liveable. There were always beautifully arranged bouquets of flowers on tables and chests of drawers. There were more than enough flowers on the huge property. Our first home together became more and more homely and comfortable. It was just a pity that we didn't have much time to relax. My wife was still working, taking the company bus to her work every day at Glaxo Laboratories. She had already worked there for more than ten years. She loved her workplace and the friendly atmosphere at the reception. The bosses appreciated Ann's reliable work and her friendly, always helpful manner. They were reluctant to let Ann go when she resigned from her long-term position in August with a heavy heart. When she left, she was paid a respectable pension.

I liked my new married life in this foreign country. Now someone was waiting for me with a smile when I came home tired and exhausted in the evening. Ann was patient and understanding, proud of her husband who cared for her fellow country people in desperate need. With her I could express myself, and relax, finding new strength. It was also an interesting time to get to know each other better and show understanding when we disagreed. We tried to understand the many opposites, our different ways of thinking. Since we came from very different countries, we judged some things completely differently. Misunderstandings were inevitable, but we learned from them. It was more difficult to make plans for the future. We still had no idea to which part of the world fate would take us next. Distant countries beyond the horizon and the Red Cross had meant well with me up until then.

The distance was still tempting. What would Ann say to that when the time came? For the time being we were still in Chittagong, and everything was fine. That was the most important thing.

I liked it better and better in our bungalow. The hilly, always green surroundings with the huge ancient trees, the exotic birds, and colourful exotic flowers, with Ann by my side, made my heart soar. But one day, as I was walking down the narrow, grass-covered steps to the pond, I suddenly heard a slight rustling in the grass, something was rapidly approaching, and I stopped immediately. Frozen as a pillar of salt, I saw a large cobra snaking up the hill overgrown with vegetation. A yard from me, it dove into a shallow, grassless ditch and disappeared. Time stood still for a moment. I swallowed hard and heard my heart pounding. Then I turned and ran back inside to tell Ann about my latest adventure. The gardener had to mow the grass to the pond more often from then on.

Ann also made herself more and more at home. Relatives gave her two cute young dogs, Barky and Tommy. Conveniently, a doghouse already existed. Unfortunately, Tommy soon died. The cook had observed how he wanted to play with a cobra in the grass, but it obviously wasn't joking. Next to the bungalow there was also a small chicken house. Ann got five laying hens, gave each one a name, and also bought a beautiful, multi-coloured rooster that she named George. This colourful Bengali George took his job very seriously. All day long he strutted around his harem as a guard with his beak always up. The hens admired their protector unreservedly. I, for my part, no longer needed an alarm clock; because very early each morning George announced the new day with several "Kiikerikiiii!" that could be heard from afar. This guy seemed to have learned German somewhere.

Occasionally, when work permitted, I would take Ann to the Jamalkhan Church for the Sunday service. I felt a bit lost here and had to get used to the unfamiliar Catholic customs. Ann became my patient teacher. She was pleased that I was willing to come with her. She also introduced me to the priest who had refused to marry us. But he remained unyielding. We had to accept that.

One day, I had an unexpectedly strong feeling of my homeland: in the port of Chittagong, a red and white Swiss flag was waving, visible from afar. The *Moléson*, a Swiss ocean-going freighter, had arrived with relief supplies. Lucien Bally from Lausanne, an extremely friendly, short man full of mischievousness and joie de vivre, was officiating on the bridge. We liked each other right away. When I told him about my recent marriage, he spontaneously invited Ann and me to dinner on "his" *Moléson*. He turned out to be a charming host, served a hearty meal with white wine from Lake Geneva and was delighted to have Ann at the table. Apart from the captain, there were only a few Swiss on board, Lucien Bally enjoyed being with us all the more. The freighter stayed in port for five days, so two days later we were invited back, this time for lunch. What a surprise! This time the Lake Geneva wine was served with a real Swiss fondue. The first engineer, a burly Dutchman, was also at the table. We, in turn, had brought a Swiss nurse with us who was in Chittagong at the time. The fondue was an unusual, exotic lunch for Ann, and she didn't seem to like it that much. The fondue was quite good, but not the "usual Swiss class," which was probably due to the Dutch cheese and the hot climate. We returned the favour and invited Captain Bally and his colleagues to dinner the next day at our favourite place, "our" Gate of London.

Cargo ships from all over the world with relief supplies of all kinds continued to arrive every week. We were informed by radio a few days in advance of the arrival date, the cargo and name of the ship. We then informed our reliable shipping agency which took care of the customs formalities for us. The radio station was housed on the ground floor of the four-storey Alkarim house and belonged to the young Anglo-Indian ICRC radio operator Patrick Mercer from Chittagong. However, he was at loggerheads with the word Switzerland. It sounded hilarious when I brought him a message and he would then radio in: "Hello Dhaka, this is Chittagong, I have a message for Swingerland." Patrick's girlfriend was my efficient secretary, Jessie Paul. They married the following year, settled down Canada and from then on lived in Toronto, where we much later visited them. In June, the Indian freighter *Jalakala* brought us an unusual cargo, which was the greatest possible present for us: 62 well-maintained, veteran Swiss army trucks, from 1941 to 1945, with a payload of 3½ tons. All Swiss quality makes by Bernea, Saurer and FBW truck factories and supplied with the original tools in canvas bags. Even the snow chains were included. The Army had discarded these proven veterans in good condition. The Swiss Red Cross bought 100 of these trucks at a bargain price of 500 Swiss francs each and had them shipped to Chittagong. The remaining trucks arrived shortly afterwards on another freighter. For me, the sight of the field-grey camions with tarpaulin hoods was a reunion. When I was in the army, I had driven 3½-ton trucks like these, earning my spurs as a truck driver on them. Here in the port of Chittagong, I immediately promoted myself to driving instructor, drove two laps around the customs building with each driver. That way I could introduce them to the correct "downshift with double de-clutching." Then I let the trucks go to our *godowns* and ordered the trucks to be parked in a very precise line on a meadow, as befitted veteran Swiss army trucks. In the Swiss army we had learned to park in a perfect straight line. But the Bengali drivers, however, looked at me in amazement. "Now the boss has snapped," was clearly to be read in their expressions. But my reawakened "military head" gleefully rejoiced at the sight of these perfectly aligned field-grey veterans. Perhaps a high-ranking

Swiss army officer would have had palpitations and promoted me to the rank of private had they seen this?

The 100 Swiss army trucks were worth their weight in gold for the Bangladesh Red Cross. They were distributed to the individual sections throughout the country and initially used to supply the countless milk-feeding stations, more quickly and more regularly. Caritas, which also operated in Bangladesh, had imported the same Swiss army trucks. Last but not least, in Dhaka there was a repair shop for trucks and other commercial vehicles. It was under the direction of the United Nations and was directed by the Swiss chief mechanic Albert Wyss. This was the perfect workshop for repairs to our trucks.

My supervisor Werner Janz left us at the end of June. He was posted to the town of Khulna, a town in the famous Sundarban. Region. It annoyed him. He would have preferred to have stayed in Chittagong for the rest of his time, in order to then resume his medical studies in Graz in Austria. Actually, I should have gone to Khulna, as I was number two in place there. That's how it was usually done. But our boss Sven Lampell decided Werner had to go and appointed me the new boss of the Red Cross League in Chittagong. He didn't want Ann and me to move from there as a newly married couple. Ann had brought me luck there too. As boss, I could have moved into a large office in the Alkarim building. But I preferred to continue operating in the *godown*, right on the frontline. Here I had a better overview of the constantly changing circumstances and problems and was able to rearrange things much quicker. The many months of experience have benefited me. Because I had always been able to meet the increasing obligations thanks to extra hours, Sven Lampell had gained complete trust in me.

Now the work had become even more diverse. It was necessary to write weekly and monthly reports, send daily radio messages, monitor the work and results of the local financial accountant Marshall d'Souza in the Alkarim building, dictate letters, coordinate the personnel activities of around 100 local employees and prepare their payday. It was no less important to negotiate the price for additional trucks hired, to settle disputes between personnel, to monitor precautions against theft and to reschedule work processes due to the circumstances. Perishable aid supplies in particular, which had priority to be forwarded, were under constant control with regard to their expiration date. I also regularly visited the Secretary of the Bangladesh Red Cross, Chittagong Section. He felt a bit pushed against the wall because we in the Red Cross League were so powerful here in Chittagong and because of the emergency situation we were "running the shop." However, the secretary felt more let down by the chairman of his own section because he was rather busy with other activities. This was an unfair, even counterproductive situation that left me sitting between chair and bench. So, I brought up this state of affairs, which was not conducive to the Red Cross cause, at the next monthly meeting and suggested that this Red Cross section must be more involved in our activities. Sven Lampell found this a good suggestion and a viable way to improve collaboration. From now on, we delivered additional supplies to the Bangladesh Red Cross *godowns* to enable them to better support the most vulnerable of the local population. The section was also assigned its own Swiss truck. At that time, all aid organizations in Bangladesh were faced with a huge emergency situation. Real development for future activities could not be started yet. First, all relief organizations urgently needed to deal with the overwhelming need. Bangladesh was only about seven months old, could not walk on its own like a child and was in urgent need of international support. So, it was imperative that each Red Cross section in the country could work well as quickly as possible. With the integration of Red Cross Chittagong, we were able to make an important contribution to this. The secretary there was very happy and things really blossomed. That, in turn, felt like a reward for me and the collaboration just got better and better. We pulled hard in the same direction. Cooperation between the Red Cross League and the ICRC also worked well. We often helped each other out at short notice with vehicles, storage, and information. Mr. Tschiffely, the new ICRC chief in Bangladesh, came to our *godown* in person twice to thank us and express his appreciation for the excellent cooperation. It was unfortunately not yet possible to build on this or even hope that a certain routine would set in over time in the daily work. Too many imponderables got in our way every day but our routines meant that we knew how to deal with issues better and even quicker.

Young Canadian, Ron Feist, my assistant, was a brilliant delegate. He was primarily responsible for supplying the poorly accessible valleys of the Chittagong Hill Tracts in the Bangladesh-India-Burma border region. It wasn't additional delegates that we needed; what worried us was the insufficient transport and loading capacity to bring the relief supplies to all the hard-to-reach areas. All the sampans, UNO mini bulkers, lighters, planes, trains, and trucks that we loaded and dispatched were not enough to meet the delivery needs. The *godowns* were overflowing with newly arriving aid supplies and we had become a bottleneck. Often only quick decisions with improvised rearrangements prevented literal chaos. Time was running out on us almost every day, and the days were always too short. But despite all that, I enjoyed managing this responsible task, leading our delightfully eager squad, keeping them in a good mood between trot, stop and canter. It was also important to me to maintain a friendly atmosphere of mutual respect among the staff. It was just as important to me to plan enough time to keep in touch with the workers in the warehouses, the drivers and the night watchmen. All of us were aware that our work, at the country's most important hub, benefited countless people in need. That was a great incentive for everyone, and it demanded respect from the bosses at all levels.

After Ann left her job at Glaxo Laboratory, she came to the *godown* office on a number of occasions as a volunteer to give me a little help, which I always appreciated. I was regularly overwhelmed by the memory of how, not so long before, when the phone had rung on April 10th at 9 a.m., and I had heard a euphonious female voice on the line. Now she was sitting here next to me, the beautiful telephone operator with great charisma, who had called the wrong number and only a little later became my beloved wife. Truly a wonderful fairy-tale had come true.

It has been raining heavily for weeks. Again and again, dark rain clouds covered the sky. Heavy thunderstorms raged non-stop and pounded the corrugated iron roofs with a roar, while violent gusts of wind shook trees and plants. *Godown* roofs and truck tarpaulins with even the smallest defects always had to be repaired immediately to protect our goods from getting wet. The streets quickly emptied during these outbreaks of natural forces. The poor rickshaw drivers, however, were to be pitied. They looked like wet mice, still pedalled calmly, while their passengers were more or less dry under the raised canopy. As soon as the sun came out again, it got hot and uncomfortably humid. Unsealed roads turned into mud. In these weather conditions, it often happened that we had to use a crane to pull one of our trucks out of the dirt or even one that had slipped into a pond.

At the end of August, I was assigned another task. Sven Lampell appointed me as a "flying trouble shooter." Twice a month, when the helicopter stopped in Chittagong, pilot Rainer and his mechanic Heinz flew me to various districts and provinces. There I met with the responsible chairman of the local branch of the Red Cross Bangladesh to discuss their current situations, problems, and immediate needs on site. Of course, I really liked being able to get away from the on fines of the *godowns* and stress of everyday life. But first and foremost, it was the direct contact with those responsible "out there on site" that were able to simplify the challenges in the very complex day-to-day business. I enjoyed these flights, which always gave me many unforgettable bird's eye views. Helicopter landings in district capitals almost always turned out to be a delicate, even dangerous, undertaking. The respective chairman knew our approximate arrival time, but often there was no barrier monitored by security guards. As soon as pilot Rainer carefully floated down onto the intended meadow, more and more excited people came running who didn't want to miss the landing of this super bird. So, the landing field was quickly smaller than needed. Even if security guards were present, they had a hard time keeping the curious crowds in check. A sweating Rainer climbed higher again, gave hand signals to move away and tried to touch down on the ground again. He often had to fly down several times before he dared to put his bird on the ground. Once that was done, Rainer breathed a sigh of relief. But he could only relax when the rotors, which were death traps in operation, had stopped. Twice I took Ann on one of those trouble-shooter flights because there was an empty seat on the helicopter. On the first morning flight with Ann, we took off from the roof of the Alkarim building, first doing a lap around our nearby bungalow on Sarson Road. The cook and the maid came running out excitedly and we waved at each other, laughing. For the first time we marvelled at our home from a bird's eye view. On the connecting flight we crossed the large factory building of Glaxo Laboratories; this was an unforgettable experience for Ann, since she had worked down here for many years, and had earned her spurs, so to speak.

Our first destination was the district capital Feni. The airfield was cordoned off, so landing didn't cause any problems. The chairman of the local Red Cross section was already waiting for us, and handed me his report on the current situation, its activities, various problems and urgent needs. Then we were in the air again to our next destination, the town of Comilla. We followed the railway line from Chittagong to Sylhet, which runs very close to the border with the Indian state of Assam and the Tripura district. Fascinated, Ann and I followed the course of this "toy train." I was happy for my wife that she got an unexpected bird's eye view of her homeland. Many of her relatives and acquaintances worked on the railroad. When I sometimes asked her where this or that of her relatives worked, Ann often said: "He works on the railway." It was mainly Anglo-Indians who had been employed by the English since the mid-19th century to build the railway network on the Indian subcontinent. Thanks to their reliability and English language training, they also operated all railways there. However, a large number of Anglo-Indians emigrated from 1972 onwards because the Muslim population became too dominant for them. Canada, USA and Australia were preferred emigration countries. Thanks to their English mother-tongue, these Bangladeshis assimilated quickly and found work in a short time, even if this rarely matched their qualifications at the beginning.

As we approached the hill-framed town of Sylhet on the Surma River, we looked out over the famous, lush green and vast tea gardens stretching across the border up towards the Indian Shillong. Our flight now took us over extensive, open deciduous forests, from whose penumbra a seemingly endless hilly carpet of landscape full of tea bushes shone; an unforgettable, peaceful fairy-tale panorama. Besides tea gardens, there were also orange groves and pineapple plantations. The first tea gardens were planted as early as 1830. At that time there was no national border. A striking number of fair-skinned people lived there, evidence of a centuries-long intermingling of Europeans and natives. Fair-skinned Indians and Bangladeshis are very proud of this privilege.

After we stopped in Sylhet, I finished my meeting with the local chairman, we sipped the wonderful Sylhet tea, then Rainer flew us to Dhaka for our monthly meeting. Soon the green rice fields disappeared in the flood tides that prevailed in this part of the country. Broken dams and overflowing rivers dominated the scene. As far as the eye could see, nothing but water, from which only clumps of trees, houses, villages, and sections of streets protruded. Here and there I glimpsed an elongated *killa* on which cattle could take refuge. *Killa* are large rectangular mounds of earth that were built by villagers working together to escape the flood. Within a very short time we experienced two worlds that couldn't have been more contrasting: in Sylhet, colourful vegetation with tea gardens and orchards, in Dhaka, wet, grey misery that threatened people and animals with its flooding. That left us mute and despondent.

I immediately took all my papers to Sven Lampell , made a report and then drove to the hotel. Ann didn't come with me; she used my monthly report time to meet her relatives. So, I spent that evening alone at the obligatory Red Cross party at Sven Lampell's house. Since we delegates, from all over the world usually only met at these end of the month report meetings, we were once again happy to be able to chat. The next morning however, there was no more room for personal talks. The meetings were always long and exhausting, as there was always a lot to discuss and coordinate together. Ann and I were lucky this time to be able to fly back to Chittagong on the Balair DC6, two hours after the end of the session. During the flight, Captain Vogel informed us that he would be flying this aircraft to Basel for maintenance in November and would be returning 10 days later. If we would like to accompany him, we are most welcome; free of course. My heart immediately beat faster. I couldn't turn down such an offer! I was entitled to a vacation anyway, the superiors in Dhaka, Berne and Geneva would certainly agree to it. A dream would come true if I could fly to Switzerland with Ann. I promised the well-meaning Captain that I would keep him informed. For the time being, however, our air trip came to an end. When the DC6 landed in Chittagong, two RK trucks loaded with relief supplies were already waiting with workers to immediately load the aircraft with sacks and boxes. A driver took us first to the *godown*, where I reported back, and then to Sarson Road. As we got out in front of the bungalow, Ann and I smiled at each other and in one voice we said, "home again!"

In the fall of 1972, almost 60,000 people were still housed in eight minority camps in Chittagong, and had to be closely guarded. The locals hadn't forgotten what had happened the previous year. For the most part, Bihari lived in these camps, and they had to be protected from popular anger. Their undoing was that they had cooperated with the West Pakistanis in the war. Only one of these guarded camps was different, the Dogra camp. Over 2,000 interned West Pakistanis lived here, eagerly awaiting repatriation to their homeland. We continued to deliver food and other relief supplies to all of these camps, some of which the ICRC had stored in our *godown*. During those weeks, a new, entirely different problem arose that bothered me. When I came home one evening, I saw from a distance that there were large posters stuck to corners of the house. On it was a message written in red and black Bengali script, signed with a stamp, date and signature. I called the security guard, paid by Volkart Brothers, and asked him what kind of nonsense this was. He reported that a man from a Ministry had stopped by that afternoon and attached the papers and also requested a complete list of the inventory. I immediately tore the papers, that looked like decrees, from the walls of the house and threw them into the fireplace. We always needed paper to start a fire. "They will get to know me," I vowed to myself. The next day another official looking paper was taped again to the *godown* gate. I also immediately tore this paper away. Two hours later, a well-dressed man showed up claiming he was from some government agency, but had no ID. He had been instructed by his boss to obtain a complete inventory of the Volkart *godown* and the bungalow. In addition, it was against the law to remove these injunctions, he added sternly. Then he handed me his boss's phone number, along with instructions to contact him. It never occurred to me to "follow the order from above." I saw this inventory decree as a kind of trial balloon – a first step, so to speak – towards possible nationalization. I would not be fooled by these "gentlemen." But first of all, I spoke plainly to the annoying troublemaker that morning. He seemed to me to be more of a Bengali rascal than an envoy from an unknown ministry. "Mister!" I said sharply, "While these are Volkart Brothers properties, the League of Red Cross Societies has been in charge since early 1972. Perhaps you are not yet aware that the entire *godown* property – including the bungalows of course – are protected neutral zones according to international Red Cross law." I let this announcement sink into him before I repeated in a boss's voice: "You and your ministry have no business or power here. Now leave this property immediately." He seemed to swallow it, not expecting the harsh and confident reaction. "You'll be hearing from us soon," he replied, rather insecurely, and walked away. Of course, I was bluffing with the neutral zone, but I scored 1-0. After that I had a break of two weeks, until suddenly notices of disposal were put up again, which I immediately removed. Now I informed Sven Lampell in Dhaka. He praised my intervention and, last but not least, that I had not allowed myself to be unsettled. If necessary, Sven promised to intervene immediately at a higher level. About ten days later I was called to the *godown* gate. The same guy was standing in front of it again. The guard hadn't let him enter. Another decree was already emblazoned on the gate, which I demonstratively tore away on the spot. "What do you want again?" I asked harshly. "Because you don't want to cooperate, we'll be forced to involve the police," the guy puffed out. "You'd better not do that," I answered in a raised voice while noisy trucks, rickshaws and baby taxis rolled past us and people stopped and stared at me, the foreigner. "I assure you, you would regret that quickly, mister!" I added meaningfully and followed up, "Should you approach with the police here, I will immediately alert my boss in Dhaka. The influential chairman of the Red Cross Bangladesh will then take the matter on, using his good contacts and will speak to Prime Minister Sheikh Mubjibur Rahman, of course with this so-called decree in hand. It's going to be very difficult for you and your boss," I assured him, swiping the ordering paper in front of his nose. "Because you are going to be fully responsible for the fact that the Red Cross is severely hampered in its task during a humanitarian catastrophe in Bangladesh!" Without a word, the guy turned on his heel, got into the nearest rickshaw and disappeared into the heavy traffic. The case was finally closed. I never heard from these obviously, bluffing people again and was able to go about my work again, undisturbed.

We had heard that a huge American ship was bound for Chittagong, loaded with vast amounts of much-needed food. It was the *Manhattan* that anchored around 50 kilometers off Chittagong as she could not approach any closer due to her great draft. The *Manhattan*, which was launched in 1962 as an oil tanker with a displacement of 115,000 tons, but soon proved to be unprofitable for the oil business; newer, even larger super tankers quickly outstripped it. Therefore, the *Manhattan* was converted into a giant cargo ship, which the US government in Washington had now chartered to send 66,000 tons of wheat, rice and sugar to Bangladesh as quickly as possible. Eight hundred tons of aid supplies were pumped into the pier ships via suction lines every day. From these, the goods were reloaded onto UN light ships and mini bulkers, in the port of Chittagong. As already mentioned, thanks to their very shallow draft, they were able to reach almost all provinces of Bangladesh via the rivers. The *Manhattan* lay at anchor for months and at the same time served as a huge floating *godown*. Undoubtedly, this quick and costly American action saved millions of Bangladeshis from starvation in 1972 and 1973. The estimated population at the time was over 75 million people. Troubleshooting or not, our Balair flight to Switzerland was fast approaching. There had been no problems when I presented my holiday wishes to Sven Lampell., "You have to grab such a good opportunity by the forelock," he decided. So, the young, confident Canadian Ron Feist took over all my functions in Chittagong. For sure, everything would take its usual, well-established course. It was also reassuring that fewer cargo ships were arriving.

In mid-November, Ann and I flew to Dhaka with Captain Schneitz. Here we met the two Balair pilots, Kurt, and Vogel, who took off the next morning with us and six other passengers for the first leg via Bombay to Dubai. A Balair loadmaster from Basel had bought a new, splendidly shiny Bengali rickshaw in Dhaka, which was now secured by ropes in front of our seats. We marvelled at the many lovely paintings on the vehicle. There were flowers, palm trees, portraits of women, ornaments and even a waterfall. A large Bengali rickshaw bell was also emblazoned on the handlebars. As soon as you pressed the bell, silvery tones rang out, like a Christmas bell.

A DC6 engine that had been recalled for reconstruction was also firmly lashed down in the long passenger compartment. There was more than enough space on this trip. After a short stopover in Bombay to refuel, we started our onward flight across the Arabian Sea towards Dubai. It was getting dark, and we tried to get some sleep. But suddenly we were startled by an unusual engine noise. One of the four engines sputtered alarmingly, then quit, began to "cough" violently, knocked briefly, and stopped. As if startled by a alarm clock, we sleepers looked at each other questioningly. Captain Herzog reassured us over the loudspeaker: "An engine suddenly became ill. I've calmed him down now. We now fly to Dubai with only three engines: just a little slower. We will look at the engine after landing." In Dubai, the engine was examined early in the morning by the on-board mechanic in the presence of the pilots. He climbed up with his toolbox and began to work on the engine. The pilots watched him and asked him their technical questions. The problem was soon found. The diagnosis was: Motor irreparably defective. Captain Herzog spoke to the Balair bosses in Basel. They decided to send a replacement engine to us in Dubai as quickly as possible. That would take at least two days. It finally became four.

For Ann and I, it was the perfect opportunity to explore Dubai – a country just waking up from its slumber. We moved to a cheap hotel near the airport and started by looking at the fishing district on Dubai Creek. Ann was amazed when she saw the many pieces of jewellery in the shop windows realizing how cheap gold was here. I encouraged her to take advantage of this. After some thought, she settled on some gold wrist bangles and a sparkling necklace. Great, belated wedding presents for my wife. For dinner we let ourselves be spoiled by delicious oriental dishes in specialty restaurants. Ann surprised me with her language skills as she conversed in Urdu with the Pakistani waiters. Our honeymoon had started here in Dubai.

Finally, a DC6 charter plane arrived from Bombay with the replacement engine. In a strange duplicity of events, this plane also suffered engine failure over the Arabian Sea and, like us, landed in Dubai with only three engines. The revised engine was quickly installed and trimmed. Unfortunately, this was not good enough, because when we finally took off for the onward flight, we had to turn back over Bahrain and fly back to Dubai. A small oil leak had sprayed the left side of the aircraft, including the windows. After adjustments and cleaning, our next attempt got us as far as Damascus. But bad luck stayed with us, the replacement engine didn't work properly. We had to fly on to Beirut, where they were better equipped for repairs. With three and a half engines, we started our onward flight; but not over the Al-Jabal Mountains, as was customary. Our experienced pilots flew leisurely through the valleys until we landed in Beirut. After we landed, several fire trucks raced along the left and right of the runway behind us and came to a standstill next to the aircraft, ready for action.

Surprisingly, the mechanical problem was solved after a short time. So, nothing stood in the way of our last section to Basel - or did it? Because Captain Herzog said quite dejectedly: "Actually, we could fly directly to Basel right now. But we have lost a lot of time because of the delays; and we pilots have to comply with strict rest-time regulations." So, we looked for rooms in a hotel in downtown Beirut and enjoyed dinner together. The next morning, we started early towards Basel, where we landed a few hours later without further incidents. I now had ten days to show Ann a little bit of my homeland and introduce her to my family and friends. In the second-half of November in Basel it was cold. Ann felt it terribly, she urgently needed winter clothes. But the first "official act" took place at the airport, where I hired a VW Beetle for ten days. Our first destination was Bruderholz street, home of Magdalena Betsche, my former Swiss RC colleague during our first Bangladesh mission. We received a warm welcome from Magdalena together with her lovely mother. We were invited to stay with them. Next morning the four of us drove to Basel to buy winter clothes for Ann at the Rheinbrücke department store. In addition to the obligatory underwear, the three women opted for a white winter coat with belt, white boots, a scarf, gloves and a wool hat. Soon Ann was standing in front of us, heavily hooded. She looked very beautiful, like a warmly smiling Bengal fairy-tale princess in winter. After lunch we said goodbye to our warm hearted Betsche ladies and drove through the romantic Waldenburger valley, which was rainy that day and up to Upper Hauenstein pass. Shortly before the top of the pass, the raindrops turned into snowflakes. Ann was startled, looked incredulously through the windshield, then questioningly at me.

From where were these dancing cotton balls coming from? I stopped in a parking lot, Ann immediately hopped out of the car and began jumping around like an excited little girl, tried to catch the thick snowflakes; and watched in amazement as they began melting on her palm. Suddenly she felt the cold and, out of breath, hurriedly got back in the car. Ann beamed, now she knew what snow was. I was happy for her and gave her a kiss. After a short visit to my old very surprised friends in the small village of Klus, we drove directly to my parents in Interlaken-Unterseen. Ann was warmly welcomed by my parents and immediately taken care of. Mother read every wish from her eyes, as she didn't speak English. Ann watched with interest as my mother, an excellent cook, prepared dinner. It was only now that we realized how tired and exhausted we were from our long journey on the plane. So, we went to bed early and slept through the night until the wonderful smell of coffee from Mother's kitchen woke me up. There was bread, butter, jam, and my favourite "Zopf," a Swiss speciality white-flour twist. Our vacation days in the bitterly cold Bernese Upperland at minus 20 degrees, went by all too quickly. I visited the snow-covered Grindelwald with Ann, showed her my parents former house in the Eschen also the church and the old school building. We made short visits to family and friends, who were all very happy to see us. Before we finally returned to Basel, we stopped by the Swiss Red Cross HQ in Berne. My boss, the charming Mrs. Zuyderhoff, was very happy to see us and congratulated us. She insisted on introducing us to her employees. It wasn't every day that a Swiss RC delegate got married during his mission abroad. We then spent the last night in my small apartment in Zurich-Oerlikon, where we also stayed overnight. Early in the morning, we drove to Basel, returned our car, and boarded the repaired DC6 and flew back to Bangladesh with the same pilots and without incident. Our luggage was full of presents, especially chocolates for Ann's family.

My deputy, Ron Feist, had done an excellent job of overseeing all activities during my absence. I thanked him with great relief. It had gotten noticeably cooler, especially at night, and the rainless Bengali "winter" had arrived. Ann reminded me that it was now Advent time. Ann looked forward to Christmas like a child and enjoyed the run-up to Christmas to the fullest. In the evenings we often sat next to each other on *murras* (stools) in front of our warm fireplace sipping tea. On Christmas Eve we sat on a bench in the Catholic Jamalkhan Church, which was decorated for Christmas and crowded with people in festive clothes. Suddenly the little church choir, conducted by Ann's brother-in-law, George Paul, began to sing Christmas carols on the gallery, invisible to us and as beautiful and solemn as I had never heard before. George accompanied the songs on a harmonium and sang some of the tunes that were also familiar to me. Most of the girls in the choir were his daughters; Pamela, Glenda, and Marina. While they sang "Silent Night, Holy Night" my eyes watered. I recorded those 1972 Christmas carols live on a little tape recorder I took to church with me. We listen to them from time to time, and this unique Christmas Eve always returned immediately to our hearts. The two of us celebrated the traditional New Year's Eve dance event in the popular "Catholic Club," opposite the Cathedral and the Convent, a worthy and deserved end for us from the spectacular year that was 1972.

In January, the hustle and bustle in goods handling gradually decreased. We could breathe a sigh of relief. My contract ran until March 31, 1973. Coincidentally, the *godown* contract between the Volkart Brothers and the Red Cross League also ended on that day. During March we received a distinguished visitor from Switzerland. Director Holderegger from the Volkart Brothers headquarters in Winterthur visited us in Chittagong. He thanked me warmly that I alone had saved all of Volkart Brothers' properties in Chittagong from getting nationalized; but also, because we had kept all the buildings in very good condition. "If you would stay longer than March 31st," asserted Mr. Holderegger, "we would be prepared to extend the contract with the Red Cross for a short time; because you are like a guarantee for us that our properties here remain in safe hands." Otherwise, the Volkart brothers would sell all their properties in Chittagong. Unfortunately, an extension of my contract could not be realized at such short notice. It stayed the same, my assignment there ended at the end of March. I regretted it but didn't know that a few months later I would be promoted to RC chief delegate on another mission.

On one of my last days at work, our cook served us a particularly tasty chicken curry. When I praised him for this very good meal, Ann asked ironically: "Do you know what that was?" "No." "That was George!" The last bite stuck in my throat from shock. Suddenly my dinner didn't seem half as tasty anymore. Poor George felt heavy on me now. Ann had asked the cook to butcher our colourful, proud rooster. Our cook didn't need to be told twice and wringed poor George's neck. Ann said to console me that she had given the hens to her sister Susie, but she didn't want loud George. The next morning, I promptly overslept because my beloved George couldn't wake me anymore. My last working day was set for March 13th. I said goodbye somewhat wistfully to my successor Ron Feist and the many loyal employees and workers. At our second last evening we had a farewell party at Susie's house. Many relatives came to say goodbye. The next morning at 9a.m., Ann and I boarded the helicopter on the Alkarim roof with two small suitcases. I asked pilot Rainer to fly over Susie's house first. All the people on Jamalkhan Road came running out of their houses. We waved at each other again and again while the helicopter flew some noisy goodbye circles. In Dhaka next morning we boarded an Air India plane and flew to New Delhi, from there we visited the famous Taj Mahal and other sights. We continued to Kathmandu, where we admired the sunrise over the Himalayan peaks one very early morning. The following day we flew to Switzerland via Bombay. There we moved into my small, rented apartment in Zurich-Oerlikon. Ann appreciated the warm central heating and quickly learned to dress warmly when going out. She was impressed by the cleanliness and order in the streets, the punctuality of public transport and even more so by the huge range of groceries at Migros and Coop. However, she also quickly realized how expensive everything was here compared to Chittagong. On a rainy morning we took the train to Geneva, boarded the bus to Petit Saconnex and proceeded to the obligatory debriefing at the Red Cross League headquarters. There we discussed the end of my Bangladesh mission with the responsible people. The next day we reported to the Swiss Red Cross in Berne. Here, too, I made my verbal reports and settled accounts; and after the medical Doctor had examined me thoroughly, I received a very good certificate. Once again, I was out on the street without a job.

For me that was no problem. The uniqueness of events, experiences and goals achieved made up for this many times over. Life has been kind to us. I was also hoping the next job was already waiting but during those first days I was in no hurry to look for it.

First, we moved to my parents in Unterseen for a few days. They loved Ann from the start, which was mutual. My mother introduced Ann to Swiss cuisine and tried her hand at teaching Ann German. My father, on the other hand, proudly showed us his magnificent garden which he had laid out years ago on a sunny slope, at the Harder Mountain rail station. Spring seed was already sprouting from all the garden beds. As a trained gardener, he was a real professional. Back in Zurich, I got in touch with Manpower again. A week later I was offered a temporary job as a warehouse clerk at Battery Oerlikon. I didn't mind being a command taker again. I was sure that sooner or later there would be work with the Red Cross again. While shopping on a Saturday, I met a dark-skinned lady with a small child in front of a shop. I spoke to her spontaneously and told her about my sometimes, lonely wife from Bangladesh. I asked her if she might have time afterwards and I would introduce her to Ann. Then her husband came, and they both immediately agreed to come home with me and meet Ann. She was amazed when I entered our apartment with Rita and Walter Schmid and their baby. Rita came from Sri Lanka and Walter worked as a bank manager in Zurich. This was just the beginning. Rita and Walter became close friends for life.

In April I received a Red Cross phone call from Berne. The Swiss Red Cross offered me a new mission; namely as chief delegate of the International Red Cross League in Sudan based in the capital

Khartoum. What a unique opportunity in my Red Cross career! I could hardly believe it at first. How could I have said no to that? There was no doubt that in Berne and Geneva I was trusted with this task; but I scarcely dared to tell Ann. I felt sorry for having to pack my bags again after such a short time. To my great relief, she took the news with her usable composure; was even happy for me and this unique opportunity. I was overjoyed. We still had a few weeks to deal with this new phase of life, because the departure towards Khartoum was planned for June 1973.

CHAPTER FIVE

Sudan and Southern Sudan, 1973-1976

SPOTLIGHT ON SUDAN

The first civil war between South Sudan and North Sudan lasted from 1955 to 1972. The reasons for this conflict were historic, economic interests in the natural resources of the South as well as ethnic and religious differences. Demands by the South for active political participation in its own region as well as in the state, further contributed to the escalation into conflict. The population of North Sudan is largely Arabic and Islamic, whereas the population of the south is mainly African, Christians although religious practice continues to include animist beliefs. The south is multi-ethnic with dozens of cultures including the Nuba, Dinka, Nuer and others. The relatively fair-skinned North Sudanese Arab consider themselves superior to the dark-skinned South Sudanese and history shows how these beliefs developed.Slave traders from

North Sudan hunted slaves in the south of the country for centuries. During it's the colonial reign Great Britain administered the north and the south separately, in an attempt to stop the trade.

In the south, the official language was English and not Arabic; Christian missionaries were also allowed to work in the region. One plan for the decolonization of Sudan included letting South Sudan become a separate territory. Another plan was to join South Sudan to its southern neighbour Uganda. But at the Juba Conference of 1947, the representatives of North Sudan and the colonial power of Great Britain decided that the provinces of South Sudan, even after independence, should remain with the territory of Sudan. The reason for this change in Great Britain were highly political, with plans to maintain influence in the region well beyond the time of decolonization. The South Sudanese were given little opportunity to contribute to this decision and the Northern government expanded administratively, and militarily into the south. Participation in the administration, direction, and formation of the state of Sudan – was largely denied to the South Sudanese. As Sudan gained independence from Britain at the beginning of 1956, immediately the civil war began. The insurgents came to be known as Anya-Nya, with the aim of fighting against the discrimination and paternalism of the North and enforcing autonomy for the south.

North Sudan's political parties rejected the autonomy and federalism demands of the South. Head of state Ibrahim Abboud came to power by military coup in 1958 and brutally retaliated against the rebels from the South to ensure the unity of the entire country. However, between 1958 to 1959 numerous villages were burned, chiefs and clan chiefs killed, and civilians accused of collaborating with the Anya-Nya, imprisoned and tortured. The military dictatorship ended in 1964 when, due to public pressure in the north, Abboud was forced to hand over power to a civilian government under al-Chatim al-Khalifah. The Round Table conference was convened in Khartoum to meet with representatives of the North and the South to discuss a solution to the "Southern problem." The fronts were so hardened, the differences of opinion so great, that this conference failed.

In the 1965 election, the South was once again absent; with the justification that the security situation was too delicate. In the years to come, government in-fighting raged and the conflict between North and South deepened. It was only Prime Minister Nimeiri who sought talks with the rebels from the end of 1971. He preferred a political solution to the conflict. In February 1972, a ceasefire agreement was finally signed in Addis Ababa. The North granted the South the desired autonomy and ended a civil war that had claimed an estimated 700,000 lives. This agreement held for eleven years, then in 1983 a second, no less bloody, civil war began.

AFRICA: SECOND OBSTACLE-FILLED MISSION

In mid-May, Ann and I went to Geneva and Berne for the briefings and to sign the contract. In addition to my mission as Chief Delegate of the Red Cross League, I was given the additional task and entrusted as coordinator for a construction project in South Sudan at Malakal, capital of Upper Nile province -for the Swiss Red Cross (SRC). This was a project between the UN High Commissioner for Refugees (UNHCR) and the Swiss Red Cross, the latter being responsible for execution. This was about the renovation and expansion of a state teacher training college in South Sudan. The company, Baustrag, in Nairobi, a subsidiary of the Swiss construction company Losinger AG in Berne, was engaged for the construction.

In the Oerlikon library I oriented myself on the history, politics, and geography of the vast Sudan. Sudan once stretched from the Egyptian border in the north to the Ugandan border in the south. A distance that corresponds with the distance from Berne to Istanbul. In this, the largest African country, Switzerland would have fit sixty times. It was the same size as Western Australia, although it lost this status when South Sudan became independent in 2011.

In the 1972 the Addis Ababa Agreement that bought the first war to an end, South Sudan, with its 650,000 square kilometers, was classified as an autonomous Region divided into the three provinces of Equatoria (main town Juba), Bahr al-Ghazal (main town Wau) and Upper Nile (main town Malakal). Malakal is around 800 kilometers south of Khartoum on the White Nile: about halfway between Khartoum and the border with Kenya. At the time, it had 40,000 inhabitants.

The north is mostly desert land or at least has desert-like characteristics. In the south, however, savannas stretch out. Along the White Nile there are huge areas of wetlands. The history of Sudan is closely linked to the Nile, whose two arms, the White and Blue Nile, unite in Khartoum. The rivers form important traffic routes, because the thin road network in South Sudan is usually impassable during the half-year rainy season. Only the city of Juba, the capital of the south had some paved roads. However, the savannas turn, during the rainy months, into huge, impassable swamps. Villages not on a river are cut off for months at a time.

There is a railway line that connects the north with the city of Wau in the south. The best connections during the rainy season were sparse and expensive. Sudan Airways flights operating with their Fokker Friendship propeller aircrafts also landed in Malakal. Although the UNHCR construction project which was the responsibility of the Swiss Red cross, was in Malakal, my base was in Khartoum, 800 kilometers away, at the headquarters of the Sudanese Red Crescent. From there I would pull the strings and report back as coordinator and liaison between Berne, Malakal, and the construction company in Nairobi. The obligatory vaccinations were done, the visas were available, and our suitcases were already packed, when I got a painful phlebitis on my left leg. A visit to the doctor was indicated. After the consultation, he asked: "Do you smoke?" "Yes, unfortunately," I confessed. "It's an annoying thing, leftover from my Biafra days." The doctor warned me, "If you don't stop, you will suffer more and more from phlebitis!" That was obviously the kick I needed. When I stepped out onto the street again, I resolutely threw the almost full cigarette pack out of my breast pocket and threw it unerringly into the next rubbish bin. That was May 28, 1973, the day of my final, irrevocable, and happy farewell to nicotine. But still, when we arrived a week late in Khartoum on the weekly Swissair flight, the inflammation in the leg was to blame.

At the customs control the Red Cross League Delegate, Dimitri Severi, was waiting for us. He brought us to the German Sudan Club which was near the airport. Here we had a room, and they also had a restaurant. We soon went to bed and slept like logs. But when we came out of the clubhouse next morning blazing heat nearly knocked us over. Unfortunately, we had arrived in the hottest season, with an average temperature of 43 degrees. On particularly hot days, this could rise to 50 degrees. Only in the rooms with air conditioning did we feel well. Dimitri Severi brought us to the headquarters of the Sudan Red Crescent Headquarters close to the city centre where my new place of work was. There we were warmly welcomed by the President Dr. Mohjeddin, the secretary Mohamed Ali Nur and the office manager Mr Fatty. That first encounter was very optimistic about the desired cooperation. I started working there two days later. On short notice I had to fly on official duty with Sudan Airways to Port Sudan at the Red Sea. The propeller plane unfortunately, had only one seat left. What a pity, Dimitri and Ann were unable to accompany me. "As a newcomer to Sudan, what can I expect in Port Sudan?" I asked myself, a little anxious. When I got off the plane there, I felt a heavy, damp heat. The air seemed sticky, and I thought I was stewing in a sun-drenched salt-air sauna. A driver came up to me when he saw my Red Cross emblem and immediately called me on board an all-terrain vehicle with a flag standard next to the aircraft. "We're going straight to the Governor's now," the driver told me. "He is expecting you!" The headwind cooled me down a bit. In front of an imposing building in the city, the chauffeur let me out and I was immediately assigned to the Governor. He greeted me warmly, had tea served and informed me about the geographic situation of the province, speaking of several years with drought and difficult development in this arid sand hill province. I was amazed at how skilfully and clearly, he conveyed this region, its problems and his ideas to me, the foreigner. What a pity Ann could not witness this lecture. Then the chauffeur drove me to the old Red Sea Hotel, built in a nostalgic colonial style. A room with a sea view was booked for me. Even a table for lunch in the restaurant was reserved. A gentleman was already there: the President of the Red Crescent Section Port Sudan and full-time seaport commander. While we ate together, he explained the program he had put together for me. The next morning, I would be driven to the port as his guest and in the afternoon, I would have the honour of opening the new kindergarten, realized by the local section of the Red Crescent. Subsequently there will be an official early dinner in the garden next door. "Further programs I will tell you about the remaining days later," he concluded his discourse. I couldn't help but be amazed. Here, in this Red Sea town, I was treated and respected like a foreign ambassador. In the evening I made some notes. No doubt I would have to say a few words at the kindergarten party. The next morning at 8 a.m., as announced, a chauffeur drove me to the commander of the port. His office was a real command centre and gave a good overview of the activity in the port with the docked freighters, moving cranes and waiting trucks. The commander was a sought-after man and got repeatedly asked for on the phone. In between he informed me about his functions, explained statistics, problems and plans for the future. Then he introduced me to Port Sudan's Fire Brigade Commander who had just arrived; he too was a key committee member of the Red Crescent Section. At 9 o'clock sharp there was a break for the traditional Sudanese breakfast, called *ful*. A woman came in with a steaming bowl with brownish stew and put it on the dining table. We four present were all given a flatbread that served as the function of the missing cutlery. Everyone then tore off a piece of bread and dunked it in the common bowl. I was immediately enthusiastic about this excellent-tasting, Arabic-spiced dish; my first *ful* breakfast. The men reacted proudly to my compliment as this one dish tasted so good to me. *Ful* is a national dish, a stew made from fava beans, peanut oil, onions, tomatoes, lemon juice and traditional spices, cooked over a fire. *Ful* even became a side note in the history of Sudan's independence. When Sudan was due to gain independence on New Year's Day 1956, the celebration was set by the English at 9 o'clock. The Sudanese, however, refused to take part at this hour. It was impossible for them because 9 a.m. is time for *ful* - for all Sudanese. For the Sudanese, their beloved *ful* breakfast was more important than the independence they had waited so long for and they arrived at the ceremony an hour late.

The official opening of the new kindergarten in the city punctually took place in the presence of numerous people, at the agreed time. Also, the Governor and other dignitaries had come. Somebody handed me a large pair of scissors, while I slowly walked with measured steps to the entrance of the kindergarten and proudly cut the red and white ribbon in two, accompanied by applause. The committee members then proudly showed me around the generously designed premises. Some short addresses were given in Arabic and a school class sang a song that sounded exotic to my ears. The invited guests then walked to a nearby flower meadow and sat down at a long, festively decorated table. While the sun slowly sank below the horizon, iced drinks were served. I was given my first glass of *karkade*, which is made from red hibiscus flowers. From then on, *karkade* was my absolute favourite drink in Sudan. Delicious lamb and chicken dishes were served, I stood up and said words of appreciation to the large, long table. I thanked everybody for the warm welcome, hospitality and congratulated the very active committee members, sponsors, and volunteers for the realization of this unique kindergarten, which was an important achievement for the residents. I also asked for a written report of the difficult drought situation in this Red Sea province. The next morning, I was picked up by the prison commandant from Port Sudan, another member of the Red Crescent. I was obviously being "passed around" for inaugural visits. I assumed that these first contacts would be of use to me in my work here and was therefore willingly and consciously involved in these valuable encounters. My companion drove us to his beautiful residence on a bumpy sandy path, a few kilometers outside of town. We had breakfast on the terrace together and had a good chat. It was my second, yet even better breakfast of *ful*. Then we drove to Suakin, 60 kilometers away, which was Sudan's only seaport until the 1930s. But Suakin had over the years become a crumbling ruin, a ghost town, nevertheless a very popular tourist attraction. Back in Port Sudan, the port commander took me for a boat trip out to the Red Sea. The next day I flew back to Khartoum, where Ann was longingly awaiting me. Thirteen years later I visited Port Sudan and Suakin a second time, this time with Ann, and celebrated a surprise reunion with the same active members from the Red Crescent Committee.

The sweltering Sudanese heat plagued us for three more weeks in Khartoum, making us lethargic and sluggish. Despite this, we never worked up a sweat because the shimmering air was bone dry. Sweat evaporated instantly from the skin. We realised, how important it was to drink water regularly, whether lukewarm or chilled didn't matter. Gradually we felt better, the lost spirit of life reported back, we felt "arrived." Now it was time to register us at the Swiss Embassy. Daniel Aviolat the charming *charge d'affairs* was happy to meet us and welcomed us with two glasses of *karkade*. As I slowly settled into my duties, Ann tried to find a suitable house or apartment for us. Most foreigners lived in El Amarat, a newer neighbourhood near the German Club and airport. This residential area was suitable for us. Three weeks later we were able to move into a simple 72 square meter apartment with a balcony on the first floor. In the kitchen, however, there was only a simple gas *rechaud*, which was not a problem for Ann. She settled in quickly and conjured Bengali curry dishes onto the table, but also learned quickly to cook a *ful* breakfast, preferably on Fridays, the Sudanese Sunday. From two foreign families who were leaving Sudan, we cheaply bought some furniture. But we bought the real Sudanese beds new. They consist of a simple wooden frame with four round feet. The mattress lies on a braided cord. We got used to it quickly and slept well. We only woke up after midnight when a plane took off and the windowpanes rattled. It took some getting used to that in Khartoum, surrounded by semi-desert, the air was never clean, dust found ways trough every crack and crevice. The worst for us were the sandstorms, which stir up the dust and rubbish lying on the ground. Approaching brown sandstorm clouds could be seen from afar. People called each other immediately warning "*Habub! Habub*" (sandstorm) and rushed home to quickly close open windows and seal the front door at the bottom with wet rags.

To change things up, we went to the cinema once a week. There were only open-air cinemas and we sat under the sea of stars on a simple metal chair with plastic mesh. At the entrance we bought two small bottles of Pepsi and put the opened bottle under the chair; until we realized that stray cats were roaming around and licking at the open bottles unnoticed. It also happened that during the events on the screen, quite slowly the moon rose, which gave the movie night a very romantic touch. The two of us loved going to the Blue Nile Cinema, between the Nile and the elevated end of the airfield runway. Even when it regularly happened that all of a sudden, an airliner took off, thundering over the heads of the terrified movie goers with its headlights on. Everyone gaped and stared anxiously upwards.

Once we were sitting unsuspectingly in the Blue Nile Cinema when sudden strong winds picked up. Suddenly and silently, it had arrived, a real *habub*, the dreaded brown sandstorm. The movie screen became unrecognizable. Everyone stood up and hurriedly headed for the exit with handkerchiefs over the nose. A typical, difficult to describe, unpleasantly dry dusty smell was in the air. We drove home cautiously in very poor visibility, fogged with sand. Unfortunately, a nasty surprise awaited us there. We accidentally had left a small window open. The sandstorm had blown in loads of fine dust into our apartment and evenly coated the living room, the kitchen and our bedroom with a thick, light brown layer. Bed covers, pillows, tables, chairs, and the floor were one sandy desert. My first official act was to angrily clear small sidewalks through the apartment with a broom. We toiled until well past midnight to make our home liveable again, at least temporarily. Now it was clear to us. A *habub* was an opponent that was anything but easy to deal with. The whole of the next day remained foggy, even the sun could hardly penetrate the fine dust still floating in the air.

The six-day week was also known in Sudan, but the pressure to work and perform was not as strong as in Bangladesh. The Red Cross League Geneva had purchased a Volkswagen Beetle for me and shipped it to Port Sudan. However, it did not arrive until two months later. In the meantime, Dimitri picked me up with the Land Rover. Thirty-six year-old Dimitri Severi was Italian from Sardinia; an experienced, patient Red Cross man who spoke several languages and was even fluent in Arabic, which made our work much easier for him and me. He had successfully worked for some time in Port Sudan and helped the local branch of the Sudan Red Crescent Committee with new ideas. Also, Dimitri had set up a new committee in Kassala. In Khartoum, Dimitri was staying at the rather old Akropol hotel in the city centre, which belonged to a Greek family. Khartoum had quite a number of long-established Greek businessmen and shops in the town centre. The dentist I soon had to see was also a Greek.

A second Red Cross delegate, the Norwegian Jakob Frick, worked in Wau, the capital of Bahr al-Ghazal Province in South Sudan. He oversaw the construction of a new midwifery school, a project of the Norwegian Red Cross. Jacob Frick was also involved in the motivation, education, and fundraising of the local Red Crescent committee. Not an easy task, after 17 years of civil war, to motivate people to take their destiny into their own hands. In 1973 beyond the city limits of Khartoum, in a country as big as Western Europe, there were only 300 kilometers of asphalt roads! The longest paved route ran almost 200 kilometers from Khartoum to Wad Medani. Only during the late 1970s, did foreign companies build an almost 1,500-kilometer-long asphalt road between

Khartoum and Port Sudan. This road led across the province on a long detour passing through towns towards the Ethiopian border. The railway line to Port Sudan, on the other hand, was much more direct when it was laid at the turn of the century. Up to the end of the 1970s, almost all goods for Sudan arrived by ship in Port Sudan. The entire Sudanese railway network back then was around 5,000 kilometers.

Before I flew to South Sudan for the first time, I reported to the Head of Department in the "Ministry for Education" in Khartoum. I was welcomed by a friendly elderly man, whose name I unfortunately forgot. He became my ministerial contact and interlocutor for the planned construction of the teacher training college. When he introduced me to two of his employees, I got a fright, because these two were sitting in a really dangerous workplace. Behind their desk chairs rose several meters of wooden frames, which were loaded with dust-covered, bundles of files crammed up to the ceiling. They could have tumbled down at any moment, burying the unsuspecting bureaucrats beneath them. History of the Sudanese education system presumably slumbered in these dust-covered files. This picture worried me a bit, because the files needed for the construction of the teachers' seminar could not allowed to gather dust. So, one week later, at my first meeting with the Sudanese Minister of Education, I firmly said: "It is of utmost importance for our construction project in Malakal to receive partnership support from the local provincial commissioner and the school board." Then I added, "This is the only way to avoid bureaucratic problems." I had the towering, dusty files in mind, yet I had no idea of the time-consuming difficulties this construction project would involve. I took my first flight from Khartoum to Malakal with Paul Osborne, a young British civil engineer from the Baustrag construction company in Nairobi. Ross Pike from the UN's Food and Agricultural Organization in Rome was waiting for us in his Land Rover and drove Paul and me to the ancient Malakal guest house. Around a dozen vultures sat staring at us in long line on the rusted corrugated iron roof like a hungry, eerie welcoming committee. A weary man in the traditional white *jalabia* robe and turban came shuffling out after some time to the entrance, handing us Arabic printed registration slips and led us to a simple room in which stood two rusty, old-fashioned iron beds, presumably leftovers from the former British colonial period. Then the man who called himself Ahmed, shuffled away then called back, "Lunch will be ready in half an hour."

Now I had to go to the toilet quickly. Following the scent, I found it outside, a small lean-to, against the brick wall. I hesitantly pressed the doorknob and opened the door a crack. Immediately I recoiled from the sickening stench, mosquitoes and tremendous flies that came darting out, swarming around me. Upset, I bolted a few meters and gasped for better air. But there was no way out, the pressure inside me demanded I enter this horribly smelly disposal site again. After washing my hands, I recommended to my partner Paul Osborne the amazingly modern guest house toilet.

Soon Ahmed called us to eat. Paul and I sat at one of the few guest tables in the dining room. On a wall, next the entrance to the kitchen, which looked like a dark tunnel, lay a big heap of broken dishes, almost a meter high. In response to our question, Ahmed replied: "These are all the broken plates, cups and bowls from the last ten years. We keep all these shards as proof that the crockery was broken and not stolen because the guest house is owned by the Sudan Railways, and they send an inspector to check every year." We smiled to ourselves and eagerly awaited our lunch. Nothing was missing, there was soup, meat, and vegetables, even a crème for dessert. The only problem was all the dishes not only had almost the same greenish colour, from the soup to the crème, it all seemed to have a similar taste.

We called our guesthouse the Malakal Hilton, as it was the first house on site when approaching from the airport side. The hungry vultures on the roof left us in peace, but the ravages of time and the many guests had badly affected the colonial beds in our room. Beneath the crushed, decaying mattresses, the metal struts had buckled sideways under the weight of countless sleepers, leaving a coffin-like pit to lie in. Turning was difficult but I did it again and again and it made me angry. The next morning, I had bad back pain and felt exhausted as I groaned from this antediluvian couch. Paul wasn't much better. We both felt older overnight, unable to loosen our stiffened limbs.

The shuffling Ahmed served us fried eggs next to the tunnel kitchen and left two flatbreads to go with it. Tired and hunched over, he shuffled back into the dark kitchen hole and brought the tea in a badly battered pot that must also have belonged to the Sudan Railway inventory, although there was no railway line at all to Malakal. The breakfast tea awakened our spirits again. We wanted to go exploring that day, but first on foot, because there were no taxis in Malakal. On the way we met slim, black South Sudanese who looked at us curiously as we observed their tribal lines scarred across their foreheads. The White Nile flowed sluggishly past us towards the north, purple-blossomed water hyacinths floating along with it. Now and then we saw a man in a dugout canoe paddling a passage laboriously between the crowd of hyacinths. Beyond the opposite bank stretched an endless plain of green, merging with the sky on the distant horizon. Soon we two hikers began sweating, bothered by the unaccustomed muggy air. Suddenly a big Land Rover pulled up next to us. A European in his thirties, smiled and invited us to join him. He introduced himself as Paavo Färm from Finland. He was leading a development project in Malakal for the Lutheran World Federation (LWF). He told us, "We educate and teach, among other things, young lads out here to become carpenters." Paavo took us to the derelict, teacher training college that had been vacant for many years. The recently ended civil war had sad consequences there and throughout Malakal. My colleague Paul was now frowning and thoughtfully scratching his head, wondering if it was right to be in this backward, dilapidated, and strange-smelling town as a construction manager. Paavo smiled and said, "I know the countless difficulties and obstacles in this sleepy place." He assured us to get in and invited us for dinner. We gladly accepted this invitation. The burgeoning doubts were blown away for the moment. Also, what good luck, we didn't need to eat dinner at "Chez Ahmed" that evening. Buoyant, we got back into the Land Rover and Paavo drove us to the Police Commander of Upper Nile Province. Paul Samuel was a handsome, dark-skinned man who greeted us kindly. He had knowledge from rebuilding and the planned enlargement of the teachers' seminar and offered us his support. "You are always welcome," he said. "I will be happy to help you if you encounter any difficulties - which is guaranteed to be pre-programmed here," he added. Then he told us about his career as a police officer, was visibly proud to have made it to the rank of commandant and have responsibility for 2,000 police officers in Upper Nile Province. He had an important function there, to ensure order and security after 17 years of civil war.

Later that afternoon, Paul and I were sitting on the elevated bank of the Nile near the seminar waiting for Paavo on the grass. Suddenly, wet, glistening heads emerged. Loudly snorting hippos with big mouths and huge teeth presented themselves to us in the most beautiful way. We were amazed like two little kids who were at the zoo, seeing a wild animal for the first time. The heavy hippos seemed to feel at home here. They snorted and pulled off an exciting nature show just for us two lucky guys. So, Malakal wasn't just a run-down town, but also had a lot of nature to offer. When Paavo picked us up, these hippos, as they are called in English, were still swimming around. Paavo said they would get out of the water at night, eating lots of grass and sometimes rounding around and heavily tramping the dirt road in front of his house. "It would be life-threatening to stay outside." We believed him without a doubt. The training workshops and Paavo's simple house stood a bit outside of the city on the elevated bank of the Nile. Paavo's blonde wife, Lena, was a warm, personable host who treated us to a delicious fish dish - Nile perch, the best and largest fish in the White Nile. We were amazed at how big and thick the fillets were on our plates and didn't ask twice. Paavo took us back to the Malakal Hilton afterwards, where we spent another uncomfortable night. At that time in Malakal there was no telephone connection with the outside world. Realising this worried us, knowing how difficult communication would be during the construction period. The Baustrag construction company provided the prefabricated buildings in Nairobi (Kenya). From there, the elements were to be loaded onto trucks and driven 1,100 Km through Kenya and Uganda to the capital Juba and reloaded there onto barges attached to Shovel steamers and shipped almost 900 kilometers on the White Nile to Malakal. How was that supposed to work without well-functioning communication? A real logistical nightmare! We had to come up with something. The best solution would be to get a radio link permit in Khartoum between Nairobi and Malakal. The next day we tried our luck with the Commissioner in charge of Upper Nile Province. He was in Juba, we were told. However, Paavo drove us 30 kilometers to the remote mission station of Doleib Hill on the Sobat River. Here we met Henry Lund, an interesting young civil engineer from Denmark. His father was the owner of the largest construction company in Copenhagen and expected that Henry would one day take over the business as his successor. For the time being though Henry was enjoying his self-chosen freedom and was working on a Danish development project. He had built his home himself, a tower-like, three-storey tree house on the Sobat River with corrugated iron siding, including the Danish flag. It could only be climbed using ladders. The top bedroom "floated" as an airy lookout with a fantastic view over the flat, wide country. In his free hours Henry, a young life artist, read his books up there, observed the weather, the many flocks of birds passing by or kept an eye out for crocodiles in the river.

The next morning Paul flew on to Juba and in the afternoon,

I boarded the same plane in Malakal for the return flight to Khartoum. When I arrived there, I enjoyed the hot "oven air" as a real benefit; a good feeling to have escaped the very unpleasant humid air in the south. Little did I know that I was going to fly another 39 times to South Sudan. Ann was very relieved to know I was safe and sound at home. She was worried because I couldn't phone her. In the meantime, she had enrolled for a German course at the German Goethe Institute in Khartoum. My Volkswagen car was meanwhile on the train from Port Sudan. A Red Crescent employee had the Arabic license plate and insurance taken care of. Now nothing stood in the way for a first ride with the new car. We took the next day off and drove along the Blue Nile, over the old steel arch bridge, then crossed the White Nile. After this bridge the two arms of the Blue and White Nile merge. We drove on just a few kilometers to the largest city in Sudan, the historic, Arab-influenced, Omdurman. Its camel market is as famous as it's many mosques. Omdurman is a residential city, unlike Khartoum which more resembles as an administrative city. Both cities are in their own way impressive.

Now I was finally motorized, I drove to the Red Crescent every morning, discussed projects, plans and ways to raise funds. My contact persons were always the secretary and the President, who arrived around noon. Nothing worked without the latter, which had advantages and disadvantages. Almost every day I typed memoranda to the Red Cross League in Geneva and reports for the SRC in Berne on the typewriter I had brought with me. Excited I opened the letters when mail arrived from Geneva and Berne. At first, I tried to call Switzerland from the main post office. A very time-consuming undertaking: it took a while before the connection to work. The responsible people in Switzerland were sometimes absent. So, I stopped trying to get in touch verbally and stuck to reporting by letter. I needed patience, but at least I knew that my letters ended up in the right place. One day, a new League of Red Cross Delegate arrived. Miroslav Kalinowski from the Polish Red Cross was about 45-years old. A Professor and blood specialist from Gdansk, he had the task of running and improving the blood donation service in Sudan. At first, he lived in the German Club, but later he got a room in our apartment block. I accompanied Professor Kalinowski from time to time for meetings with doctors in Khartoum hospital. He fought to have the Red Cross League in Geneva approve an apparatus to produce dry blood plasma. The dilemma was: such a facility would be very expensive but would be of great benefit to the huge country of Sudan. Miroslav tried tireless persuasion. He also flew to Port Sudan, Juba, and other cities, spoke there with hospital doctors and bureaucrats, made suggestions for improvement, and informed them about the latest developments. For its part, the Red Cross League appealed to national Red Cross Societies to raise enough funds for the purchase of a blood plasma machine. All of this dragged on for a long time and was ultimately unsuccessful; to the great disappointment of Professor Kalinowski and the Sudanese doctors.

On Fridays, our day off, we often had lunch at the German Club. A particularly good meal - a "Sunday meal" so to speak - was served. We also got to know other resident Swiss people, such as Emil Iseli from Zurich and his Mexican wife Rosita, whom he met during his many years in Mexico City where they had married. Emil worked

TO THE HORIZON AND BEYOND

in a weaving mill that processed cotton and trained local employees. They worked with the Swiss company Saurer Arbon, which had developed an embroidery machine that operated via a punch card system. During a visit to the factory, Emil proudly showed us how this punch card machine could conjure up beautifully embroidered, multicoloured flowers and ornaments on a piece of cloth. He also led us into the huge hall in which 300 rattling machines created an unbearable noise. Here, large quantities of cotton were processed, which generated so much dust that one could hardly see the end of the hall. The countless machines literally shook the floor. Young, dust-covered women with headscarves sat bent over these infernal machines and worked on them like resigned slaves. I felt sorry for them. It seemed inconceivable to me that these young women working for hours, in the midst of such noise, dust, heat could concentrate on their task with a rattling floor. They seemed to me exploited and tortured by machines for the sake of a meager salary. At that time, Sudan was one of the largest cotton producers in the world. In the vast plain between the Blue and the White Nile, the Ghezira, stretched over a length of almost 300 kilometers, the cotton field were laid out like a chessboard. The white, woolly cotton had to first be collected then processed before being exported to all over the world. Hearing the word cotton I remember this inhuman, noisy dusty working environment.

Our Swiss national day was also of great importance in Sudan. Before the 1st of August Daniel Aviolat always sent out invitations for a cocktail party. Of course, the Swiss people were invited and guests from other embassies as well as representatives from the Sudanese Government. Here we got to know the German

Ambassador Michael Jovy and his wife Linda, who came from Guyana in South America. Linda and Ann hit it off straight away and soon became very good friends. Linda was an excellent cook. From then on, she regularly invited us to dinner at the Ambassador's residence. Sometimes Ann helped her in the kitchen and studied some of Linda's cooking. At that first cocktail party, Ambassador Michael Jovy told us how, in early March, he had very luckily escaped a terrorist attack. He had attended an important meeting with other ambassadors at the Saudi Arabian embassy but had to leave early because he himself had guests from the German Bundestag and had to look after them. Just fifteen minutes after Michael Jovy had said goodbye, a Palestinian squad from Black September stormed the Saudi Arabian embassy, taking the diplomats present as hostages and demanded for the release of Palestinian prisoners in Israel as well as the Baader-Meinhof Group in Germany. A day later the last ultimatum had expired, and US President Richard Nixon had refused to negotiate - the terrorists shot the American Ambassador Cloe Noel, his first secretary and a Belgian diplomat. The one they had hoped for, the most important hostage escaped them: the German ambassador.

We were often invited to cocktail parties by foreign embassies, usually on their national holiday. Ann always moved with confidence and ease among these dignitaries. We didn't like standing around alone with a glass in our hand, so got practiced in asking questions to interlocutors and receiving useful information. In between, we quickly picked a small snack from a tray or grabbed a new drink. Here we met diplomats, ministers, civil servants or representatives of foreign organizations and companies. For the first time I met East German diplomats from the former GDR or

East Germany. Although, or precisely because I am opposed to the communist system, it interested me to talk with one of their representatives. But I was disappointed, because apart from general phrases, nothing illuminating was heard.

As I was driving around dusty Khartoum every day, I needed to go to the traffic office for the driving test. As the officer in charge was reading my Swiss driver's license with all the vehicle categories listed, he waved, smiled, and pulled a new Sudanese driver's license out from a drawer, wrote down my personal details in Arabic and stuck a passport photo on to the last page. This driver's license was a green 25-page booklet that described traffic regulations by means of drawings and brief instructions. For example, it was made clear that before turning left, you must stretch your left arm horizontally out of the window. Before it was necessary to turn right, stretch an arm out of the window and wave your hand to the right. I didn't need to signal like this, my VW had its own indicators.

In Sudan at that time, traffic was driving on the left side and there were no traffic lights anywhere. You only saw a tiny traffic jam occasionally in front of railway barriers, which usually remained closed indefinitely. Huge areas in Sudan are desert and my desire to drive through a desert grew. Ann immediately agreed to come along. Early on a Friday morning Dimitri provided us with his Safari Land Rover for the adventure. So, we drove with 20 liters of drinking water, food, a full reserve petrol can, and headed north with a shovel and some wooden boards. The area quickly became lonely. Now and then a miserable shrub stood near the few lanes in the sand. Soon we were all alone in an endless plain. All around and as far as the eye could see, nothing but sand. In the distance, the horizon as a fine line.

At first, I was careful to stay on the lane, my only clue. Soon, however, I began to boldly drive around, a feeling of infinite freedom gripped me. It was a wild escape from everyday life. I could hardly believe it. For the first time, literally nothing stood in the way of my life. I started singing out loud. Ann listened with a smile, then happily hummed along. Then I stopped and we got out and let the indescribable expanse of sand affect us. Sand, nothing but sand and sky and in between the horizon line, plus we two little humans with a Land Rover. I took Ann's hand, and we walked a little away from our vehicle, but only so far that we could still hear the engine running. I had not dared in this seclusion to turn the engine off. Like Adam and Eve, we seemed to be the only people on earth here. Too bad I forgot to bring an apple. It wasn't until I took Ann in my arms and kissed her in this otherworldly place that we suddenly felt how hot the sun was beating down on us. We walked back to the Land Rover and drove on, following the wheel tracks in the sand, towards the horizon, which refused to come any closer. Then it came to me the thought of letting Ann drive a little. Here in this boundless desert hardly anything go wrong. With somewhat mixed feelings, Ann sat on the driver's seat. I slipped her another pillow, gave her the necessary instructions on how to use the clutch and operated the shift for her. When the heavy Land Rover started humming, Ann got visibly nervous and looked at me questioningly. I encouraged her to accelerate, take slight curves, then brake a little again, continue and follow the tracks in the sand. Ann's worried frown lines slowly smoothed out, she seemed to gain trust. Suddenly a small, white cloud of dust rose on the horizon and slowly got bigger. A truck or bus seemed to be coming towards us but was certainly still several kilometers away. Ann yelled, "What am I supposed to do now? Please help me!" I had to smile because my poor wife was afraid of a distant cloud of dust rising behind the horizon. So, I asked her to stop, and we changed seats. Soon, two fast-moving trucks came into view. Because of the huge dust that was thrown up, we crossed at a great distance. Shortly thereafter, I turned around a long 180-degree curve to make our way back home. Apparently, this little desert adventure had triggered something in Ann because a few days later she expressed her desire to take driving lessons. The next day before sunset we drove to the city in the Volkswagen, where the semi-desert begins. There Ann got back behind the wheel and began to carefully drive around the bushes. Some skinny rabbits appeared suddenly and ran away looking for cover elsewhere. A week later, Ann booked driving lessons at a Sudanese driving school and sitting at the steering wheel of a Morris Minor car, with a large L on the hood, began driving around downtown with an instructor. At that time there was still little traffic. There was only one traffic light at one crossing. Ann progressed quickly and asked the driving instructor to teach her how to reverse as well. He waved it off: "We don't need to practice that; reversing is not required at the driving test!" But Ann replied: "I want to learn it for myself!" The guy remained unapologetic: "Don't you worry, that is why!" At the driving test a little later, everything went well, but when the examiner directed Ann into a dead end in front of a wall and let her stop, her misfortune was imminent. With a bit of luck, she nevertheless managed reversing, and Ann passed her first driving test with flying colours. I was happy for my wife and finally also for me; because she then drove me once or twice a month, at 5 o'clock in the morning to the airport when I had to fly to South Sudan.

The teacher training program in Malakal began more and more to be the centre of my task. A Cessna chartered by Baustrag had civil engineer Paul Osborne and his wife Joyce flown from Nairobi to Malakal. They rented in Malakal town, a simple but solid house, where I was also allowed to stay when I visited. "Chez Ahmed" was now history for me.

The actual start of construction was delayed, however, because the requested sand from Juba had not arrived. On the White Nile in South Sudan old paddle wheel steamers operated, transporting passengers and goods, with side-mounted barges dragged along behind. It was planned that our sand should be brought to Malakal with such a boat. But for some time, there had been no shipping traffic on the Nile. The countless water hyacinths floating on the river blocked the ships, because these water plants clogged the paddle wheels. The 900 kilometer long river path between Juba and Malakal passed through the Sudd, Africa's longest wetland.

Brought many years before by the British colonizers as ornamental flowers, water hyacinths became more and more of a plague. They spread rapidly into the inaccessible swamp areas. They were chemically controlled by boats and low-flying airplanes that sprayed them and they then sank. But in the swamps, themselves they grew rampant and from there they kept entering the White Nile. During the years of civil war, the hyacinths spread rapidly and became far worse. Paul Osborne finally made the decision to look for sand closer to Malakal. As if prospecting for gold, his workers began digging deep holes in various places along the banks of the Nile in the loamy earth. In vain, there was no sand anywhere. Only at the last test drilling – just near our notorious guest house "Chez Ahmed" – they finally found sand deep down. However, the sand was heavily soiled with earth. Digging out the soiled sand by shovel, then flushing the earth out with Nile water was a long and sweaty task.

That was one problem solved, but the second was already pending; because sand alone is not enough for building, it also requires cement. So, we urgently needed at least 30 tons of cement. This in turn was rarer than gold in Sudan.

There was a cement factory located in Kosti on the White Nile, 400 kilometers north of Malakal and a huge paperwork conflict broke out between me and the Sudanese authorities. In order to produce the 30 tons of cement, the cement factory required the appropriate permits from two ministries. I had to accept this and added copies of the UNHRC project contract with the cement order. But the Sudanese bureaucrats were even slower than the sluggishly flowing Nile. Their answer was always the same: *"Bukra"* (tomorrow) while smiling at me meaningfully. At 2 p.m. they closed their office and that was it for the day. It was the "end of the show." In addition to promises, many *"bukras"* and later "nos," I tried to apply more pressure. One day I went to the historic government palace on the bank of the Blue Nile, decorated with huge elephant teeth. Michael Jovi, the German ambassador tried to help and sent me a letter of recommendation to the Government. A senior official promised to present this to the responsible ministers. It was of no use in the end, my one-man fight against the Sudanese lethargy continued. At least the people I spoke to in the ministries were always very friendly, showed understanding and benevolence, which, however, was of no use for our struggle. It always reminded me of my time in Anatolia when I waited in Government offices drinking tea. In Sudan, I was presented with a glass of water. I decided to visit the cement factory myself. Dimitri was immediately willing to accompany me. A chauffeur driven Land Rover was the order of the day for Dimitri. Ann came along too. We drove at full speed, leaving a long trail of dust clouds behind us on the flat desert landscape to Kosti, 350 kilometers away. The cement factory there was running at full speed. According to the statement by the Director, each cement order always took longer than planned, because the priorities always had to be set according to orders from Khartoum. We also wanted priority but of course this could not be achieved in Kosti itself. The managers on site were only order recipients. So, after our return I asked again and again for a meeting with the Minister of Education. I could hardly believe it, when he granted me a short audience, even letting his first director to attend. Maybe some pressure had been exerted on the minister from other quarters; because I had fully informed the directors of the local UN development program, as well as UNHCR, about the sluggishly unacceptable bureaucracy. So, whatever it was, the minister knew, I didn't need to repeat it. For this I demanded with all clarity, the delivery of our 30 tons of cement must be lifted to the highest priority. On the same day I doubled my request by confirming my request in an urgent letter to the minister. However, it took another two months until the 30 tons of cement was finally ready in Kosti. So, this fight alone had taken a full six months. Now it was just a matter of organizing the transport of the cement. To my great joy help was offered by our good friend Paul Samuel in Malakal, the Police Commander of Upper Nile Province, when he offered us the spacious police ship. There was only the need to pay for the fuel and other modest, expenses that were incurred. Paul Samuel had acted with foresight, given his great interest in the war-ravaged and neglected South Sudan. He knew exactly how important the teachers' seminar was for the future of the region. During my next visit to Malakal, this police ship had already been provided for the trip to Kosti. Paul and Joyce Osborne and I did not want to miss this opportunity and got permission to go on board to reserved cabins.

The next morning, this older ship, 30 meters long and powered by a diesel engine left early. An eight-man uniformed crew was on board. Well decorated and clean, the police ship, with its cabins and toilets presented itself as a small nostalgic steamer. The three of us felt like guests; especially because we were served from the small kitchen with simple, tasty meals. The long journey down the Nile, through mostly flat landscapes was rather monotonous. Only now and then were there a few huts on the bank. The helmsman on the other hand, had to be careful to dodge around the many floating water hyacinths. On the other hand, many crocodile varieties seemed to be sleeping on the muddy shores. The captain watched these dangerous creatures very attentively, but that time none seemed a risk to us.

Late afternoon the prominent steel railway bridge at Kosti appeared. Our ship docked at one of these bridge piers in the middle of the White Nile. It was a hard climb for Paul, Joyce and me up narrow steel ladders onto the bridge. Beside the railway line was a road but without traffic, so we three walked to the Kosti railway station. As I was planning to return to Khartoum the next day, I asked the stationmaster when the next train would arrive and was told that evening at 9 pm. Wow, that was perfect I thought and immediately booked a seat. I said goodbye to Paul and Joyce, who wanted to spend the night in a local hotel and return to Malakal the next day with the cement on the police ship. However, my overnight train from Wau in the south did not arrive as scheduled. It arrived at midnight - three hours late. When I previously had complained to the station manager about this long delay, he laughed: "This is the train that should have arrived a week ago. It is seven days and three hours late!" The train was hopelessly overcrowded as a result. Pretty tired, I got in and moved to the compartment that was reserved for me. It was stuffed to the ceiling with all sorts of wooden furniture. All the seats on the whole train were overcrowded. The conductor shrugged his weary shoulders when I gave him my reserved ticket and pointed meaningfully at the crowded compartment. Undeterred, he shuffled on. I had no choice but to lie down on the hard, dirty floor in the corridor, with my travel bag for a makeshift pillow. In the hours that followed, fellow travellers kept stumbling over my feet and legs. Sleep was out of the question. Then and again the train squeaked to a halt at a station. At the town of Sennar, we reached the Blue Nile. The slow, nocturnal journey continued and stopped at Arabic sounding stations like Hag Abdullah, Wad Medani and El Hassaheissa. At five o'clock in the morning the train stopped again, but oddly enough nobody left or entered. So, I got up and looked out of the window. I was amazed to find the train had stopped in the middle of the desert. As I looked around to ask why, one passenger was happy to explain to me: "The loc driver is praying!" Indeed, when I leaned out of the window, I saw a man kneeling on a small carpet in the sand in front of the engine, praying in the direction of Mecca. At the end of this sleepless night, the train finally pulled into Khartoum station. Ann stared at me in disbelief when I came home in a cab, saw my dirty clothes and the tired, unwashed face with reddened eyes. A long shower and a quick breakfast woke my spirit for life again; however only briefly. Quickly, I was overpowered by the need for some well-deserved sleep.

We had been living in Khartoum for more than a year by then. Holidays were due, if possible in a cooler place than a Sudanese oven. That's why we decided on the Ethiopian highlands. We flew on August 1974 with Sudan Airways to Asmara, a city located at 2,400 meters altitude, (Asmara is now the capital of independent Eritrea). We were pleasantly surprised at how well Asmara presented herself. How well dressed and friendly the self-confident people were towards us. The cool temperatures under the bright blue sky did us good. They were like a refreshment and for three days, we wandered through that beautiful city with its large range of goods. We went to the cinema and twice to church. Naturally, we also tasted the Eritrean cuisine in the restaurants. We enjoyed these holidays and made other short visits to various cities in Ethiopia becoming acquainted with the culture of these countries. In the back of my mind however, was my work.

We rounded off our vacation by taking a flight to Nairobi to discuss the Malakal project in the Baustrag AG office there. The most important thing at this point was the search for improved communication between Nairobi, Malakal and Khartoum. The conversation was not encouraging. This much was clear, this problem would continue to exist for the time being. There was no quick fix in sight. It was reassuring that the problem was identified, and a solution was being sought.

The next day we flew back to Khartoum, home to the familiar dry heat. A week later I flew back to South Sudan, this time to Wau, the capital of Bahr el-Ghazal Province. This is 450 kilometers southwest of Malakal. Here, in the new midwifery school, the first thirty students had passed their requested exams. Jakob Frick from the Norwegian Red Cross requested that I, the Chief delegate, should hand over the certificates to the young midwives. During a solemn ceremony I gladly fulfilled this task and found joy in these radiant young professional women who, to great applause from the many relatives and guests, received their certificates. The Norwegian Red Cross and its busy Jakob Frick was also proud of this, as this sole midwifery school had made an important contribution to the development of a region severely damaged by the civil war. Two days later, Jakob and I drove in the Land Rover, with three reserve canisters of petrol, on narrow dirt roads to Juba: around 650 kilometers. After a two-day, sometimes adventurous journey, we arrived at our destination and looked around the Nile port.

The first wooden elements for Malakal had arrived on trucks from Nairobi a month before; after a 1,000-kilometer-long journey through Kenya and Uganda. The problem we now had was: the large articulated trucks were not allowed to cross the White Nile. The steel bridge was too weak. The prefabricated narrow bridge was a recently constructed gift from the British Government. I got a queasy feeling every time I drove over this shaky bridge. It's inconceivable how it could withstand a semi-trailer truck heavily laden with wood! All the material therefore had to be reloaded onto smaller trucks for the last 15 kilometers to the Nile port and then stored in a shed for months because there was no transport to Malakal for an indefinite period. The old Nile paddle steamers, which were in need of repairs, sailed to Juba irregularly, and the barges were also rare. Even if we were awarded an empty barge to load with the components – a lot could still go wrong before the finally refuelled paddle steamer left the next day. Possibly, the captain refused to sail for flimsy reasons, which sometimes happened. Either he had priorities to obey which we did not know about, or he had been swayed with bribes. What we did know only too well, was that Mr. Nile Captain had the final say. More than 1,400 kilometers away in his office, the Minister of Education had no influence at all. Even the Police chief of the province of Upper Nile, who had been so kind to us, was powerless. All these difficulties caused great delays in the construction of the teacher seminar.

Once, in Juba, I waited for two days for a scheduled flight to Malakal. The plane showed no signs of arriving and a truck driver, leaving early in the morning for Malakal offered a seat in his empty truck, which I gladly accepted. The over 700 kilometer gravel road was narrow and bumpy. There was almost no traffic, and we regularly saw wild animals. In Bor, close to the White Nile, the driver decided to spend the night on a large meadow. We ate our sandwiches and drank the clean water the driver stored in a large bladder. I spent an uncomfortable night on the hard and dirty floor of the truck. Next morning at 6 am while washing my face at the water hyacinth infested White Nile, I could suddenly hear the roaring of an engine. A large dark green biplane came flying around the bend of the White Nile, at best about 10 meters above the water, spraying big clouds of chemicals onto the floating water hyacinths. I ran like a sprinter back to the truck.

On this long trip to Malakal, we drove through two or three villages were children and adults walked around completely naked. This obviously was their traditional way of life. To my eyes it looked entirely natural and I felt proud that I'd had a unique chance to see that far into the past of humanity, to see "beyond the horizon."

About an hour later we saw two people walking on the gravel road in the distance. When we came closer, they were not people but two emus', running away at full speed. Later our truck noise stirred up a herd of gazelles. Just 20 meters from my window seat, they graciously jumped high and far, trying to compete with the speed of the truck. What a pity I didn't have a movie camera to record these beautiful gazelles trying to overtake us, crossing the road, and disappearing into bushes. The driver eventually slowed down to let them pass.

It was a very hot day and we had to drink a lot of water from the bladder hanging near the front of the truck. The bladder unfortunately seemed to leak and we eventually ran out of water and became very thirsty, but Malakal was still far away. Eventually we reached the village of Duk Faiwil where villagers led us to a soak well and pumped up a bucket of water. From the bucket they filled us two glasses. I couldn't believe what I saw. The water in the two glasses was almost dark brown. I wanted to drink and quench my thirst, but hesitated, afraid of what I saw. Bystanders smiled at me, and I realized I had no choice. The driver had more courage and quenched his thirst, even asking for a second glass. Now I overcame my fears and began to drink. The surprise was the water was not only cool, but it tasted good. Now I also drank a second glass and smiled at the bystanders. Before we left, I even drank a third glass of brown Duk Faiwil water. The driver said, we had to hurry on, because the last ferry over the Sobat River, before Malakal, was leaving at 5 p.m. The driver drove on faster and faster on this bumpy, curving dirt road, while I was praying that the brown water in my belly didn't create problems. It didn't. The brown soil in the water from deep in the grown was obviously pure. Unfortunately, we reached the Sobat River too late, the ferry was already on the other side at Doleb Hill. So, we slept a second night in the truck. We reached Malakal safe and well next morning and this bumpy truck journey from Juba was indeed one of the most fascinating trips of my life.

When the first building materials finally arrived in Malakal, the rainy season had already begun, and the torrents from the sky turned the site into a mud bath. Despite this, site manager Paul Osborne tried with his six professionals from Uganda and Kenya, the local workers, and henchmen – as best they could, and the circumstances permitted – to advance work.

A Cessna came every five weeks or so, flown in from Nairobi, carrying food, tools, and more materials for the team. These flights were very important for us because there was almost nothing to buy on the local market; now and then it had potatoes, onions, or tomatoes on offer. Even in the few shops you could hardly find essential groceries. The locals lived mainly on millet, which they grew themselves. If we foreigners hadn't been taken care of from outside, the project could hardly have been realised. The Swiss engineer came on the supply flight from Nairobi to talk to Paul and to discuss further work and upcoming problems with me. As before, the only means of communication we had was the lengthy postal route. By the time the letter arrived, the problems described therein were no longer relevant. So, I had to regularly fly to Malakal with Sudan Airways to discuss issues with Paul Osborne in person.

Even if Malakal was a remote, boring place, there were also beautiful things to see there. For example, the glorious sunsets during the rainy season, when the red-gold shining sun on the horizon slowly disappeared into the distant swamps. The best location to take photos was the elevated bank of the Nile near the river port. Sometimes, in addition to the low sun, spectacular lightning flashed out of the thunderstorm clouds, or distant flocks of birds flew slowly through them in wedge formation.

One day we met Conradin Perner, a Swiss from our Bangladesh deployment. He had worked for the ICRC as Chief delegate in Chittagong, in the local delegation. He had already been to Congo and Vietnam before. Conradin, from Davos, was a professor of literature and taught French, from 1974 to 1976, at the University of Khartoum. He told me he was planning to go to a remote area in South Sudan, and intended to live with the Anyuak tribe to research their way of life, culture and language. A difficult and challenging undertaking for a European. But Conradin was fascinated by going there, living with a not yet explored tribe in the wilderness and remoteness of South Sudan. The area closed to the outside world for several months a year because of the long rainy season. I was amazed when Conradin explained his plan to me, admired him because he had the courage and determination to be a loner and embark on such a difficult research mission. He spoke of his plan rather casually like it was nothing special. Just him, with a backpack, living with a tribe in the distant wilderness. Nearly forty years passed before I found out how successful Conradin Perner was in South Sudan. Gifted the name *Kwacakworo*, he had become a highly respected and honoured man there. Five days after South Sudan became independent in July 2011, in the capital Juba, he was awarded honorary South Sudanese citizenship by President Salva Kiir Mayardit. During a long civil war before independence, Kwacakworo became famous in South Sudan for gathering thousands of child soldiers and leading them to safety in a week long march to the border of Ethiopia. He also wrote four large volumes of books from his studies and experiences with the Anyuak. We continue to be in touch with each other until this day.

At the end of 1975 we received a surprise visit from an old acquaintance, also from our time in Bangladesh. Kurt Herzog, the Balair's chief pilot, with his partner Annemarie Kuhn, came to Sudan to witness a commemorative plaque. On the evening of May 15, 1960, two crews on board a Balair DC4 departed Khartoum on an empty, return flight to West Africa. That night the DC4 crashed into a cliff at Jebel Marra, near Nyala, in the Sudanese province of Darfur. All twelve crew members died. For Kurt Herzog, the journey to Jebel Marra was an affair of the heart, he had known both crews well. The commemorative plaque was professionally installed at the crash site, in the village of Toli and Kurt and Annemarie were warmly welcomed. Kurt told us after returning that the residents had salvaged a lot of debris from the DC4 and used it to forge cookware.

In November 1975, Ann and I had been in Sudan for two and-a-half years. The Arabic characters on the monthly electricity bill I could now decipher, but I still struggled with the language itself. My time as chief delegate here was coming to an end. Dimitri Severi, Jacob Frick, and Professor Kalinowski had already returned home as the Red Cross League programs had all been completed. I stayed until the SRCs Malakal project could finally be finished. My flights to South Sudan continued unabated in that time.

* * * * *

On one return flight from Wau to Khartoum I had a real stroke of luck. I happened to be sitting next to "His Majesty" the Minister of Communication. On these flights there is only one class, namely economy. My neighbour, a large tall South Sudanese, with tribal marks carved on his forehead, had recently been appointed as minister. I had the unexpected chance to lay out all our Malakal problems. He showed interest and shortly before Khartoum he promised to give us permission for a radio station in Malakal. "Bring me all the documents and write an application," he encouraged me. I didn't need to be told twice. Two days later I handed in this weighty post at the ministry. Then it took another two months until the approval came; but it came. This radio connection was a quantum leap for the project. Paul Osborne was finally able to discuss the problems with his bosses in Nairobi on a daily basis, however this worked only for a limited time. The suspicious Sudanese security office overheard and sometimes interfered in the conversations, because these were direct talks between South Sudan and Kenya.

They seemed to distrust the talks, and probably considered them to be sharing of secret information. For this reason, the permit for this very important radio traffic was unfortunately revoked after just two months.

In December 1975, Ann and I flew to Switzerland with Swissair. We needed a vacation and spent most of our time in Interlaken with my parents. Ann could now speak German with them since attending the language course at Goethe-Institute in Khartoum. A few times I took the train to Grindelwald to ski, speak and hear the familiar Grindelwald dialect. Before the return flight we visited my superiors at the Swiss Red Cross in Berne and reported on the extremely difficult progress in the Malakal Project.

Back in Khartoum, the end of the Malakal project gradually became apparent, and we began to make plans for the future. This time we wanted to stay in Switzerland. Ann deserved to find a new home and to settle down even though I still didn't have much "seat leather" myself. Finally, something happened in Juba. The sustained and increased pressure from various quarters on the river port authorities there finally had an effect. Excuses were no longer accepted. When Paul and I flew for the umpteenth time to Juba, two barges were just being loaded with our material. The paddle-wheel steamer that powered the side-mounted barges on the Nile, almost 900 kilometers to Malakal, was ready to leave. We were happy and relieved, but still only cautiously optimistic, because things could still go wrong on the four-to-six-day river journey. The Steamer only needed to have a defect, a leak or hit a sandbar or the river be covered with water hyacinths. For all these reasons I had no interest in going. Paul and I preferred to fly back to the construction site in the twin-engine Cessna, the next day from Nairobi, and land in Juba. Eight days later, the Nile steamer arrived in Malakal with our components. A happy day for all involved. The buildings were erected in record time within a few dry days. When the concrete floor was dry, desks, tables and blackboards were taken to the various classrooms. The prospective young teachers were finally able to start teaching. We were amazed, how many future teachers arrived in a short time. There must have been hundreds. The school authorities organized a modest opening party, which unfortunately I was unable to attend, as I had to take a return flight. No other airline have I flown as often, as the twin-engine Sudan Airways Fokker Friendship. I boarded one of these planes a whopping 120 times, and always felt safe and in good hands.

A few weeks before our journey home to Switzerland, Ann and I went through the most difficult week of our Sudan years. At dawn on July 2, 1976, a "Sunday Friday", Ann and I were rudely torn from sleep by the sound of gunfire. It came from the direction of the airport, barely 800 meters away. Something was obviously going on there. Also, from the city we heard explosions, possibly the launching of heavier weapons. It was becoming light, the phone line was dead and Radio Omdurman was no longer broadcasting. We saw armed soldiers and civilians hurrying across the nearby sandy field and away from the noise of battle. We were forbidden to leave the house for three days, and we had to ration our food supplies. It quickly became clear that an attempted coup was going on as we kept hearing gunfire and explosions. More than a thousand armed mercenaries trained in Libya, from the Libyan Ma'tan Es-Sarradrove in fifty heavy trucks drove through the desert landscape of the Libyan Sudanese border, through Kordofan and Darfur towards Khartoum. The commander was the Sudanese, ex-Brigadier Mohamed Nour Saad, head of operations for the former Sudanese Prime Minister Sadigel Mahdi, exiled in Libya. The rebels attacked strategic points in Khartoum and Omdurman. Around noon, a Hercules transport plane suddenly appeared over the airport. We watched from our balcony as the dark machine made several low altitude circles above the airport building then disappeared again. It turned out later that it had been a Libyan military plane, which probably had the "government-in-exile" on board. However, without the agreed landing signal from the ground and it flew back to Libya.

Throughout the day strategic heavy fighting occurred. In the afternoon of the following day - the fighting was still going on - President Nimeiri stated on Radio Omdurman that the army was about to defeat the attackers. This was not an attempted coup, but a foreign invasion, according to the President. Over 100 Sudanese Army personnel and an unknown number of mercenaries died in those battles. Countless mercenaries were captured, around 100 of them sentenced to death and executed. Gradually order returned to our lives. Although we had always appreciated the Sudanese people with their warm-hearted hospitality both in the North and South, after these war-like days we looked forward to leaving Khartoum and Sudan.

After we had sold the furniture and household effects, it was time to say goodbye to our friends in the Red Crescent, in the ministries and in the German Club. Our cooperation had been extremely pleasant. After more than three years in Sudan, Ann and

HANSRUDI BRAWAND

I boarded on August 15th, shortly before midnight, the Swissair plane and roared at full throttle over the Blue Nile Cinema and the darkened Blue Nile River. We looked back at the sea of lights of Khartoum and Omdurman for the last time. An interesting chapter in our lives came to an end and the future awaited us in Switzerland. But first went to Istanbul because I wanted to show Anatolia to Ann. She was fascinated by this historic city. Two days later we boarded a bus that, after many hours of driving, many stops and the company of the well-known Anatolian love drama melodies, to Kütahya. I wanted my wife to see some of the schoolhouses which I had built in this province five years earlier. The porter at the entrance to the sugar factory recognized me immediately and called his director who welcomed us into his office. We were allowed to stay in the guest house and eat in the restaurant. The waiters were happy to see me, and I was greeted everywhere in the factory with the euphonious, "*Hosh Geldenis*" (welcome). Hairy Bey, my old friend and chief electrician invited us to his family for dinner the following evening. To my great joy, the next day I met my former translator Ferid, at the building authority. We then paid a visit to the new provincial governor. Ferid informed him about my previous work in the province. The governor immediately arranged for us to have a chauffeured vehicle made available in order to visit some of "my" schoolhouses. The next day, together with Ferid, we drove the next day to Kiraspinar (Cherry Stone), and then to Ikesöyük (Twin Hills) and further to Büyüksaka (Big Sparrow). I was really impressed and delighted at every place. In all three villages, their new school buildings, prefabricated in Switzerland, had been well maintained and cared for. The villagers had built stone walls all around and planted trees. Many residents flocked to our arrival at the Büyüksaka Swiss school buildings. Their serious faces lit up when I greeted them happily. Ferid introduced them to Ann, who immediately took centre stage. The children approached her curiously, with shy eyes. All men greeted me with the familiar "*Hosh Geldenis*" and grasped my hand. These were the first two schools erected under my direction. At that time, without anyone knowing, I had passed my Anatolian "Master's Examination." Now the long, green-clad buildings looked prettier than ever, fitting well into this landscape in front of the old village. The lesson was over when we arrived. In the five classrooms order prevailed. The walls were clean and decorated with drawings and Turkish words were written on Swiss blackboards. Ferid assured me that our school buildings were also good in the more distant villages. Two teachers drummed-up a whole crowd of students to say goodbye to us with a euphonious Anatolian farewell song.

The next day we drove back to Istanbul and flew out the same evening to Athens. We stayed there for a week and saw many sights. At the end of our visit to Greece, we boarded a ship in the port of Piraeus that would take us through the Corinth Canal and via Corfu to Bari in Italy. From there we continued by train to Rome, where we stayed for five days.

For Ann, the devout Catholic, a visit to the Vatican was a very impressive, lasting experience. I was happy for her. Once we were strolling through Rome in the evening, and a man suddenly ran after us and called loud: "Hansrudi!" It was Ross Pike, the FAO man in Malakal. He was sitting in a pizzeria when he saw us walking by outside. The world can be so small!

Arriving in Switzerland, the obligatory debriefing visits soon followed, first to the Red Cross League in Geneva and then to the Swiss Red Cross in Berne. Here, from Toni Wenger, the Swiss Red Cross department manager, I was issued a very good certificate and words of thanks. The medical examiner put me through my paces but was not enthusiastic about my state of health. In Sudan - probably in Malakal at "Chez Ahmed" and unnoticed by me, I acquired amoebic dysentery. The cure of which was soon taken care of in Zurich by a tropical-diseases doctor.

The years in Sudan had drawn to an end and we set out to gain a foothold in Switzerland

CHAPTER SIX

Zurich, Switzerland, 1976-1979: Native Soil

SPOTLIGHT ON ZURICH

Before 1983, the original municipality of Zurich only included the area of today's old town. With two large urban expansions in 1893 and 1934, numerous surrounding villages were incorporated, which grew together more and more over the course of the 19th century. Today the city of Zurich is made up of twelve urban districts, which are numbered from one to twelve.

After three interesting years in Sudan, we were happy to be home in Switzerland, my treasured homeland. We settled down in the beautiful city of Zurich, at the shore of its great lake, surrounded by hills, forests and great walking tracts. I had previously lived here, knew the town like my pocket and had many sports friends. We stayed a few days with friends until we found a small, temporary furnished apartment in the suburb of Schwamendingen, close to a

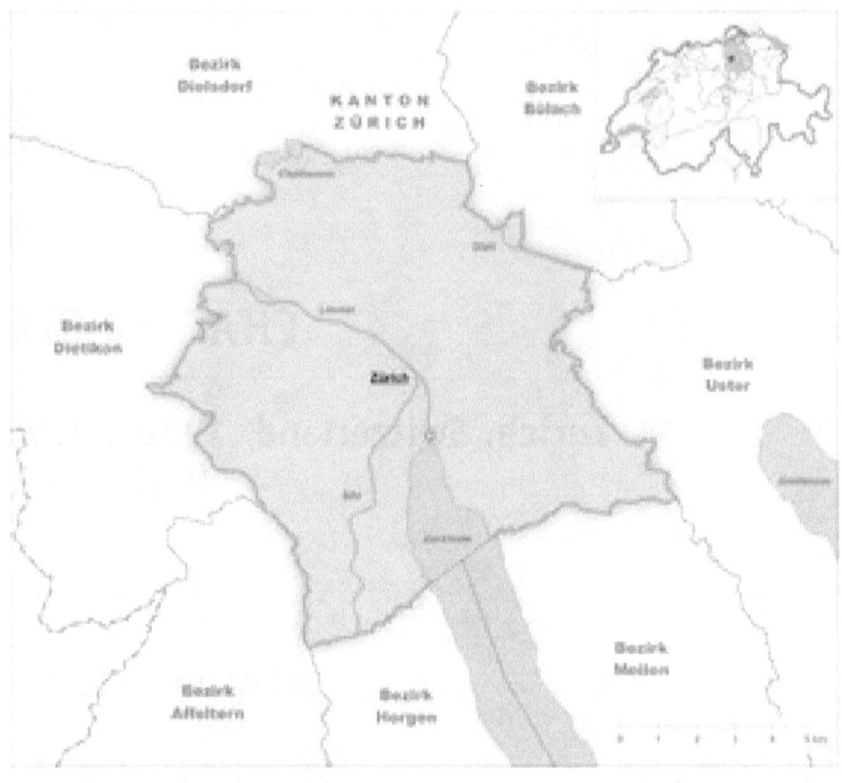

Zurich [4]

hilly forest. The search for a more suitable apartment was now a priority, and we soon found nearby, a nice three-room place in an apartment block for six families. Now we had to look for furniture and household goods to complete our new home. No problem for Ann with her good taste, nor did she shy away from patiently bargaining down prices every time; just as it was common in Asia and Africa. In a short time Ann made our home comfortable. In the meantime, we had even found work. This was an exciting time for us. I started working as a warehouse employee at Bührle Oerlikon.

---

4 https://pl.wiktionary.org/wiki/Zurich#/media/Plik:Karte_Gemeinde_Z%C3%BCrich_2007.png

TO THE HORIZON AND BEYOND

In this well-known factory, I went from being a Red Cross man to a guy who used a crane to move gun barrel blanks and other components from the warehouse onto trucks - from Red Cross to warrior. This was the same factory which manufactured 20 mm Antiaircraft cannons, the ones I had pulled on my truck in the Swiss army during my younger years. I had even been able to practice shooting with it.

Ann had found work as an egg beater through Manpower; namely at the Eier (Eggs) Schmid company north of Zurich. She had to crack fresh eggs all day long, separate the egg white and yolk, and discard bad eggs. Of course, that wasn't a dream job either, but it was a start. My wife was soon looking for more interesting work, which she found in the Oerlikon factory Precisa, assembling calculators. As she was always ambitious since a young age, Ann looked for higher-paid work and undertook a course as a data typist. It soon paid off. In the city centre of Zurich, the well-known company Dosenbach Shoes employed Ann as a data typist. She loved her well-paid new job. I was very proud of my wife, in a rather short time she had successfully assimilated well in German-speaking Switzerland. To familiarize herself with Swiss cuisine, Ann also signed up for a cooking class. For two months, I took her to the Zurich cooking studio every Monday evening. I was amazed at how quickly Ann - thanks to her pronounced self-confidence - found her way around her new home. However, I had some problems finding myself at Bührle AG. The problem wasn't the work, it was easy to do; too easy for me. Sometimes I got bored. Added to this was the fact that I immediately felt cramped when I started work early in the morning. Not a good feeling. My supervisor at the metal parts warehouse was a veteran warehouse manager; kind and conscientious, who luckily had a sense of humor. However, I just wasn't used to the time passing so slowly. I missed interesting work with responsibility. Counting and preparing orders and other paper works was easily done. After that, I sat next to my boss in the office for a while and listened again to the long-past episodes and arguments of his 32 years at the company.

My pride and joy as a 44-year-old, was my first car. We had ordered our blue Opel Ascona while still in Khartoum and now repeatedly enjoyed trips into the country side with it. However, once a month we spent the weekend with my parents in Unterseen-Interlaken. When the weather was good, we drove 25 kilometers to Grindelwald, (were I was born), or we indulged in a boat trip on Lake Thun. Ann also enjoyed helping her beloved mother-in-law in the kitchen. The two women could now converse fluently, in High German and liked to laugh together. They had a really warm relationship.

In Zurich, early on Saturday afternoon, we had gotten into the habit of driving to the huge Glatt shopping centre, for lunch and grocery shopping,. After our three years in Sudan, this shopping centre appeared to us like a paradise; with the difference that in Switzerland everything was costly compared to Sudan. All of what was offered, on several floors, was unbelievable. But we were shocked to see how so much food was carelessly thrown away. There was a boom in Switzerland, people could afford a lot. In Sudan, Nigeria and Bangladesh, in spite of income problems people seemed somehow more relaxed. They were also thrifty and hardly threw anything away.

TO THE HORIZON AND BEYOND

I made contact with my old sports friends and soon joined them most Wednesday late afternoons at a sports ground, were we changed into our running gear for a 10 kilometer training run. Everyone was happy I was back in the country taking part in their activities. But something seems to have changed in me. The years in Africa and Asia had left their mark. Compared to the high standard of living in countries of Western Europe, I had experienced the poverty and short-comings of other countries. Strangely, I even felt sometimes a little bit like an outsider in my homeland. Maybe my sympathy was now flowing towards the poverty in the developing world, because I cared for these under-privileged human beings. My thoughts kept wandering between my beautiful, well-ordered homeland and that other world. But I also had made up my mind to stay there in Switzerland with Ann, and settle down. I knew the many memories of my experience in Africa and Asia, would always accompany me and would never let me go. I found it fulfilling. Less good was a certain inner-restlessness I also felt. My homeland seemed to have become smaller and narrower. During this time we were also plagued by great worries about our dear father. An inoperable tumor in his esophagus was giving him more and more problems. He was only able to swallow small chunks and was losing weight. On the 9th of August 1977 he was relieved of his pain and allowed to die. My beloved father had worked very hard all his life for our family and had faced many difficult years with his plant nursery. First, the great depression years during the early thirties and then in 1939, when World War II broke out. My parents had booked our passage for 1st October 1939, on the passenger ship Windhuk, to immigrate to South Africa via Genova in Italy. But this never happened, because the war broke out one month before our departure. My father immediately had to put on his army uniform and leave Grindelwald by train to join his army unit at the border of Italy. Our poor mother had now to care for us two children as well as the plant nursery.

In autumn 1977 our travel fever returned, the distance was calling both of us. So we decided to spend our holidays in Perth, Western Australia, where Ann's eldest sister Susie and some of her nieces lived with their families. Ann had previously visited Perth in 1974. We combined the vacation weeks of two years and left just before Christmas, with Swiss chocolate and gifts packed in our luggage. When we landed in Perth, after what seemed like an endless journey, I had the feeling that I arrived at the end of the world. A welcoming committee of Ann's relatives awaited us. Sister Susie, nieces Una, Hazel and other relatives couldn't wait to hug us. We were lucky enough to be able to live with Una and her husband Edgar. The two had been our guests when we got married in Chittagong. Actually, we had planned to rent a car in Perth to go on excursions, but unfortunately, I forgot to bring my driver's license with me. No ID, no car. That annoyed me, but I quickly looked for a solution. Who knows, maybe there was a chance to get an Australian driver's license? Driving was my forte after all. But in Australia it was left-hand traffic, which reminded me a lot of my Red Cross years. The next day, December 20th, I took the city bus to East Perth and spoke to the Chief of Examiners Mr Bracken. Unfortunately, a driving test was no longer possible before Christmas, all their examiners were fully booked. But he offered to make an exception and personally take my driving test on December 22nd. "But only if you have passed the theory test beforehand," the nice man stated. I assured him of that, thanked him and booked the theory test for next day. Before I left for this test, Una's husband Edgar gave me a booklet about the traffic rules that apply here. I went through it hastily during the bus ride and noticed a few special features. At 2:00 p.m., I sat at a desk with around twenty other – almost exclusively young – examinees and was assigned the questionnaire by an expert. I tackled the task with full concentration. Luck seemed to be on my side: the three or four questions I had memorized on the bus were asked. While collecting the questionnaires, I sent a prayer to heaven, which was answered: I passed my first Australian exam with only two wrong answers out of thirty. Late afternoon I drove around the neighbourhood streets with Edgar in his car for a quarter of an hour. The next morning, Edgar brought his car and at 9 a.m. sharp, the Chief Expert began to guide me through the busy city center. Half an hour later he congratulated me on passing the exam. All I had to do was take the eye test. Only 58 hours after my first arrival in Australia, I proudly held my new driving license in my hands; a real Christmas present.

Christmas, 1977, was an unforgettable experience. Many of Ann's relatives who in 1972 had still lived in Chittagong were now based in Perth. When the new state of Bangladesh was proclaimed at the end of 1971, the Christian Anglo-Indian minority no longer felt comfortable under the new Islamic government. A slow but steady exodus of reliable, Christian professionals began. Whole families emigrated, some to England, others to the USA, Canada and Australia. The formerly close bond and kinship of Anglo-Indians in Chittagong was torn apart. Susie, Ann's eldest sister, was now living with her daughter Hazel in Perth. Her three other daughters Una, Marietta and Maxene also lived there. Duncan, the only son, served in the Australian Army as a tank driver. He always spent Christmas in Perth. Three of Ann's other nieces, Jeannie, Marie and Patsy, as well as other relatives we had known from Chittagong who also lived in Perth. They all lived in their own houses with a garden. That impressed me a lot. Switzerland had significantly fewer homeowners. "A house with a garden, that would be something," I quickly began to dream. On Christmas Eve we attended the solemn midnight mass with our relatives. Then there was tea and cake at Hazel's house. The midsummer Christmas days flew by with food, drink and Merry Christmas wishes. After the Christmas celebrations, Edgar and Una drove us to some of Perth's many attractions.

First, we toured the wooded 400 hectares of Kings Park, next to the city, which is slightly elevated. From up there you have a wonderful view of the nearby city and down to the Swan River, which there, is very wide. The city center was decorated for Christmas, but somehow the midsummer heat didn't suit it. In vain I looked in Perth for centuries-old buildings, ancient churches and monuments, that are common in Europe. It was not surprising, because this beautifully situated city at the Swan River, with its friendly atmosphere, was only 149 years old in 1978 and the population was almost 900,000.

The more trips we made, the more I liked it, the people acted carefree. It was also striking how friendly and helpful they were; and that they called each other by their first names. During the conversation nobody wanted to know my last name, I was immediately called Rudi. Their Australian dialect, however, sounded unfamiliar to me. Especially when they spoke quickly, I had to prick my ears. When we first saw the deep blue Indian Ocean in the suburb of Scarborough, I was amazed. A light grey sandy beach stretched to the left and right as far as the eye could see. We visited this beautiful beach several times, always in late afternoon. We happily lingered there until the huge yellow-orange or sometimes deep red sun slowly sank into the ocean. Excursions in a hired car took us to the South West, to Margaret River, and from Pemberton down to Augusta where the Indian and Southern Oceans merge. A really beautiful region with wine farms, stalactite caves, rocky beaches and huge forests. Every now and then I wondered if I could live in this strange, far-off land. There was a lot to be said for it: the warmth, the vastness, the strange newness, but also the light-heartedness of the people. But the most attractive thing however, was the possibility of owning a house with a garden. However, this would be a bold step to dare a new start so far away from Switzerland – at the age of almost 46. Ann was very surprised when I first confessed these thoughts to her. Her spontaneous answer brought me back to earth: "You must be crazy!" This topic was off the table for the time being. But a few days later, Ann suddenly came up with the idea herself. She had also thought about it in the meantime, since many of her relatives now lived here. She always had a particularly close bond with her kind-hearted oldest sister Susie. While we took some time to reflect, we also informed ourselves about the different immigration categories. It quickly became clear to us: the conditions were strict and our professions were not among the ones they were looking for.

Unexpectedly, Ann had to see a dentist because of a dental problem. Coincidentally, this Dr. Chew had arrived from Malaysia five years earlier. Ann jumped at the chance to ask him for immigration advice. He suggested that we should also apply in the business category, in my case as a pastry chef, to open a Swiss bakery here. That was a very thoughtful suggestion that we took back with us to wintery Switzerland at the beginning of February. Now it was harder for me walking through the Bührle factory gate at half past six every morning to the monotonous work in the warehouse. The almost nine hours of work passed painfully slow. I would much rather have worked 12 to 14 hours in Chittagong again, where my life had been full of activities that needed achieving as time was running out. Here at Bührle, the work was orderly, organized and slow, there was hardly anything exciting to experience; except maybe when the boss recalled past controversies with employees or superiors.

Ann and I took our time with project Australia. Such a giant step had to be considered very carefully, many things had to be considered. We wrote lists with all the pros and cons, discussed them again and again from beginning to end, up and down. We also contacted the Australian Embassy in Berne, which sent us information sheets and visa forms. Our pendulum swung slowly at first, then more and more towards Australia. However, we hesitated because we wanted to try business visas. The crux was that I hadn't worked in my profession for a long time. So I urgently needed new practice as a baker's pastry chef with the appropriate certificate. For this purpose I contacted my old friend Arnold Metzler, an Austrian from nearby Bregenz. He owned a flourishing bakery and confectionery in Zurich. Maybe I could brush up on my old craft with him? Arnold immediately agreed to help me. So, I worked every Friday evening, from midnight until 9 am on Saturday morning, in the warm basement bakery. Arnold was not only a tireless worker, but also an accomplished master of his trade. It was quite exhausting, as I had worked at Bührle all week, came home at 5:30 p.m. on Friday and then had to work a strict overnight shift. It took a while before I got back on my feet with the baking trade. First, making the different doughs in the machine, letting them ferment, weighing the pieces of dough and shaping them into loaves and then letting them rest in the prover on a large wooden board covered with a cloth. After a while, I placed all the raised dough into the oven, only to pull them out again at the right moment as brown, wonderfully smelling loaves of bread. Finally, the many small pastries such as rolls and *gipfeli* (croissants) came along. It was always "Hurry up!" Not a minute was wasted. Towards morning it was turn for the sweets: fruit cakes, Russian braids and small pastries. Dead tired, I returned home at 9:30 am, surprising Ann with fresh bread and sweet pastries; products of that long night. After a warm shower I fell into deep sleep. I stuck to this Friday night work out for three tough months, before I threw in the towel. My professional knowledge and practical skills were sufficiently refreshed. Arnold wrote me the important certificate and gave me some of his tried and tested recipes to take with me. Shortly thereafter we sent our visa application for Australia to Berne. We had no more reservations about venturing into a new future "down under." Ann could "go home" to her extended family in Perth and I would certainly find work. Distance had given me happiness, blessings, more self-confidence, motivation and youthful vitality so far. So I was full of optimism and good cheer.

Two months later we drove to the Australian embassy in Berne with the additional documents that had been requested. An officer was waiting for us. During the interview he finally said that if our application were to be approved, we would have to pass a driving test in Perth. When I then pulled my Australian driver's license out of my pocket and told him how quickly I had passed the driving test, he was amazed and quickly wrote a note in our file. That seemed like a plus for us, a sign that we knew how to help ourselves. Some weeks later an official letter arrived from the Australian Embassy in October. What was in there? Yes or no? We were sitting at the kitchen table, our hearts were pounding and we hesitated for a while before opening this "hot" letter. It was clear to us: our future, our destiny lay in this unopened envelope. We looked at each other. I put my hand on Ann's hand: time stood still for us. Finally, Ann pulled herself together, got up and got the letter opener. Now we held the official letter in our hands, read it together in slow motion and fell into each other's arms. Our visa application had been approved! We were given twelve months to leave Switzerland and immigrate to Australia. It was several days before we were able to "return to earth" and come to terms with this new situation; realising that we had an unimaginable amount of work ahead of us in the coming months. It had been two years since we had returned to Switzerland from Africa, set up our household to gain a foothold in my homeland again. Now we would soon be breaking up the tent again; this time forever! Unimaginable and also unbelievable and yet just right, because one thing was certain:

TO THE HORIZON AND BEYOND

Biafra, Turkey, Bangladesh and the Sudan had turned me into a restless wanderer, who after a certain time had to set off for ever new horizons. In other words, the grass seemed greener and more promising on the other side of the fence. I had become a nomad, always looking for a new meadow. I hated standing still, it put me to sleep. Ever since my apprenticeship, I had always been urged to change, even if I was satisfied with the job in question. I refused to stay in the familiar. Staying in an apparently secure job for many years was something I resisted all my life, it felt like standing still. This was certainly one of the reasons why I blossomed during my temporary Red Cross assignments and limited jobs in between. To continue with this unique kind of nomadic life however was only possible after my marriage with Ann, because she always supported and encouraged me all those many years. She understood and accepted my way of life, my dreams to carry on working beyond the distant horizon, bring support and hope to refugees and the under privileged. They were all suffering exotic strangers at first, but they motivated me to work harder. It was there that I was able to fully develop my potential and prove it with good performances. But my greatest happiness as a restless wanderer was and remains Ann. I had found a miracle, my dear wife and soul mate who went along with me. It would be unimaginable if she had not changed from her original shock at my idea of immigrating to Australia, with her "You must be crazy," statement. But now we both faced another big turning point, one after many discussions we wanted with all our hearts. First, we were faced with lots of new challenges. Not an ordinary one, like from one neighbourhood to another, but from the northern to the southern hemisphere. That meant clarifying, planning, calculating, attacking the savings – and scratching your heads. This also meant giving up a secure job as a middle-aged man and looking for a new job in distant Australia. But that would definitely not be a problem, we were optimistic. At our workplaces we had not yet announced anything about our big plans. My mother didn't say anything when we informed her, she just looked at us with sad eyes. That hurt us, and made us think. We briefly doubted whether our decision was the right one. The sports friends, on the other hand, were quite surprised because I was again standing on a stepping stone. They weren't sure if I would really go through with this "emigration forever." The last months before departure passed quickly. We visited our mother as often as possible. She and Ann always cooked my favourite dishes. At the end of March 1979 we ordered a truck to move our household items, new Swiss furniture and souvenirs, to a Swiss customs, duty-free warehouse. There we loaded a sea container with our possessions saving as much space as possible. Our calculations were correct, everything fitted and as a final step I hung a thick padlock on the container door. Two days later I brought our Opel Ascona to the private car market in Oerlikon. I was lucky there too: I got more for it than I had paid three years before.

We took the train to Interlaken one last time. Since winter had returned, I used April 4th to once again enjoy downhill skiing in Grindelwald on rented skis. Glittering powder snow in the sunshine made it a bit difficult for me to finally say goodbye to my beautiful, so-called glacier valley surrounded by high mountains. The memories of my youth made me feel nostalgic that day. But soon I composed myself. When I was a little boy, didn't I always wonder what it may have looked like behind these giant mountains? Where there also people living there I had wondered? Well, I now knew and was ready for a new start into a very far away future together with my beloved wife Ann. Saying goodbye to my mother at Interlaken train station was very difficult. It hurt both of us to hug my mother, say goodbye and see her tears. Was it goodbye forever? I immediately banished that thought. I just couldn't think about it, instead I looked forward and trusted that she would be with us for a long time.

First, we drove to Basel and boarded a late evening night express Basel-Calais (France) – as the first stage of our trip to Australia. In Calais, without having slept well, we dragged our suitcases laboriously over long, steep stairs to the ferry, which took us to Dover. From there we continued by train to London, where we stayed in a cheap hotel with breakfast. We stayed in London for four days, picked up our prepaid tickets to Singapore and from there to Fremantle-Perth by ship. In London, we also visited Ann's former neighbours in Chittagong; Aunty Eileen and her daughter Yona. We then flew on to Singapore with British Airways, where we boarded the small passenger ship *Kota Singapora* (City of Singapore) on April 19, which was supposed to take us to Fremantle near Perth. Although this ship had a capacity for 300 passengers, only 57 were on board for this seven-day voyage. Shortly after nightfall, the gangway was pulled up, the ropes loosened, and our first sea voyage began. At dinner we got to know three Aussies, Mike and Kevin at the shared table. Both worked as prison wardens in the district town of Geraldton, which is 400 kilometers north of Perth. Victor, another West Australian, was also at the table.

That night we slept well, felt free, relaxed and confident. At breakfast the next morning we ate a lot, the sea air was obviously increasing out appetite. The voyage took us from Sumatra and Java through the Sunda Strait, which connects the Java Sea with the Indian Ocean. Here we passed the volcanic island of Krakatau and looked over devoutly. Only a stump remained of this once-giant volcano after a monumental explosion blew up the uninhabited volcanic island on August 27, 1883. The devastating bang was so loud that people in Western Australia were roused from their sleep. Only a 10 square kilometer stump remained of what was once a 33 square kilometer island. The eruption cloud rose 30,000 meters high and the area remained pitch black for 22 days. A massive, 36 meter high tidal wave rolled over the neighbouring islands of Sumatra and Java, destroying 300 places. Over 36,000 people lost their lives. The tsunami then rolled on to Africa and South America. We couldn't imagine such a catastrophe day, because the sun was shining, the sea was glittering blue, small white clouds crowned the sky and a light breeze caressed our skin. Soon Java and Sumatra disappeared into the distance and the immensity of the Indian Ocean captured us; all around up to the horizon nothing but sunlit, blue water and above us the cloudless sky. Again, I was overcome by this great feeling of vastness, infinite freedom and bliss, just like when we first drove through the desert near Khartoum. Somewhere during this voyage we also crossed the Equator.

This first voyage on the high seas was an unforgettable experience. Among others I raised my hand to be baptised after lunch. Victor, our table mate, acted as the Sea God Neptune with his three prong fork as we crossed the Equator that day. He baptised me appropriately as Codfish. Afterwards I was told to sit at the swimming pool, where a waiter poured spaghetti mixed with ice-cream over my head; big fun for the onlookers.

One morning the captain announced there would be a costume competition that night. We both quickly went into action after we had decided what kind of dress we would appear. I looked for a thin white carton, cut it out like a crown and put it on Ann's head. Now she only had to fold a bed sheet and wrap it around her like a long fashionable dress. I dressed in my white Sudanese *jalabia* and head scarf and put on sunglasses. We appeared on the stage as Ali Ben Rudi and his wife Queen Soraya. We won and received a bottle of champagne. One day the call "land in sight" came out of the loudspeaker. We ran to the rail, peering ahead. A long narrow white shoreline stretched out on the horizon. This could only be our new homeland, the vast 2½ million square kilometers of Western Australia. Sixty times larger than Switzerland. I embraced Ann, we looked at each other questioningly. Our future was finally here in front of us. We had faith in God and hoped for good times. It took two more days for the ship to make its way south along the White Coast, down to the port of Fremantle. It had long since gotten dark when we docked on April 26, 1979, at 7:30 p.m.

Our reception committee was already waiting for us. Ann's relatives stood among hundreds of spectators on the pier, craning their necks and scanning the railing with their eyes. We shouted loudly and waved vigorously until they recognized us and waved back happily. Ann beamed and I was happy for my beloved wife, for this moment was like coming home emotionally after such a long journey. After customs formalities, we lay in the arms of our welcoming committee and heard over and over again: "Welcome to Australia!" In six cars we all drove from Fremantle to the house of Ann's niece Una and her husband Edgar in the suburb of Girrawheen, 30 kilometers away. Here we were entertained and had a lot to tell each other. We didn't go to bed until well after midnight, but we found it hard to sleep because of the excitement. The turbulent months of making the decision "to emigrate, yes or rather no?" the challenging relocation work and even more so the eventful mental ups and downs and saying goodbye had left their mark on us; more than we had expected. Now we had arrived here in our new chosen homeland. It was overwhelming and still hard to grasp. Rather, it was like this: we had arrived with great joy but we weren't yet there. It would be a while before we felt that was a fact.

CHAPTER SEVEN

Perth, Western Australia, 1979-1980: To New Shores

SPOTLIGHT ON WESTERN AUSTRALIA

The state of Western Australia is located west of the 129°E meridian. It is divided from north to south into the diverse Kimberley Plateau with the Bungle Bungles, the Great Sandy Desert, the Hamersley Range (1235 meters), the western part of the Great Victoria Desert and the Nullarbor Desert. Western Australia can be divided into ten geological regions: Perth with Fremantle, Peel, South West, Great Southern, Goldfields-Esperance, Wheat belt, Mid West, Gascoyne-Outback Coast, Pilbara and Kimberley. The total land area of Western Australia is 2,529,880 square kilometers, making it seven times the size of Germany. It's main metropolitan area is the city of Perth. Today it consists of 30 independent municipalities with their own administrations (Local Government Areas). The actual city is comparatively small. Among other

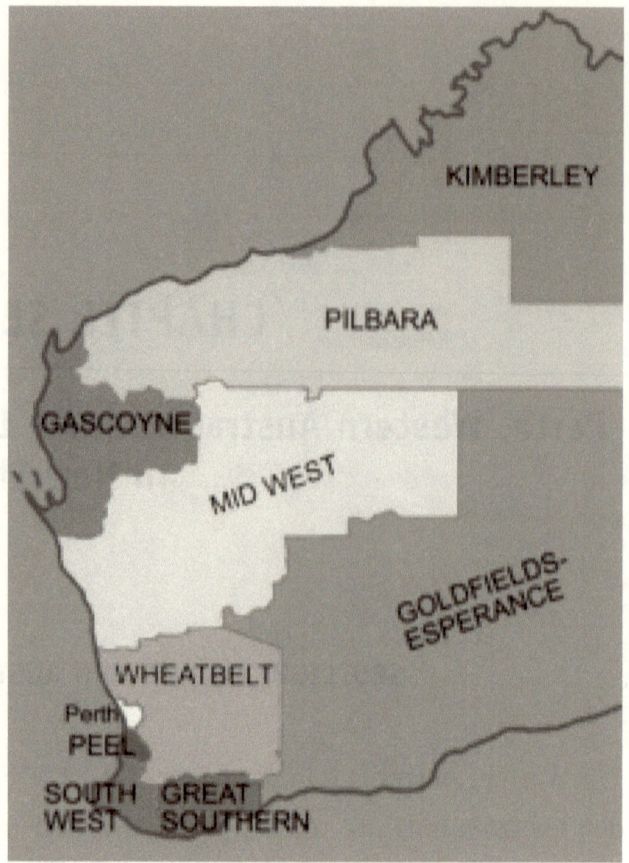

Western Australia [5]

things, it houses the banking district and the stock exchange, the Northbridge entertainment district, a pedestrian shopping street (Hay Street/Murray Street) and the seat of the state parliament, with only 12,000 inhabitants.[5] The Chairman of Perth City Council is also the Lord Mayor and the highest representative of the entire city. Perth is the seat of the Catholic and Anglican Archbishop and, among

---

5   https://commons.wikimedia.org/wiki/File:Regions_of_western_australia_nine_plus_perth.png

other things, an important financial center. In addition, the Perth Mint is one of only two mints on the Australian continent. Perth is also the western terminus of the trans-Australian railway, the Indian Pacific Railway, which runs through the Nullarbor Desert to Sydney.

PERTH: CENTER OF LIFE

We spent the first day in our new adopted homeland with "*dolce far niente*", (carefree idleness), slept in and let ourselves be spoiled by Una's culinary arts. We quickly realized that we absolutely needed a car. The metropolitan suburbs stretched out endlessly, and the bus connections were complicated and time-consuming. But for the time being we had no choice but to visit car dealerships by bus. Used car dealers in Perth had a bad reputation at the time, so we bought a new Datsun Stanza. This was the first step towards a new life, and many more followed quickly. We opened an account at the Commonwealth Bank, registered with the authorities, completed the mandatory medical examination as immigrants and became members of the national health insurance system. Then we started looking for an apartment to rent – although we would have preferred a house. To our great delight we found this in Girrawheen, the suburb where Una and Edgar also lived. Our first rented home down under was a simple three room house. Since the container ship with our furniture and all the household effects had not yet arrived, we made do with the essentials. We could hardly wait for the ship to arrive.

Looking for work was next. Every day we drove to the local employment office, where vacancies for all of Perth were advertised on the walls in the lobby. I immediately started applying to various companies, be it as a store clerk, dispatcher, pastry chef or an office job, and I was able to introduce myself to various companies. It quickly turned out, however, that new immigrants who did not belong to a desired occupational category had few chances. Because I couldn't produce any Australian certificates and my good Swiss certificates and references counted for little, it became difficult to find work. To fill this period of unemployment, I killed two birds with one stone and took a few driving lessons on trucks and trailers, passing the exam at the beginning of June. The following day I had good news in the mailbox. The New Zealand Insurance company in the city invited me to an interview. The sympathetic personnel manager Mr. Clive Lewington offered me the vacant position as stationary officer/manager. He explained that, thanks to the excellent Red Cross certificates, he saw me as the right man for this position of trust, despite lacking the practical experience in Australia. Of course, I said yes straight away and thanked him for his trust. Ann beamed and hugged me when I came home with the good news. I had my first day at work the following week and took the bus to the city centre. New Zealand Insurance was based in the heart of the business and financial district. Mr. Lewington welcomed me and hence forth called me Rudi, because Hansrudi was far too long for him. In Australia, as I soon discovered, many things are abbreviated: Philip becomes Phil, Patricia becomes Pat, Samantha becomes Sam, even a poor 'km' is demoted to a single 'k'. Jack, the outgoing stationary officer, stayed on for another week and briefed me on the various duties and introduced me to the other employees on both floors. Getting off the bus just before

8am I would first have to pick up the padlocked New Zealand Insurance mailbag at the main post office in Forrest Place. At the office I would then open all the letters – except those addressed personally –and take them to the various offices. I was also responsible for all the office supplies, and reordered or purchased them myself when needed. Further tasks consisted of updating statistics and working in the archive. Even the replenishment of spirits in the guest room was my responsibility. The fridge also needed to be regularly de-iced and refilled with cans of beer and Coke. Courier services to other insurance companies and brokers in the area were also part of my duties. Delivering and picking up files, franking outgoing mail before closing time and taking it to the post office rounded off my daily work. I enjoyed walking around outside in the fresh air during working hours. I really liked my job at New Zealand Insurance because I was able to work fairly independently and there was a friendly working atmosphere. The salary, which was paid every second Friday, was unfortunately a bit meager. That didn't bother me too much though, as it was enough to make ends meet. The main thing was: I had a job.

Our container finally arrived in mid-July. We immediately drove to Fremantle, and reported there to the Kuehne and Nagel agency, where a juicy surprise awaited us. The responsible man did not want to hand over the papers to us. We would first have to pay 2,000 Australian dollars in extra costs, he told us. The reason given by the man was that the container had to be shipped via Hamburg. He held the corresponding letter from Zurich under my nose. In a flash, I felt catapulted back into my SRC missions. I refused to pay. Since it was still night in Zurich, I couldn't call them until the afternoon. When we returned the agent made another call to Zurich and repeated the $2,000 request. Now it was my turn to speak to Zurich, and I did so for several minutes, in a loud and energetic Swiss German. The fierce dispute was worth it, as was the information that we had already contacted a lawyer. There was silence on the other end of the phone for a few seconds, then my interlocutor said that in this case he would withdraw the request, and that Kuehne & Nagel Zurich would cover the extra costs. I thanked him and requested that he communicate this decision here and now to the local agent in English. A minute later the papers were handed to me. Financially, that phone call was the most valuable of my life. Ann was impressed and gave me a grateful kiss.

Two days later, one of our friends hired a container truck and took us to Fremantle. A crane heaved the container onto the truck and we happily drove to "our" house. Relatives helped us unload. Finally we slept in our own beds again, were surrounded by our familiar furniture, and enjoyed having all our household goods around us again. Ann had her hands full for days unpacking and getting everything in place. The following weekend, when all of this was done, and our rented home was truly a home, we invited our relatives to a house-warming party. Each family brought something to eat and by 10 p.m. all the beer had been drunk. Immediately someone fetched supplies from the nearby tavern. As much as we enjoyed finding suitable housing, we didn't want to remain renters forever. We dreamed of a house built just for us. But how could we make this happen? Each suburb had its own pricing structure. Land was cheaper to buy here in Girrawheen than anywhere else. Ann's sister Susie and three nieces lived here. So we decided that

Girrawheen would also be the right area for us to really settle down. Every weekend we looked at plots of land, so-called blocks, ranging in size from six hundred to 1,000 square meters. After a long back and forth, we bought a 760 square meter block on Whitworth Avenue in Girrawheen, on a gently sloping former vineyard with a magnificent view. The block was full of wild lupins and dandelions, with a few old vines surviving. We got the property for $12,700– slightly cheaper than advertised. At that time it was about 21,000 francs. Today, such a property in this location costs over 400,000 dollars. We were filled with great pride of ownership when we held in our hands the official property document with our names on it. It was an unbelievable, unreal feeling to own a property in order to be able to build a house. We started by inspecting the model houses of proven construction companies. These companies bought all the blocks in a street in a new suburb and built their different model houses there. Buyers could choose a model and have it built on their own property block with certain modifications for an additional charge. We particularly liked a large four bedroom, 160 square meter home with no cellar, but a garage. Cellars are hardly ever built in Australia. But we also had to consider the extra costs for fencing, concrete for the driveway, sidewalks around the house, the corrugated aluminium sheets for the court yard side, a garden shed for tools, wheel barrows and other things. When we had extrapolated all the costs for our dream house - several times back and forth, critically examined and checked - we spoke to our bank. They gave us a mortgage at a high interest rate and we paid the rest in cash instalments. Now things happened in quick succession.

On October 1, 1979, the foundations were laid, a week later the masons, known as "brickies", began construction. Often we drove to the construction site after work and enjoyed the amazingly fast progress. For Ann and me, building this house was an important high point in our lives. The house was handed over in mid-December, only 11 weeks after the start of construction. Together with the managing director of the construction company, we inspected the whole thing, and had nothing to complain about. Then we held the keys to our own house in our hands. What a fantastic Christmas present! A great dream had come true for us in that moment. We hugged and thanked the Lord that everything had gone so well. We moved in on December 15th. Thanks to my truck driver's license I was able to rent a large, covered truck. Relatives helped make the merry move from Alison Drive to Whitworth Avenue, half a mile away. Telephone, electricity and gas were all connected. All I had to do was mount the green aluminium letterbox on the street. We had bought it months earlier at the Glatt Center near Zurich. After quickly sticking the number 47 and a small white and Red Swiss coat of arms on it and our move was officially over. Our new house was no longer just a house, a home now, our home. From time to time, when we stood on the street and admired our home in the following days, we thought we were still dreaming. For a long time it was almost unbelievable for us that this large, friendly, red-orange glowing single-family house was our own home that belonged to both of us.

Celebrating Christmas in our new home for the first time was something special; especially because the thermometer showed 41 degrees and the air conditioning was running at full speed. That spoiled my Christmas spirit a bit. Nevertheless, we enjoyed these days. On Christmas Eve, Ann and I attended midnight mass at Girrawheen Church. Afterwards we met all our relatives over cake and tea. Then on Christmas Day, everyone met again for lunch and a festive Christmas party with the opening of the many presents. Dancing was the order of the day on New Year's Eve. Ann and I went to a ball for the Anglo-Indians who had migrated here, most of whom were from Chittagong. A nice opportunity for Ann to see old acquaintances again and to renew friendships. The two of us really had every reason to welcome 1980 confidently. A new year and with it a new decade.

A lot of work awaited us at the beginning of the year, especially around the house. The slope below our house, overgrown with weed and old rootstocks, was waiting to be cleared and transformed into a garden. A truck also dropped 10 tons of so-called moss rocks behind the house. These were brown, natural stones of all shapes and sizes, weighing between 5 and 20 kilograms, some covered with decades-old lichens. I had it in my head to build a 22 meter long, 1.2 meter high exposed wall along the slope. Most of the time I worked on Saturdays or after work. As a complete beginner, learning by doing was the order of the day. The mistakes I made taught me to choose the most suitable stone, to work it with a heavy hammer if necessary, then to insert it and connect it with mortar. My first born wall grew a little every week, but 22 meters is long and finding the right stones took time. When the last cornerstone was finally anchored and the many steps concreted, Ann invited me to the cinema as a thank you. In the meantime the cooler autumn had settled in and brought some rain. At the weekends we visited the large nurseries, took advice and gradually bought young fruit trees, bushes, roses, lantana, oleander, bougainvillea and various native wild flowers to green our property. We started by planting young fruit trees, got carried away and ended up with limes, apricots, lemons, mango, plums, guava and pomegranates in our hillside garden. Ann also grew her beloved chilly, parsley and chives. We had to add a lot of manure, fertilizer and compost to get a decent harvest. Memories of father's garden center in Grindelwald returned and I was happy to kneel down, work up a sweat and learn new things.

A nice time for us beginners, we stayed in the garden every day, nurtured our newly planted protégés, encouraged them and were rewarded with wonderful fruits for years to come. Buds, blossoms, green and yellow lemons hung all year round on the fast-growing lemon tree, a natural perpetuum mobile.

I soon got into an everyday routine: after breakfast I walked ten minutes to the bus stop, twenty minutes later I got off in the city center and took the short walk to the main post office to pick up the company mailbag. In the office ten minutes later, I unlocked the mail bag and sorted around a hundred letters. At 4 pm I franked and dispatched the outgoing mail. Shortly after 5 p.m., I came home to Ann and she immediately poured tea for me. After a quick shower I continued to work in the large garden. However, the effortless, routine work, as easy and comfortable as it was, was eventually becoming more and more boring to me and the desire for change was being awakened in me again. Opening a bakery, as we had written in the visa application, was out of the question at the time. The financial risk was too high, and the night work put me off. My train of thought kept drifting away to Asia and Africa. I could do better things there, my inner voice whispered to me; I would be challenged, even if I had to leave my comfort zone in exchange for the conditions of the developing world. A trigger preceded these considerations. Ann had visited a fortune teller, recommended to her weeks earlier because of her interest in the subject. After this visit, Ann reported that the fortune teller said, among other things: "I see your husband. He'll be on a plane at the end of the year and flying somewhere." Of course I listened, but at that moment I couldn't imagine travelling again any time soon. Nevertheless, these words remained "said" and kept haunting me. Although I had long since found the distance I had been looking for, I sometimes asked myself, "Where do I actually belong?" The answer wasn't that easy, because in every country I'd lived and worked, up to then, I'd found for myself a piece of homeland, despite the different climate, cultures and people. I had arrived as a stranger, enjoyed the new, the different, got to know many people, left friends behind every time I said goodbye and always took countless precious, indelible memories with me.

The quiet longing for a "distance," new adventure had returned. Ann sensed the unrest, guessed the cause and said: "Let's talk about what's bothering you, I think I know what it is." I found it difficult to tell Ann about my dreams and aspirations. Admitting to her that I was bored with this well-ordered life – despite the dream house and large garden – made me feel guilty. We were very fortunate to have fulfilled so many dreams in such a short time, yet I wanted to leave again. How could I ask my loved one to move away from here as soon as she had properly "arrived"? How could I be so selfish as to want to take Ann, who felt so at home here in the midst of her many Chittagong relatives, back to any country where I hoped to be of some help; Asia or in Africa with the threat of famine, refugee movements or even civil war. A country where I could help alleviate suffering human beings in need of urgent support. A new task for an experienced Red Cross worker where I develop further my proven potential.

All of this was nagging at me, grinding me down, and I told Ann the same. But I also confessed that the psychic's testimony had been permission for me to engage with these thoughts that were already dormant deep inside. Thanks to the fortune teller, they prophesied. I confessed to Ann that I craved real challenges. "You know, like it was in Biafra, Turkey, Bangladesh and Sudan," I said. "Of course it was never a cakewalk, more often a struggle than work," I continued. "And yet I knew every day how important it was to win this fight." This conversation made it clear to me how important this struggle was to me. That was a difficult challenge for me: in the long term could I stand up to the urge to pull away from my planned, everyday, ordinary life? "It's like sports," I summed up my feelings. "It's a fight with a view to winning." Ann understood very well what I meant. She too had had her thoughts over the past few weeks when she noticed I was often deep in my thoughts. However, she had gotten much further than I dared to and her suggestion overwhelmed me: "You will contact the SRC in Berne tomorrow and register your interest," she said firmly. "Who knows, maybe the SRC will respond quickly, maybe not." It was immediately clear to me that Ann had decided in my favour. "One way or the other," she continued in a firm voice, "You can accept the job that suits you, but I'll stay here for the time being." It was important to her to "hold the fort." "It's important to me," she had said at the end. I couldn't believe that Ann had not only given me permission to go on an SRC mission, but actually understood my need to do so.

The next day I contacted the SRC Berne and said I would like to work for the Red Cross again; preferably in a country that was new to me. The answer was not long in coming. "We are looking for a Deputy Chief Delegate in Somalia, based in Mogadishu." To my great delight, I also learned that Sven Lampell was chief delegate in Somalia. That seemed like a good omen to me. The uneasiness and guilty conscience was still plaguing me, by Ann's moral support allowed me to accept. After that everything happened quickly. I quit my job with New Zealand Insurance and got ready to travel. As always, the SRC in Berne took care of visas and all the other trimmings. Once in Berne I would receive health checks and the information about my area of responsibility in Somalia. But first Ann and I had to get through the goodbye. It was difficult, as we had no idea when and where we would see each other again. What reassured me was the fact that Ann was in good hands with her sister Suzie, nieces and all her other Chittagong relatives who lived here.

I was warmly welcomed at the SRC in Berne. "It is a wonderful coincidence that you are about to embark on a new mission right now!" was the message everywhere I went. The formalities were a habitual matter of course, however I also had to go by train to Geneva to the International League of Red Cross and Red Crescent Societes as Somalia was a mission for the International League of Red Cross. After Geneva I still had one extra day visiting my beloved mother in Interlaken. Then I was on my way. I rejoiced deep inside me. "Somalia, I'm coming!"

CHAPTER EIGHT

Mogadishu, Somalia, 1980-1981

SPOTLIGHT ON SOMALIA

The history of Somalia and its people, are deeply entwined with the history of the neighboring people in Ethiopia, Kenya and Djibouti. It begins in earlier millennia, which cave paintings remind us of, then takes winding paths through various sultanates, the colonial period up to the various civil wars. The British, as colonial masters, initially saw Somaliland primarily as a meat supply station and restricted themselves to indirect rule. The infrastructure was hardly expanded under them. Until 1942, the administrative center of their colony was the port city of Berbera, through which cattle exports were processed, while the interior of the country remained largely untouched. Other colonial masters, the Italians, built banana, sugar cane and cotton plantations in southern Somalia, among other things, and founded several settlements, such as Jawhar. Slavery was abolished under colonial rule, but after the fascist takeover

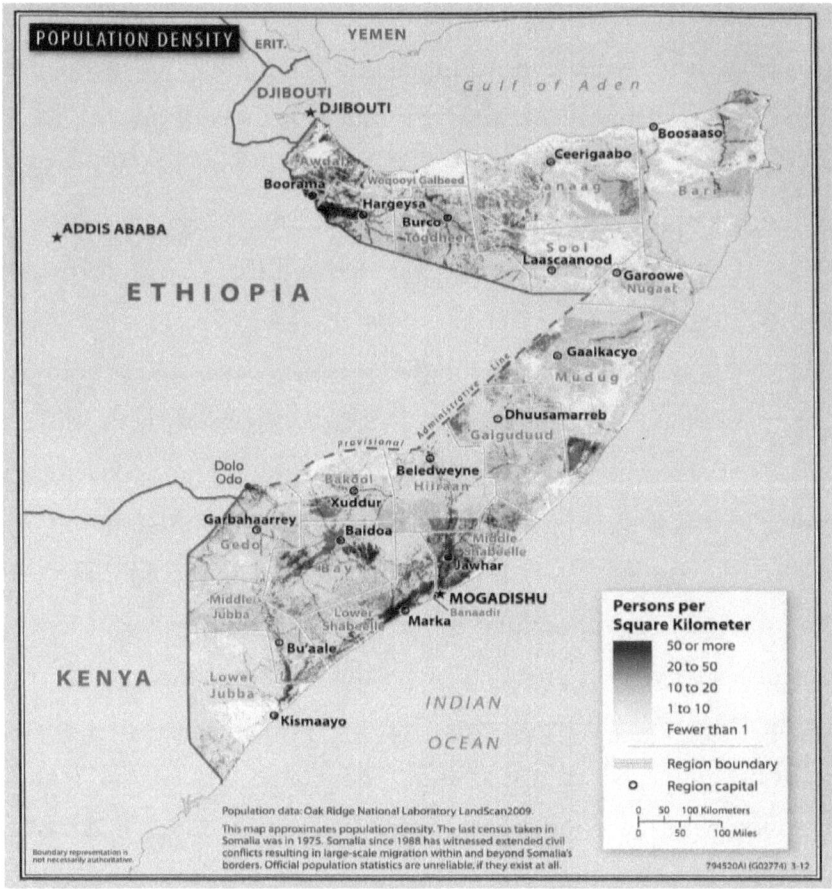

Somalia [6]

in Italy, the Bantu in particular were used for forced labor on the plantations, since only a few Somalis were willing to do voluntary wage labor.[6] After Mogadishu was made the capital of the colony, trade flows increasingly shifted there. Ports in the northeast, like Hobyo, lost importance. There were efforts within the Somali population to end the division of the area and to unite all Somali in one state (Greater Somalia). The Somali Youth League (SYL),

---

6   Source https://maps.lib.utexas.edu/maps/somalia.html

founded in 1943, and the first political party in Somalia, supported this goal. It played a significant role on the road to independence and thereafter; mainly because they was able to work towards their goals across clan boundaries. British Somaliland, which became independent on June 26, 1960, united on July 1, 1960 with Italian Somaliland, which became independent on that day, to form the state of Somalia.

In general, the Somali population was very interested in politics. National integration, however, presented difficulties, as the differences between the underdeveloped north and the more developed south and east were pronounced. The north, inhabited mainly by the Isaaq, saw itself disadvantaged compared to the South in the overall structure of Somalia. In the course of the 1960s and 1970s, more-or-less violent guerrilla or border wars flared up again and again. The many clans accused each other of nepotism and the political guard, which was split into 60 parties, of electoral fraud. On October 21, 1969, pro-Soviet military leaders, under Siad Barre, seized power. This initially leaned on the Soviet Union, tried to introduce a "scientific socialism" and push back the traditional influence of the clans. However, he continued to base his power on his own clan and on the Ogadeni and Dolbohanta Darods - the so-called "MOD Alliance." Barre fought another war over Ogaden against Ethiopia in 1976–78, which Somalia lost. In this war, Ethiopia was supported by the Soviet Union and Barre by the USA. The dramatic consequences of the Ogaden war were thousands dead, high costs for Somalia and the influx of over 650,000 refugees from Ethiopia. From 1980, Somalia granted the USA the right to use airfields and port facilities (including Berbera in the north of the country), in return the government received extensive support, military and development aid from the USA and other western countries. During this time, heavily indebted Somalia, like other developing countries, transitioned from socialism to an economic policy that worked according to the guidelines of the International Monetary Fund. Corruption and nepotism increased sharply during this period, while the economic situation deteriorated due to the effects of war, persistently high military spending, drought and unsuccessful economic policies.[7]

ARRIVING IN MOGADISHU

A cool breeze blew in from the nearby sea as I got off the plane in Mogadishu. We passengers marched in single file to the airport building and passport control dragged on. The uniformed officer, who was holed up behind a lattice, looked at every page of my passport very carefully, eyed me suspiciously and asked questions. After a moment's hesitation, he stamped the visa page and wrote something on a piece of paper. He handed this to me along with my passport and ordered me to show it at another counter. There I was handed the next piece of paper, which I handed over to another officer in the next room. Only now was I able to queue for baggage claim. The suitcase was also searched very carefully but I finally got through the passport and customs controls. A friendly, young Somali with a Red Cross badge was waiting for me outside. He introduced himself as Abdul acting as "Welcome Officer"; a job that I soon took on myself. Abdul took care of my luggage in the

---

7   Source: Wikipedia

trunk of a black Fiat that was already quite old, and then we drove towards the city center with little traffic. At the headquarters of the Red Cross League I was warmly welcomed by the English secretary Kay Spellman. "You're finally here," she beamed at me with a sigh of relief. "I'm so glad because we're drowning in work, your predecessor left a few days ago." Hearing my voice, the Swede Sven Lampell, formerly my boss in Bangladesh and now chief delegate in Somalia, came out from his office. We hugged each other warmly and his first words were: "Welcome Hansrudi, we urgently need you here. How is Ann?" And immediately I was in the middle of the situation, with Sven describing it in detail:

"More than 80,000 Ethiopian refugees are already living in the border area and thousands are joining them every day," Sven informed me. "The widely scattered refugee camps house an average of around 30,000 people, the vast majority of whom are women and children." "Certainly the 1978 war, the constant unrest and inflation are largely to blame. But the main reason for these ongoing streams of refugees are years of drought." The refugees would reach the camps totally exhausted, malnourished and completely dried out from the days of marching. Now I knew theoretically what to expect on site. I had already received the extensive catalogue of tasks in Berne. Here in Mogadishu I was responsible for the administration of all expatriate Red Cross personnel working in Somalia. It all started with looking after colleagues on arrival and departure at the airport. I was also responsible for telex communications abroad, daily radio communication with delegates and medical teams in the field. Obtaining visa extensions and photo IDs was just as much a part of my duties as booking and paying for plane tickets and organizing trips to the field. I was also responsible for renting and maintaining the residential and warehouse buildings in Mogadishu; and even more so the entire human resources and payroll system with regard to the Somali employees. Cooperation with the employment office, the Somali Red Crescent Society and the local UN organizations was also part of my daily work, as were regular trips to the field, to northern and southern Somalia. In addition, as a clerk for special projects and as deputy chief delegate, I had to deal with a wide range of other tasks in the absence of Sven Lampell. One thing was clear: there was a fair amount of work waiting for me. I didn't have to fear boredom here.

Fuel shortages prevailed in Somalia at the time. I found out what that meant the next morning. It was still dark when Abdul drove me to a fuel station at 5a.m. and parked the Fiat at the end of a line of several dozen cars. However, the fuel station did not open until two hours later. We were forced to line up once or twice weekly at 5 a.m. or even earlier, to be sure of being able to fill up with between ten and 20 liters of petrol. Nevertheless, it happened that the fuel station was pumped empty just before it was our turn. So I tried the following morning arriving even earlier. From then on I drove very early to this fuel station whenever I was in urgent need, in order to stay safely mobile. The other delegates in Mogadishu also became early risers in order to get fuel, one even had to refuel the car of Sven Lampell as well. As soon as the fuel station opened, everyone pushed their car forward a little by hand. I quickly learned not to leave objects on the seats while we drivers were chatting and waiting. Little boys hung around in the dark, stealing from the seats anything they thought of value that was worth selling. When you finally reached the only petrol pump, it was the order of the day for these rascals, smiling mischievously, to offer you the stolen things for sale. They knew exactly from which car they stole what. So I bought back my sunglasses twice and my hat once.

I was allocated a room in one of the houses rented by the Red Cross. We had a cook who also did the housework. The old black Fiat that Abdul used to pick me up at the airport became my vehicle and Abdul my trusted assistant. We were only a small number of delegates in Mogadishu. Most of the other Red Cross people were doctors, nurses, orderlies and field delegates in the distant refugee camps bordering Ethiopia's Ogaden region. Every day more people crossed the border to the nearest camp. The food transports by the UN organizations for them became more and more urgent, but were difficult to organize due to the lack of infrastructure in the interior of the country. The Somali government under its dictatorial President Siad Barre was also suspected of artificially inflating the number of refugees so that more food was donated, part of which could be diverted to the army. As a "Welcome Officer," I spent a lot of time waiting at the airport to attend to Red Cross people or official visitors who regularly arrived or left. I organized accommodation for them or their onward journey in Somalia, and helped those leaving with the time-consuming check-in process. I was soon to feel the effects of the several years of Russian presence in Mogadishu. All the passports of the more than 50 foreign delegates were safely stored in our office safe. I regularly took passports to the relevant ministry for visa extensions. Black-clad Somali officials with sunglasses were already lined up at the entrance, staring at me with cold poker faces and asking unfriendly questions. Inside the building, too, these guys hung around on every floor. In general, the atmosphere in this building was chilly and oppressively uncomfortable. Usually I had to wait a long time in front of the visa room. The fact that there was hardly any seating didn't make things any easier. My gut feeling told me that years before the Russians had set up their notorious KGB system there, and it continued to work well, even after they left.

Once again we celebrated Christmas away from home; quite simply in the team house, where the cook had prepared a wonderful roast for us. With a few puny candles, flowers and plant branches, we tried to create a modest yet heartfelt Christmas spirit. We gave out small presents, sang two or three Christmas carols and thought of our loved ones at home. In February, just before my birthday, a small Christmas present arrived from the Swiss Red Cross; late, but I was no-less pleased. The Swede Tim Nilsson, a journalist from the well-known newspaper "Dagens Nyheter", also worked in our Mogadishu team. He was our information officer, while New Zealander Sidney Smith, was our accountant. In February, Per arrived, our new transport officer from Denmark. Slowly but surely we were able to spread the day-to-day work over several shoulders. That was very important and helped to master the ever-increasing tasks to some extent.

For a long time, calling abroad was extremely difficult. I tried twice to call my Ann from the main post office, but I couldn't get through. I telexed Vreni Wenger at the Swiss RC in Berne, asking her to contact Ann to calm as she must have been worried in Australia. In the evenings I often wrote letters or postcards to her.

On February 25th, her birthday, I really wanted to surprise her with a phone call. Despite the bad experiences I had had so far, I drove to the main post office at 1 p.m. and asked the officer in charge to call Ann's number in Australia. "It might works today," I thought hopefully. After a twenty-minute wait, the duty officer sent me to cabin one. Excitedly, I picked up the phone and happily called out "Hello!" No answer. So I kept waiting. Every few minutes I would hear a crackle on the line that made me hope and again call out "Hello!" Finally a distant voice said, "I'm connecting." My tension rose and I continued to wait hardly daring to breathe. Again the line cracked and I heard a voice saying they would put me through. After 20 minutes I gave up and went to complain. The officer tried again to establish the connection. Again the cracking, again "I connect", but again nothing happened. The minutes turned into what felt like hours, and I broke out in a sweat. I was still hoping fervently that Ann would suddenly answer. As I stepped out of the booth, shaking my head, the officer responded with an encouraging, "Okay, now I'll try via Sydney instead of Singapore." New hope germinated in me. But for the time being, the long wait continued unabated. Finally, a voice answered from the central office in Sydney and called out to me: "I'll now dial the number in Perth!" Now my heart began to pound when the phone was ringing "at home" at Ann's. I waited excitedly - but suddenly I was seized with doubts: Maybe Ann wasn't at home after all? Perhaps she had been invited to dinner by her sister? After all, it was her birthday. I let it ring full of hope many more times, but in vain. Deeply saddened and at odds with myself, I put the receiver back on the cradle. The clerk just shrugged his shoulders indifferently and sent me to the cashier next door to pay for my phone call. However, a huge shock awaited me: the cashier actually asked for 150 US dollars for this unsuccessful call. I was flabbergasted. All my assurances that there had been no conversation at all went unheeded. I was in no more shape for further puzzles and vehemently and vociferously refused to pay this outrageous amount. In the meantime, many onlookers had streamed in not wanting to miss this loud argument between a Somali and a foreigner. Feeling well-supported by this, the officer then threatened me with the police. That was finally enough for me. Angrily, I ended the conversation with a decided "I don't owe you anything," and the cashier called the boss, to whom I told my story one more time. The supervisor listened quietly and ordered the large wall box with the automatic recordings to be opened in the next room and my statements to be checked. Another 30 minutes passed before a specialist trotted up with a long roll of paper on which the recorded conversations and numbers were listed. But the wait was worth it: this man confirmed that no telephone connection had ever been established. The cashier then caved in and apologized. With mixed feelings, I said thank-you and rushed out into the fresh air, where another horror awaited me: my Fiat was gone, simply gone. I stood there completely frozen. I couldn't believe someone had stolen my car. I immediately went in search of my indispensable vehicle. I quickly walked down the street and low and behold: about 50 meters ahead I saw my car standing abandoned on the side of the road; the driver's door open. As I got closer, I saw the mess: loose copper cables were hanging down under the dashboard. Whoever had taken the car fortunately didn't get far with it. After several attempts to connect different cables together, the engine started when I turned the ignition key. That was music to my ears! With a sigh of exhausted relief, I drove back to work. Getting up twice a week at 4:30 a.m., queuing at the fuel station for petrol, three hours later having breakfast and then tackling a tough day at work was draining.

At the beginning of March, I flew in a Somali Airlines Fokker Friendship to Hargeisa, 1,500 kilometers away. During the colonial period, as the capital of British Somaliland, this was the second largest city in the country. Peter McGeniss, an Aussie from Queensland, welcomed me in Hargeisa, which lay in a wide, arid basin of sparse vegetation at 1,300 meters. The climate was dry and pleasant, not as humid as in Mogadishu. The next day Peter drove with me towards the Ethiopian border, via Nabadeed, to the border at Borama. Here we were only 120 kilometers from former French Somaliland, which only four years before had become the new country of Djibouti. On our way back from Borama we stopped at the border crossing of Tug Wajale where we witnessed more emaciated refugees slowly crossing the border from the Ogaden. We wondered how many family members may have perished on these endless escape routes. The landscape in the Ogaden appeared barren, dry and hilly. Peter confirmed that it was extremely difficult for UNHCR to bring enough food supplies to the constantly growing refugee camps. All medical teams also had similar supply problems with regard to the urgently needed medicines. Transporting refrigerated vaccines was even more problematic.

In Hargeisa, I visited the German Red Cross car repair shop. The German mechanics under the direction of Erich Offner did heavy work here for the maintenance and repairs of the transport vehicles of several aid organizations. Bad roads and dusty air put a heavy strain on all vehicles. With a long list of urgently needed spare parts and lots of valuable information, I flew back to Mogadishu.

In April, I wrote two express letters to Ann requesting her to quit her job as a receptionist at the Parmelia Hilton Hotel and come to Mogadishu. On May 28 she left Perth. She first flew to Bangladesh with the aim of making a stopover in Chittagong for several days to visit relatives and friends. Listening to BBC News on my shortwave radio as usual on the morning of May 30, I was shocked: a few hours earlier Bangladesh's President, General Zia, had been assassinated by army officers at the Circuit House in Chittagong; just a few hundred yards from the house where Ann was staying with her friend Iris Pereira. A *coup d'état* was in progress and a curfew had already been imposed. So, I had to assume that Ann was stuck in Chittagong and might have missed the onward flight to Nairobi. Thanks to BBC News I was able to follow further events in Chittagong. General Ershad took over the presidency of Bangladesh in Dhaka and called on coup leader General Mansoor to step down. But he fled after most of his officers surrendered, and was caught and shot shortly afterwards. Ann had reached Dhaka in time and was able to fly on to Nairobi via Air India. Since our boss Sven Lampell was also in Nairobi at the time, he promised to take Ann under his wing. Ann was stuck in Nairobi for six days because at short notice, Somali Airlines had pre-dated its weekly Nairobi-Mogadishu flight by one day without noticing Air India in Dhaka. During Sven Lampell's absence, I was acting Chief Delegate in Somalia. When I returned to the office shortly after noon on June 4th, our secretary Kay casually mentioned that a plane with relief supplies for another aid organization had landed and was soon flying back to Nairobi empty. Now I pricked up my ears and immediately checked whether this corresponded to the facts. It was clearly the case. So I asked Kay to get my passport from the safe. I wanted to try to catch this flight. As the current boss, all I had to do was ask my own permission; and I gave myself the green light with a smile. Our people in Mogadishu could be without me for a few days, they all knew very well what work to do. Abdul drove me towards the airport, took a small detour to my house so that I could quickly pack a travel bag with the essentials. When we arrived a little later at the big gate at the airport, I saw a young pilot marching towards a small plane standing far behind. We decided to follow him asking where he was flying to: "Back to Nairobi," he said. "Can I fly with you?" I asked hopefully. He looked at me in astonishment: "Yes, I have space; but that would cost you $150!" I was fine with that, but I had one tiny problem: customs clearance. "There's nobody there at the moment, they're taking a break," the young man stated dryly. He had already completed his formalities and was therefore ready to go. Now I hesitated for a moment. What should I do? Departing without customs clearance and an exit stamp in your passport? I knew this was rather risky. Would I be able to enter the country a second time with one visa? But I pulled myself together: the opportunity to soon be able to hug Ann after seven months of separation was worth the risk to me. I quickly gave Teddy, the young American pilot, traveler checks worth $150, and took a seat next to him in the elegant twin-engine Cessna. I peered out of the cockpit, a little concerned. No one had yet noticed that a Mr Brawand was about to leave. Less than 15 minutes after illegally entering the airport, we were airborne on our flight to Nairobi. When the Cessna reached cruising altitude, Teddy switched to autopilot, sat back comfortably, and began to read a book. My stomach started to growl, so I ate the bananas I'd cleverly packed. After a while, Teddy called Nairobi to tell his wife that he would be home for dinner just before 6 p.m. Then he continued reading his book while I, lost in thought looked forward to seeing Ann again. After a while, when I saw the peak of the white Kilimanjaro summit sticking out of gray clouds, I was pulled out of these dreams for a short time. I immediately recalled in my mind's eye the morning of January 21, 1970, when I was standing there on the highest mountain in Africa. Then and now this seemed to me an adventure from another life. I found it unforgettable and enriching to have done this mountain tour; and yet I felt no desire to turn the clock back and undertake more such projects; because now I had Ann. The greatest of all gifts fate had given me. Shortly after 5 p.m. we landed at the small Wilson airfield in Nairobi. A customs officer looked in vain for the entry visa in my Swiss passport, so he asked for 80 Kenya shillings to issue a visa. But I had no shillings and the bank at the airport was already closed. The officer grew impatient. "No money, no visa," he made it clear to me with his words and even more so with his demeanour. So what to do? I thought feverishly how I could still get this visa. Suddenly the brilliant idea hit me: I was a Red Cross delegate and for once a desperate bluff was called for: "Sorry sir," I turned to the customs officer and diligently showed him my Red Cross identity card. "I'm chief delegate in Somalia," I enlightened him. "In the Luq Genana refugee camp on the Juba River, the kitchen section, got completely destroyed by fire," – which unfortunately was true. "In this emergency situation, I came to Nairobi today as soon as possible to procure some new kitchen equipment, which I am sure will cost more than a million shillings." This however was a bluff. Now the customs officer beamed at me. "Why didn't you say so straight away?" he asked reproachfully. "In such a case I can give you a free visa!" With these words he hammered the appropriate stamp into my passport. I thanked him warmly. This hurdle was over. But the next one was already waiting: How did I get into the city without money? I tried hitchhiking at the airport exit gate and waited quite a while. Suddenly a big Chevrolet with its top down glided up, with three young Europeans in it. I explained to them my plight. They just laughed and invited me on board. Teasing and cracking jokes, they drove me straight to the hotel where Ann had found shelter. Relieved, I got out and suddenly felt my heart beating wildly. Excited, I stepped into the lobby. Only now did I really realize that Ann had no idea that I was on my way to her. I asked a young man at the front desk for Ann's room number. He looked at me regretfully: "Sorry sir, Mrs. Brawand doesn't stay here anymore. She only stayed one night." I was stunned. When I asked if he remembered Ann, he nodded vigorously, "Oh yes, I remember her. Her English wasn't good." I didn't think I heard properly and replied indignantly: "How can you say such a thing! My wife speaks very good English." He took my criticism lightly and replied with a shrug: "Oh well, her English was better than yours." Now it was enough for me: "Thank-you very much but where did my wife go?" Now the young man got more specific and was able to report that Ann had looked around for a cheaper place to stay. "I recommended the Ambassador nearby," he explained. "She promised me a tip if I carried her suitcase." Which she did, he proudly said, but had first to remove his own hotel badge from the shirt. I had heard enough now, I grabbed my sports bag and marched over to the Ambassador. Ann wasn't in her room. She went out again after checking in, I was told. My face grew longer again, my legs a little weak. The situation overwhelmed me, I had to sit down. Full of hope I kept looking at the entrance and trying to see Ann. Later, I ate a little something in the restaurant, but didn't like it. Then I started pacing in front of the hotel. Suddenly I was surrounded by three young prostitutes so quickly fled back to the first hotel in the hope that my boss Sven could give me some information. But he wasn't in the hotel either. Suddenly a new thought struck me: Could it be that Ann was on a safari with him and his companion and wouldn't be back until tomorrow? That possibility allayed my anxiety a little. Night was slowly falling and I urgently needed a room. Back at the Ambassador, I asked permission to stay in my wife's room, but was flatly refused. I asked to speak to the manager, who immediately welcomed me to his office for an interview. But he also categorically rejected my urgent request for that room. I didn't give up, produced my Red Cross ID and passport and told him credible details about Ann and me. After a strenuous 20 minutes he finally gave in hesitantly, got the key and accompanied me to Ann's room on the 4th floor. When he saw a framed portrait of me on the bedside table, his last doubts vanished; and he wished me good night. When I opened the cupboard, I saw Ann's familiar clothes hanging. They smelled beautifully of Ann!

Now all restlessness fell from me, overcome by an unspeakably great tiredness. Today's experiences and especially the emotional ups and downs of the past few hours took their toll. After a refreshing shower I slipped into the wonderful double bed and fell asleep immediately. The next morning I treated myself to an extensive buffet breakfast while hoping Ann would return soon. I instructed the concierge to tell Ann that someone was waiting for her. From the room balcony I had an excellent overview of the large square in front of the hotel. During the afternoon I watched like a sparrow hawk for newcomers. It was just before 4 p.m. when I saw Ann. I recognized her from afar, immediately stepped back into the room because I wanted to surprise her, I lay down on the bed and waited. A few minutes later Ann opened the door and froze when she saw me. We hugged and kissed each other, we could hardly let go of each other. We hadn't seen each other for seven long months and missed each other more than we had given ourselves credit for. Ann laughed and told me that the concierge had mischievously told her there was a man waiting for her in her room. But she couldn't believe that. I roughly told her my story and how it came about that I was now standing in front of her. As suspected, Ann had been on safari with Sven and his companion. Now she took a refreshing bath and rested a bit before we went to eat. It turned out to be a long and hearty meal, we had so much to tell each other. When I looked at Ann's beautiful eyes, I was no less in love with her than I had been nine years before when we first met on April 10, 1972. We experienced the completely unexpected holiday together in Nairobi like a young married couple and wholeheartedly enjoyed being close to each other again. Ann told me that Air India paid her bill for five nights Ambassador Hotel, while I just paid the difference between single and double room. Clever Ann had gone to Air India in Nairobi to claim they were responsible for not informing Dhaka of the Somali Airline flight schedule change. The boss did not agree, but Ann refused to leave his office until he finally agreed to pay.

On Wednesday we flew back to Mogadishu with Somali Airlines. We had concocted a strategy so that I could enter the country a second time unmolested, because officially I had never left the country. Before getting off the plane, I pinned my Red Cross badge to my shirt. First, Ann handed her passport to the customs officer. When she got it back stamped, I stuck my passport through the window and the officer immediately started leafing through it. At that moment, Ann came back and asked him a question to distract him. He looked at her and answered. As if she hadn't understood, Ann asked him a second time and got the same answer. He looked at me now, then at the passport in his hands, seemed to consider where it had gone. Then, spontaneously, he grabbed his stamp and slammed it onto a blank page. I breathed a sigh of relief, my secret trip to Nairobi had been a success from A to Z. Ann wasn't thrilled when I carried her over the threshold of the little house I'd rented just for the two of us. Because of my hasty departure, it looked anything but comfortable. Ann shuddered when she discovered the dust lying everywhere. It took her two full days to fix that house as she said "to make it liveable." Because of the green shutters, we named our Somali home the "Green House." It was in a suburb oddly named Km 4, about the distance from the airport.

Many Pakistani's lived in Mogadishu, most were businessmen. They had their own private school speaking Pakistani Urdu, but were short on teachers. When a shop owner heard that my wife was fluent in Urdu, he arranged with the school administration to meet Ann. After that, the principal offered her a job as a teacher in a lower grade. Ann accepted gratefully. From then on, every morning I would take Ann to Mogadishu's old "Arab town." We walked the last 150 meters through winding narrow alleys to the multi-storey Ithnasheri Madressa school. Here Ann taught the youngest of the students English. Ann's methodology was more child-friendly than the old one and the children liked their lessons with her. They eagerly participated with great interest. Ann really enjoyed her new task. The other teachers also liked my wife and appreciated her teaching. Even the rector listened when she recommended improving the cleanliness and order in the toilets and in the corridors. The tip was implemented immediately. Soon Ann began receiving invitations to family gatherings. Ann once learned from one of the grandmothers that her granddaughter, always talked about the new teacher after school, and gave detailed reports about the color of her dress and lipstick. Even a new handbag was noticed. One evening when Ann went into a jewellery store looking at the display, a boy came out of the back room and excitedly said to the shopkeeper: "Daddy, look, that's my teacher!" The father was very happy and complimented Ann on her manner of teaching and in return offered her a discount on his jewelery.

On a Sunday morning, we Red Crossers went on a trip to Merca on the Indian Ocean in a hired eight-seater car. Over 100 kilometers south of Mogadishu, it welcomed us with a spectacular water show at the rocky beach. Big breakers hit the jagged rocks shooting huge white waves high into the air with a roar, we couldn't get enough of it. While eating the sandwiches we had taken with us I started to feel uncomfortable. During the long drive back I got really sick, with headaches and dizziness. When we finally reached Mogadishu, I felt really weak. At home I took a shower, then dragged myself to bed. The headache got worse. Ann brought me water to drink. What was the matter with me? I could barely sleep, an inner restlessness didn't allow it. In the morning I had diarrhoea, and was unable to eat anything. Now body aches also set in and a severe headache tormented me. Ann began to cool my painful forehead with ice cubes, which relieved the intense pressure somewhat. However, my condition made it clear that medical attention was necessary. Since all Red Cross doctors worked far away in the refugee camps, Ann had to look elsewhere. She contacted a young doctor from *Médicins sans frontières* to whom she described my symptoms. "Your husband probably suffers of dengue fever," he diagnosed, adding: "There are still no medications for it." He could only recommend cooling with ice and painkillers. In the afternoon he gave Ann the pills but flatly refused her request to come for a home visit. He may have thought it was contagious. The situation was really difficult because we were in the middle of the hottest season and it was very humid. In addition, we didn't have any air conditioning, just two small fans that were able to move the hot air a little. For four days I drank only water. Unable to eat anything at all, I suffered from a constant feeling of fullness. The bathroom scale showed that I lost eight kilograms in just four days. The constant pounding headache – especially in the forehead area – continued unabated. Sometimes I felt like something was about to burst inside my forehead. On the fifth day, Ann found me deliriously stumbling naked in another room. It seemed to me that I was slowly but surely losing my mind. Ann literally sacrificed herself for me. Regularly, even at night, she put fresh ice cubes in a plastic bag on my forehead. She suspected bad things when she looked into my suffering eyes. Every few minutes I kept turning to the other side. Ann never wanted to leave me alone and stopped going to school. She became my nurse and guard. Even today I have no doubt, Ann literally had saved my life back then in Mogadishu.

Finally, on the 12th day, the pain became just a little more bearable, but I felt completely drained and dead tired. I was so weak that I had to lean on the back of a chair in order to at least independently "push" myself to the toilet at a snail's pace. If there had been rollators back then, I would have been the first to buy one. Ann's constant loving and motivating care helped me to very slowly to regain my courage. I had to, and wanted to, get well as soon as possible, because the team needed me, and of course Ann needed to recover from the round the clock stress of nursing me.

Just three weeks after the onset of getting ill, I went back to work part-time for a maximum three hours a day but gradually increased working hours. There was so much unfinished work, I had to force myself to continue, owing it to my team mates and our Red Cross responsibilities. Most of the time I was in bed dead tired by 7 p.m. and slept 12 to 13 hours straight. Eventually, but very slowly I regained my strength back. It wasn't until four months later that I seemed to have fully recovered. Luckily, during my illness, Wolf Reifenrath, a coordinator for the mechanics team, arrived from Germany. He was a veteran Red Cross man from Göttingen, who lent a hand with the most urgent work in the office. We became friends and stayed connected for many years.

One day we received an order from the Ministry of Foreign Affairs to present all foreign passports on site. The next day, with no fewer than 52 passports, I made my way to the den of the Somali KGB lions. As soon as arrived at the entry of the building, I was harshly asked what I wanted and that I should identify myself. I took the two tied-up passport bundles out of my bag and handed them to this lout hiding behind black sunglasses and said, "Here, Sir!" Because I had deliberately said Sir, he must have assumed I was afraid of him. Holding the two bundles in his hands, he stood threateningly in front of me and said harshly: "What's all that about? Give me your passport now!" "You already have it in your hands!" I replied calmly. "Which is your passport?" he asked impatiently. I said "It is in one of these bundles," while staring into his mirrored sunglasses. Again he said, "I want to look into your passport!" "Ok, hand me all passports back." He did, and I now said loudly: "Listen, if you do not immediately let me pass into the ministry, the International Red Cross will complain to the Minister about your misbehaviour here today. What is your name?" That helped. The guy immediately got decent, called a second man, and told him to escort me to the passport department. Once again I had to wait a long time there; however, this time there was a chair I could sit on. When I was finally let in, an unfriendly official awaited me behind a massive desk. I could see in his face that the Russians and their KGB henchmen had exorcised any decency years ago. I gave him the 52 passports with a list of our people's names and nationalities. "When do we get them back?" I asked the middle-aged man who took himself so seriously. "You'll hear from us," he growled back, gesturing appropriately. I quickly left this frosty office with an oppressive feeling and stepped out of the building into the warmth, breathing a sigh of relief.

Two weeks later I was back to that building on an urgent matter. I had to reclaim the passports of two Scandinavian nurses returning home. But I was told I wasn't able to pick up these passports for another four days. It was pure harassment and the nurses had to postpone their departure by a week. Ten more days passed and I went to pick up the remaining 50 passports, I only got 49 back. The only Icelandic passport was missing. When I trotted back two days later, to my surprise, there was an attractive young Somali woman sitting behind the desk smiling kindly. What a difference! Not only did she smile, but she credibly promised to look for the missing Icelandic passport and notify me. When I came back two weeks later, without having received a message, the young woman apologised, unfortunately they couldn't find this Icelandic passport. I quickly suspected that this passport had deliberately "disappeared" in order to use it for another purpose.

While welcoming a newcomer at the airport one day, I caught my breath at the sight of him: I thought I was shaking hands with the famous film star Donald Sutherland. Driving into town, I mentioned his striking resemblance to the actor. "I know" he said and laughed. "It often happens to me when I'm travelling, especially in hotels, where I'm regularly greeted as Mr. Sutherland," said the Swedish doctor who was to visit our medical teams. The doctor smiled as he shared his stories. "Whenever I present my passport at a hotel lobby, it's often, 'Of course, I understand Mr Sutherland you prefer to remain incognito. That is no problem, we are giving you a particularly nice, discreet room!'" At such moments he always happily accepted.

TO THE HORIZON AND BEYOND

On our only day off, we drove to the Mogadishu beach in the morning, changed at the UN clubhouse and plunged into the cool waves of the Indian Ocean. Sometimes I also jogged along the water to improve my fitness. After the swim we sat down in the clubhouse and treated ourselves to a beer. One day I heard a familiar voice and when I turned around, we recognized each other immediately. It was Allan Williams, the Enugu Poacher in Biafra. He was working for Oxfam, a British NGO. We were very happy to see each other again, so unexpectedly, and exchanged memories.

Our weekly swimming pleasure came to an abrupt end one day. The sun was already burning hot, when I got out of the water at 10 a.m. and went home. Two hours later, Wolf Reifenrath came and reported to me, in a very agitated way, that fifteen minutes after I had left, a shark attacked a Somali in waist-deep water and bit his thigh: at the very spot where I always cooled myself in the water. Wolf, a trained paramedic, helped tie off the heavily bleeding leg and quickly drove the man to the hospital. There was only one young doctor on duty, who was sitting on a chair outside, smoking a cigarette enjoying himself. When he saw the deep leg wounds, he just shrugged his shoulders. Wolf was outraged, "The guy said he could not help and couldn't even be persuaded to call another doctor." My colleague was very upset; he had watched helplessly as the unfortunate young man bled to death. Over the next four days, three more Somalis became victims to sharks at this popular bay. The reason was quickly discovered. Two kilometers away, just above the beach, a newly built slaughterhouse had been put into operation a few days earlier. Its bloody sewage was poured into the ocean, attracting sharks that now made their way through the reef. From then on swimming was taboo for us. However, from time to time I jogged along that beach and twice I saw a huge shark in deeper water – at most 20 meters away – slowly patrolling up and down. I got goose bumps both times. Abdul then recommended a narrow bay 10 kilometers south of Mogadishu. Here we could safely swim in the morning for an hour on our day off, but after that it quickly got too hot.

In October I traveled to Hargeisa a second time. The first leg took me by plane over the rocky Horn of Africa to Berbera, which lies on the Gulf of Aden. There I was picked up by the Red Cross employee, Joyce Rebeiro, and drove with her on a steadily rising asphalt road through barren land to Hargeisa, 180 kilometers away. We had to stop again and again because turtles the size of a football slowly crossed the road.

Joyce Rebeiro from Melbourne, organized courses in midwifery and baby care in Hargeisa. In order to acquire knowledge in this area as well, I took part in such a course. I was impressed by how motivated and active the young, colorfully-dressed women took part, asked many questions and also talked about the risks of traditional births in remote villages. On this course, I saw practical examples of how urgently educational work and low-level training opportunities were needed in this country. Courses of this kind – conducted parallel to the work in the refugee camp crisis centers – were by far the best way to help people to help themselves. In addition, the great interest shown by the young women reinforced to me how important all of our commitments on behalf of the Red Cross were; and how much they were appreciated in the field. This new knowledge accompanied me from then on. If I occasionally had slight doubts as to whether our work wasn't just a "drop in the bucket," I pictured the young women listening eagerly to Joyce Rebeiro and peppering her with questions. For their part, the medical Red Cross teams in the still growing refugee camps on the border to the Ogaden, continued to work with dedication and helpfulness. I admired the personal strength with which our people coped with all this misery day after day, week after week. Deeply impressed, I flew back to Mogadishu a few days later; a detailed report and a materials order list of considerable length, in my luggage.

On an autumn day, I welcomed Vreni Wenger, the clerk at the Swiss Red Cross in Berne, at the airport. Two days later we flew with the UNO-Pilatus Porter to Lugh Genana on the Juba River to visit the large refugee camp there. Nurses from the Swiss Red Cross were working here. When the subject of the burnt down kitchen was mentioned and Vreni asked about the reasons for this fire, the camp manager said laconically: "The cook was cooking." We all laughed heartily. Then I told the story of my trip to Nairobi, where I was issued a free entry visa thanks to the burnt kitchen. In the meantime, the kitchen had been rebuilt and everyone was relieved that only material damage had been reported and that no one had been injured. After the evening meeting and a simple dinner, my visitor and I walked to our beds in two small round huts. We wished each other a good night, but something kept me from going to sleep. The comfortable nightly temperature was too tempting. So I stepped in front of my little hut and looked out into the moonless night. What I saw in the sky was an impressive fairy-tale world like something out of 1001 Arabian Nights. Billions of yellow, silver and reddish stars glittered, sparkled and flickered above me, creating a unique atmosphere. Never before had I experienced a night sky like that, the huge Milky Way shimmered so brightly. I was moved, overwhelmed and in awe. The countless stars shone so clearly. I even thought I heard some heavenly sounding whispers from this eternal wonder. Despite the nightly darkness, I was able to perceive countless delicate colors floating in space in the soft light of the stars. With wide open eyes I looked into the eternal infinity of space. Every now and then, gloriously glowing shooting stars raced through this nocturnal arena at lightning speed. Heaven was alive and well. My eyes, my consciousness, my soul, everything in me opened up to this heavenly miracle. I thought I saw eternity in the distant depths. Deeply moved and tiny, I stood down there on earth and stared, enchanted, at this monumental, nocturnal spectacle above me. It must have been midnight when I was finally able to break away from it. I lay down on the plain bed in the African hut, continuing to gaze at the stars through the doorless entrance, slowly slipping into a restful sleep. Even today, many years later, this unforgettable, magical starry backdrop in the Somali hinterland regularly returns to my consciousness and the stars begin to shine again in my memory. These were without a doubt one of the most wonderful and impressive moments of my life, compared only with the moment smiling Ann looked at me, in 1972, and said: "Yes Hansrudi, I am going to marry you!!!

My Somalia mission ended at the beginning of December 1981. From then on, Wolf Reifenrath took over my complex tasks. He was the right man for it. I was happy to return home and relax; because the serious illness five months earlier had cost me a lot of substance and it was still somehow lingering. Ann resigned from her position as a teacher at the end of November. The principal was reluctant to let her go and gave Ann a very good certificate. We enjoyed a happy farewell party in the "Green House," and Abdul drove us to the airport the next day. After the complicated check-in and various customs formalities, we finally stood with the other passengers in front of the gate. As the glass door opened and the first travellers filed out, a female customs officer approached from behind, and nudged Ann brusquely on the shoulder. She ordered Ann to follow her for a body search. No sooner had they both disappeared into a cabin, I was also picked up for a search. They had only chosen the two of us and found nothing forbidden. We were very relieved we could now get on the plane and make our way home.

The unusual 13 months on the Horn of Africa remain unforgettable for us. We experienced so many highlights, surprises and problems in this short time, and we got to know countless interesting people from other countries. Some have remained friends for life, and we remember the good team spirit from many others and the work we did together. The hard-working Red Cross teams in the distant refugee camps were always at the center of it. To support them, to facilitate their self-sacrificing work, that was always our goal.

After arriving in wintery Zurich-Kloten, we immediately opened our suitcases to put on warmer clothes. It was cold and gloomy here, and we immediately missed the Somali sun. In the city we suddenly encountered thickly hooded people who were in a hurry; Christmas was just around the corner. This changeover came far too quickly for us and was a bit of a shock. Christmas trees and decorations downtown, and bulging shelves in stores all seemed so unreal. None of this could create festive anticipation with us. I thought of the other world, of the refugees in Somalia; I saw them standing anxiously in front of their round huts woven with branches and twigs. This discrepancy between Switzerland and Somalia really bothered us both. In the afternoon we took the train to Interlaken for a warm reunion with my mother, who served us with a delicious dinner. Two days later we reported to the Red Cross League in Geneva to discuss the Somalia mission. The next day, the final meeting at the Swiss Red Cross in Berne was on the agenda. In addition to a very good job reference, I also got the "green light" at the final medical examination. The bad dengue fever was finally over and had left no after-effects. We still had three more days to spend with my mother and, my brother Fredi's family in Matten. After that, Ann and I – with loads of the famous Swiss chocolate in our luggage – happily flew home into the summer heat of Australia to celebrate Christmas there. A lot of work awaited us there. The tenants had moved out weeks ago, and the large garden was full of weeds, but we were happy to be home in our beautiful house. A new, as yet unknown chapter of our lives was upon us. We were unemployed again, but still unconcerned and confident that 1982 could begin!

CHAPTER NINE

Perth, 1982-1984: New Perspectives

SPOTLIGHT ON PERTH

Perth sits near the mouth of the Swan River in the Indian Ocean and was founded by Captain James Stirling on August 12, 1829. Stirling's aim was to prevent the French from settling in Western Australia. However, Perth was not officially founded until 1856. At the request of the British Secretary of War and Colonies, Sir George Murray, the city was named after Murray's birthplace, the Scottish city of Perth. The area of Australia's fourth largest metropolis is now larger than 5,400 hundred square kilometers and stretches from the beaches on the Indian Ocean eastward to the foothills of the Darling Range. The centre is located inland, about ten kilometers as the crow flies from the Indian Ocean. The actual city is where the Swan River expands into a lake. As early as 1886, hydraulic engineer C. Y. O'Connor expanded the estuary into a port, which however, belongs to the independent city of Fremantle.

HANSRUDI BRAWAND

Many Perth residents refer to Kings Park as the "soul of the city," a 400-hectare site on the outskirts of the city that consists largely of original Australian bushland. The southern part of the park is occupied by the botanical garden. There is a restaurant, sports facilities, monuments, an open-air cinema and space for picnics and hikes. From the height of the park you also have a view of the Swan River and its said lake, but also of the glass and concrete buildings on its banks. This impressive skyline is the result of the West Australian natural resource boom. Many old buildings had to give way to these modern buildings. The most impressive of these buildings is the Central Park skyscraper with a height of 226 meters and 51 floors. This is followed by the Bank West building with 214 meters and 52 floors. Despite this modernity, there are still old buildings from the Wilhelminian period to admire in Perth,

A black Swan with her youngsters in the city of Perth, circa 1990. [8]

such as the Government House (1864), Deanery (1859), Town Hall (1864), and the His Majesty's Theatre (1904). The oldest park is Stirling Garden (1845), the oldest building is the Old Courthouse (1836).

Perth is considered a metropolis of sailing and water sports. The water temperature of the Indian Ocean is always around 20 to 22 °C due to an ocean current coming from Antarctica. A popular excursion destination – also for divers, among others – is the offshore island Rottnest Island ('Rotto' for short in the local dialect).

2017/18: NEW PERSPECTIVES

Having landed safely at home, we spent a peaceful Christmas and happy New Year with our relatives. We consciously recharged our batteries in order to repair our neglected household – in a hot mid-summer January. In the house and garden, everywhere, there was an abundance of work waiting for us. Days passed in the house cleaning, washing, repairing and painting. Outside in the garden; weeding, mowing the lawn, cutting back hedges, bushes and trees. There was a lot of administrative work waiting for us, such as filling out tax returns and it was also time to start earning money again.

Three times a week we drove to the nearest employment office to study the advertised, job offers. Ann immediately found work, this time with the city welfare office. I worked again for a while in short-term temporary jobs. Because I didn't like this anymore, I thought about alternatives, for example, take over a business,

---

8   Source https://tr.wikipedia.org/wiki/Swan_Nehri_(Bat%C4%B1_Avustralya)#/media/Dosya:Swan_River,Perth,Western_Australia.jpg

become self-employed. Of course, this was associated with financial risks that should not be underestimated. So we set out to know more about it. The bank was willing to give us a loan if needed. So far, so good. We gathered all the information we could, studied brochures, talked to businessmen and brokers, and even attended a short seminar. After a lot of back and forth and some deliberation, we decided to venture out with a "lunch bar." We looked at some of these bars for sale, started comparing, discussing and doing the math. We imagined taking that first step was as easy as dreaming of having your own business. At that stage there were no consequences. But did we really want to take the second step and actually make the decision to buy a business? This required a great effort, even daring, but we did it—we took that big step.

In April, after receiving a corresponding mortgage from the bank, for 25,000 Australian dollars we bought "Rocky's Lunch Bar" from a couple returning to Serbia. Our store, with its own gaming room, was on the 601 Albany Highway, a busy arterial road, across from the old-style Victoria Park Hotel; about 20 kilometers from our home. Many smaller businesses such as car dealers and motorcycle shops lined both sides of the street. Not only did their owners and employees visit every day, but many of their customers also took the opportunity to come for a delicious lunch, snacks or drinks. Paul and Anna, the two previous bar operators, introduced us to the work for two weeks. Every beginning is known to be difficult. We newcomers became aware of that. But we learned fast, and our self-confidence grew every day.

Our lunch bar opened Monday to Friday, from 7.30 a.m. to 6.30pm; on Thursday evening until 9 p.m. and on Saturday from

TO THE HORIZON AND BEYOND

7.30 a.m. to 4 p.m. As soon as we opened the door in the morning, the first hungry customers were already queuing for breakfast. Bacon and egg, large hamburgers or hot sausages were in demand early in the morning. Lucky for us that customers could park in front of the store. That brought us more of them. With Ann in the spacious kitchen, and I with the service and behind the cash register we were always in a hurry. Five tables with chairs were available in the shop for the customers who preferred to eat their food there rather than take it away. A jukebox with 30 popular hits provided entertainment. Although we also sold tobacco products, particularly cigarettes, we were fortunate to have the largest turnover from the sale of sandwiches, hamburgers and pies, sausages and chips. We also sold cold drinks, coffee and ice cream cones. Next to the counter was a heated glass display case with the hot snacks. At noon, Ann cooked a simple lunch, such as spaghetti, lasagne or a rice dish and chicken was also in demand in large quantities and Friday's menu was always and only fish and chips. Ann was able to really live out her love of cooking here. She soon earned well-deserved praise. I myself blossomed into the barista of all kinds of coffee, but above all I shone as a "chef de cappuccino." I bravely went into the production of ice cream cones and soft serves. In short: I was in my element and enjoyed it when the customers praised us both and congratulated our management. We didn't produce the round Aussie pies, a traditional pastry, they were delivered to us and we sold tons of them – almost always a small portion of tomato sauce on the side.

At that time a typical Aussie bloke, or rather his caricature, looked like this: Tall, skinny, unkempt, unshaven, dressed in shorts and a singlet and wearing "thongs" on their feet – a rubber sole with a small strap between the toes – also known as flip-flops. In his left hand he held one of those typically round pies, and in his right hand, a stubby (a small bottle of beer), with a cigarette butt hanging from the corner of his mouth. When asked how he was doing, he said straight-faced, "No worries, mate," which means "no worries, mate." This "no worries, mate" still conveys a good feeling of togetherness. I myself feel a kind affection when someone addresses me as "mate," i.e., buddy.

In the large adjoining room was the gaming room with 30 slot machines, which consisted of two meter high boxes with a screen. A game cost a 20 cents coin. No money could be won, but the more skilfully a player used the buttons, the longer the fun lasted. The machines belonged to a company who every Friday sent someone to collect the coins, half of which were given to us. The gaming room was a good thing for our lunch bar. Instead of waiting for their ordered to be prepared, many customers went and played the slot machines. Other customers came to play a game and ordered something to drink or eat as well. You could call it a win-win situation. However, significant business expenses were also incurred. Accurate book-keeping was very important in order not to slip into the red. We learned how to be economical with money, because even small things could make the difference between success and loss. We were aware of that from the start. A decent profit could only be achieved thanks to full commitment, teamwork, innovation, a good, varied range of quality food and respectful interaction with customers. The downside was that we had little free time. At the weekend, the unfinished work in the house and garden awaited us.

But there was the bookkeeping to do and the menu plan for the coming week had to be created. A weekly bulk purchase was made from the wholesale markets at 6 a.m., on a Monday morning. But all in all, for the two of us, the risk of buying the lunch bar with an adjoining gaming room paid off. I was far from bored; on the contrary. It was good, it was fun to work in a team with Ann and to achieve something together.

In the autumn of 1982, I filled out the multi-page application forms to become naturalized, we wanted to become "real" Australians. After two and a half years in the country, new immigrants were eligible to apply, but we had to wait four years because of our mission in Somalia. In March 1983 the time had come: To our great joy, we received an invitation to the naturalization ceremony. On the evening of May 3rd, we put on our best clothes and drove to the northern district town of Joondalup. It was already dark when we drove through bush terrain where a yellow warning sign unexpectedly appeared at the roadside. It read in large letters: BEWARE Of KANGAROOS AND EMUS! Was I dreaming? How did we end up here? As a genuine Grindelwalder at heart and even more so as a seasoned Red Cross worker in distant countries, one sentence got burned into me: "Beware of exotic animals!" We were obviously very, very far from glacier valley's in the Swiss mountains. At that moment, the steppes and deserts of Africa seemed much closer to me. Yet we were in Australia and about to become new citizens of the country called "Down Under." Briefly, only very briefly, I felt a little queasy. However, this strange feeling quickly gave way to joyful anticipation when an official welcomed us at the entrance to the district building in Joondalup. Around 30 Aussie aspirants had already gathered in the large hall in tense anticipation. Western Australian politicians spoke, and the responsible minister was also present. A portrait of Queen Elizabeth hung on the wall, with the Australian flag next to it. After the politician,s speeches, all newcomers were asked to come forward and take the oath. Everyone echoed to the speaker: "Here today, I pledge my loyalty to Australia and its people, whose democratic beliefs I share, whose rights and freedoms I respect, and whose laws I will uphold and obey." After this oath to the Constitution of Australia we were individually called to the front where we received, with applause, the certificate of citizenship. For Ann and I, this was a remarkable milestone in our life journey together and we were also eligible to apply for an Australian passport. For Ann, Australia was her fourth nationality after Pakistan, Bangladesh and Switzerland. However, we would never be like original Aussies. As citizens of this country, we knew that with certainty in our first hour. Our speech was a little too polished for that. My edgy Glacier valley accent would stain my Australian English forever. But decent and helpful citizens, that's what we wanted to be.

On October 28th we received deeply sad news from Switzerland. My brother Fredi called to report the unexpected death of our beloved mother. Her death affected us deeply. It took us a long time to process the loss. Switzerland without our mother? That was unimaginable for us a long time. Flying quickly to Interlaken for the funeral was unfortunately impossible. We were too dependent on each other because of our busy shop. I could not leave Ann alone. But it was comforting that the funeral service for my dear mother was scheduled for All Saints' Day at 11 a.m. in Switzerland, while here in Perth it would be 6 p.m. when a catholic mass was being held in nearby St.Gerards Church. Ann had informed the priest about my mother's funeral in Switzerland before mass began. The priest asked that I stand and then informed the church-goers that my mother's funeral was happening in Switzerland at that very same moment. This way I was able to pay my last respects to my kind-hearted, beloved mother, albeit from the other end of the world. When Ann and I were the last to emerge from the church, a large number of unknown churchgoers awaited us, to offer us condolences and to express their sympathy. This proof of charity and consolation was unforgettable for us.

Our work in the lunch bar was slowly becoming too much for us, so the job centre provided us with Tanya, a young apprentice girl who was willing and quickly brought desired relief for Ann. It was particularly important that we could trust her and she also became a reliable helper at the cash register. Ann became more and more courageous with the new menu offerings. She began making Asian snack's, particularly vegetable samosas flavoured with paprika. Whoever tasted them came back and asked for more. For Ann, that really lifted her spirits.

One day a German man came into our shop and sat down on a table. Ann called me to talk to him. His name was Hans Joachim Burzlaff, a structural engineer by profession. He had a small construction business in Munich, where he lived with his family. He intended immigrating to Western Australia, had already purchased a block of land in York around 100 kilometers from Perth and started to build a house there. Hans was indeed a very interesting person. We liked each other, but didn't know yet, we would become friends for life. I went with him one day to the immigration office in Perth. A high ranking officer from Canberra, told Hans that Australia was interested in highly-qualified professionals like him. Unfortunately Hans forgot to ask this Canberra VIP officer for his business card. A huge mistake, because other bureaucrats in Perth later strangely rejected Hans immigration application.

Every now and then even Swiss tourists found their way into our lunch bar. I quickly recognized them by their accents. When they sat down at a table to eat something, I did not identify myself. Only when collecting the money did I suddenly ask in Swiss German, but without my Grindelwald dialect: *"Händsi no es Brötli gha?"* (Did you have a bun, too?) The very surprised guests first stared at me, then burst out in happy laughter realising I was a Swiss too.

In mid-1984 time was right to start thinking about our future. We couldn't afford vacations and felt a great tiredness. Enthusiasm and positive drive at our lunch bar had given way to a monotonous routine. In short: it was time to hand our business over to someone else. We found an agent who put it up for sale. Through clever trading we were able to increase the turnover, which in turn increased the market value of the lunch bar somewhat. We hoped to achieve a good selling price. Every now and then interested parties came by, but they always tried to negotiate the selling price down. We declined, preferring to wait. In the fall, a serious prospect finally got in touch. Twice a husband or his wife came to the store for a few hours to check the sales figures that had been sent to them. They appeared satisfied and shortly after we came to an agreement and sold Rocky's Lunch Bar with gaming room, making the small profit we had hoped for. We stayed in the shop for another two weeks to train the new owner and his family. We were free again and enjoyed our new freedom for a few weeks. Ann quickly found work in the administration of the health insurance company HBF in the city. But I decided to paint the rooms in our house. Only then did I realize how big 150 square meters of living space is, including walls and ceilings; and how much preparation went into such a "prank project." Week-long gymnastics movements, up and down ladders with paint kettles, rollers and brushes – accompanied by local folk music bands - brought me back fitness and enthusiasm. Not surprisingly, I started thinking about Africa again. When, with Ann's consent, I telephoned the Swiss Red Cross in Berne, Vreni Wenger immediately laughed when she heard my voice. She seemed to know the reason for my call before I even got to it. I loved it when she said bluntly, "Yes, there's a good chance we'll have something for you soon. In eastern Sudan more and more Ethiopian refugees are coming across the border." Ann immediately understood what that meant. She was already used to letting me pull into the distance. Reluctantly, she let me go; hoping to catch up one day.

The postman with the telegram was not long in coming: the SRC offered me the post of administrator in the Swiss Red Cross medical team in eastern Sudan. I was scheduled to start work on January 15, 1985. With Ann's consent, I immediately agreed. At least we could still celebrate Christmas together. Then on January 5th, a scorching hot day with 40 degrees in the shade, I flew to Singapore to connect to the flight to Zurich. After the taking off the captain informed us that the temperature in Zurich was minus 19 degrees. When I got out in Zurich-Kloten, the thermometer showed minus 20 degrees. "Well," I said to myself, "now I'll have to run swinging my arms at high speed." A drop in temperature of 60 degrees within 24 hours was indeed extreme. I stayed in Switzerland for a whole week, did the obligatory meetings with health checks at the SRC in Berne. This was a seasoned Swiss Red Cross programme, no need to also go to Geneva. But of course I made a short trip to Interlaken to pray on my parents' grave and visited my brother Alfred and family. It never got "warmer" than minus 15 degrees that week. In my thin raincoat I marched through the streets of my homeland, frozen through and as swift as the wind. Every few minutes I'd take refuge in some store, rubbing my hands to warm up. I couldn't wait to fly to warm Sudan.

CHAPTER TEN

Kassala, Sudan, 1985-1986

SPOTLIGHT ON KASSALA

Kassala is located in eastern Sudan, around 400 kilometers from Khartoum, however the distance by the winding road is much further. Kassala is on the eastern bank of the Gash River, near the Eritrean border. Kassala is at 495 meters altitude, at the foot of the much higher Taka mountains. Kassala is the third largest city in Sudan outside Khartoum and Omdurman, with a large number of different ethnic groups. The long-established Beja ethnic groups include the Hadendoa, Beni Amer and Halanga. In the 20th century, emigrants from the neighbouring countries of Yemen, Eritrea, Ethiopia and Somalia arrived, as did some Indians. From the late 1970s, during the liberation war against the Derg regime, thousands of Ethiopian refugees settled in extensive temporary settlements on the outskirts of the city. In the mid-1980s, black African refugees fled famine in South Sudan to Kassala. Kassala

The state of Kassala in Sudan. [9]

The city centre of the capital Kassala with the inviting Taka mountains. [10]

has a high population percentage from West Africa. Among the first settlers in the city were Kanuri from the region around Lake Chad and Fulbe. Some West Africans, often grouped together as "Nigerians" in statistics, also got stuck in Kassala on the pilgrimage to Mecca and are called *Takarir*. Others hired themselves into the Madhi's army, with which they were sent to Kassala later to settle in the area depopulated by the war. In the 1993 census, around 23 percent were Nigerians for the city of Kassala.

ZURICH TO KHARTOUM

In the fight against refugee misery, I boarded a Swissair plane in Zurich on January 12, 1985 that would take me to Khartoum. In a good mood, I looked out from my window seat at the snow-covered Alps. The only downside was that Ann couldn't travel with me: she would have been happy to see her Sudanese friends in Khartoum again after nine years.

Shortly before landing in the evening, the hostess handed me a whole stack of Zurich daily newspapers at my request. I wanted to bring them to the Swiss Red Cross Team in Kassala. Stepping off the plane in Khartoum, the familiar scent of this city on the White and Blue Nile hit my nostrils. It smelled like slightly rotten straw and to me that smell felt like coming home. A Sudanese from the Red Cross League brought my entry visa to customs and then

---

9   Source: https://en.m.wikipedia.org/wiki/File:Kassala_in_Sudan_(Kafia_Kingi_disputed).svg

10   Source: https://sh.wikipedia.org/wiki/Kasala#/media/Datoteka:Kassala_center_Totil.jpg

drove me to the old Hotel Akropol. But before that, a customs officer told me to unpack my suitcase and spread the contents out on a table. I later remembered this woman in Kassala and cursed her from the bottom of my heart. Apparently practiced and very skillful, in a flash and at a favourable moment she had made the special batteries for my camera her property. Two months passed before I was able to return to Khartoum and get new batteries to finally start taking pictures. On January 14, I boarded a fully occupied bus travelling the 750 kilometers to Kassala on a new asphalt road. My heart rejoiced: now I was once again on the way to a new task, in a place that was still unknown to me. We were driving here on the close to 1,500-kilometer-long road that led from Khartoum to Port Sudan on the Red Sea, a lifeline of the vast Sudan, it was used mainly by heavily laden articulated trucks. On the way I looked at the changing, desert-like landscapes. We drove past mountains up to 400 meters high and my eyes were already looking for possible ascent routes. Every two hours, the bus stopped at a teahouse so passengers could get some warm food. I, too, got hungry over time and chose the Sudanese national dish *ful*, which I already knew from Khartoum and Port Sudan. I ate the bean dish with a flatbread from the wood-fired oven and drank tea. As we drove on, I soon felt an unpleasant rumbling in my intestines, something was wrong, my stomach was upset. The pressure increased, what should I do? The bus drove here at 100 kilometers per hour through the endless semi-desert. Soon there was nothing left to think about because disaster was approaching. I got up quickly, ran to the driver and begged him to stop immediately. When he saw my tortured face, he slammed on the brakes and the bus screeched to a halt. No sooner had the door opened fully than I was out with a long leap, running as fast as I could from the bus to a bush for cover; just in time to avoid an embarrassing accident. I hurried to get back to the bus because there were over 40 passengers waiting to continue. Some smiled understandingly when I thanked the driver with a relieved "*Shucran*." The asphalt road led from here in a long, wide curve towards the Ethiopian border. After a while a large and wide building appeared on the horizon, reminiscent of a mighty cathedral. But as I got closer, I saw that it was a huge, rectangular silo. We were now approaching the town of Gedaref. I had heard that here were also refugee camps for Ethiopian refugees. That meant we were only 200 kilometers from Kassala. At Showak, for a change, we drove through a long, green deciduous forest, soon after we reached Girba, where we crossed an irrigation canal. Here began the province of Kassala. A refugee camp already existed near Girba, 26 kilometers away near New Halfa, it was jointly managed by the Red Cross League and the Swiss Red Cross. This area presented itself as very dry, dusty and flat. But as it was the Sudanese winter the temperature was now very comfortable. We only had 100 kilometers to go before Kassala would appear. Finally, my eyes spotted mountains again, which rose behind the horizon. Those must have been the Taka Mountains I had heard about. My heart began to beat faster as the bus left the main road to Port Sudan on the Red Sea. Here the bus turned right towards the fast approaching Kassala. The impressive Taka mountain range was beautiful to see. For several kilometers they stood in rank and file like a huge wall with gaps in between. The rounded peaks, sloped steeply, reminding me of my mother's big sugar cane candy. She had to lock it up during the war so I couldn't chew on it.

It was immediately clear to me: climbing some of these peaks without a rope would be impossible. But maybe you could let off steam in front of and between the mountains, where steep scree slopes with large boulders piled up. It was already clear: I would undoubtedly like it here. But I didn't come here to climb mountains, but rather as a team member that helped alleviate the great need of refugees. I was really looking forward to this work, integrated in the medical team with people from various countries. On the outskirts of town, the bus drove over a two-lane concrete bridge that crossed the wide bed of the dried-out Gash River. This river only carried water during the Ethiopian rainy season. I got out at the big market square and asked about the Red Cross team house. For a fee, a man carried my suitcase to the building a few hundred meters away, which was near the entrance to the army garrison. In the team house, where the long table for dinner was just being laid, I was greeted first by the somewhat older nurse Josefine (Josy) Harder from Zurich. I immediately liked her and it was the beginning of a lifelong friendship. Then I was introduced by Josy to the team leader and Swiss doctor Dr. Martin Weber and his wife Susanne and warmly welcomed. Martin had been working here for a few months, while his medical practice in Berne was run by a deputy. Susanne, his lovely wife, who worked in Berne as a laboratory assistant and scientific draftswoman, was the team administrator and therefore my predecessor. Since the Weber couple's assignment would end at the end of January, Susanne had to familiarize me immediately with my various tasks. I was relieved that the experienced Swiss nurse, Erika Wachter, was staying on site and she also knew the ropes. We got along very well right away and I would always be able to turn to her or Josy, if I had any questions or uncertainties. From then on, I was busy on various fronts: in the office of the team house, in the warehouses and shopping directly in the town centre. The Wad Sherifay refugee camp, where the Swiss Red Cross Medical Team works, was about 13 kilometers behind the Kassala mountains, near the border with Eritrea, which then, was still part of Ethiopia. The dirt road passed between the mountains behind Kassala, and flat desert tracks to the dry Gash River which was lined with bushes and trees. From there the large refugee camp of Wad Sherifay, spread out on desert soil. This ride took around 30 minutes. Our team could not manage the entire and rapidly growing refugee camp. The American Red Cross Team (ARC) had taken responsibility for a certain part of the camp. I drove to Wad Sherifay myself at least once a week. On my first visit, Martin Weber led me to a bed under the makeshift sunroof[11] hospital on which an old Ethiopian woman was sitting with her granddaughter, who was around nine years-old. Their extended family of fourteen had left their village a weeks before and tried to walk to the rescue of Wad Sherifay. Only the grandmother and her granddaughter made it. All the others perished on the long journey from lack of water, food and exhaustion. This was a shocking testimony of a precarious situation for so many unfortunate refugees. In the coming weeks and months, the situation in Wad Sherifay worsened dramatically. More and more exhausted refugees reached the camp. The next

---

11   A sunroof is made out of thick layers of straw which rest on wooden beams, supported by wooden stems.

time I arrived at the hospital, a little girl had just died. The little body was already wrapped in a white cloth and the father carried his dead daughter out with a serious expression intending walking to the somewhat distant camp cemetery to bury his daughter. I spontaneously opened the passenger door of my Land Rover and gestured for him to get in. The man looked at me, nodded and got in the car. We drove slowly towards the cemetery on the dusty camp roads. The silent, wordless mourning of this father was almost unbearable. So I lightly touched the sorrowful father's arm and offered my condolences on this sad journey. He couldn't understand me - and yet he understood, looked at me and nodded slightly. As infinitely sorry as I felt for him, I was glad to be able to pay this unfamiliar man's daughter my last respects. In the sandy cemetery with its many mounds, each with a stone as a marker, the father laid his daughter in an already prepared depression, prayed, then covered the grave with his bare hands and remained kneeling in front of it. Meanwhile, I slowly drove on, sad and deeply in thought.

As an administrator, I was also responsible for local purchases and drove to the market every day in a badly run-down green Peugeot station car. There were large amounts of food on my shopping list every day, especially fruits and eggs. Every day I bought at least 300 pounds of bananas and 100 pounds grapefruit, which were loaded onto the nurses' vehicles the next morning. I also became the biggest buyer of eggs in Kassala, ordering up to 750 daily, but I hardly ever got this number delivered. These eggs and fruit saved the lives of many malnourished mothers and children cared for in the mother/child departments of the camp.

At the end of the month, the wages for the more than 100

Eritrean employees were due. After I had calculated the total wage bill, I picked up thick wads of Sudanese pounds from the nearby bank. Most of the time I only found time to count the payroll and put it in the appropriate bags after dinner. The payroll grew longer each month, eventually reaching nearly 300 names. As an accountant, walking the tightrope between being in the black and being in the red became more difficult every month.

Luckily there was air conditioning in my office, but it was of little use if a *Habub* (sandstorm) darkened Kassala. The dust got through all cracks, covered the typewriter, the desk, documents and my white Red Cross shirt. On such days, our Eritrean cleaning lady had to come every 20 minutes to dust and clean everything off. Despite such adversities and the ever increasing monthly workload, I would not have switched places with anyone. Like everyone else in the team, I wanted to be part of this life saving team. In this situation personal commitment, dedication and willingness to help counted twice. Someone who doesn't fully engage with these qualities or prescribe to them with heart and soul was out of place in an emergency situation and put strain on the whole team. We all pulled together, showing respect and cared for one another. In everyday situations like those in Kassala, the best of a person comes out. That doesn't mean that everything always went like clockwork. Sometimes there were personal problems and incompatibilities. One of the doctors couldn't stand a nurse, she annoyed him every day. Once, completely beside himself, he said to me: "On the day this woman finally returns to her country, I am going to personally carry her suitcase to the bus. I want to be sure that she actually leaves!"

After our team leader Dr. Martin Weber and his wife had left, a couple of doctors arrived from Belgium; Jean-Marie Tromme, the new team leader, and his wife Dr. Martine Tromme. They had brought with them their twin sons, who were only about three years old. One was always a little sickly. When Martine had to travel to Khartoum a few months later, she took her weaker son with her to be on the safe side. When she returned three days later, she suffered a huge shock: her second son had suddenly died in her absence. It was a terrible personal tragedy amid the suffering the medical team was enduring every day.

A month later, I drove Martine back to Kassala from Wad Sherifay. She asked me to drive first to the OPD, the Swiss Red Cross outpatient clinic in Kassala. She wanted to visit the patients there. When Martine came out again, she was crying bitterly, inconsolable. I couldn't do anything but sit with her in silence and wait. When she had recovered a little, she told me that she had been worried for a while about the twins of an Eritrean woman who were born there a few weeks before. And now one of these twins had died that morning. All the pain about the tragic loss of her own little son, which she had to repress in her stressful work in the refugee camp, suddenly and unexpectedly broke out. I felt so sorry for her. I tried to comfort her, even though I knew there was no real comfort possible. In those minutes I could only guess what a *tour-de-force* this quiet, very kind woman performed day after day as a doctor in Wad Sherifay and Kassala during her own bitterly sad time.

The Swiss Red Cross medical Team became more and more international. We had nurses from Canada, Germany, Belgium, France and Switzerland on duty. Two paediatricians also arrived: the

Norwegian Dr. Eigil Sörensen and for the second time the Bernese Dr. Elmar Heimgartner. The latter regularly conducted further training courses for the local Eritrean medical staff in Wad Sherifay. Not only the heat, but also the regular sandstorms made work in the camp difficult. There were few closed rooms. The work was done under braided sunroofs. But a sunroof of course can not seal off a sandstorm's sand, dust and wind. The tired nurses often returned in the afternoon covered in dust, as if they had been working all day in a flour silo. Nobody complained, everyone took on every hardship in their exhausting work for the sick and needy. From time to time I looked longingly at the nearby Kassala mountains, which beckoned to me. The long working days hadn't allowed for a mountain tour – at least for the time being. One evening, after dinner, I asked the group if anyone was interested in a mountain tour, and my compatriot, the male nurse Klaus Dissler and the Belgian nurse Giselle, immediately got in touch. So it was clear that as soon as there was time and opportunity, we would try climbing.

On a Friday afternoon (our day off) the time had come. In order to try climbing there for the first time the three of us drove a two kilometers to the foot of a rocky hill that looked to be a relatively easy climb. The ascent in a T-shirt and shorts was not difficult for us, we made good progress on steeply sloping, still hot rock slabs. It soon became challenging and steeper, and we began sweating. But once at the top, we were royally rewarded with great views down onto Kassala town and across the flat countryside to the hazy horizon. We cheered for joy. Tired and sweating, but deeply satisfied, after two hours we returned to the team house. The sometimes very stressful situations in our work that had occupied us before this mountain tour had vanished. The physical exertion and sweating, the joy of climbing up this strange mountain world had relieved and freed us of some pressure and stress. After a shower, we felt reborn and grateful. We had found the right therapy for us. Sleep overcame me quickly that evening, I didn't have to count sheep.

Our local auxiliaries were recruited from among the Eritrean refugees, including medical staff and their training, by our doctors and nursing staff, was ongoing. "Some did very well and became so-called "advanced dressers," i.e., barefoot doctors. They even held consultation hours and became a great relief for the Swiss team. I have many fond memories of these very capable, dedicated Eritrean medical staff, including the chief midwife, Senet Abdu, and the pharmacist, Abrehet Asfaha. The latter conscientiously managed and protected the essential medicines delivered from Berne to Wad Sherifay. I happened to be nearby when a uniformed Sudanese captain was on his way to the pharmacy. As soon as he entered it, I heard Abrehet scolding him loudly. The officer immediately came out, stumbling backwards with a red face, completely overwhelmed, saying to me: "That's not a pharmacist, she a tigress!" There was no tampering and zero tolerance was the order of the day: the drugs were only allowed to benefit refugees, no one else at all. Our beloved Abrehet Asfaha made sure of that with body and soul, with every fibre of her being.

In mid-April I drove to Khartoum to pick up our boss from Berne Mrs. Noa Zanolli. She wanted to get her own picture of the rapidly changing and escalating situation. She brought a priceless gift for me: my wife, my beloved Ann! I could barely believe it when

I hugged and kissed her at the airport. The joy was even greater because Ann was now also a team member. The Swiss Red Cross had hired her as an administrator with special tasks. From now on we worked together for the SRC. Nothing could have been more beautiful and satisfying for both of us! Our team now numbered 13 people who had to be well fed for such strenuous and stressful work. Ann was immediately responsible for the daily menu, did the shopping and supervised the two local cooks preparing the food. She was also responsible for the maintenance in the four team houses and helped me in the office in between tasks. Ann and I lived here like before in Mogadishu, also a green house , but here we shared with Josy Harder. There was no shower, we made do with a water barrel and jug; or we showered with the hose in the garden behind a bush. The outhouse stood at the end of the large garden, which at night we had to access with a flashlight.

One day the representative of an English NGO came to me and offered us a delivery of 50 tons of spaghetti, which I was only too happy to accept. However, I remained skeptical because a lot could happen during the shipping from England to Kassala. But it worked. A few months later, two trucks arrived from Port Sudan, but not with spaghetti. They delivered instead 50 tons of lasagne sheets packed in no fewer than 200,000 packets of 250 gram. These sheets of lasagne quickly became popular and were enjoyed by all the children and adult patients we catered for. It was always a pleasure to watch the smiling cooks at the Wad Sherifay kitchen, carefully stirring the steaming pasta in large cooking pots. Outside of Kassala town there was an airfield. One day a cargo plane that had taken off from Amsterdam landed there and brought us 10 tons of biscuits packed in large tin cans. Our truck delivered the first two tons directly to Wad Sherifay, where the still cold biscuits were received with great joy.

A Swiss NGO from Basel sent an ophthalmologist to Gedaref, 200 kilometers south of Kassala. This generous eye specialist was using his own holidays to treat countless African eye patients free of charge. He really deserves to be mentioned here for his amazing generosity. I got several assignments to bring eye patients in a 30-seater bus from Wad Sherifay to this doctor in Gedaref. A long sea container was there with the appropriate technical equipment, in which eye patients could be treated. As a rule, the patients had one eye lens replaced. I was even allowed to watch one such procedure for a moment. In the late afternoon, all 30 patients were back on the bus for our return journey. All of the operated eyes were bandaged. If I looked in the rear view mirror during the bumpy ride home, I saw thirty "one-eyed people," swaying from left to right like ears of corn in the wind.

One day Urs Schneider, a young Swiss doctor arrived in Kassala to join our team. The young Lucerne native was enthusiastic about the Kassala mountains and turned out to be the best climber when he went on a tour with Giselle and me. Urs and Giselle chose more difficult routes, while I as a latecomer, preferred less dangerous routes. Sometimes, when a cliff stopped us, we could find cracks that appeared inside the mountain. Whole labyrinths opened up to us in the semi-darkness and we gained height . With due caution and mutual support, this was not dangerous. There were enough safe ledges climbing slowly higher and eventually down again. Bathed in sweat, satisfied and relaxed, we returned to the team house. However, we did once get caught by a violent sandstorm on a descent. Visibility immediately became poor. Very carefully we found our way down, while staying close to each other. Covered in dust, when we arrived at the team house, we caused laughter and joking. These climbing activities in our free time quickly helped dissolve all our work stress.

* * * * *

More and more refugees needed medical help, but our makeshift sunroof hospital was no longer appropriate. The team requested permission from Berne to urgently look for a better solution. The SRC in Berne decided to build a larger, more suitable hospital in Wad Sherifay. The motto was that only local material must be used. After calculating the relatively modest cost of five long buildings, we got the go-ahead from Berne. The procurement of materials was again my task. Shambel, my reliable and knowledgeable assistant, was of vital help. First we mixed short cut straw with loamy sand and water, filled it into wooden moulds to form thick adobe bricks. We then let them dry in the hot sun. We also needed straight, solid tree trunks, as well as wood for windows, doors and rafters, and a large amount of brushwood for the grass roof. All of this was purchased in Gedaref 200 kilometers away. To our great relief, the five buildings or rather called wings could be erected according to schedule without any major annoyance or quarrels and to the delight of all, we moved beds into it within a reasonable period of time. The doctors chose one of the five hospital wings as the children hospital.

The new hospital hadn't long been in operation when a team from Swiss television arrived and shot a film in Wad Sherifay interviewing team members and refugees. Some of my Zurich friends afterwards wrote to me that they got excited to see me on TV in front of the new hospital and hear me speak. Wad Sherifay became increasingly well-known internationally. Almost every week European TV and radio crews visited the huge refugee camp behind the Kassala mountains. Our experienced Josy Harder quickly became famous for her competent interviews. The media people always wanted her to interview. On my small shortwave radio, I could regularly hear how our Josy – surrounded by refugee mothers and children – describing the difficult emergency situations under the straw roof in the Mother/Child section. Josy thus became an important ambassador for our work in Wad Sherifay and far beyond. Gradually, celebrities and political greats took notice and travelled to Wad Sherifay, which now had become by far the largest refugee camp in Africa. Bob Geldof visited and after that he used his highly-acclaimed international concert appearances to collect money. When he was still vice-president, George Bush senior also visited. The Swiss Jean Pierre Hocké, my former boss in Biafra-Nigeria, also honoured us with his visit and happily remembered me. He had an impressive, very steep career behind him. He came to Wad Sherifay as the highest UNHCR official for refugee affairs. Another visitor was Leon Stubbings, an Australian VIP who for decades had been the General Secretary of the Australian Red Cross. Ann and I invited him to dinner at a restaurant. Despite the tough steaks, we spent a pleasant evening with stimulating conversations.

TO THE HORIZON AND BEYOND

* * * * *

During this time Klaus Dissler our experienced nurse, and his twelve Eritrean helpers performed a first-class feat. Klaus was responsible for the sanitation in the ever-expanding refugee camp. So Klaus and his staff scoured the refugee camp on bicycles every day, visiting all the refugee families in their modest, self-built little huts. These young men were constantly on the move, tirelessly teaching about hygiene– and how important it was to observe. With these regular visits, Klaus and his followers were able to ensure that the important sanitary regulations were taken seriously and implemented. These were very important measures to preventing an epidemic. Nevertheless, despite all these efforts, in May 1985, the Cholera broke out in Wad Sherifay. Officially however, we were not allowed to use this frightening word in radio and telex messages. The word gastroenteritis had to be used.

The first patients were being treated in the hospital, but more and more people fell ill. An isolation ward was quickly set up one kilometer away from the camp – under large tents directly on desert ground. A doctor and two nurses were delegated there, as well as Eritrean medical staff. The American Refugee Committee (ARC) also sent personnel to assist. When I arrived at the isolation station for the first time, an electrician was just laying cables for a generator so that work could be done 24 hours 7 days. When I entered the big tent, I was greeted by a terrible stench which was at first almost unbearable. It what also was the hottest season of the year. There were 40 beds under the hot tent roof. The wicker beds on which the patients lay had a circular hole cut out in the middle, with a bowl or plastic bucket placed on the sandy ground below. All the diarrhoea fell or splashed directly into the container. A second bowl stood next to each bed to catch the vomit. In order to relieve the very busy nursing staff, I helped to change any almost full container and carry the smelly contents outside to pour down a narrow deep hole. Rather slowly my nose got used of the penetrating stench in the cholera tent. Nevertheless, I still feel proud and grateful for having experienced such a unique situation once in my life but I also very highly admired everyone who, for six months had kept up a strenuous 24-hour non-stop operation under very demanding conditions. Day and night they simply persevered without any "if's or buts." Over 60 medical professionals and paramedics performed their duties at this desert station for months, 24 hours and 7 day weeks. They had received a cholera vaccination at the beginning of the outbreak. Nevertheless, strict hygiene with hand-washing and constant disinfection was the top priority. Luckily, none of the staff fell ill during the epidemic. Using a tanker, a 15,000 litre water tank had to be filled up every two days. Most patients were given fluids intravenously first because they were so dehydrated. Once the greatest danger was averted, they were allowed to drink again by themselves. It was of the utmost importance that newly-infected people– sometimes more than 50 a day – were immediately taken to this camp where they recovered relatively quickly. The epidemic lasted from May 30 to November 20 in 1985, with a total of 1793 patients, 32 of whom died, which was a surprisingly small number. For the team, this was an extraordinarily trying time; much more stressful than the usual, so-called normal. every day. Nobody at the cholera station, Wad Sherifay or Kassala itself had enough recovery time during those weeks and months. At the end of November, we were all just very tired. And yet, as soon as we thought about how many patients could be saved, that alone gave us energy and impetus. And if we just imagined the constant stream of patients, big and small in need of help, tiredness and tension disappeared almost by itself. Without our medical staff most of them would have been sentenced to death. They couldn't allow that. We were all here to fight as a dedicated team of the Swiss Red Cross and the American Red Cross.

At the beginning of 1986, we foreigners decided as a team that we would finally wanted to learn basic Arabic. So we hired an older, retired Sudanese school teacher at our expense. Once a week on Wednesday evenings from 7 to 9 p.m., we were sitting like excited school-children, armed with notebooks and pens at the long table in the team house. As we were unable to read the exotic Arabic letters, we wrote down words, phrases, verbs and sentences by ear. Abdullah, our teacher went to great lengths to introduce us to this unfamiliar language. The following week, we tried to repeat what we had previously written down, and then listened to new words or sentences. At the next lesson a week later, we had great difficulty remembering what we had learned. Most of the time we had forgotten almost everything from the week before, even though we had written it down. We were all simply too tired and worn out in the evening to try repeating what we were supposed to have learned and .. do our homework. After two months we all regretfully agreed to quit. What remained of Abdullah's patient teaching could only be described as very modest: *Bukra* = tomorrow; *Malesh* = sorry or never mind; *Yawash* = slow; *Wahid, Itneen, Talata* = one, two, three. Our minds simply had to concentrate on our much more important work. Every six months we received from Switzerland a container full of medicines via Port Sudan. But in the spring of 1986, the container ship encountered a severe storm en route and our medicine container fell overboard along with other containers. This put us in a very delicate position. At least we found out about this accident in good time, and were able to narrowly avoid a bottleneck with an express repeat order.

Eritrean rebel groups had been fighting against Ethiopian rule for over 25 years. Eritrea, a former Italian colony, wanted independence. By 1986 the conflict had turned into trench warfare in the mountains of Eritrea. Countless determined Eritreans including women, fought there on the front lines. The Eritreans had for some time rented a multi-storey house in Kassala for their soldiers to have a rest there. Unarmed men and women with no insignia of rank, they could be recognized by their khaki uniforms.

The ICRC maintained a workshop for prosthetic legs in Kassala. I watched with fascination on various occasions as these Swiss experts took measurements and produced appropriate prostheses and then, after a trial further adjusted and refined them. I will never forget the bright eyes of those Eritrean war victims when they made their first attempts to walk without crutches. The three Swiss technicians were no less pleased when they saw the result of their tinkering and precision work.

Lavina, a popular South Sudanese woman, also worked at the ICRC in Kassala; a very capable physiotherapist and midwife, she cared for our patients at Wad Sherifay as well. With her sincere, cheerful nature, she won many friends. Lavina had a big dream of her own: she really wanted to work in Switzerland. We all supported her – and indeed she managed to go to Switzerland. However, she was not allowed to take her own small tools with her. Josy Harder, Klaus Dissler, Kathryn Grünig and I later brought them to Switzerland for her. Lavina, who spoke English and Arabic, quickly found a job at the regional hospital in Biel and learned French, German and Italian. Her professional experience and willingness to continue training helped her to have an amazing career in her new home country. Her employer soon sent Lavina abroad for further, specialist training. Then she married a Swiss man and later, successfully set up her own physiotherapy practice.

The work for and at Camp Wad Sherifay did not diminish during the first half of 1986. But the cholera epidemic the year before seemed to have been a kind of turning point for all of us. No matter how heavy the workload was, or how imponderables always brought additional pressure, we always managed to cope with it. Everything seemed manageable to us - so long as no other epidemic appeared.

In September 1986, Ann and I received an inquiry from the Swiss Red Cross in Berne. Completely unexpectedly, our employer offered us a new very tempting task: to work as Swiss RC Delegates with the Red Cross of Bangladesh to set up a development program for the poorest population in the coastal area and islands at the Bay of Bengal. Ann as a development worker in her old homeland! It sounded like a gorgeous dream! Of course we said yes straight away. We first couldn't believe it and were overjoyed, looked forward to this mission in Bangladesh with great anticipation – from day one with my Ann.

CHAPTER ELEVEN

Dhaka, Chittagong, Bangladesh, 1986-1989: A Homecoming

SPOTLIGHT ON CHITTAGONG

The city is also the administrative seat of the Chittagong district and region of the same name. The port in turn is the largest in Bangladesh and one of the largest in the entire Indian subcontinent. Chittagong is located in the southeast of the country at the foot of the Chittagong Hill Tracts. The region is characterized by a rich biodiversity. In the Hill Tracts there are still many plants and animals that have otherwise become rare in Bangladesh. Examples include elephants, leopards and bison. The forests of the Hill Tracts are severely endangered by the ongoing deforestation. 14 kilometers

---

12   Source: https://www.tide-forecast.com/locations/Sandwip

TO THE HORIZON AND BEYOND

Chittagong is the second largest city in the country after the capital, Dhaka. [12]

Hill Tracts

south of the port is Patenga sandy beach. This is a tourist attraction and known for spectacular sunsets. Chittagong is located on the banks of the Karnaphuli river between the Hilltracts and the Bay of Bengal. The greater Chittagong area has a population of 5.2 million people in 2022. It hosts the biggest seaport on the Bay of Bengal and is one of the oldest ports in the world, with a natural harbor. Chittagong appeared on ancient Greek and Roman maps. During the Bangladesh liberation war in 1971, Chittagong became the Site of the Bangladesh declaration of Independence.

* * * * *

For me, Bangladesh, the "Land of the Bengalis" is a country of sparkling waters and blue-green rice fields dissolving in the haze of the distant horizon. The people are friendly and frugal who have to work hard in the rural areas to support their large families. Their numerous children are the old age insurance - one day they will have to care for their elderly parents. However, Bangladesh is also a country with dangerous cyclone, massive floods and is over-populated. The latter in particular poses major problems for development aid. Corruption is, unfortunately, also widespread, the victims of which are primarily the poorest. Personally, Bangladesh which had to pay a very high price (in blood) for its independence, has become something of a third homeland for me, next to Switzerland and Australia. A country that changed my life and even more myself. It gave me my beautiful wife Ann and with it, happiness and well-being and thirteen years after leaving, we came back to our other home –Chittagong! In the capital Dhaka the traffic had increased massively since our departure in 1973. My many years of driving experience were no longer of much use to me. With passive considerate driving, you couldn't get anywhere in this metropolis. It was like an anthill: countless rickshaws, baby taxis and pedestrians fought for their right of way. Respectful, considerate driving was seen as weakness and your way was immediately blocked. Whenever I stopped to give way, drivers behind me would furiously honk. As before, the horn was more important than the brakes. Clearly, the law of the largest vehicle ruled. Since I wanted to avoid this unnecessary stress, I quickly hired a driver. From then on, I sat next to the chauffeur now holding a green coconut with a drinking straw, and following the hair-raising traffic in a relaxed manner. I was looking forward to leaving Dhaka and its noisy and smelly traffic chaos. Full of anticipation I waited for the time we could leave for the much healthier coast, to start the first inspections of the low-cost housing development program.

The officer responsible for this program at the Swiss Red Cross HQ in Berne was Claude Ribaux, an experienced development worker from St. Gallen who knew Bangladesh well. After he also landed in Dhaka, Ann and I drove to the coast with him and Mihir, the representative of the Bangladesh Red Cross. Once there, we waded bare foot through a thick, gray mud slick to an old passenger boat that was waiting to take us to the island of Sandwip. This island is located near the mouth of the Ganges, which flows into the Bay of Bengal, and is locally called Meghna. At the landing site we loaded the two 125 cc Honda motorcycles we were taking with us. They were best suited for us to thoroughly explore the island. We also wanted to see the houses that had already been built for the Swiss Humanitarian Aid Unit (SHA), development program which was headed by Bernhard Bosshart.

The afternoon was already advanced, so we had to hurry. I was a little worried because I hadn't ridden a motorcycle in twelve years. In addition, there were hardly any dirt roads here, only bumpy cart and footpaths. And there was really no time for me to practice on the motorcycle. In the meantime, a few dozen residents and their children had rushed over to see us driving away. With a worried Ann as my pillion passenger and our two bags on the rack, I stepped on the starter lever. Somewhat unexpectedly, the engine started immediately, and I drove off swaying and quite uncertain. Ann let out a scream and grabbed me, her fingers digging into my stomach. Mihir and Claude followed us on the second machine. Shortly after we took our first corner, I immediately caught my breath. To my horror the path narrowed and led to the top of a high dam. Uncultivated rice fields glistened on either side – a long drop from the path. There was no turning back. We were already bumping along the wet, glistening crest, barely a foot wide; trying carefully to ride in the middle. Ann clung tighter to me and yelled angrily, "If you throw me down here, I'll go straight back to Dhaka!" I felt like Karl Wallenda (circus acrobat and tightrope walker), but that Karl, by the way, didn't have a trembling wife glued to his back. Suddenly, I hit a hole and the front wheel sank into the earth next to a narrow crest. But I accelerated in a flash and was able to bring the swaying bike back onto the barely 30 centimeter wide path. Imagine if we had fallen into the muddy water? A wet marital quarrel would have been inevitable. Luckily, I somehow managed to pass over this dam safely. With a sigh of relief, we turned onto a much wider dirt path, and the pressure from Ann's embrace eased noticeably.

The much quieter ride continued past groups of trees, farmhouses, ponds, banana trees, cows, and waving children. Towards evening we reached our destination, a farmhouse where we would spend the night. The farmer's wife, whom we didn't see personally, cooked us a simple dinner. After that it was time to lie down on a bed of straw. It stung a bit but that didn't stop our well-deserved night's rest. After our cat wash the next morning, Ann was allowed to go into the kitchen to help the farmer's wife prepare our breakfast. Ann found out how lonely this woman's life was because she hardly ever left the house and, as a Muslim, was not allowed to speak to strangers. Ann later told me that this woman was genuinely pleased being able to talk to her and had become brighter and quite lively as she did. When saying goodbye two days later, she hugged Ann with sad eyes.

For three days we looked around the island. As mentioned, the Swiss Humanitarian Aid Unit (SHA) had already started the cheap housing program here. Excavation and landfill had occurred in some places made, and other houses had been built with walls made of bamboo mesh. Since other building sites had been marked out, we were able to estimate the distances between the individual building sites. This gave us a first, important impression of how the development program would be completed. With the status of this construction work in mind, we now began our own, extremely time-consuming inspections of the entire coastal area. We went in search of building sites, wherever the poorest families lived. Between the protective dam and the water, they were completely exposed to the danger of tidal waves.

Our next destination, this time without Ann, was the island of Hatyia, a two-day journey from Dhaka. This time we travelled with a Land Rover. But the last stretch from Maizdi to the coast was the most difficult part of our exploratory trip. For what seemed like forever, we rumbled at walking pace along a brick-covered dam causeway full of holes. Finally arriving at the coast, we waited for two hours for the so called "Sea truck" a strange, unconfident looking watercraft; a kind of rectangular landing craft with a wheelhouse that could dock on banks that were not too steep, independent of the tides. The front wall was simply folded down to get in and out. The "Sea truck" also offered space for our vehicle and a few dozen standing room passengers.

This sea truck made only slow progress in the water and the swaying crossing to Hatiya took almost three hours due to the strong current of the mighty Meghna (Ganges) which flowed further down into the Bay of Bengal. When we finally arrived at Hatyia Island's steep, heavily eroded shore, workers had already dug a steep driveway into the tough clay, closely watched by countless curious onlookers. It was only thanks to this temporary driveway that we were able to drive our Land Rover off the craft and drove off immediately to Roffique, the head of a local aid organization and were able to spend the night there. The next morning, we climbed down a concrete staircase into the pond next to the house to wash and shave. In those rural regions, there are hardly any bathrooms. As mentioned in my first Bangladesh mission, most rural houses have a pond next to the house. The pond fills itself with water after soil is excavated to build a raised platform as a foundation of the house. Mostly these ponds are used for fish farming.

TO THE HORIZON AND BEYOND

We set off early, but only made slow progress on the pitted road, which was badly paved with bricks. At the market in Char Chenga we made our first stop in front of the tea house. As soon as we got out, we were surrounded by staring men. However, they willingly made room for us as we pushed our way into the almost empty teahouse. It got dark in a flash because the curious men in their traditional loin clothing (*lungi*) also pushed into the tea house, sat down or stood close to watch us with serious, motionless faces as we might have looked at strange animals in a zoo. This behavior did not worry us in the least. We were aware that Europeans seldom found their way onto this remote island, so we understood how exotic we looked. The same thing kept repeating itself over the next few days. Wherever we went we were surrounded by local people who curiously stared at us with spellbound expressions; totally fascinated by us and our behavior.

We drove back and forth across the island, walked long distances to the shore, ate bananas, drank coconut water (dab water) or tea and talked to other responsible aid agency people and of course to the village elders; always looking for suitable building land for the housing program. Three days later we took another old-fashioned passenger boat to the secluded, mangrove-covered island of Nijhum Dwip (Quiet Island). It lies on the edge of the Bay of Bengal and is completely vulnerable to hurricanes and tidal waves. Around 500,000 people lost their lives in this region in November 1970, the most devastating hurricane disaster at the time. Of 500 inhabitants, only six survived on Nijum Dwip. That disaster contributed to the separation of East Pakistan from West Pakistan a year later because the government in West Pakistan had failed to provide urgent needed aid. It quickly became clear to us: we really wanted to build there.

Back in Dhaka, we informed the Secretary General of the BDRC (Bangladesh Red Cross) Major Quoreshi (retired) and director Akram about our construction plans and discussed the next steps with them. Because this was a partnership program, it was entirely up to the BDRC to approach the state for the land needed for building. The SRC was responsible for the concept of the development program, its financing with small loans to the beneficiaries and the broad-based teaching and motivation of the program.

Christmas was just around the corner and on December 23rd, full of joy and laden with gifts, Ann and I travelled by train to Chittagong to spend our Christmas and New Year holidays with Ann's relatives, as we had done 14 years before. A very big surprise awaited us in Chittagong that would change our lives. We learned from Ann's younger sister Elsie, that their late brother Aldrick's two young daughters had recently been placed in the care of the Catholic orphanage. That worried us a lot. Our thoughts kept circling around Ann's two young nieces. What could we do? We knew we had to get to the bottom of this sad story, otherwise it would never let us go. So, on December 26th on St. Stephen's Day, we took a rickshaw to the orphanage and reported to Sister Bernadette the matron. It was a wonderful coincidence that it was the same Sister Bernadette who had spoken so warmly and kindly of Ann to me 14 years before, after I had asked her for advice. She was very happy to see us again after many years, listened to our request and asked us to sit and wait at a table while she fetched the two girls. During those minutes of waiting, an almost unbearable tension overcame us. With great inner uncertainty we asked ourselves what awaited us now. How would the two girls react to us?

After a while a door opened, and Sister Berneadette carefully pushed two little girls into the room. She introduced us to Janet, who had turned six days earlier, and her smaller sister, Hazel, who was four. Then she left us alone with the children. There they stood hand in hand in front of us, two poorly dressed little girls with very short hairs, looking at us mutely, seriously, and shyly with large questioning eyes. Ann immediately smiled at her two little nieces, hugged, and kissed them both, stroking their heads. The children remained tense; waiting and silent, what could they say? Both looked so terribly thin in their faded skirts. When Ann spoke Bangla to them, Janet and Hazel listened carefully. Slowly they seemed to relax a little, but they couldn't elicit a smile; even when they received two small gifts and a bag of candy. As timidly as they had come in, they fled through the door silently and hastily, when the matron came for them again. That was our first encounter with Janet and Hazel. This visit touched our hearts, stirred us up and triggered a storm of thoughts in our minds. We were even more shocked when we heard from Sister Bernadette about the traumatic experiences behind Janet and Hazel. Both girls became seriously ill after their father's death. The mother, who lives as a member of a tribe in a remote, hilly area bordering Burma and India, had no other option than to take the two girls to an orphanage. From there they were soon taken to the large orphanage in Chittagong, where they could be better cared for, and they slowly recovered.

A few days later, Sister Bernadette allowed us to pick up Janet and Hazel at the orphanage and go shopping with them. Ann really wanted to dress her little nieces better, and bought each of them two nice little dresses, underwear, and sandals. The two still couldn't smile, they just kept looking at us shyly with big wondering eyes. We both felt that these children needed a lot of time, personal care, patience, trust, attention, and love to be able to gradually process their traumatic experiences. We both knew that in these last days of 1986, independently of one another, both Ann and I felt a desire to care for Janet and Hazel. This probably didn't go unnoticed by the matron of the orphanage either. So, one day she gently informed us that the two girls also had an eleven-year-old brother named Charles, who worked for a farmer in the Hill Tracts as a hired boy. This information was a huge surprise which overwhelmed us and forced us to rethink everything from the beginning. We were sure that we could take care of two girls who were still young and traumatized. But to take in three children at once, one of whom was an eleven-year-old boy with an even more burdensome life story to carry. Were we up to it? How could we do justice to all three children without overtaxing and losing ourselves? We were both in our 50s and had limited experience with children. Simultaneously and instinctively, we both realized that we urgently needed a marching stop; take some time out and distance to think about the new situation thoroughly. At the same time, it became important to deal with eleven-year-old Charles. We could only decide which path we wanted to take if we included him and his life in our thoughts about the future. Did we want to become a family of five, or would it be better if we supported the children in other ways? A first hurdle that was not to be underestimated was a visit to Charles. The Hill Tracts were a restricted area at the time. So, it took an elaborate plan to get there. The main town of the Hill Tracts is the town of Rangamati, which lies on the scenically very beautiful lake Kaptai; surrounded by many bays and green islands. At that time, only indigenous tribes lived in this remote, hilly jungle region bordering India and Burma. Tensions with the native tribes had led to the Hill Tracts being declared a restricted area. Foreigners were therefore forbidden to travel there. Ann went anyway in March 1987; namely with the local bus and accompanied by her nephew Ronald Gonsalves. Ann wore a poor, faded sari with a headscarf so as not to be recognized as a "foreigner." Her common sense forward-planning, as always, was once again successful. After some back and forth on site, the head nurse of the local orphanage in Rangamati, had Charles brought in. And then, standing in front of Ann, who was waiting anxiously, was her rather short, nephew Charles. He reacted not only reservedly, but suspiciously and negatively. Unlike his two younger sisters, he was not shy and scared. His facial expression – and especially his eyes – showed even more that he must have experienced far more bitter sadness in his short life than an eleven-year-old could be expected to bear. Although he answered Ann's questions in monosyllables, he showed no interest in a longer conversation. It was obvious: Charles was strongly influenced by his previous life. Upon her return, Ann told me in detail about her feelings on that first visit. The "raised wall" that she had felt very well with Charles made her think and unsettled her. She kept wondering if it would be any good for Charles if we took him out of his current circumstances to offer him a so-called "better life." Could he cope with it, and use the chance? Ann doubted this, she was rather opposed to taking Charles with us. I, on the other hand, voted in his favor, because I felt it was unfair to exclude him as a brother to Janet and Hazel. I also counted on the fact that at eleven, Charles was still young enough to put his bitterly sad childhood behind him and embrace his "new life." On the other hand, when he met Ann for the first time, he had of course no idea at all how important this meeting with his Aunt Ann was for him. Well, I just felt he should get a chance. It was good that our work had to be at the top of the priority list during those weeks. So, we didn't rush into anything, or push ourselves to make hasty decisions about a "family of five." It had to wait a little longer, meanwhile, we visited Janet and Hazel.

Just as we had to exercise patience in our private lives, our work also required a lot of us. Every journey from Dhaka to the coast took time because we had to cross the Meghna in two places with chronically overcrowded car ferries. We looked longingly across the river, where concrete pillars protruded from the water. Japan built gigantic road bridges over the Meghna. But the difficult construction had dragged on so, we would probably never be able to drive over these bridges. On the first day of each trip, we only ever got as far as Noakhali, where we stayed in the Danida guest house. Even "everyday little things" could cause some hardship. For example, an evening power failure in the hottest season of the year, meant there would be no air conditioning in the guest house in question. In many places in Bangladesh, power stations had too little capacity and could therefore only distribute rationed electricity.

After a long and often nerve-wracking day at work, it was a kind of limbo for us. It was even more stressful when the weather suddenly changed. This was also the case when I travelled with

Mihir to Hatyia again on the sea truck. The weather suddenly deteriorated unexpectedly. A gusty wind picked up waves grew higher, the sea truck rocked violently, the boat seemed to literally be pounding in the dirty brown water. Because of the strong lateral current, we hardly made any progress. Land was nowhere in sight; to make matters worse, the cloud cover began to turn yellowish. "Not a good sign," Mihir stated dryly: "I suspect there's a cyclone brewing." The worried faces of other passengers made me feel uneasy. However, the skipper did not want to turn back. Hours passed, the island of Hatyia should have appeared hours ago. It seemed as if we were lost in the endless expanses of a brown ocean. Could it be that this strong current pushed us out into the Gulf? We standing passenger got obviously further concerned. Twilight was already setting in, and hunger was making itself felt. The captain finally informed us that we were still heading for Hatyia but were making obviously slow progress because of the strong current, headwind, and higher waves. Those words didn't really calm anyone down. The oncoming darkness contributed to the fact that passengers began to shiver and stood closer together. At least the hard-working diesel engine continued to roar soothingly, making the jet-black water surface look a little less threatening. Finally, someone with a relieved voice called out "Light!" pointing ahead. Indeed, a faint light could be seen far away. The mood rose immediately, the relief was palpable, everyone began to chatter. Mihir raised his right hand and released a "high five" on mine. It was already 9 p.m., a whopping six hours late, when our struggling sea vehicle finally docked at Hatyia. What a unique, wonderful feeling, after endless hours standing on unsteady legs in this rocking tub, we felt extremely relieved to be standing again on solid ground. At our colleague Roffique's home we were able to enjoy a small, late dinner with some rice and vegetables before lying down. The next morning everything was quiet. There was no breeze, and we looked worriedly at the sky: the yellow cloud cover didn't bode well. We were sure: something was brewing somewhere. Hopefully far away. There was a peculiar, unusually quiet, almost oppressive mood in the air. Nevertheless, we didn't let ourselves be annoyed, put our Hondas in motion and drove off. But already in the second curve of the dirt path my rear wheel slipped on the dewy clay, and I fell to the ground. The only injury I suffered was a slightly damaged ego. From then on, we did our daily program more carefully, without falling. However, the yellow clouds that had stayed with us hadn't disappeared the next day either. But we were lucky again this time, the cyclone raged further away, Hatyia stayed in its fringe zone.

After Claude Ribaux had flown back to Berne, I visited other islands with Mihir in the Meghna estuary. All of our trips were similarly time-consuming: we spent precious hours waiting for a boat, often didn't reach the destination until it was dark. Then Mihir had to find a family who was willing to cook us a simple meal at a late hour that we happily paid for. After that we lay dead tired and unwashed on some sort of straw bed. After a morning bath in the cool pond followed with a cup of tea, we got on our Hondas, let the wind caress us on narrow, uneven dirt roads and happily waved to the farmers in the fields. Despite these limitations: I really liked these journeys in the freedom of beautiful Bangladesh. Whenever I was in coastal areas, Ann would take care of the administrative needs, attend meetings, while also looking out for a cheap house.

We finally decided on a simple house with a garden behind the market in the suburb of Gulshan 1. Hansrudi Wittwer, another Swiss Red Cross delegate and compatriot of ours, lived in the same suburb in the Green Goose guest house. He was working on the same program as us but in North Bangladesh. In this way, we were able to continuously exchange our experiences. Peter Amacher, head of *Enfants du Monde*, also lived near us with his charming wife Eva. The exchange with them was also good for us; especially at this time when the topic of children was so important to us. During these days and weeks our thoughts often went to Janet and Hazel at the orphanage. We both were on a real emotional roller coaster ride. We were a childless couple in our mid 50s. Caring for the two girls would change our lives from the ground up. It would demand hitherto unknown sacrifices from us, and burden us with responsibility which would result in unforeseeable consequences. It was a difficult decision; how should we act? This question did not leave us. There were days when we both feeling positive and felt strong enough for this new challenge. Then there were days when either me or Ann, or both at the same time, doubted whether we were in fact capable for it. There was still some time left to decide. But every further visit to the orphanage also had an effect. The tip of the scales slowly but steadily moved in the direction of our hearts, away from the equally important, sober headed decision. Charles was still not fully involved. It was even uncertain whether he would be "released." We now cautiously took step by step, deliberately moving in the direction of taking over all three children. In the weeks that followed, Ann made further clarifications, obtained information, and finally received the required forms to fill out and submit. After that the waiting began. Since our daily work absorbed us so much, this waiting didn't seem as torturous as one might imagine. Mihir and I were always on the go, we were travelling a lot. When we once again reached distant Nijum Dwip with a rented boat, we had to wait 300 meters before the canal entrance for the incoming tide. Shortly thereafter we suddenly witnessed a very fascinating natural spectacle as I had never seen before. The sea water suddenly began bubbling non-stop quite far around the boat. It had started slowly, then more and more. It was like a very wide pan of water was boiling. Mihir explained to me, this is the exact time when the low tide stops and turns into high tide. Amazed, I couldn't get enough of this. We anchored here in the middle of millions of bubbles glittering in the sunlight. Then suddenly all the bubbling stopped, and the water appeared again as smooth as glass. Sea God Neptune may had taken his giant pan off the gas stove. The tide was now slowly raising, still it took another hour before we were able to enter the canal. In order to gain extra time two days later, we decided to sail out to sea during the nightly high tide. It was bitterly cold at two o'clock in the morning when we switched on a flashlight and trudged through a forest to the canal where the three-man crew awaited us. But the skipper and his helpers were unable to start the cold diesel engine with the pull line. They tried again and again for almost an hour. The engine refused to start, only loudly coughed a few times and stopped again. The skipper murmured some encouragements and patted the engine a little. But after further unsuccessful attempts, his patience gave out and he cursed the stubborn engine with loud, angry words. By now we were all really shivering. A quarter to three, our frustrated skipper, announced: "We're going to try it now for the very last time. If it still refuses to work, we'll all go back to sleep!"

The men pulled the strap again with the last of their strength. But this time the engine began to cough loudly and let stinking exhaust fumes shoot up into the dark air with irregular but deafening bangs. After that, the stubborn engine started working. We beamed to each other, and suddenly felt less cold. In good spirits we drove carefully slow through the narrow canal in the glow of the flashlight. But ten minutes later, just before the mouth to the gulf, we got stuck in the mud, because the low tide had already started. The loss of time caused by this stubborn boat engine gave us this additional annoyance. Two headscarf-wearing helpers, wearing only their thin loincloths and a woolen blanket knotted around their shoulders, spent twenty minutes shivering in the night wind desperately trying to push the boat out of the mud with bamboo poles. With a sigh of relief, we finally got away and headed out into open water. However, the freezing cold night wind continued. The night sea became more and more restless, high waves set in and we were constantly driven up and down. For once, it was good to have an empty stomach, there was nothing to sacrifice. The bearded skipper was undeterred, and held the rudder firmly, staring grimly at the next wave, and spreading as much confidence and trust as possible. We braved this merciless ascent and descent for two long hours, frozen to the bone. Had the boat capsized, the strong current would have swept us out into the Gulf, never to be seen again. This knowledge made this strenuous adventure one we would rather not experience again. When the southern end of Hatyia finally came into view in the first light of dawn, Mihir and I had only one wish: to get off! We were shaking and felt really miserable. We both agreed: next time we would rather walk. So, the boat dropped us off and we told the crew we would walk from there and could they send our driver with the Land Rover to meet us on our way. It was very reassuring and even more invigorating to be able to step on solid ground and start walking to warm up. Nevertheless, we felt a certain tiredness and heaviness, which we attributed to the strenuous boat trip. But we liked walking forward between fields, trees, bushes, and creeks, waving at the farmers and children in the fields, who had also got up early. As we passed a palm tree, a man was just descending the ladder, carrying a small jar of juice. This sap, which he had extracted from the tapped palm tree, would now be boiled down until it crystallized into a tasty sugar. For a small fee he filled a cup for us. The slightly sweet juice tasted good and invigorated us. Cheerfully we marched on until suddenly and menacingly it started to rumble in my intestines. Drinking sweet palm juice on an empty stomach was probably not such a good decision, or could it be that a bird was sitting up there on the juice jar and dropped some poo into the sap juice? I began to run faster, desperately looking for a protective bush. This was immediately noticed from far. Children quickly came running in high spirits to catch up with this white stranger. Tensely I ran on, with urchins laughing and shrieking at my heels. They didn't know the dire need I was in. Out of breath I was finally able to disappear into a group of bushes that saved me. The children walked away, laughing happily. I was lucky, though, that I hadn't disturbed a snake in those bushes. Relieved, we hiked on and after this adventurous trip with all its pitfalls and the long cold up and down boat ride taking its toll. The amount of time it took to make these important exploratory trips to the coast and islands was a challenging problem. With every trip the more we realized only a boat of our own, a trawler, would speed everything up. I knew the Danish aid organization Danida had been building these wooden fishing trawlers in Chittagong for years. So, I asked the Danida accountant in Noakhali for a cost estimate before submitting an application to the Swiss Red Cross in Berne. The offer was convincing: a 13-meter-long trawler with a loading capacity of five tons was available for the low price of 13,000 Swiss francs. This trawler had a small wheelhouse, well-covered bench seats on deck, was powered by a reliable Yamaha diesel engine and a two-man crew was enough to operate it. With Berne's consent, I was able to order such a trawler in spring, to the delight of all of us. Two months later we received our new ship in Chittagong and named it *ML Red Cross* and added a signboard which said: Donated by the Swiss Red Cross.

With our experienced crew of two, Ann and I set sail with Mihir for the first time. On board we had 12 coconuts, a large bunch of bananas, drinking water and sandwiches. First, we sailed from Chittagong to the island of Sandwip, then on to Changpur on the mighty Meghna (Ganges) river. At last, we had become independent seafarers, no longer wasting long hours on hired boats. But we depended on a reliable crew and their experience. We knew from experience that it was essential not only to hear the weather forecast in this cyclone region, but also to be able to interpret it with foresight. Trips to the coastal area were still taking hours but were much easier to plan with our own ship. However, they remained strenuous, especially during the sweltering hot summer months and our primitive, nocturnal resting places didn't help. But I was happy to accept all that because I really enjoyed travelling around in this open flat expanse on land and on the water. The conversations with these simple, destitute people had a motivating effect on me and gave me an additional boost. Here we were able to ensure that many of these poor families, exploited by rich landowners had a greater future ahead of them.

Once we ventured with our trawler on a particularly long route from the island of Hatyia to Sandwip. Claude Ribaux, our boss from Berne, stayed with us those days. To save time, we chose to sail directly to Sandwip before reaching Chittagong. The weather was good, and a strong wind blew out from the gulf, and the current pressed on the other side, but we made good progress. But halfway, when no more land was in sight, our boat suddenly ran aground on a sandbank. We were stunned that this was possible here in the open sea. This was a tricky situation because strong winds made our trawler stuck in shallow water, tilt to one side. We couldn't expect outside help, the crew knew that. But Mofiss, our skipper, calmed us down. "Soon the incoming high tide will lift our boat out of the sand," he said. Patience was now required; Ismail the second crew member jumped into the water; it was only 1 ½ meter deep! He managed with a solid bamboo pole to stop any further inclining of the boat. We were impressed how our crew, as a well-established team, kept an overview and calmly observed the sandy subsoil. Almost an hour later we breathed a sigh of relief when, after a few unsuccessful attempts, the trawler was finally able to detach itself from the sandbank at full throttle. When we finally reached Chittagong, Claude Ribaux left us here, flying back to

Dhaka and then back to Switzerland. When Mihir and I reported a second time to the local BDRC office in the district town of Lakshmipur, there was a pleasant surprise: The team leader there was Salauddin, who had been one of my most trusted field officers in Chittagong 15 years before. We wanted to visit Char Gazaria Island on the Meghna (Ganges) to explore the opportunities there. Salauddin summoned a surveyor and helpers to assist us. The six of us set out the next morning on the *ML Red Cross*, crossing the mighty Meghna and docking at Char Gazaria Island. We set off barefoot, wandering for hours under the burning sun, back and forth across the flat island, which is roughly ten kilometers long and six kilometers wide. On muddy trails between flooded rice fields, we made slow progress in single file. There were hardly any dirt paths, we had to walk straight through the flooded rice fields and hop across streams. We greedily drank water from hand pumps at farmhouses while Mihir gathered the information we needed from the farm people. He always asked the same questions that we had set out in a list. We wanted to find out where the poorest families lived outside of the protective dams in the endangered river areas. Mihir also inquired about the ownership of the land from the peasants; whether large landowners were in charge, and also asked for names of the local officials. It was no less important for us to find out to which *upazilla* (sub-district) the respective area belonged and what the main problems were there. Wherever we found suitable building sites, they were surveyed by the specialists accompanying us and sent to the BDRC. We waded further and further between rice fields through deep water. Sometimes the murky water rose above our knees. Often, when I was at the front of our one-on-one column, I would spot the heads of small snakes sticking out of the water, ten to twenty meters ahead, staring in our direction. They dived under like lightning when I approached with my troop. A little later, with an uneasy feeling, I waded barefoot through the murky broth at the very spot where the snakes had just disappeared. After a quarter of an hour, I had seen enough diving snakes in front of me and let somebody else to the front. Walking at the back I felt safer.

After five hours walking in burning hot humidity, we finally arrived in a small village at the other side of the island, where our trawler and crew was already waiting. While a village woman cooked us exhausted walkers a tasty fish curry, I noticed a tiny creek with clear water flowing down a little slope and starting walking through that cool water. Just when I lifted one foot for the next step in this clear water, I saw a small black and white snake in the cooling water and quickly jumped out of the creek sideways and ran away. I didn't need to know if it was poisonous or not–that day I had seen far too many snakes. Shortly after sunset, with much relief, we arrived back in Lakshmipur.

It was June 1987 when Ann received a letter stating we had permission to take care of Janet, Hazel and Charles. We were thankful and happy and looked forward with mighty respect of the challenges and responsibilities that awaited us as foster parents of three children. Janet and Hazel had come to know us well by then. They trusted us and looked forward to the day when they could leave the orphanage to live with us. Both had been lovingly motivated and inspired by Mother Superior Bernadette and Ann to join us as their foster parents, and form a new family of five including Charles.

One day the 80-year-old Matron Sister Adolphe from the orphanage in Rangamati arrived with our Charles at the Chittagong orphanage; here I met Charles for the first time, but could not yet talk to him, as he didn't speak English. Of course, he had been informed of the plan to bring him to Chittagong to meet his two little sisters, then travel by train with Ann to Dhaka and become a member of a new family. It was not easy involving him in small talk. He often seemed confused, or wondering, and observing. I had to drive back alone to Dhaka.

I could not leave the car in Chittagong, and it was safer for Ann and children to travel by train.

Ann boarded the Chittagong-Dhaka train two days later with Charles, Janet, and Hazel. After a while Hazel suddenly asked Ann who this boy Charles was. Little Hazel no longer recognized her older brother.

Late in the evening, I was excited when I welcomed my new family at Dhaka train station and drove them home. Now it was a fact, we really had become a brand-new family of five. WOW! What an over whelming milestone in our turbulent life. Ann had to use her precious time carefully. She had so much work and responsibility caring for and teaching the children. But Ann was also a Swiss Red Cross delegate, who had to rise early morning, remain in constant contact with the BDRC and other official duties.

Janet and Hazel appeared to like their new home, while Charles needed a bit more time to feel right and accept it. Ann spoke Bangla to them, expressing our love, care, and protection of them. Janet and Hazel showed us sometimes in the evening what they had learned in the orphanage, singing and dancing graciously. They were happy and trusting of us. Ann began to teach all three English and contacted the nearby Tinkerbell school and registered all three. They enjoyed walking to school every day. I was surprised how fast they began talking in English, enabling me to also converse with them, and listen to what they had learned in school. Charles also began open in gup, obviously realizing he had arrived at last in a safe place. He even began to teach Janet and Hazel himself.

Charles, Janet, and Hazel were blessed we had welcomed all three and formed a new family. They had shared a tragic fate, like the majority of poor country children, this seemed to be the rule and not the exception. At the time the state provided schools, hospitals, and social services to poor and helpless rural families. But it was precisely the poorest and therefore neediest families who could not benefit from this because they were not members of an agricultural cooperative. Illiterate, there was no way for them to get a loan from a bank at an interest rate they could afford. A family with little or no land could not count on any outside help and was caught up in a daily struggle for survival, unable to build a better future. Even families who owned some land could easily lose it if they had to take out a loan to survive. Because the banks ignored the landless and small farmers, they had to turn to the local money lenders. These were always influential landowners whose usurious interest rates were deliberately so high that the money lent could hardly ever be repaid. So, the small holders were forced to cede their small pieces of land to their money lenders. But that was not all: in order to survive, these poor men had now to work as dependent, cheap day laborers for these usurers. They were even forced to become thugs to violently achieve the corrupt ends of such landowners. Corruption and bribery were the order of the day. Even Police, military and civil servants were part of this scandalously corrupt system. It was easy to get fake land ownership documents. The Dutch, who have been involved in this region for years with a land reclamation program using dykes, campaigned for the landless and their rights at various levels. They aimed to giving the landless poor families the new, fertile land gained through the construction of the dykes and avoid it falling into the hands of corrupt landowners. But they couldn't guarantee that. These rich landowners had the power and even involved the landless in fights against thugs, police, and military. There were dead and many wounded. We too, saw how cleverly the rich and powerful tried to trick us. When we came to Char Gazaria again, we were welcomed on a hill by about 100 farmers: along with the young secretary of one of those rich money lenders. They too had personally come from the mainland. This secretary now rose to become the advocate for the farmers. The secretary responded immediately to all questions that Mihir deliberately put directly to the poor farmers. The farmers remained silent. I watched this game for a while, and eventually stopped it in a harsh voice. Now I wanted to know from the secretary on what terms loans were given to the farmers. He said that for every 100 *taka* of a loan, the farmer would have to repay a *"maund"* of rice after six months. That corresponded to a value of around 400 *taka*. In case of late repayment, an additional 50 *taka* per month would be due. It was obvious: even if the farmer could pay it back after six months, this was a criminal annual rate. When I asked the young man about this, he wanted us to believe that he had tried unsuccessfully to lower this high interest rate, but the system could not be changed. After that appearance on the hill, we found out that he had brought most of the 100 farmers with him from the mainland to fool us into believing they all were property-less and poor local Char Gazaria farmers. He wanted to foist them on us for our home program. I felt like slapping the bastard afterwards. But at least we were now warned: We had to be particularly critical and selective. We later did build houses on Char Gazaria. Unfortunately, a very tragic accident happened during construction. I will write about that fatal accident later.

Even if the aid organizations repeatedly had to accept setbacks of one kind or another, little by little there was some progress. To put it figuratively: the dyke construction by the Dutch allowed fertile land to develop. Seeing this as the first seed, it is fair to say that this seed was a bit slow to sprout, but it did eventually. Over the years, more and more development programs for the poor rural population emerged. In 1983, for example, mathematics professor Muhammad Yussuf from Chittagong founded the Grameen Bank (village bank) to help poor families with reasonable interest rates on loans. "People don't have to go to the bank, the bank comes to the people," that was Professor Yussuf's convincing slogan. Normal banks never do that. The Grameen Bank representatives speak to people in their familiar environment, primarily to women because it had been shown that poor women were more likely to invest money for wealth-building and social purposes than men. It is not material possessions that are required for a loan, but the social security of a group. The interest rate was adjusted to the possibilities of the group and its members. A group can have a maximum of 5 members, everyone must be able to write their name. Only the poorest ones were allowed to form such a group and elect a chairman. The two most in need of the group received the first small loan of 500 taka (25 Swiss francs) at an interest rate of 12 percent. Whether they used this loan to raise chickens, but a cow, a water buffalo, a spinning wheel, a sewing machine or whatever, this was entirely up to the borrower. As soon as they started paying back the loan, the next one in the group received his small loan and so on. Women quickly found additional opportunities earning money with their loan. Each member also had to make a modest weekly contribution for social and risk insurance. It had been shown again and again: women are more imaginative and combative when it comes to liberating themselves and their families from poverty. The Grameen Bank thus succeeded in freeing countless landless people who joined an organized group from the clutches of the exploitative money lenders. The repayments made were very impressive at over 95 percent; and a compelling proof that the motivated poor are indeed credit worthy. The Swiss Red Cross and the Bangladesh Red Cross decided to also introduce this promising Grameen Bank system in their new Red Cross village programs. This required a lot of training, motivation, and supervision from the BDRC people in the field, and was difficult at first. Many residents of our newly built villages only got to know each other time. There was for a while a lack of neighborly togetherness. The responsible BDRC people tried to promote unity in the individual villages. A development program involving the granting of loans can only be successful if those responsible in the field are well trained, honest, put their hearts and souls into it, and work incorruptibly according to plan.

As this part of the development program in North Bangladesh

had already started, to gain initial practical experience, I flew up north to Saidpur with the two development workers responsible for us, Mr. Bimol and Ernest Roy. We visited some of these new villages near Kurigram at the Brahmaputra River and were pleasantly surprised at how well group building and lending seemed to work. A lot happened in our private life as well: We urgently needed a cook for our family, because Ann was overwhelmed with the children and her Red Cross work. On recommendation, we hired Francis, and he came to live in our house. He quickly became a real relief for Ann. Every morning he got money to go shopping. To our great delight, he was an excellent cook. Francis would also regularly nimbly climb up one of the three tall palm trees in the garden and throw down the heavy green coconuts that provided my favourite drink. Shortly after moving into this house, I planted a young banana tree, which shot up in a short time. A year later the first bunch of bananas had ripened. In the presence of the whole family, I cut off the heavy bunch with a large knife and counted 72 bananas. What an event for a Swiss! Neither before nor after had bananas tasted better to me than these first ones I had grown.

Finally, excavation could also begin on the island of Char Gazaria. The more houses were built in a settlement, the wider and longer the pits became. Dams were built with the excavated clay, on which the houses then came to stand. Many of the men working the excavation had to be transported to Char Gazaria daily and brought back to the mainland in the late afternoon. During one such voyage home, a terrible accident happened on the Meghna, not far from the mainland shore. Water entered the boat through a leak. The workers became frightened and pushed to the bank side, causing the boat to list. Now panic broke out among the men, many of them jumped into the water. Tragically, seven of our workers drowned. Had they kept calm and stayed on board, nothing would have happened to them, because at the last minute the trawler reached a safe bank a little further down. The accidental death of these seven men shook us all deeply. My priority was to help the affected families from four different villages quickly and on a long-term basis. So, I applied in Berne to build one of our houses for every widow in her village, to give a sum of money and to support these families with food, especially rice. This was quickly approved, and I set out with Mihir on one of our difficult to bear walks, to these villages. We expressed our heartfelt condolences to every widow and every child. We felt extremely sorry for these grieving women and their children. It was difficult to find words of sympathy, to let them feel that we mourned, sympathized, and want to help. Emotions overwhelmed us more than once when we saw the sadness, sorrow, and pain in their eyes. This extremely sad duty was repeated seven times during this long day, always surrounded by other villagers. We gave each widow a large sack of rice, flour, cooking oil and other foodstuffs, as well as an appropriate amount of money. And we promised to build them a new house to give them some comfort, confidence, and hope. They all thanked us. But could they believe that we would further support them and build the promised houses and not abandon them? The gifts and promise of further support personally helped me a little to process these profound encounters. This was by far my most difficult and sadist day in the service of the Red Cross. Although it was not our fault, this accident and its consequences weighed on me for a long time. The construction of the seven houses for the widows and their children was now our first priority. We later visited the seven families twice more and were happy to see them again in their newly built Red Cross houses. Their thanks and quiet sparkles in the eyes meant a lot to us.

The annual August/September rainy season made travel more difficult and slowed down our program. Again and again heavy rain clouds darkened the sky. Countless thunderstorms fell while violent gusts of wind shook trees and plants. Streams and rivers turned brown and quickly burst their shallow banks. Dirt roads and paths turned into morass, nobody left a protective roof without a compelling reason. In August 1987, Bangladesh was hit by particularly severe flooding that lasted for several weeks. Dhaka was not spared this time either. Once when I drove to the northern outskirts of Dhaka, I thought I was at a sea shore. Nothing but water as far as the eye could see. Only trees, telephone- and utility poles and some ridges of houses stuck out. The arterial road north to Manikganj had disappeared. Many quarters in Dhaka were deeply submerged. On a Friday we travelled in a boat through some suburban streets, encountered rickshaw drivers struggling to push their vehicles without passengers through the water in search of higher ground; only the steering rod and hood remained visible. Road traffic had turned into boat traffic for passengers and goods. Often only the chest and head of a few pedestrians were visible. Lakes formed in many places, a soccer field had become a pond, the water level reaching midway up the goal posts. Ann and I were rather lucky: the water only flooded our garden, the floor in the house stayed dry. But many other houses in our neighbourhood were soaked in water for weeks.

A few times I accompanied employees from the BDRC on a boat taking food and drinking water to the many families staying on a roof. A Bengali proverb says "Water is the mother of our land. It brings life and not death;" an allusion to the fertility of the soil. Thanks to the annual floods and progressive silting up by the sea, rice can be planted later.

It was foreseeable that in a predominantly Islamic country like Bangladesh, the name Bangladesh Red Cross would eventually change. In the spring of 1988 that time had come. The Major Quoreshi, Secretary General of the BDRC informed us that the name Bangladesh Red Cross will soon be changed to Bangladesh Red Crescent. This was probably done at the request of the government, since Islam was the leading religion. On April 4, 1988 the entire cadre, the employees of the BDRC and other foreign Red Cross delegates gathered in front of the flagpole in the courtyard of the Dhaka headquarters. Most of those present looked thoughtful, sincerely regretting this name change. They felt connected to the Red Cross in the white field, this famous and ubiquitous symbol of charity. They hardly identified with the Red Crescent. Nevertheless, it was a solemn and dignified ceremony when our familiar symbol, the Red Cross flag, which fluttered for the last time that day, slowly moved down the flag pole. This was a contemplative and emotional moment for everyone present. Nobody said a word, and time stood still. Our familiar Red Cross flag was untied from the rope, folded for the last time and handed over to the clearly moved, General Secretary Quoreshi. A new white flag with the Red Crescent symbol was now attached to the rope and slowly raised. All eyes followed this Red Crescent symbol representing the same principles of the

International Red Cross, on behalf of Islamic countries. As the new flag began to flutter in the breeze, we found our voices again. Even if this symbolic act moved us away from the Red Cross towards to the Red Crescent, it was comforting for all of us: whether the Red Cross or the Red Crescent (in a white field), the underlying idea of our work remained the same.

Our family life offered me very welcome time out, especially during stressful days. Taking care of our children, doing things with them, it always helped me to get back on the "right track." There was the German club in our neighbourhood, with a clubhouse and a swimming pool and there we taught the children to swim. They quickly became enthusiastic water lovers. One day in the clubhouse I met a good friend, Axel Pawolek from the German Red Cross. We knew each other from our Kassala Mission in Sudan. On Christmas Eve, Axel officiated in the clubhouse as Father Christmas, dressed all in red. He called each child by name, drew gifts from his big sack and gave them to the children with warm words. At that moment, Ann and I thought of the year before when we had said goodbye to Axel in Sudan. Back then, nobody could imagine a year later we would be parents of three children and Axel would be handing over the Christmas presents to them in Bangladesh.

Still not knowing how long our Bangladesh mission would last, Ann approached the Australian Embassy early on with visa applications for Charles, Janet and Hazel. But the okay from Canberra was not forth coming and we became concerned. But Ann didn't give up. Ann was a very loving and caring mother to the children, encouraging and protecting them, gently teaching them good manners, cleanliness and responsibility. She always stayed consistent and never forgot to praise them, while not wanting to spoil them. It was much easier for her than me to find the right approach. But I also learned something new every day. The five of us needed time to slowly learn how to form our family. Charles, Janet and Hazel loved going to school, and over dinner they told us what they had experienced and learned that day. They really made an effort to catch up on what they had missed during their early difficult years. When the Australian visas for Charles, Janet and Hazel finally arrived, we breathed a sigh of relief.

In order to be at the forefront of implementing our house program as often as possible, Mihir and I got back on our motorcycles more often. We drove from place to place with verve and vigour, looked at the progress in the settlements and solved pending problems on the spot. By now we knew almost all the bumpy roads, paths and tricky passages. The pot-holed brick streets could no longer harm us. I liked the temporary "nomadic life" in the fresh air, green nature and glittering waters. It provided a healthy appetite for the evening's curries and aromatic fresh fruits. The long trawler journeys on the water also offered time for recovery; to plan, think, talk and last but not least relax in the midst of this endless expanse glittering in the sunlight. My heart opened up. I felt contentment coupled with the joy of existence and gratitude. Here I lived in the country of my beloved wife, my Ann. We had achieved so much together, supported and encouraged each other, worried and even suffered, but still bravely set out to face new challenges. What more could I ask for? Working for the poorest people in these far-flung coastal areas never seemed like a job to me, rather it was a privilege. In the Gulf of Bengal amongst the crooked estuary delta of huge rivers, I was able to live out my youthful dreams full of joie de vivre. The simple sleeping places were basic, but I happily accepted it. Travelling, duties and ever changing challenges inspired me. I seemed to be better able to cope with daily problems, and found ways to speed up the construction work to save costs.

An example of our home program was the widows' village in the Nalchira area of Hatyia. There were many very poor elderly or lonely widows for whom we built a colony of 22 houses. These women were motivated paid workers for the excavation of the clay. I marvelled watching how they spent hours carrying pieces of the gray-coloured clay – in baskets on their heads – up the steep slope, knowing this clay became the foundation of their future homes. Without being asked, the BDRC development workers in Hatyia and Laksimpur showed me the lists of names of the poorest families who were supposed to get one of our houses. I was assured; as planned, it was mainly families who had to live dangerously exposed outside the embankments. The first families had already moved into two villages, and two community development groups had also been formed. I only heard positive things from Mihir and the on-site RC supervisors in response to my specific questions. Unfortunately, I could not check whether the information was correct. But sometimes their body language made me somehow suspicious. One day I took Ann with me to be part of these conversations. Now my interlocutors could no longer quickly agree on something among themselves in Bangla. Ann very soon realized that some of what these RC workers were saying couldn't all be correct. She now recommended to hire a neutral person to investigate. Our choice fell on Ann's nephew Rony Gonsalves from Chittagong.

I knew him well and could not think of a more honest, reliable assistant. Rony agreed to help us.

The cooperation with the Swiss Humanitarian Aid Unit (SHA) was very fruitful and very valuable for us. Together with an engineering office in Dhaka, the SHA had developed a rectangular settlement concept of a so called *killa* hill on which a concrete cyclone shelter stood. We adopted this concept, but without the expensive shelter, so we could build more houses instead. We also had visitors from Switzerland. First our Swiss Red Cross boss Toni Wenger arrived, who wanted to get an idea of the progress of the village-house program on site, in the north as well as in the south. He was also interested in conducting important meetings "with practical relevance." At the same time Toni Frisch, head of the Swiss Disaster Co in Berne arrived. Both were pleased with the progress, and thanked us for our ongoing commitment at the coast. Hansruedi Wittwer in the north, like Ann and I here in the south, took the opportunity to just "empty the craw." Our new collaborator Rony Gonsalves kept us updated on his local inquiries in Hatyia, Sandwhip and Laksimpur. As feared, he had bad news regarding the previous work of the BDRC people in the field. It wasn't encouraging: unfortunately, corruption worked there too. Even if it had been made clear that families living outside of a bank protection wall must get priority for a house in one of our villages, some of the BDRC Red Cross people working there had evidently smelled money; because they took bribes from unauthorized families to be put on the list. For this reason some of the most endangered families outside the protective embankment missed out. Rony had spoken to some of these unauthorized families, who openly told him how much the bribe was that they had paid to get on the list. It had also explained to these BDRC field officers that only the beneficiaries living in the RC houses would be eligible to use the village pond for fish culture. But in some of the new settlements, the BDRC field officer took over the fish farming and pocketed the proceeds themselves. I was flabbergasted by these devastating reports, annoyed beyond measure. A consolation for me was: I now knew. When I confronted these gentlemen, they became subdued and tried to explain themselves with lame excuses. I didn't leave it at that. Ann and I called a meeting with General Secretary Quoreshi and the directors in Dhaka. As we brought up these facts and mentioned names, there was a deep silence in the room. Ann and I were able to answer their questions clearly, nipping any possible doubts in the bud. Those present were obviously very embarrassed that a foreigner and his wife were able to prove this corruption by their employees in the field. Mr. Quoreshi promised to investigate this shameful matter and take appropriate action. But this was also a blow to Ann and me. Our joy at being instrumental in this important program for the poorest families suffered a painful setback. Some of these young BDRC field officers obviously lacked passion, dedication and integrity to take their work seriously to conscientiously build the village development. A chain is only as strong as its weakest link. Ironically, some of these people in the field lacked the integrity to train the new villagers in a gradual and ground-breaking manner for the subsequent loan program. This fact was probably our biggest disappointment. Repeated requests in Dhaka to hire better, more honest people were not immediately implemented. Bureaucratic mills grind particularly slow in developing countries; moreover, the coastal area is far away from the centres of bureaucracy. So we undertook the task ourselves: Rony and I put these BDRC field officers under the greatest possible pressure and controlled their work on the loan program very closely. We demanded that future borrowers instructed and led without becoming dominant; because each group would later continue to work independently. A problem we couldn't solve were the islands that were far apart. Travel by water was dictated by the tides, while broken or flooded roads and paths on these islands often impeded progress. We rarely had enough time to stay in one place. Lack of telecommunications also made things difficult for us. Roffique on Hatyia island had a telephone, but the connection to Dhaka rarely worked. Very long work and travel times remained the norm. Ann was always worried when I was eight to ten days at the coast unable to call her.

The Bangladesh Red Crescent HQ in Dhaka was most days busy like a bee hive to cope with the workload of development programs initiated and financed by various foreign Red Cross societies. We were not the only ones. Several foreign Red Cross societies provided development aid in the country. The International Red Cross League (Renamed later RC Federation) in Geneva was strongly involved, always in cooperation with the BDRC. This included the extensive coastal cyclone preparedness program led by Director Irshad Hussein. Last but not least, its experienced general secretary Quoreshi, a man with very good specialist knowledge, played an extremely important role. Regular courses and practical exercises were carried out for countless volunteers in coastal areas. Material such as megaphones, drinking water containers, radios, boats and other essential emergency material were stored in coastal areas and islands. This also included the construction of more and more concrete cyclone shelters on concrete stilts. On April 26, 1989, one of those feared emergencies occurred. A massive tornado devastated the district town of Manikganj north of Dhaka. This tornado went down in history. The BDRC immediately rushed to help with a medical team and food. I also drove to Manikganj, only 40 kilometers away, to find that this powerful tornado had levelled over 100 villages around Manikganj and turned Manikganj itself into a vast wasteland of rubble. I had never seen such devastation before. As far as the eye could see, nothing but a colossal tangle of wood, corrugated iron, wires, iron sheets, rubble, household effects and clothes. Only here and there a badly damaged brick house still protruded from the huge field of rubble. Residents searched feverishly for victims and belongings. The BDRC had set up a large tent on the outskirts of town where medics treated the wounded while helpers distributed plastic bags with food. In the meantime I drove further afield. Most of the trees had fallen victim to the storm. You could only see large splinters of wood towering above the roots, or the trees lay uprooted on the ground. Remains of the simple houses were scattered widely. At full force the storm had torn the corrugated iron sheets from roofs, deforming them into large, sharply jagged balls. At high speed they hurtled like bombs through the fields. It looked like a battlefield with dead victims laying under uprooted trees.

When my Red Cross Land Rover appeared in this wide spread horror, survivors came running from all directions. I let as many injured people as possible ride with me to the huge, white BDRC tent and pointed others in its direction. This was the deadliest tornado in Bangladesh's history, killing an estimated 1,300 people and injuring 12,000. Over 80,000 people lost their homes. In 153 villages and three towns, 90 percent of the houses were destroyed. When I was on my way back to Manikganj after my reconnaissance trip through the devastated area, an army helicopter was doing several laps over the destroyed town. Apparently it was General Ershad Hussein, the President of Bangladesh, who wanted to see the catastrophe for himself. Half an hour later I was stopped on a narrow dirt road by an army motorcyclist. He told me I had to wait there. So I got out, stretched my legs a bit and waited. After ten minutes a large army Land Rover drove up. When the driver saw my white RC vehicle and me, he stopped, got out and walked over to me. To my great astonishment, it was General Ershad Hussein, the President of Bangladesh himself. He greeted me warmly and wanted to know who I was. As President, he was also the highest patron of the BDRC. He wanted to know where the BDRC tent was, which I pointed out to him. I also informed him of what I had already seen, the photos I had taken and the emergency calls I would be sending to the Swiss RC, as well as informing the BDRC. He thanked me, gave me an appreciative pat on the shoulder, walked back to his vehicle and drove on. I knew that General Ershad liked to drive his Land Rover himself. It was his way of showing up unexpectedly early during mornings, accompanied by cameramen, to talk to the working people and listen to their problems. He was often accompanied by his wife. After a day like this, both of them appeared in the evening news, giving the impression of constant contact and dialogue with ordinary people.

HANSRUDI BRAWAND

At the end of our mission, we were proud of what we had achieved in the coastal areas. We had built 583 houses with latrines in 16 new villages, as well as an additional 33 community houses, some of which also served as school houses. It was important that the new residents had a place where they could meet to discuss, learn and improve. A place which made them feel like part of a new community. The community houses also served to form small credit groups and discuss their activities. It was only in retrospect that we were able to really grasp what had been accomplished in this in-house program: All the earthwork had been carried out laboriously by hand with spades and carry baskets. A slow time consuming task, but with a rewarding outcome. On the distant island of Nijumdwip hundreds of workers had, for weeks, patiently carried these heavy loads of clay to build platforms for two large villages and it also enabled them to earn some money. More than 7,000 young trees purchased in Chittagong were planted in all of the new villages. Twenty groundwater pipes were sunk and fitted with hand pumps. Without the huge distances in the coastal area, we could have built even more of these villages. We looked back on an overall complicated and costly Red Cross mission at the Bay of Bengal. It was a joint effort by three partners: the Swiss Red Cross, the Red Crescent Society of Bangladesh and the Swiss Disaster Unit. Working together to free very poor families from the claws and criminal exploitation of rich landowners, to give them a better future and achieve something very valuable in the long term, was a great satisfaction for Ann and me. For Ann it was a particular satisfying reward, she had arrived and worked in her native homeland like an accomplished Red Cross Ambassador and even became the proud new mother of her two nieces Janet and Hazel and nephew Charles.

It was now left to the people of the BDRC to continue and oversee this program. For us, however, it was time to say farewell once more to the other delegates who were close to us, to the many employees of the Bangladesh Red Crescent and of the many close relatives and friends of Ann. First, we flew to Switzerland with the children, then drove to Berne for the so-called "debriefing." Everyone was happy to meet our children. Toni Wenger said: "Hansrudi, Bangladesh has been very kind to you! In 1972 you arrived here with your wife Ann and now you both came with your three children!" I could only confirm that. Our years of commitment and fruitful cooperation with the BDRC were warmly thanked in a letter from Mr Quoreshi to Mr Wenger. Once again we received excellent certificates. Our final medical examination by the medical examiner, our old friend Dr. Martin Weber, went smoothly, our employment contracts ended and we were unemployed again. Of course we used our stay to visit my siblings in Interlaken and Lucerne and make a few trips. In Grindelwald, the children marvelled at the high mountains, which, from their point of view, reached into the sky. The ice grotto tunnel in the lower Grindelwald glacier left them completely speechless but excited. They experienced the first snow on the Susten Pass, which immediately encouraged them to have a snowball fight. When we heard cowbells during a walk through a forest near Lucerne and stepped out to a meadow, we saw a wonderful landscape. Lake Lucerne glittered from far below and in front of us lay a fenced, lush meadow with grazing cows and their familiar sounding cowbells. Here Janet spontaneously called out: "Daddy look, this looks like a cartoon!"

We combined a visit to our close old friends in Klus near Balsthal with a hike up to Old Falkenstein Castle, which towers high above the village. The old weapons, antique furniture and the ceramic vessels in the museum there made an impression on our children, but also caused disappointment. "This must have been a poor king living here. He didn't even have any gold." Again it was Janet who stated it dryly. A little later we boarded Swissair in Zurich for the long flight home. Customs officials at Perth Airport took their time with the children's immigration papers. We were both tired and excited when we finally took a taxi through the familiar, nocturnal streets. Yet, we were still uncertain of our family future here. It was long past midnight when we pulled up to our beautiful house. We quickly put up mattresses and bedding stored in one room on carpets, and pulled out night dresses from our suitcases. After almost five years away, it was a great moment to be home again, in the house that we had built ten years earlier. Luckily it was big enough for our family of five. Plenty of work was waiting for us now. First, Ann got school places for the children. There were two primary schools very close, and our three youngsters were admitted to one of them. Ann collected the school uniforms, and with the satchels and writing materials they had brought from Bangladesh, just five days after our arrival, she accompanied the children to school which was only two minutes away—and again, I began looking for a job.

CHAPTER TWELVE

Kassala, Sudan & Perth, 1989-1991:
At Home – With Wanderlust

SPOTLIGHT ON KASSALA TOWN

The new centre of the city (Al-Mowgif al-Aam), with its bustling market district, lies about two kilometers east of the broad Gash river bed, which is dry between October and June. The intercity bus station is five kilometers to the east in the Souq as-Shaabi district on the through road. In between, along the river, a wide strip of arable land, *Sawagi* (gardens) divides the city areas. The former British district of Sikka Hadiid (near the disused railway station) is located directly on the east bank of the Gash. There you will find a daily wholesale market (Souq Gharb al-Gash) where agricultural products are offered. Residential areas stretch for several kilometers to the north and south. Visible from afar – the symbols of the city – are the round granite peaks, which are called Taka, Totil or simply the Kassala mountains. On the (eastern) far side

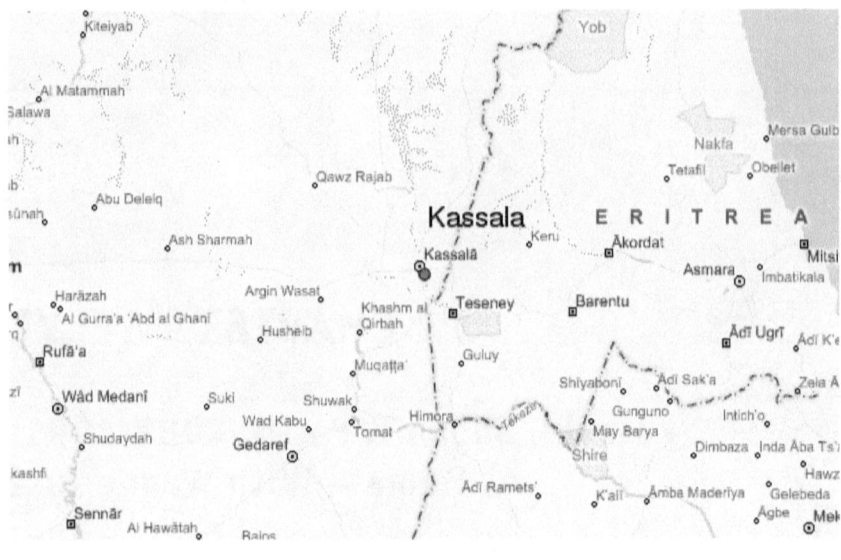

Kassala [14]

of the mountains, a flat sandy desert stretches in the direction of Eritrea and to the north is the Nubian desert. Nevertheless, a large area around Kassala is one of the most fertile regions of Sudan. In the 19th century, agricultural yields were still dependent on the annual inundation caused by the Gash in food. Over time, irrigation canals were laid, which are supplied with groundwater from wells via diesel pumps; a big plus for agricultural production and thus for the supply of the population. During the summer months, the floods of the Gash are redirected into these irrigation canals and used in agriculture. In many fields, a harvest is possible even in the dry winter season thanks to irrigation. Sorghum, sesame, fruit and vegetables are grown, mainly oranges, bananas and onions. Cotton is grown on large areas in the direction of Gedaref. Flooding from the Gash River however, also risks submerging town and country. After heavy rainfall in the Eritrean tributary area, a spring tide is to be expected in Kassala three days later. Precautionary measures have so far failed due to the hostility between the two countries. Disaster floods occur about every five years, the last being in 2003 and 2007.[13]

THE SUDAN FOR THE THIRD TIME

Settling into Perth also worked out well for the children. Charles, Janet and Hazel were speaking good English and they seemed to have forgotten their Bangla. Unfortunately, they regularly argued in their school class. On Ann's orders, Janet was promoted to a higher class and Charles, four years older than Janet, was sent to a more distant, age-appropriate school. Ann made sure the three of them did their homework. She took pride in being a caring mother to the children, teaching good manners, hygiene, responsibility, respect and decency. They also had to do their little jobs in the household because we definitely didn't want to spoil them, but Ann, a talented hobby seamstress, started sewing beautiful dresses for the girls.

Shortly after our arrival we held a big party to introduce our children to Ann's many relatives. Charles, Janet and Hazel were a little overwhelmed meeting so many people they didn't know. I hadn't found work yet, but didn't see it as a problem, rather a challenge. Taking on new tasks in a different environment and getting to know people was exactly what I wanted. Sometimes it was enough to read

---

13   Source: Wikipedia

14   Source https://www.google.com/maps/d/u/0/viewer?mid=1HfGv9NKNT5RZId00431VgBxAVuQ&hl=en_US&ll=15.585297902416098%2C37.334289378906256&z=8

the job advertisements for temporary work or spontaneously stop by a job agency. However, a workplace could not be too far away and a vehicle was also a requirement; for the capital, Perth, had expanded in the years of our absence. With suburban trains and buses, some trips to work became far too time-consuming. With temporary jobs I earned enough to take care of the family. Then one day at the end of 1990 my friend Hans Burzlaff called from Munich. We had met each other years before at our lunch bar. He also wanted to immigrate to Western Australia. But the visa he applied for didn't work out, even though he was a civil engineer and owned a small construction business in Munich. A few years earlier he had bought a 1,000 meter square plot of land in York, 100 kilometers from Perth, and started to build a house on it. But only the outer and inner walls were built. Now Hans wanted to know if I would like to finish building this house as a site manager. Of course I agreed and drove to York with the family over the weekend to see the site. From then on, I drove to York two or three times a week, got the required information I needed from the building department and spoke with the tradesmen. Founded in 1831, two years after Perth, the provincial town of York is Western Australia's oldest inland city with a population of just over 2, 000. This nostalgic town with several well-preserved buildings from the Victorian colonial era is situated on the Avon River, in the middle of a lovely hilly landscape. The people of York, like everywhere in the Australian outback, are extremely friendly and helpful. Local tradesmen such as plumbers, carpenters, pavers, electricians, tilers and roofers offered me their cost estimates, which I discussed with Hans in Munich over the phone. Then I wrote the corresponding contracts. The construction was slowly gaining momentum, but the 200 kilometers round journey took a lot of time. Regardless, I liked the varied rides through long forests, over hills and past farms with surprising views. It gave me a feeling of freedom, happiness and distance.

I painted the interior walls and ceilings myself, but soon realized how big this house really was with four bedrooms and other rooms. A young painter finally came to my aid. The neat house with the modern beige exposed bricks looked inviting. After all the work had been done and everything around the house had been tidied up and put away, a real estate agent put the house up for sale. Just two months later, a buyer was found who bought it at a reasonable price and the proceeds were transferred to Munich.

A short time later I was hired as a dispatcher in a transport company. Of course, I liked that job, as organizing had always been my strength. Ann also had ambitions, she didn't just want to be a mother and housewife. In a class at World book, an American company which sells encyclopedia books for school children, she learned how to sell encyclopedia's to families with schoolchildren on a consignment basis. Not an easy task. Talent, persuasiveness, perseverance and self-confidence were required. Ann was a quick learner, enjoyed using documentation to convince parents of the value of the various subjects taught to their children. The first sales successes soon followed. She was able to organize her working hours herself, which was a big plus. I would accompany her to the monthly World book meetings where Ann later won several awards for selling many encyclopedias.

At the weekend we loved to take the kids to Bullsbrook, 40 kilometers away, to our 3.5 hectare property on the Jess road. There we sat under one of the several hundred year-old trees for a picnic. The hilly and wooded surroundings with countless eucalyptus trees, their green-blue leaves hanging down, put us in a calm mood every time. We planned to build a house there and set up a small hobby farm. If we would move and live in Bullsbrook, the village school was two kilometers away.

I thought that this was actually the time for me to deposit my Red Cross wanderlust in a box and turn the key twice in the lock. But after a while, despite the family, my gypsy blood began to simmer again. Wanderlust was returning and it made me think. What was the matter with me? Why couldn't I sit still and rejoice being at home? Everything was set up perfectly; and in the coming year I would already be 60. Why was I still dreaming of the next mission in the unsafe distance? Once again, Ann felt this condition early and clearly, guessed the reason for my restlessness and thoughtfulness. When I then confessed this to her, Ann said sadly that she knew me too well not to feel it herself. My passion was dormant for the time being, but she didn't want to stop me. I immediately felt guilty. The fact that Ann was once again willing to make a sacrifice – this time as a mother – bothered me and put me in a dire quandary. But I also knew that Ann would rather let me go than have a husband at her side whose thoughts drifted more and more into his beloved distance. So one day I pulled myself together, called the SRC in Berne and spoke to Toni and Vreni Wenger. Both were happy that I wanted to approach that distance again and for my many years of experience in the field. While I was on the phone, Ann agreed. Just a few weeks later it was definite: I was offered a third assignment in Kassala, Sudan; From January 1991, for a maximum of six months. The limited contract had been my condition. I didn't want to and couldn't leave any longer.

In mid-January, I said goodbye to my family with mixed feelings and once again flew from the hot Australian summer to wintry Switzerland. In Berne there was a warm reunion with Toni and Vreni Wenger, the coordinator Verena Kücholl, medical examiner Dr. Martin Weber and many other old acquaintances. In Zurich, Josy Harder gave me a long letter for her former team members in the Wad Sherifay refugee camp. This time I flew with Lufthansa to Frankfurt first. When I strolled into another terminal while waiting for a transfer, I suddenly stopped in amazement. Sven was standing right in front of me! I could see his profile as he was checking in. I recognized him immediately from his striking stature and white hair. It was really and truly Sven Lampell, my former Red Cross chief from Bangladesh and Somalia. We greeted each other warmly. The old warhorse was now 71, but still at the height of his creativity. The Red Cross was his life, his passion. In 1980, we had celebrated his 60th birthday in Mogadishu. This former Swedish Air Force colonel had already achieved an unbelievable amount. Years before, during the fighting in the Congo, he led a Swedish air squadron – on behalf of the UN. Later he was active in countless foreign missions for the Red Cross League in Geneva, always in a leading position. Now he was on his way to Afghanistan as chief delegate. Sven looked at me and said spontaneously: "Hansrudi, we urgently need an administrator in Kabul. I'd be happy to contact Geneva and request you." Regretfully, I told him that unfortunately that was not possible. "I'm taking on a temporary job in Sudan because I don't want to leave my family alone for much longer."

Good Sven could absolutely understand that. So we said goodbye and each of us made their way to a crisis area. Nobody knew what awaited us there.

The Lufthansa plane to Cairo was full of Egyptians and Sudanese, I only saw two or three Europeans and they got off in Cairo. From there to Khartoum I was the only pale face. Not surprising, Western governments had urged their citizens to leave Sudan. The country had become a terrorist hotbed, with suspected training camps– a risky place for foreigners. Still, I wasn't particularly worried. Our plane landed in Khartoum at 10:30 p.m. As soon as I got out, the familiar smell of Khartoum made me feel like I'd arrived home.

Mamoun Abdelatif from the Red Cross League was supposed to be waiting for me at customs with my entry visa as we had previously been arranged. But I didn't see him anywhere, maybe he was late? The customs officials made me wait. An hour later Mamoun still hadn't shown up. Who knows, maybe the guy fell asleep at home? I had now been awake for 18 hours and had become really sleepy. The customs officials treated me kindly, let me sit in the manager's office and I was served tea, but his boss warned me: even an RK delegate would not be allowed to enter the country without a visa. I'd have to fly back to Cairo, at three in the morning, on the same plane. "Then you could get off in Cairo to apply for a visa at the Sudanese embassy," the caring man comforted me. But I didn't have a visa for Egypt either. Now it was time to act. Luckily I had the private number of the Swiss *chargé d'affaires* with me. I rang him out of bed at midnight and reported the situation to him. He wanted to help me but couldn't come because of the curfew.

However, he promised to alert the Red Cross League immediately. I should call him back in an hour. I called back to the minute and was given Mamoun's phone number. But the sleepyhead did not stir. I kept trying, letting it ring without success. Now it was getting tight for me: In an hour I would be back on the plane. I washed down the anger with delicious Sudanese tea. The customs chief was sorry because he couldn't help me during the night. Now I let Mamoun ring non-stop. I dialed his number over and over again. Finally, still sleepy, he answered, but he was wide awake as soon as I read him the riot act. He'll come straight away with the visa, he promised. A really heavy Sudanese stone fell from my shoulders. Fifteen minutes later, the Lufthansa passengers were already walking to the plane, when Mamoun showed up waving my visa, apologizing in embarrassment. He had fallen asleep on the sofa and only woke up when the night watchman banged more and more violently at the front door–he had heard the repeated ringing and realized that something wasn't right. But the odyssey was not yet over. A customs officer had meanwhile taken my suitcase to a distant hangar. There, a young customs officer demanded to open the suitcase. But my stubborn head wouldn't allow that anymore, as I was now too tired and frustrated after waiting so many hours. The cup was full and pretended I couldn't find the little key anymore. But he insisted that he must be able to check the contents of the suitcase. For my part, I didn't want to allow any more interventions. Six years before, a customs officer had stolen special batteries from me at lightning speed. My stubborn Bernese skull finally won. The officer grudgingly gave in and said, "Okay, you go." I now had to lug the heavy suitcase all the way back to the waiting Mamoun, who at least had a night curfew permit. On the way we were picked up twice at roadblocks, stopped at gunpoint. It was four o'clock in the morning when I could finally go to bed in the Red Cross League building, relieved and very tired.

I got up at 10 a.m., washed, was served the typical bean-dish breakfast *ful* with bread and tea. Outside the sun was shining, and life looked positive again. It was now the pleasantly mild winter time in Sudan. Mamoun took me to see Norwegian Kyell Holte, the chief delegate of the Red Cross League, to discuss the current situation. I stayed in Khartoum for two more days before tackling the bus journey towards the Red Sea. Excited like a little boy, I was happy when the striking mountains of Kassala became vaguely visible on the horizon. Reason enough to hum the Grindelwald song to myself. After five years away I returned to friends and many acquaintances. Mohamed Abubaker, known as Shambel, was waiting for me in the green team house in Kassala. We hugged each other enthusiastically. Shambel had been my best and most important Eritrean collaborator in 1985/86. Now he introduced me to the current team leader, Ali Saeed Boss, a light-skinned, black-bearded North Sudanese, in a flowing white *jalabia* robe and perfectly wrapped turban. But Ali Boss was a genuine native of Berne, who spoke Arabic fluently and was happily married to a young black Sudanese woman. Having converted to Islam years ago, he obviously felt at home in Sudan. He already had a new job with another NGO, so in ten days I would be taking over as program manager.

The next morning we drove out between the Kassala mountains to Wad Sherifay refugee camp on the Eritrean border. While Ali Boss sat at the wheel of the dust-raising Land Rover, I peered up at the towering mountain peaks, recognized the ascent routes we had climbed years ago. Upon arrival in front of the hospital, Jemal Abubaker, Unit Manager and barefoot doctor (advanced dresser) came out to greet us. "Hansrudi has come!" This cry spread through the camp like wildfire. I was delighted to find that the efficient and experienced Eritrean medical professionals I knew well were still at work. Together with the petite but extremely assertive pharmacist Abrehet Asfaha and the midwives, they all came to greet me. They bombarded me with questions about Ann, and wanted to know how the legendary Josy Harder was doing. I was very happy to hand them a long letter that Josy had written to the Eritrean workforce, along with many greetings. The "Out Patient Center" that Josy had managed for a long time was still in operation and had been called the Josy Center for years. In the hospital I was welcomed by the friendly Sudanese doctor Dr. Bedredin, who was now the sole doctor on the SRK team and was appreciated by staff and patients alike. The refugee and detention centre had become smaller but still offered shelter to around 66,000 people. Despite this, new refugees continued to arrive from Eritrea and Tigre, even though the decades-long war there was now in its final phase. The SRC medical team continued to run their well-organised tasks in the desert hospital that had been built 1985 with only local material. It was a huge improvement, compared to the original quickly built makeshift straw-roof so-called "hospital." But there was also an outpatient clinic, a mother-child health clinic, a "Home Visitor Program" and a feeding centre. These still were mostly under straw roof covers. Great importance was also attached to prevention and health care.

HANSRUDI BRAWAND

* * * * *

Ali Boss introduced me to his self-developed financial accounting and all other tasks. Inaugural visits to the local authorities and other NGOs followed. Soon Ali Boss and his wife said goodbye. I enjoyed my work in Kassala and regular visits to Wad Sherifay, but my thoughts often flew to my distant family. Sometimes it depressed me to be so far away although Ann had it a lot harder than I did. I couldn't even phone her. At most, short reports by radio via Khartoum–Geneva–Berne were possible. Of course I wrote letters home regularly, but they took up to three weeks to get there. Nevertheless, I felt comfortable and in the right place. One of my most important tasks as de facto manager was to leave as many administrative tasks as possible to suitable Eritreans. The high number of Eritrean staff in Wad Sherifay also had to be reduced wherever possible in order to reduce costs. As always in my SRC missions, a good relationship and good cooperation with the local authorities was very important; just like the trusting cooperation with the representatives of the other NGOs and of course with the extremely motivated, well-organized Eritrean workforce.

Every day I was fascinated by the Kassala Mountains, rising steeply out of the desert floor and standing like protective defence towers between Kassala town and Wad Sherifay. But nobody wanted to come climbing with me. So I went there alone on a day off, but for safety's sake I always stayed in visual and call contact. At 4:00 p.m., I would climb briskly up the west side over the many steep slabs of rock. Knees and thighs soon protested, but with every breath I took, the distant views and the silence filled me with intense happiness and gratitude. After climbing up to 300 meters higher, I sat down and watched the pale red sun slowly sink behind the distant horizon. It was the right moment for heartfelt thoughts of my distant family.

Irene and Elke, two German women who had rented what was known as the "blue house," also worked in our team. I shared their house with them and the costs. A Sudanese cook took care of the household and prepared good meals for us. In the evening we told each other about our lives and enjoyed the comradely get-together. From time to time we went out in the evening to eat out with other friends; preferably charcoal-roasted, tantalizingly fragrant small pieces of meat with side dishes.

At noon, Irene, Shambel, Ahmed and I sat under a straw roof in Wad Sherifay to discuss upcoming work, problems and plans. Irene, who was ten years my junior, was an interesting, highly intelligent woman with great charisma. From 1982 to 1987 she did field research with the Dinka tribe in South Sudan, earned her doctorate with this work and wrote the book *The Cow Shed of God* about her studies.

Here in Kassala she was responsible for the neglected Sudanese villages in the border area, where she built up a program of self-help. She taught the women how to prevent or cure diseases, helped them with vaccination programs and brought much-needed medicines. It was also important to Irene to show the women how to organize themselves so that they could form committees. These operations out in the villages made it clear again and again: the SRK not only wanted to support the refugees, but strengthen the population in this area. Our self-help programs in the villages created a lot of goodwill, not least among the authorities. This, in turn, always benefited our work and even more so our plans.

Every now and then we got visitors from Berne. Our boss and program, Verena Kücholl, also wanted to get an idea of the current situation on site and discuss any upcoming problems with us, the authorities and other NGO representatives. She had traveled to eastern Sudan regularly in recent years. We awaited Verena with great anticipation, her visits were important to all of us; because only on site could Verena get a realistic overall picture, and make decisions that were adapted to the given circumstances.

Before daybreak I drove off to pick up Verena in Khartoum and also – to the delight of Irene and Elke – to buy some delicacies such as sugar, canned cheese, butter and jam for the team house. During the eight-hour return journey the next day, Verena and I had plenty of time to discuss the situation. Eritrea's thirty-year struggle for independence seemed to be nearly over and we would feel this quickly. The Ethiopian army was still occupying the Eritrean capital Asmara, which was surrounded by the EPLF (Eritrean People Liberation Front). When no more supplies of food came through from Ethiopia, around 88,000 Ethiopian soldiers broke out of Asmara and fled in vehicles, buses or on foot in the direction of the Sudanese border, which was almost 400 kilometers away. The Eritrean soldiers pursued and engaged the fleeing army in bloody battles along the way. Around 33,000 Ethiopians surrendered, but an estimated 50,000 soldiers reached the safe border of Sudan, around 20 kilometers from Wad Sherifay. As soon as we heard about it, I drove there with Shambel straight away. In a border village we met hundreds of soldiers who, in an apathetic state, were looking for shade in houses and under thorn bushes. They had come from cool Asmara, 2,300 meters above sea level and were completely exhausted after such a long trek and fighting the sweltering heat of Sudan (45 degrees in the shade). Some even suffered from infected gunshot wounds. A soldier lost his shoes and burned his feet in the burning sand. He got my shoes. Two others were missing their uniform jackets. We gave them our shirts. The water bottles and sandwiches also found takers immediately. We drove back to see Dr. Alert Bedreddin and the advanced dressers. The Kassala garrison and authorities had already begun to bring aid; especially tankers with life-saving drinking water and plastic buckets. But there were too few tankers and the few were too small to continuously supply so many dying soldiers. A tragedy began to loom. The scorching heat quickly dried out the weakened bodies of the soldiers who suffered terribly under the modest shade of thorny bushes. A SRK medical team was formed in Wad Sherifay, which drove to Alafa the next morning, where most of the Ethiopian soldiers had crossed the border and were now lying listlessly under the thorn bushes. Dr. Bedredin and the dressers immediately put together a team that, from the next morning onwards, drove to Alafa and other villages every day to take care of the dying and the wounded. Because the Gash River had not dried up completely and could not be crossed, they had to drive 45 kilometers via Kassala; a detour that took twice as long. This emergency team was now absent from the camp, so it was time to improvise, with immediate effect. Time off for all staff came to a stop. On the fourth day I counted 312 small mounds of sand between the bushes near Alafa. They were soldiers graves who had died of thirst or had succumbed to their wounds. For several mornings I accompanied Kastro, one of our most experienced barefoot doctors, on the drive to Alafa. Methodically, he examined the most critical dehydration cases. Kastro used two fingers to lift a piece of skin on his chest or arm. If the skin remained like this, immediate help was needed. As soon as the loading bridge of our pickup truck was full of seated patients, I drove to the schoolhouse, which was now an emergency hospital. Kastro meanwhile examined other patients. I carried the barely reacting, exhausted soldiers one by one into the school building and laid them on the cool cement floor among other patients. They were light like 14-15 year olds. The last man I lifted off the truck appeared to be unconscious. As I carried him in, he opened his eyes. As I gently lowered him to the floor and straightened up again, I saw something like gratitude in his eyes. That touched me deeply. So I didn't want to just leave this seriously suffering fellow human being and asked a Sudanese caregiver to bring him a saline solution immediately. In the vehicle I got a small pillow, which I put under the soldier's head and pressed my water bottle into his limp hand. At the door I looked back at him again. His eyes had followed me. Now, with effort, he raised his hand slightly and waved at me to say thanks. I waved back, touched. For me this thankful waving by a semi-conscious probably dying soldier was an unforgettable moment in my Red Cross life. I don't know if he survived. I couldn't find him the next day. Instead, terrible cries of pain came from another room, as if a person were being tortured. A nurse sadly said the Sudanese doctors had run out of narcotics. They had no choice but to try to get the bullets out of the ulcerated gunshot wounds without anaesthetic. The terrible screams haunted me for a long time. The helpers who fought against this human tragedy at the time will never forget this stressful time. But they can also have the certainty that they helped these people in need; as much as they could. Nevertheless, I experienced something there that made me smile. In a border village cared for by our SRK team, I heard a loud cry of pain upon my arrival at one of the unoccupied houses. In front of the house were wounded but already medically treated soldiers. When I entered the house, our portly chief midwife, Senet Abdu, greeted me with a syringe in her hand, while at the same time baring the buttocks of a soldier and shoving the needle roughly in. He immediately yelled "Ouch!" and turned his head angrily to Senet. When I asked her why she gave the tetanus shots so roughly, she laughed at me mischievously and said: "I'm a proud Eritrean. And these Ethiopian soldiers were our enemies just a few days ago. Here's where I can return the favour, a little bit, and cause these guys some pain!" So far so clear.

Our SRK team members were by no means the only Red Cross volunteers who worked for the soldiers who had fled. Along the long border I met the European nurses from the Red Cross League and also from the ICRC in Geneva. They worked overtime and gladly sacrificed their days off to save the men from dying of thirst. There were helpers who set up their own stalls in various border villages and distributed saline solution during the critical phase; even during an annoying day-long dust storm that fogged the area a dull yellowish, they didn't give up. My admiration for these women was great. That's why I also sent a radio message to Khartoum, to the ICRC and to the IFRC in Geneva saying: "Be proud of your nurses! They also volunteer their days off at the border, even during day-long sandstorms, distributing life-saving saline solutions to dying Ethiopian soldiers."

HANSRUDI BRAWAND

After the Ethiopian army fled Asmara, a great frenzy broke out in Wad Sherifay. Countless refugees sang and danced in front of our desert hospital, rejoicing like children because the end of this merciless war was finally approaching. A few days later, the countless Eritreans in Kassala organized a big procession through the main street. Already in the morning numerous groups marched past our office and warehouse. Others rode along on slow-moving trucks, standing and waving flags. I ran to the street and started taking pictures from the side of the road. When I had filled the first roll of film, I returned to the office for another film and continued shooting. After the third snapshot, a plainclothes policeman put his hand on my shoulder from behind and said no photos allowed, I had to go with him. My RC ID was of no use to me, the law enforcement officer ignored it. Shambel saw what was happening and came running to intervene without success. My camera was confiscated at the police station, a policeman wrote my personal details in a thick book, then he grabbed a clanking bunch of keys and ordered me to follow him. So we walked down a corridor together, and at the end he opened a heavy cell door, asked me to enter, locked the door behind me and walked off. Stunned, I found myself behind bars like a criminal. That was not expected, imprisoned in Africa with the family in Australia completely unsuspecting. In the cell there was an old wooden bed, a wormy chair, and a small, rickety table in the corner. My predecessors had scribbled their business cards on the crumbling gray cement wall. But the best thing was the open, densely barred little window. I could look out into a small side street. Every now and then someone would walk by. After a while a familiar voice outside called my name. When I answered, a laughing Shambel appeared at the window and inquired about my state of mind. As a captive photographer, I laughed along. I was experiencing something new again, a day off from work in the jail! Shambel said not to worry, he'll try to get me out. He then asked if I was hungry or thirsty, to which I said yes. I also asked him for writing paper, a pen and a long nail. He soon returned with the requested items, but had trouble squeezing the food and plastic bottle through the bars. Then we discussed what still needed to be organized and I wrote down work orders for him for the next day. I grinned to myself as I did all this, thinking of mafia bosses who issue orders from prison. After dinner I wrote a long letter home, then I scratched my business card into the cement wall with a nail: "Hansrudi Brawand, Grindelwald, was here May 1991." Then I lay contentedly on the musty-smelling bed, on which I soon fell asleep.

Shortly after 5 p.m. the clanking key of the duty officer opened the cell door and he silently led me to the boss. Dressed in civilian clothes with a white shirt and tie, he appeared with a very dismissive KGB expression. My camera was on the desk in front of him. He snapped at me, "Why are you illegally taking photos?" To which I replied wittily, "I'm new to the fact that it's not allowed to take photos in Kassala." "By photographing this parade, you made yourself suspicious," came the gruff reply. "It was just a peaceful procession of Eritreans because their capital, Asmara, was liberated," I countered in a soothing manner, which seemed to help. "I could have you expelled from Sudan immediately, but I won't because you work here for the Red Cross." But he demanded that I give him the film from my camera. I followed this order immediately and carefully placed the film with only three frames on the desk. With that I was mercifully dismissed. Angered yet relieved, I ran back to freedom, the nap behind bars had done me good. In the office I pulled the rescued first roll of film with 36 frames out of a drawer and showed it to Shambel with a smile. Now we could both laugh freely and heartily.

The hours of driving to Khartoum and back were never too much for me. I saw it more as relaxation than work. There was a lot to see on the way, mountainous, then flat landscapes with small and larger villages, waving children or people waiting for a bus. The cooling wind invigorated the senses, and made me feel carefree. Thoughts wandered in all directions, including Australia. Apart from heavily loaded trucks, there was hardly any traffic. A young Sudanese doctor once traveled with me. While we were eating in a tea house, he showed me four rifle bullets he had removed during an operation, wrapped in a handkerchief. Bother Ethiopian soldiers; two of them without anaesthesia, which had been an ordeal for him too.

The day of my journey home was approaching. Because my Swedish successor hadn't arrived yet, Shambel temporarily took over the reins. Saying goodbye to the many Eritrean friends and acquaintances in Wad Sherifay was not easy for me. For years, the entire staff had worked with all their might for the well-being of the refugees, who, after all, were also compatriots. I would no doubt miss them all, as I would the mountains. "The longer in Sudan, the deeper the sand" says a Sudanese proverb. I can only confirm that.

On the eve of my departure, Shambel and Tsegay invited me to a farewell dinner with Eritrean specialties at Shambel's house. It was an evening among good friends, just the way I liked it. As I took the bus to Khartoum the next morning, I was filled with countless unique memories, but little did I know that I would return.

When I arrived at the SRC in Berne, Toni Wenger and Verena Kücholl instructed me to fly to Sweden immediately to prepare my successor Ture Andersson comprehensively for his task in Kassala and Wad Sherifay. I accepted this job with pleasure, as it was my first trip to Sweden. In Stockholm, Ture was waiting for me at the airport. We greeted each other as old friends who had always stayed in touch. We first worked together in early 1972 when we ran the Red Cross League warehouses in Dhaka, Bangladesh. In Sweden, Ture worked as a trade school teacher in the town of Linköping, 200 kilometers from Stockholm. The drive there flew by, and the shared memories made us happy. I stayed in Linköping for four days, and we sat together for several hours every day, intensively discussing the situation in Sudan, Kassala and Wad Sherifay. I explained the problems, tasks, accommodation and that very experienced Shambel is at the moment doing the Administrator job, capable for complete support. I also showed Ture various documents and photos I had brought with me. Ture's lovely wife, Astrid, an excellent cook, spoiled us with her Swedish cuisine from morning to night. When I arrived back in Berne, the obligatory debriefing followed, as always with the final medical examination by Dr. Weber and followed by a good job reference. Then I said goodbye to my dear friends at the SRC in Berne. Secretly, I was already hoping that this mission might not have been my last. Cheerfully, the backpack heavy with Swiss chocolate, I boarded a plane at Zurich Airport and made my way home to my family.

CHAPTER THIRTEEN

Ljubljana, Slovenia & Zagreb, Croatia, 1992-1993

SPOTLIGHT ON THE BALKANS

The Yugoslav wars (often also called Balkan conflicts) are a series of wars on the territory of the former Yugoslavia towards the end of the 20th century, which were associated with the disintegration of the state. In detail, the important period here was the 10-day war in Slovenia (1991), the Croatian war (1991-1995) and the Bosnian war (1992-1995). After referendums, which did not, however, take into account the obligation for mutual agreement when reorganizing border changes, Slovenia and Croatia first declared their independence in June 1991, followed by Macedonia (November 1991) and Bosnia and Herzegovina (March 1992). In the course of the conflict, the Yugoslav People's Army (JNA), under the leadership of Veljko Kadijević and BlagojeAdžić, tried to thwart the independence efforts in Slovenia (a 10-day war) and Croatia militarily. In 1992 the war also spread to Bosnia and Herzegovina.

TO THE HORIZON AND BEYOND

Croatia [15]

In 1991 Slovenia became independent and proclaimed a republic. Ljubljana became their capital. On the one hand, Ljubljana resembles an Austrian city, but has a special Mediterranean flair due to its old town, the many cafés by the river and the moderate climate. Ljubljana is the most important economic center of Slovenia, it is the seat of the Ljubljanskaborza, the country's only stock exchange, as well as most of the large companies in Slovenia. Zagreb is the capital and largest city in Croatia. A Catholic archbishop, the Croatian Academy of Sciences and Arts and important administrative and military authorities reside in Zagreb. As a commercial and financial center, the city is of national and regional importance.

---

15 Source: https://en.wikipedia.org/wiki/Informbiro_period#/media/File:SocialistYugoslavia_en.svg

HANSRUDI BRAWAND

LET'S GO TO THE BALKANS

It was well past midnight when the plane began its descent. Perth's golden sea of lights spread out before my eyes, which made my heart pound happily. The urge to travel far away had been satisfied for a while. Before disembarking, a customs officer marched briskly down the aisle spraying two cans of foul-smelling bug spray. Who knows, maybe some dangerous Swiss mosquitoes flew with me! With a sigh of relief, I sank into a taxi a little later, which quickly took me home. With a gentle kiss, I woke my sleeping Ann, who gratefully embraced her safely returning gypsy. The excitement kept us from falling asleep for a long time. There was a lot to tell. Charles, Janet and Hazel woke me up in the morning before going to school. They are beaming and seemed happy that daddy was back.

The first few days at home gave me trouble, the jet lag plagued me to the utmost. There was a lot of work waiting for me, minor repairs had to be made and weeds sprouted in the garden. In addition, relatives, friends and neighbours came by every day wanting to know what I had experienced.

Again I quickly looked around for work, which I found as a holiday replacement in a large warehouse. At the weekend I motivated the children to do take up running. We started with a light jog through the bush or walked along the beach. Charles enjoyed it and soon became a good runner. When there was a 7 kilometer fun run in the huge Whitemans National Park, we both ran in different categories. A few months later we even attended the annual 10 kilometer bridge run along the Swan River. Although I was now an "also running" participant, I was fit again.

On Sunday we all went together to Girrawheen Church to see Rev. Tom Gayne whom we knew well. He was a native of Ireland and very sympathetic. When I apologized for coming to his Catholic church as a Protestant, he laughed, patted me on the shoulder and said, "Welcome Hansrudi, you are a better Catholic than many who are in name only." Ann wished that the children would be altar servers and registered them with the pastor. Two months later we rejoiced when Janet and Hazel, in white robes, proudly walked down the aisle with the cross for the first time and performed their duties during Mass.

On Valentine's Day 1992, we invited all of my relatives to a party to celebrate my 60th birthday. I made the big birthday cake myself. I was sixty now and still not the least bit tired. The gypsy blood was still flowing through my veins, foreign countries, many people and red crosses were swimming in it, making me tingle all the time. In the middle of an Australian winter I received a surprising request from Berne. It increased the tingling and brought some unrest to the family. The SRC offered me a new and attractive position in the Balkans, the client was the International Federation of Red Cross and Red Crescent Societies in Geneva. After the collapse of Yugoslavia, new states had emerged: Slovenia, Croatia, Macedonia and Serbia. "You could work as a head of delegation in the Slovenian capital Ljubljana for six months," Toni Wenger told me on the phone. I began to swallow, asked a few questions, but also said I needed to consult with Ann. I hung up the phone, promising to call back as soon as possible. It was immediately clear to me: this was my only chance at an opportunity like this, and in Europe at that. So it was a matter of making a quick decision.

Once again, Ann was willing to make a great sacrifice and let me go.

In high spirits but worried at the same time, I said goodbye to my family at the beginning of August. In Berne at the SRC, I met Michael Sidman, who I immediately liked and who was responsible for the country. Since the task in Slovenia was an aid program of the International Federation of Red Cross and Red Crescent Societies IFRC, I went to Geneva. There I was received by the program manager Martin Zak, a bearded Czech. He was responsible for the delegations in Ljubljana, Zagreb and Macedonian Skopje. My task was to open an IFRC office in Ljubljana and to work closely with, and support the further development of the now autonomous Slovenian Red Cross SLRK. This included helping to look after around 70,000 Bosnian refugees in the country and supporting the SLRK in coordinating its winter program for the refugees. I was also responsible for the constant flow of information and reporting to Geneva. Loaded with orders and instructions, I flew off in the direction of my new place of work.

At Ljubljana airport I was welcomed by a representative of the Slovenian Red Cross(Rdeci Kriz Slovenjie). He drove me to their headquarters where I was warmly welcomed by everyone. The secretary TadejaUmek (called Phta) introduced me to the general secretary, Mr. Jelinek, who unfortunately spoke neither English nor German. But Tadeja acted as an excellent translator, she could even speak Swiss German because she had gone to school in Zurich for a while. Mr. Jelinek was pleased that a representative of the IFRC was now in the country. He promised me to do his utmost to get a fruitful cooperation; for the benefit of countless refugees and the further development of the still young Rdeci Kriz Slovenjie. I soon

TO THE HORIZON AND BEYOND

felt that good spirit reigned in this RK house and humor was a welcome guest. Ljubljana and Slovenia were so different from my previous missions in Africa and Asia. I immediately liked Ljubliana, which used to be called Laibach. The medieval, well-maintained old town exuded history. "It must have looked like this many centuries ago," I thought during the first walk over the famous three-part bridge called Tromostovje, which leads to the old town. Impressed, I admired the venerable churches, buildings and monuments, and looked up at the old castle, which towered protectively over Ljubljana on the forested Castle Hill. The Ljubljanica River, slowly flowing through the city center, reminded me of old paintings and completed the historical impression. Later I regularly climbed the steep path to the castle and lookout tower, looked down on the venerable city and further out into the hilly landscape.

In Ljubljana, I experienced the five-day week for the first time, a welcome bonus after the arduous six to seven-day weeks in Africa and Asia. On Saturday mornings I liked to visit the big market next to the cathedral. There I saw burly peasant women carrying their fresh produce in baskets on their heads to market. I fell in love with the delicious sauerkraut, Slovenian farmhouse cheese, juicy sausages and the wonderfully fragrant, very dark brown bread from a wood-fired oven. I truly regretted that Ann could not be there. I would have loved to have shared this stay with her. One of the first tasks was to open a representative IFRC office. With a bit of luck, not far from the SLRC headquarters, I was able to rent a spacious, furnished office in the Institute for Electronics and Vacuum Technology; with telephone and fax connection. The institute had previously conducted research and developed equipment for the Yugoslav state. The employees in what used to be a big company had hardly anything to do and treated me like a welcome guest. In addition, they were extremely helpful. Since I was looking for staff, this suited me very well. I hired the bright young Mitja to run errands and much more. As my secretary I chose the young, already experienced Barbara, who spoke excellent English and French. On the way home in the evening I often sat down in the Franciscan church. Sometimes I sat there all alone on a pew and let the quiet church atmosphere sink in. In this peaceful stillness I found comforting peace and security, and time for inner reflection. Once it happened that the pastor sat down next this lonely stranger, and began to talk to me. Sometimes I was asked into the sacristy, where the priest filled two small glasses with delicious Slovenian *slivovitz* (plum schnaps). So we chatted on, there was more than enough to talk about. I didn't want to stay in the hotel room that the SLRK had booked for me for a long time. So I started looking for a small apartment. Every morning I walked from the Union Hotel through the winding old town to the Slovenian Red Cross building. One morning, while waiting at a traffic light, I struck up a conversation with an elderly gentleman. As we marched off at the green light, we continued talking, stopping on the other side and introducing ourselves. After a while, the friendly conversation partner asked me, completely surprisingly: "Do you like the hotel, or are you looking for an apartment?Maybe I can help you, friends of mine are looking for a tenant," he replied and immediately wrote my name and contact number on a piece of paper. I thanked him warmly, ran to the office and discussed it with my people. Tadeija even knew the landlords and she offered to come along with me to meet them. I was only too happy to agree. I made an appointment, drove there and looked at the nicely furnished two-room apartment with a balcony on the first floor of a newer building behind Tivoli Park. The rent was cheap, so I quickly came to an agreement with the friendly landlords, an elderly couple, and happily moved from the hotel. A Danish driver brought me a new, duty-free vehicle from Denmark. A superb white diesel car spray-painted with 'International Federation of Red Cross and Red Crescent Societies' lettering in red and the appropriate RK and RC emblems. From now on I was mobile, which made my work a lot easier. Meetings with UNHCR officials, authorities and the SLRK Secretary General were the order of the day. Tadeja accompanied me as a translator on trips to the local RC sections and far-flung refugee centers. I kept meeting many refugee women who were doing all kinds of handicrafts in groups, knitting sweaters, hats, socks or sewing curtains. Before the war, Slovenia had been the largest Yugoslav industrial province and employed many workers from Bosnia who had lived here for years. They now housed relatives and friends who had begun refugees.

Traveling through the hilly eastern Alps, whose mountains and glorious views reminded me of Switzerland, seemed like a princely addition to the work; a luxury almost in the life of a Red Cross delegate. On nice weekends, I liked to drive to the nearby mountains, chose an ascent route and climb up the forest paths adventurously. Never had I been able to enjoy so much free time on my RC missions abroad and the hills and mountains were waiting for me, so to speak, on the doorstep. The Slovenian forests magically lured me. Late on a Saturday afternoon, when I was descending into the valley after a Saturday mountain hike on a sparsely wooded ridge, suddenly, from the left side of the valley, distant church bells rang out. I stopped, happily surprised, and sat down on a moss-covered boulder. Then more bells rang out from the other side of the valley. The gentle sounds proclaimed peace, unity and forgiveness. It was just before 6 p.m. and the bells were calling the faithful to prayer in the villages below. Deeply moved and grateful, I listened to the wonderfully forgiving ringing, which, with their harmonious unison, peacefully called to reflection and warmed my heart. Only when the festive bell concert gradually fell silent and a cool wind could be heard in the fir tree tops did I find my way back to the present. It was time to grab my backpack to descend further.

My most important tasks were the close cooperation needed for the further development and strengthening of the Slovenian Red Cross, who had been operating autonomously for a year, and helping to support approximately 70,000 Bosnian refugees in cooperation with the UNHCR and authorities in Slovenia. This also included bilateral cooperation with the Swedish Red Cross, which ran a targeted winter program for them. The energetic Slovenian and RK delegate Vida was responsible for this. She lived in Sweden with her Swedish husband and had returned to her old homeland for this task. Vida, was a nurse, and part of our delegation. She organized targeted refugee aid and was constantly on the move. Later, another Swede, Jan Ljlja from Stockholm, came to us as a financial accountant. One day, as a complete surprise, I received an invitation for an interview from Alojzij Sustar, the Archbishop of Ljubljana. An ecclesiastical dignitary, he had previously held high positions in central and eastern Switzerland and later in the diocese of Chur for 27 years before he was called to his old homeland as archbishop. He also mentioned, with a smile, that he also has a Swiss passport. He then informed me about the current, still difficult situation in Slovenia. He told me he was proud to be appointed archbishop, especially now that Slovenia had become a sovereign country. It was a major challenge for the newly elected government under President Milan Kucan to transform Slovenia from the previous communist regime into a functioning, western-oriented democracy. In old Yugoslavia, politicians and bureaucrats didn't have to make any particular efforts; the state automatically compensated for deficits, the Archbishop reported to me. Slovenia was an industrial province even before, there were industrial companies even in larger villages. Up to the turn of the century, Slovenia had supplied the whole of Yugoslavia with its industrial products. Now, after the end of Tito's Yugoslavia, there were many unemployed and the government was urgently looking for new outlets abroad. However, the churchman continued, first of all, the quality of the products had to be improved, since the quality standards in communist Yugoslavia were at best average, they would not be accepted in the West. This exchange of ideas was very valuable to me, as it gave me a deeper insight into this war-torn country.

Representatives from foreign Red Cross societies came to Ljubljana regularly, first contacted the Slovene RC, before they came to inquire about our programs in the country. These conversations with like-minded people were always inspiring. Dr. Christian Marte from the Austrian Red Cross (ARC) was one of these always welcome guests. That year, the Austrian Red Cross, the WCC, Caritas and the Austrian radio stations launched a large, very successful aid program for the needy people in the Balkans with the program "Neighours in Need."

One day I also received a surprise visit from the President of the Spanish Red Cross, Señora Carmen Mestre, accompanied by its director, José Sinovas, and another time I was able to meet the Icelandic doctor and Vice President of the IFRC, Dr. Gudjon Magnusson and informed him about our activities. The German DRC department head Jürgen Kronenberger also honoured us with a visit. The meeting with Basel National Councillor Remo Gysin and Charles Raedersdorf, the popular head of the Swiss Humanitarian Aid Unit, was a real highlight for me. These two well-known Swiss had been heavily involved in humanitarian aid for years. Our exchange of ideas over dinner was correspondingly helpful and interesting.

In September I flew to the former Yugoslav provincial capital of Skopje, now the capital of the new state of Macedonia. There I took part in meetings lasting several days with other heads of delegations from Zagreb, Skopje and Belgrade, led by our boss Martin Zak from Geneva. We had a lot to talk about; the constantly changing situation, the exchange of experiences and the coordination of the various aid programs.

When I drove through Skopje for the first time, I thought I had arrived in Turkey. The old houses were all built in Turkish style, because the former Ottoman Empire had extended to Skopje in its days. A few times I drove with Vida to Zagreb, formerly Agram, 130 kilometers away for cross-border meetings. It took some getting used to for Vida because after about 100 kilometers of driving to Obrezje – on the former provincial border of Slovenia and Croatia

– there was suddenly now a permanent customs post with a barrier for passport control. This border crossing there is probably also the eastern dividing line of the cheerful Alpine folk music, because foreign-sounding exotic plaintive melodies begin on the Croatian side. In each country, people express their landscape, uniqueness and tradition with music their appropriate music and dance.

The Slovenian Red Cross urgently needed a truck to transport the aid supplies arriving from abroad, to the refugee centers and SLRC sections. I applied to the IFCR in Geneva, as well as to the SRC Berne and the German Red Cross for funds to purchase a truck. I had already obtained offers from the Slovenian truck factory TAM in Maribor, (formerly Marburg). The SRC in Berne, my employer, finally agreed to cover the costs of around CHF 50,000. Some months later the new truck, painted blue, arrived. Mr. Jelinek organized a small party at the warehouse for the handover of the keys. "Donated by the Swiss Red Cross" was written on the driver's door and on the tarpaulin was written in large letters RDECI KRIZ SLOVENJE, a very effective mobile advertisement for the Slovenian Red Cross. My secretary Barbara was also an excellent driver. That was very helpful to me on trips, because we could take turns to drive. I went with her three times for meetings in the Croatian city of Karlovac, (formerly Karlstadt), where the bitter war between Croatia and Serbia had started in 1991. The old town of this city, around 20 kilometers from the border, was severely damaged. Even then towards the end of 1992, there was no peace. We were twice in Karlovac the ugly crack of shells falling on the city in the evening were heard: some times closer, then further away. Serbian paramilitaries had advanced within artillery range from the south-east and were holding the city in suspense. But we also witnessed more pleasant scenes in Karlovac. It was already dark when, after hours of driving, several buses with relieved, emaciated Croatian men arrived in front of the Red Cross building. Long held captive in Serbian concentration camps, these men stepped off buses with serious faces and downcast eyes. Many relatives had come in the hope of finding their father, son or brother again. Sometimes there was a shout of joy when someone was recognised and relatives ran over and hugged him with tears. A great reason for joy for everybody. Nevertheless, the atmosphere in the poorly lit semi-darkness remained oppressive. The after-effects of the reign of terror in the concentration camps were still clearly felt in these returnees. Many families were bitterly disappointed. They bombarded those who had been released with questions in the desperate hope of finding out something about their loved ones. The great uncertainty, the fear and anxiety weighed heavily on the relatives and this bitter war went on, with no end in sight.

One day I was on a UNHCR plane from Zagreb to Belgrade with about 20 Red Cross and UNHCR people. Serbia and Croatia were still enemies, and Belgrade airport had been closed since the outbreak of war, but our plane had received a special permit. Apart from two bored Serbian customs officers and cats roaming around, we saw nobody in the arrivals hall. We had come for meetings with the IFCR and ICRC teams, but I had also some free time and used it to walk around in Belgrade. I noticed how serious and reserved the faces of the passers-by were. Only in a busy downtown square did people seem to lose some of their tension. A huge chess board had been set up at this large square, and people commented on the score and moves played. That's when I realized: Belgrade was the scene of the World Chess Championship, a duel between the Russian Boris Spassky and the eccentric American Bobby Fischer. The latter had defied the US sanctions against Serbia. Despite the ban and threats of punishment Fischer played and won. Bobby Fischer left Belgrade as the new world chess champion, however he could not return to the USA because he would have been arrested. So, this chess genius also became a refugee and died in Iceland in 2001 at the age of just 64.

Becoming a refugee is a colossal turning point in a person's life. War, persecution, violence or famine forced them to leave their home and seek shelter elsewhere. In the new place they cannot work or move freely, their live practically comes to a standstill. The long and uncertain wait is hard to bear, all they have left is hope.

In Slovenia and Croatia refugees repeatedly told me why they had to flee. Neighbours who belonged to another ethnic group, with whom they lived peacefully side by side for years and attended the same school, one day came with guns and threatened to shoot if they didn't leave their house within a very short time. An electrician told how he and his wife had worked in Switzerland for 15 years. They returned to Bosnia with their two children and built a beautiful house with their savings. Shortly thereafter, war broke out and they had to flee. He didn't know if his house was still standing, and that uncertainty was very difficult to bear.

After a very hectic week, on a Friday evening, I received a visit from three people from an English NGO. This visit was the trigger that caused a few embarrassing problems, narrowly missing the notorious devil's kitchen. These three were trying to help a group of 200 Bosnian refugees to immigrate to England. Their spokesman claimed that Mr. Jelinek , General Secretary of Slovene Red Cross had already given his consent. They claimed all these refugees had met all the conditions for travel to Great Britain. All they expected from me was a few lines of confirmation to an English MP. Since it was already quite late and all offices were closed for the weekend, I was no longer able to contact Mr. Jelinek or the UNHCR. This fact made me hesitate for a long time, as I was used to always discussing things with local partners. We discussed their request intensively for a whole hour. Since time was obviously of the essence, I finally allowed myself to be persuaded to write this fax confirmation. In retrospect, I have wondered whether I was too tired in those minutes to think critically and analytically as usual, or I was simply too trusting. Anyway: When I came into my office at the beginning of the new week, I got a fright. The floor by the fax machine was covered with countless messages. Most of the reports came from Martin Zak from Geneva. I quickly realized that my letter to the English MPs in London and Geneva had caused a real storm. The phone rang and Martin Zak said in an angry voice that I had exceeded my authority with this letter. The English press keeps calling him, everyone wants more information. "My department is under siege, it's like in a bee house here, an apiary," he reported, unnerved. But that was just a small matter in contrast to what had happened in the English House of Commons in Westminster. Martin Zak described it to me graphically: "I saw on television how the member of parliament you wrote to waved your letter triumphantly in front of Prime Minister John Major and yelled: 'I have here a letter from Hansrudi Brawand, the Red

TO THE HORIZON AND BEYOND

Cross chief in Ljubljana, saying that the 200 refugees in Slovenia meet the requirements to enter England.' However, the government did not want to know anything about it, whereupon the opposition cited my letter as a reason to demand a vote of no confidence. I swallowed empty a few times, I had to let this information sink in a bit. What could I do other than formally apologize to Martin Zak? Somewhat mollified, he simply demanded that the English journalists should not be given any information if they called. I had obviously triggered a kind of avalanche that threatened to roll over these politicians. I felt really bad. Sprinkling ashes on my head didn't bring any relaxation either. Those were my thoughts as the phone rang several times. The English journalists had found me. "No comment, thank you," was my stereotypical answer to their questions, and I hung up the phone with relief. These few actually meaningless lines, which Hansrudi Brawand – late at night on a small rickety table – typed in Ljubljana, were apparently enough to cause a sensation in the English House of Commons; if not to overthrow a shaky government. Barbara tried in vain to cheer me up after I revealed the story to her. I vowed to myself that I would no longer write letters to politicians for the time being. Of course, that didn't solve the current problem. A few days later, the English House of Commons in Westminster actually voted and John Major's government survived the vote of no confidence. For their part, the 200 refugees in Slovenia could not leave the country, they were stuck here. The English NGO people, who had deliberately deceived me, did not give up and instead contacted now the Austrian province of Carinthia.

I found out exactly how the vote in the British House of

Commons went a little later, at a last-minute Red Cross conference in Budapest, where I met Patrick Healey, the British Red Cross's international aid chief. He told me that he had received an order to help the government. Literally he said: "For the last three days before the crucial vote, I did nothing else but lobby as many MPs as possible to vote for the government; because it really was on a razor's edge." That this was the case is shown by the fact that the government barely survived by just three votes. It is obvious that these three votes were due to the lobbying of Red Cross man Patrick Healey. After some back and forth, these 200 refugees were finally allowed to travel to Austria were they found shelter in the towns of Klagenfurt and Villach. Some remained there, but the majority were eventually allowed to immigrate to England. My letter had changed the future of all those families. The head of the English NGO later sent me a letter to my home address in Australia, explaining his procedure. Among other things, he wrote verbatim: "If the opposition had overthrown the government in the vote of confidence, I would have been enthusiastically celebrated in England." I would certainly not have gone to England being celebrated. Shortly before the end of my mission in Slovenia, Michael Sidman from the SRC Berne came for a visit. As country manager he wanted to get a personal picture of the situation in the countries of the former Yugoslavia. Michael was also a guest at the farewell dinner that SLRC arranged for me. My successor, an American, was also present. SLRC President Prof. Jure Gartner presented me with a painting of Ljubljana's old Town and Castle as a thank you, and Secretary General Mirko Jelinek surprised me with a medal and the following dedication: "The Slovenian Red Cross Society presents

Hansrudi Brawand with the Silver Order Medal in recognition of his achievements for the development of the Rdeci Kriz Slovenjie."

Two days later I travelled by bus to Zagreb to work briefly as an advisor to the Croatian Red Cross and the 23 strong IFCR delegation. Here I met the energetic Swedish delegate Per Nehler, whom I knew from Karlovac. I found accommodation with two other delegates in a spacious apartment in the city centre. Most of the time I was only there on weekends, as I was constantly on the road with Croatian RC companions. Croatia is scenically very beautiful, but after the collapse of Yugoslavia and the ongoing fighting, tourists stayed away. The hotels along the Dalmatian coast and on the offshore islands were empty. Arrangements were made to provide the empty hotel rooms for refugees from Bosnia. But the rooms had no heating because most hotels were only open from spring to autumn, so electric heaters had to be bought. One of my tasks was to check whether this heating program was really working. The refugees were very grateful for the radiators, which made their existence more bearable in winter. They all hoped that the war would end soon so that they could finally return to their homeland Bosnia, even with the risk that their house might had been destroyed or inhabited by strangers.

Despite the winter cold, trips to Dalmatia and the holiday islands were a unique opportunity to get to know this popular coastal area. On the way, I discussed the many problems that arose with the local leaders of the CRC sections. UN troops and UNPROFOR (United Nations Protection Force) were also stationed in Croatia. In Dalmatia we once sat at the same lunch table with soldiers from the Ukraine and while driving to Osijek in Eastern Slavonia, we were stopped at a roadblock behind Bielovar by soldiers from Argentina—and checked with a smile. Osijek, the fourth largest city in Croatia, had suffered a month-long battle the previous year and the damage was visible on many buildings. A bridge over the river Drau lay destroyed in the water. But Osijek, in German Essegg, remained in Croatian hands.

One day, with two young RC companions, we drove from Zagreb to the town of Vinkovski, 270 kilometers away. We had loaded medical equipment that was urgently needed in the hospital there. The chief surgeon greeted us in a large basement room that was now being used as an operating theatre. He thanked us for the valuable cargo and led us behind the hospital, where shocking images awaited us: the windows were missing on all floors. For months Serbian units had used the hospital as a target, systematically sending thousands of shells into the huge building from a distance of just 300 to 400 meters. The hospital building consisted now only of a solid reinforced concrete skeleton. The doctor led us up half destroyed concrete stairs to the upper floors. Everything that could not had been taken to the basement rooms at the beginning of the bombardment lay smashed in the perforated rooms. Valuable medical apparatus, equipment and beds were destroyed, strewn with glass shards and splinters. What senseless destruction caused by human hatred! It was a miracle that the building hadn't collapsed. During our visit it was quiet, but the shooting could start again at any time. It was only thanks to what the staff were able to hastily move into the overcrowded basement rooms and long corridors that underground, emergency operations continued. The chief surgeon said with justifiable pride that thanks to dynamos, they continued to operate in the basement, even while artillery shells exploded upstairs.

For the return trip we chose a different route to visit some CRC branches in Croatian Slavonia. Gloomy and silent we drove slowly through various villages and ghost towns where the houses had been either destroyed, burned, badly damaged and covered in hate graffiti. Shell-spitting Serbian tanks were said to have passed through there, using every house as a target. When I turned off the engine, there was no sound. We saw neither people nor animals, not even any movement of birds. The dead silent atmosphere wasn't just scary, it was downright spooky.

Shortly thereafter, the IFCRS considered the somewhat daring plan of trying to drive some flagged Red Cross vehicles in a convoy from Vinkovski through Serb-held territory to the destroyed town of Vukovar at the river Danube, 20 kilometers away. I was supposed to lead this convoy. However, the project was cancelled shortly before the scheduled date, as those responsible seemed to think the risk was too great.

I was enthusiastic about the long journeys through varied Croatian landscapes and the informative discussions with the leaders of the CRC sections along the way. Many impressed with their dedication, initiatives and enthusiasm to help the suffering population. There were those who didn't want to wait for the relief supplies from Zagreb to finally arrive. They independently sent calls to other countries for help and appealed for urgently needed emergency aid. That wasn't the correct way, but the winter emergency situation really needed quick action. These sections got overwhelmed with so many donations that they were also able to supply other sections. The visits and conversations with all my fellow combatants remain unforgettable for me. I was deeply impressed by the Croatian Red Cross, their passion and willingness to help. The friendly cooperation with young, energetic RC colleagues, who often asked me for advice, was also important to me and I was able to share some of my experience. Every Friday after 5 p.m. we sat together with the CRC people in Zagreb for a friendly meeting, exchanged our reports and experiences, discussed new plans and cultivated our cross-border togetherness under the banner of the Red Cross. We also attended a sold-out classical concert together in the Vatroslav Lisinski Hall. Pieces by the popular Croatian conductor and composer Lovro von Matatic, who died in 1985, were played. It was a very welcome change for all of us. However, I celebrated my 61st birthday all by myself.

That Sunday morning, I strolled to the nearby Hilton Hotel and treated me to a fantastic gourmet breakfast buffet that lasted a full two hours. Then I read the foreign newspapers in the lobby and called Ann in Australia. She was close to leaving to meet her gypsy husband in Europe and said she couldn't take it any longer. We agreed that Croatia would be my last mission. A week later I hugged Ann at Brnik Airport near Ljubljana. Then we drove together to Zagreb for my last week of work. I really wanted to share my last tasks on the coast with Ann, she deserved it. Last visits to local CRC sections and a number of control visits in the hotels inhabited by refugees made this week fly by. We also travelled visiting CRC branches on the very long island of Cres, then by ferry to the island of Pag visiting the CRC section and refugees. We could not go further east, as the war was still going on up the coast. On the way back to Zagreb, an icy snowstorm hit. Poor Ann had imagined her visit to Croatia would be warmer.

My seven-month, highly interesting ex-Yugoslavia mission ended in Zagreb. On the last evening we celebrated my farewell to Croatia with RC companions. It was a worthy conclusion to my long Red Cross career. Then we travelled back to Ljubljana, said goodbye to the friends from the Slovenian Red Cross and flew back to Switzerland. The de-briefing took place in Geneva with Martin Zak. Then we attended a press conference in Berne together with Michael Sidman and Karl Schuler, where we provided information on the various programs and activities of the SRC and IFCRS in the countries of former Yugoslavia.

During the meeting with the SRC in Berne, Toni and Vreni Wenger made a surprising proposal to me: the very long-standing SRC refugee program Kassala-Wad Sherifay in East Sudan was to be handed over to the Sudanese Red Crescent at the end of 1993. The SRC would be very grateful if I could take on a three month mission to organise the hand over. Ann and I looked at each other and we knew each other's thoughts. But Ann being Ann, after a while, agreed to my very last mission. She had worked in Wad Sherifay herself knew the local team, the situation and also knew how important an orderly handover would be for the team.

Now it was high time to fly home! The next day we boarded the plane to down under, where Charles, Janet, Hazel and their governess, Ann's niece Hazel David, eagerly awaited us.

CHAPTER FOURTEEN

Kassala, Sudan, 1993-1994: The Last Mission

PERTH: THE FINAL PUSH

The most beautiful thing about every trip is the safe return home to the bosom of the family. The children were very excited and had so much to tell. They all wanted to talk about their school experiences at the same time. After a week's rest, I went back to looking for work. Temporary jobs as a freight forwarder, buyer and dispatcher followed. I still liked the variety and the quick familiarization with new tasks kept me fit and flexible and meanwhile Ann and I hatched new plans.

In Walliston, a small suburb in the bush on the Stirling Range, south of Perth, we had Swiss friends who owned a chicken farm with 6,000 laying hens. We really liked the forest landscape up there and decided to buy a house in the area. Every weekend we drove up to Kalamunda, Gooseberry Hill and Lesmurdie, looking

TO THE HORIZON AND BEYOND

Perth [16]

at houses for sale. We found what we were looking for at Robins Road in Kalamunda: a two-storey house with large rooms, a swimming pool and ancient trees on a 3,600 square metre plot. With our Girrawheen house sold, and a new mortgage approved, the move to Kalamunda began. It was an exciting time for the whole family and the school was only a ten minute walk away.

Kalamunda has retained its rural character to this day. It presents itself to the visitor as a village in the bush. In the Aboriginal language, Kalamunda means "home in the forest." On the western side, where the land drops away, there are fantastic views across the vast metropolitan area to the distant Perth City skyscrapers. At night it sparkles as an endless sea of lights.

The children quickly settled into the new school. The priest was happy to welcome three new, but experienced altar servers to the old Catholic church. Sometimes all three served simultaneously

---

16   Source https://www.weekendnotes.com/top-driving-roads-in-perth/

during Sunday Mass. During these services, the same thoughts struck me again and again. For many a year now, as a Protestant, I had attended Catholic Mass. It seemed to me, that the time finally had come to convert to the Catholic faith. Ann was delighted when I told her. We had never been married in a church. The pastor in Chittagong had categorically refused in 1972 to marry the full-bearded Protestant Grindelwalder and the devout Catholic Ann Martha Cecilia Gomes. We finally wanted to catch up on that. We talked about it with our friend, Rev. Tom Gayne. As I had expected, I would first have to take a course to get to know the Catholic faith better. So once a month I went to Girrawheen to see Father Gayne's secretary Margrit. She gave me the book *The Catholic Religion*, then an hour's lesson and left me with homework for the following month. However, I wasn't an avid learner, to Margrit's slight disappointment. Nevertheless, after only three months, the celebration of my entry into the Catholic Church took place on a Wednesday at 11 am in the Girrawheen Church. We had invited a dozen of Ann's relatives. Just a few minutes after I officially became a Catholic, Father Tom Gaine married us in church. My beloved Ann looked enchantingly beautiful and happy as a bride in her snow-white dress. For 21 years she had followed me everywhere through thick and thin. It was very important for her to finally get married in church. Unfortunately, my stubborn Bernese head had resisted it for much too long. Now this ecclesiastical conversion came from my own will and was a good thing. After this double celebration we invited Father Gayne, his secretary Margrit and the relatives to a restaurant for lunch. Later in the afternoon I drove to a city hotel with Ann. There we sat down in the evening, just the two of us, for a celebratory candlelight dinner in the restaurant. Then, like the newly in love, we retreated to the specially decorated room for our second, officially-certified wedding night.

Our new home in Kalamunda became the starting point for many hikes and on weekends I explored a variety of hiking trails with the children. Sometimes, at 6 a.m., I would jog down and back to Forrestfield, 250 altitude meter below and back, or trot over to the rushing Lesmurdie Falls. There was also plenty of work waiting on our large property. Many bushes and trees had not been cut back for a long time. I often spent hours sawing and chopping firewood to have enough "fodder" for the wood stove in winter. We used the dry leaves for a campfire, which inspired the children to help out. Janet and Hazel really wanted some chickens. When the chicken coop was built, we bought six laying hens. Both girls were responsible for feeding and collecting the eggs. Soon there were mice that liked to feast on the chicken feed. A little later, the dangerous Dugite poisonous snakes appeared – the mice had attracted them. That was too dangerous for us, so the magnificent hens – to the chagrin of the whole family—ended up in Ann's cooking pot one after the other.

*　*　*　*　*

In mid-October 1993 I once again said goodbye to my loved ones and flew to Switzerland to take up my commission to organise the hand over the long-standing SRC program in Wad Sherifay to the Sudanese Red Crescent. After I received the detailed order in Berne, I flew to Khartoum as usual. This time the long bus journey to Kassala was uneventful. My Eritrean comrades and friends were waiting for me, the reunion with the big team in Wad Sherifay was, as always, very warm. But the mood among the workforce had changed. Shambel, Ahmed and Abrehet seemed withdrawn to me. The fact that the Swiss Red Cross was about to withdraw had depressed the entire Eritrean workforce. Everyone knew that under the Sudanese Red Crescent much would change to their disadvantage. My predecessor had already left, unfortunately and carelessly without leaving clear directives and documents with Shambel. This had a severe impact on my work from the beginning. The handover required a lot of preparation from us with the taking of the considerable inventory. In addition, the new Sudanese government under President Bashir had already asserted its influence over the national Red Crescent. It seemed to me that absolute neutrality was no longer observed. Even before the takeover by the Red Crescent, new directives came from Khartoum, which revealed this state influence and clouded the general mood.

Christmas was soon around the corner. We German speakers in Kassala celebrated Christmas Eve with a simple chicken supper in the candlelit front yard of the team house. Thinking of our loved ones far away, we sang some Christmas carols. It was a modest and therefore all the more impressive Christmas party. The official handover was fast approaching. It took place under a large tent with the front side open so interested refugees could watch too.

The Swiss Red Cross program was now officially handed over in writing to the Red Crescent along with the part run by the Red Cross Federation. Delegates from the Red Crescent and UNHCR, as well as Representatives of the Kassala authorities attended the dignified celebration. The official speeches were given in Arabic, while my speech was simultaneously translated by Shambel into Arabic. Dr. Ismail from the Sudanese Red Crescent, our Dr. Bedredin, Chris Lee from the Red Cross Federation and myself from the Swiss Red Cross were all honored with a shoulder ribbon. I was also handed a glass case containing a colored plaster model of the Kassala Mountains as a reminder of my many Kassala mountain tours. I had a faint hope that the Red Cross and Red Crescent principals, which are lived worldwide, would continue to exist in Sudan. I wished that with all my heart for those in need, but also for Shambel and the whole very dedicated Eritrean team.

* * * * *

For me there remained one very last official duty as a Red Cross Delegate. To drive with Shambel to the capital of Eritrea, Asmara to meet Vreni Wenger, a Director of the Swiss Red Cross in Berne, for a meeting with the Eritrean Red Crescent representatives for possible future programs in this mountainous country. We both very much looked forward to this exciting tour.

SPOTLIGHT ON ASMARA, CAPITAL OF ERITREA

The city is at 2325 meters, on the edge of a high plateau that drops steeply towards the Red Sea. With around 869,000 inhabitants (as of 2018), Asmara is the largest city in the country. Until the 1880s, there were a number of small villages in the area of today's city, before they were conquered under Yohannes IV and Ras Alula

Asmara [17]

and expanded to become the capital of the Ethiopian province of Hamasia. In 1889 Asmara was occupied by Italy and in 1900 it became the capital under Italy's colonisation of Eritrea. Under Italian fascism, Asmara gained in importance from 1932 when it experienced rapid growth – mainly due to immigration from Italy. The population increased fivefold to almost 100,000 inhabitants, more than half of whom are Italians. Older people in particular still speak Italian very well and many Italian expressions such as "*Andiamo*!" (Let's go) or "*E allora*?" (So what?) are common in everyday speech. On April 2, 1941, after the Battle of Keren and the Italian Army surrendered, the British Army occupied Asmara without a fight. From 1942 to 1952, the British occupation pursued

---

17   Source: https://whc.unesco.org/en/list/1550/gallery/

a rigorous policy of dismantling the country's infrastructure and the city was badly damaged. By allying itself with the Abyssinian Empire in 1952, Asmara lost its role as the country's capital. With Eritrea's independence in 1991, Asmara regained its function as the capital. All of the country's central authorities are based here. [18]

* * * * *

One last task was still ahead of me: Vreni Wenger in Berne wanted to meet me and Shambel in Asmara to discuss possible new projects in Eritrea. What a unique opportunity for me to get to know the homeland of the refugees and Wad Sherifay's employees better!

With our trusted Abdul as our driver, we planned to drive the 440 kilometer route, up from 300 meters to 2,400 meters above sea level, then down again to Massawa on the Red Sea. We looked forward to this trip like children, and loaded enough provisions, water and important spare parts into the Pajero.

A few minutes after Wad Sherifay we reached the Eritrean border post at a small shelter. After the identity check and the questions about where we came from and where we were going, they let us go. As we drank tea in the border town of Tessenai, the familiar sounds of Eritrean folk music rang out. Shambel and Abdul immediately beamed. Our destination for the day was Agordat, 220 kilometers away. The route led between rocky hills on bumpy dirt roads through former war zones and when outside of the car, caution was advised because of risk of landmines.

After 110 kilometers we reached the town of Barentu. Shortly

---

18   Source: Wikipedia

thereafter, driving down into a green valley, we passed several destroyed tanks. Hungry, shaken and dusty, we finally reached Agordat on the Gash River three hours later. Here we met Ibrahim, Wad Sherifay's long-time driver. He had recently returned home to help his father, who owned a large banana plantation. We found lodging and food in a simple inn. Shambel ordered a typically Eritrean meal. The basis for this is *injera*, a thin sourdough flatbread. In Eritrea, most people eat by hand. A piece of *injera*, is pushed into the spicy dishes, serving as cutlery. The onward journey the next morning led steeply up into the mountains to Keren, which is 1,300 meters high. On the mountainside above us we saw bridges, viaducts, and high walls. It was the old railway line built by the Italians from Massawa on the Red Sea up to Asmara and down from Keren to Agordat. But the sleepers and railway tracks had been torn out during the decades-long war against Ethiopia and used to build bunkers and shelters.

We drove past dry stream beds, rock faces, screes and camel caravans, and a rocky wild mountain landscape that led us to Keren, the second largest city in the country. There were still 90 kilometers to go to the high-altitude Eritrean capital. Asmara is also called the beautiful Eritrean, or the southernmost city in Italy. Connoisseurs praise Asmara as the most beautiful city in Africa because of it's distinct buildings, which were built during the Italian colonial period from 1925 to 1941. The main street of Asmara is an impressive avenue lined with towering palm trees. At that time more Italians lived there than Eritreans. The climate is ideal with an average of 23.5 degrees and a deep blue sky.

We met Vreni Wenger in a hotel and days of long and intensive discussions followed in the house of the Eritrean Red Cross. Eritrea was still experiencing much difficulty. The 30-year war had bled dry this mountainous country. Eritrea had fought its way free from Ethiopia with incredible determination and was recently independent. For the first time colonial borders had been changed in Africa, but Eritrea remained one of Africa's poorest countries.

Before returning to Kassala, we drove down to Massawa on the Red Sea with Vreni Wenger. The Italians had built Eritrea's lifeline there with the sometimes very steep road. A true architectural masterpiece, which rose from sea level up to 2,300 meters. Back in Asmara we said goodbye to Vreni Wenger and drove back to Kassala. The trip to the Eritrean highlands was a moving conclusion to my missions in Sudan. It was difficult for me to say goodbye to the many friends with whom I had worked closely during three missions in Wad Sherifay and I knew we would never see each other again. Tsegai and Shambel took me to the bus to Khartoum. A last warm handshake, a last wave and Kassala was history. Again and again I turned my head to "my" Kassal mountain'suntil they finally disappeared behind the horizon. For the 700 kilometer final journey to Khartoum, kilometer by kilometer I said my last farewell to Sudan. I had spent almost six eventful, unforgettable Red Cross years there – in this fascinating country in Africa. I would never forget these times, the difficulties, setbacks and achievements as well as the many interesting people and the friends I now leave behind. They all still live in my memories. But my thoughts also jumped back 25 years to my very first assignment in Africa during the terrible civil war in Biafra. The place where I had found the fulfilment I had longed for and earned my first Red Cross spurs. The joy and energy that I felt on that first mission never let go of me. I was inspired and strengthened from then on. Working in a team, organizing what initially seemed impossible, tireless energy coupled with optimism, even in difficult times, these were the ingredients that were needed on every mission. More so was inner the strength to come to terms with the immense human misery that one encountered at every turn, day after day. The protective shield for this was the certainty that this immeasurable suffering could be counteracted with powerful, well-organized teamwork under the flag and care of the worldwide Red Cross. Whether in Nigeria/Biafra, Anatolia, Bangladesh or Sudan, whether in Somalia or during the Bosnian war, these strengths were indispensable everywhere. Sometimes there were planned missions that had to be cancelled for safety reasons. In Angola, where I would have traveled a lot more, but the risk of mines was too great. In Vietnam, a mission in Da Nang was planned, but the war front was rapidly approaching the city, this mission was also cancelled. In Yemen I should have led a food convoy through a distant desert trail to another ethnic group. This project was also canceled due to the risk of landmines.

With 62 eventful years under my belt, I finally had drawn the line under my exciting Red Cross years. I could no longer justify putting all the family chores on Ann. In addition, a certain tiredness had spread through me, which I felt as a welcome relief. The decades-long, stubborn calls to travel far away, the inner restlessness that kept sending me on trips, had both slowly faded away. A need to settle had set in, which was a great gift for both of us. In my retirement age, which I bridged with temporary jobs, I also paid voluntary contributions to the Swiss federal old-age insurance scheme called AHV in order to be a little better protected in old age. My gratitude and my eternal love keeps flowing to my Ann, who always loved, supported and strengthen me. She sacrificed so much to make me happy and grateful.

AFTERWORD

When in March 1997 the first payment of the age pension arrived from Switzerland, this was the beginning of our senior years, an exciting milestone in our turbulent life together. Because we lived abroad from Switzerland, we were not entitled to receive any company pension from the Swiss Red Cross. This unfair rule was later changed, unfortunately too late for us. Our family was now smaller. Only 16 year old Hazel still lived with us. Knowing that she would eventually also leave, we realised it was now time to down size, our big Kalamunda property was now too large for Ann and me. We decided to look for a property not too far from Perth city. We soon found a newly built double storey house with great views, six kilometers from the city. We sold our Kalamunda property and moved with Hazel to Yokine. We loved our new smaller home and the perfect city views with its high rise buildings.

After Hazel had completed high school she did a course in TAFE, which is a Government organisation providing technical and further education after high school, and took a work experience job with the company Boral. They seemed to like Hazel there and a female director offered her a full time job, but unfortunately Hazel declined. She didn't seem ready yet to start working full time, which we very much regretted. Soon after she left home and stayed with Janet as the government supported school leavers with various grants.

At last, Ann and I planned to travel to visit our relatives and friends in Bangladesh, Switzerland, Germany and North America, and just drive through countries we had never been. This was pure happiness, we felt free like birds. These travelling years turned out to be our happiest times. While travelling in rental cars, buses or trains through Europe and North America, we mostly stayed with old friends or Ann's relatives of. In the USA we enjoyed travelling through 16 states between New York and California. On the Caribic island of Antigua, during a cruise, we were welcomed by my old schoolfriend Hans Ryter from Grindelwald. In Vorpommern, northern Germany, we regularly visited our closest friends, Hans and Ruth Burzlaff. In the peaceful Peene valley, they owned a huge old farmhouse that was over a hundred years old and during our visits we helped our good friends with the restoration of their historic building. Each time we arrived there the villagers said: "The Australians are here again!" This was the same Hans Burzlaff we had met for the first time in 1983 as a customer in our lunch bar. Over the years we developed a life-long friendship with the Burzlaffs.

Our three children Charles, Janet and Hazel are all in their forties now and married with children. Janet's oldest son Michael is already 20 and lives on his own. We now have seven grandchildren. It is the children who make us aware how fast the time is passing.

TO THE HORIZON AND BEYOND

A SONG OF PRAISE FOR ANN

Many of my memories have never faded. But by far the greatest happening in my life took place in the evening of the 10th of April 1972 when, thanks to a very lucky chance, I met Ann, my future wife for the first time in Chittagong. It was a rendezvous which changed our lives into new directions, and brought us love, fulfillment and gratitude. But her stationary life suddenly ended with our marriage and together we became nomads. Wherever we later settled down for a while, Ann was always respected and highly regarded. She never wanted to remain a housewife, and always looked for ambitious new tasks. Her mother tongue is English, but she also speaks perfect Bangla and understands Hindu and Urdu well. And in the Goethe Institute in Khartoum she also learned German. She also gained her driving licence there and later in Switzerland and Australia. Ann owns four passports from four different countries, Pakistan, Bangladesh, Switzerland and Australia. They are all now expired as our travelling years are finally over. She was born in British India, but the year 1947 marked the end of British Colonial rule and two new independent States were founded, India and Pakistan. Ann grew up in a settled Christian family, always ready to help other people and blessed with a strong self confidence, life energy and masters difficult situations easily. From her modest salary as a telephonist she gradually bought parcels of land, which she later presented to her nephews and nieces. Without Ann my life would have continued differently. Ann brought me good luck, satisfaction and assurance, made a better human of me. Her love never expired, was always self-sacrificing when another Red Cross mission was calling. When possible she followed me and even became a Red Cross Delegate in her own right.

We have grown together, walked through thick and thin together and overcame obstacles together too. For all her loving virtues, sacrifices and achievements, Ann deserves my life-long gratitude and love.

Hansrudi Brawand
Perth, Australia
2022

TO THE HORIZON AND BEYOND

Ann with our best Hen, Maggie, in 1972

HANSRUDI BRAWAND

*At our wedding reception in Hotel Agrabad
in Chittagong with driver Abdul, 1972*

Just ten days married

Just married. An official RC Photo of 1972

1975 in Malakal South Sudan. H.R. with a worker at the site of the new Teacher training institute (H.R Mitarbeiter).

HANSRUDI BRAWAND

Grindelwald where H.R. was born in 1932 and spent the first 16 Years of his life. (Source: https://en.wikipedia.org/wiki/Grindelwald)

Biafra 1969, Dr. Speedy Gonzales from Columbia, H.R white dress is made out from empty wheat bags by a Taylor.

TO THE HORIZON AND BEYOND

H.R. as Muezzin Singing the prayers for the praying villagers on the ground, H.R was given the unique honour of building a new schoolhouse, 1971.

HANSRUDI BRAWAND

H.R. with most of over 100 employees in Enugu 1969, Biafra 1969.

On the island of Hatyia we built several villages like this one in Sonadia, 1988.

TO THE HORIZON AND BEYOND

H.R. in Biafra, 1969, with the two orphans Eze (right) and Nhwafor (left) who each had sneaked alone through the front lines in the bush.

HANSRUDI BRAWAND

Two of three School houses we built in Dunlupinar, Turkey in 1971.

1987 arriving with our trawler ML Red Cross at Hatiya Island. The blue ship on the right is a coastal steamer.

TO THE HORIZON AND BEYOND

1988 in Gulshan (Dhaka). Charles, Hazel, and Janet just returned home from school.

HANSRUDI BRAWAND

In Anatolia, the Asian part of Turkey, visitors from Switzerland including journalists came to see the progress of the Swiss Red Cross schoolhouse program led by H.R. Brawand.

1988 on Hatiya Island, Bangladesh. The lady in red is Bina, the caretaker of all these ladies. They are all widows. We built a house for each one here in the widow's colony.

TO THE HORIZON AND BEYOND

1975, Malakal, South Sudan. Roof work at the teacher training institute.

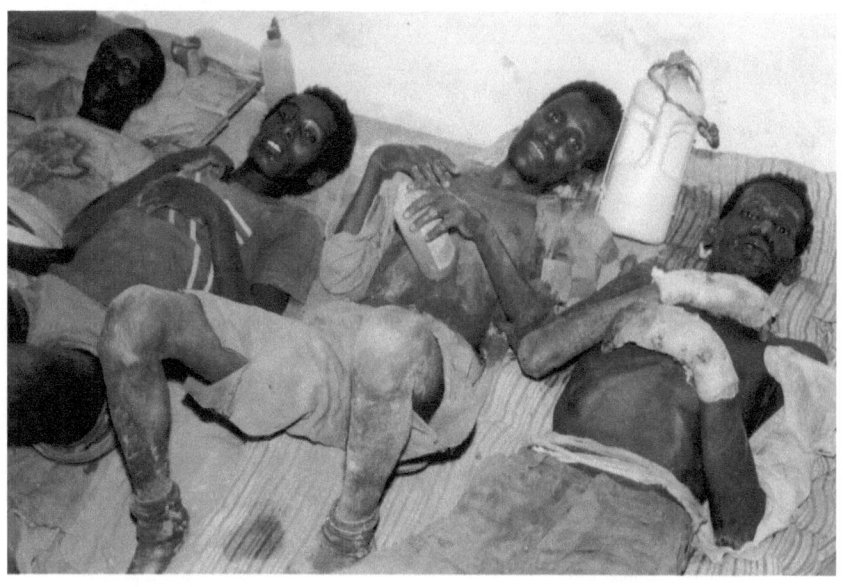

Wounded Ethiopian soldiers in Eastern Sudan, 1991.

HANSRUDI BRAWAND

H.R.'s superiors in Berne. From left to right: Dr. Martin Weber Verena Kücholl-Münzenmeier, Vreni Wenger, and Toni Wenger, our highly respected big Boss in the SRC HQ.

Hansrudi's entry permit to Chittagong port.

TO THE HORIZON AND BEYOND

H.R. and Siddiki in action at Volkart Godwown in Chittagong, 1973.

Monthly Red Cross meeting of a league of Red Cross delegates in Dhaka, Bangladesh, 1972.

HANSRUDI BRAWAND

Chittagong Airport, 1972. Loading of relief goods into a Hercules transport plane.

Our lunch bar in Perth, 1983.

TO THE HORIZON AND BEYOND

Ljubljana Slovenia, 1992. H.R. just handed over the keys to a brand-new truck donated by the Swiss Red Cross to the secretary general, Mr. Jelinek.

INDEX

Aadorf 195
Aargau 110
Ababa 303-304
Abakaliki 38, 41
Abboud 302-303
Abdelatif 488
Abdu 428, 497
Abdul 379, 381-2, 388, 400, 403, 531
Abdullah 171, 330, 435
Abo 88
Abrehet 428, 491, 528
Abubakar 11
Abubaker 490-491
Abyssinian 531
Accra 17-18
Adam 324
Adana 184
Addis 303-304
Aden 400
Adolphe 460
Advent 296
Aegean 112, 186
Aetti 268
Afghanistan 487
Africa 8-9, 14-5, 17, 23, 25, 36, 39-40, 89-90, 93-8, 104, 106, 190, 224, 228, 337, 346, 349, 356, 360, 372-3, 389, 400, 403, 411, 415, 419, 432, 498, 507, 532-3
African 17-18, 33, 96, 98, 101, 103, 301, 304, 402, 417, 430
Africans 419
Afyon 112, 172
Agbo 41, 50
Agordat 531-532
Agrabad 210-211, 235, 252,

262, 265, 267
Agram 512
Agricultural 314
Ahaba 72-73, 75
Ahmed 122, 126, 129-130, 136, 145, 153, 180-1, 187, 314-5, 493, 528
Akram 446
Akropol 312, 420
Akwa 65
Alafa 495-496
Albany 408
Albert 280
Albula 106
Aldrick 249
Aletsch 271
Alfred 416
Alhaji 60
Ali 126, 145, 170-1, 191, 234, 248-9, 306, 361, 490, 492
Alison 51, 370
Alkarim 218, 231, 235, 258, 266, 278, 280-1, 285, 298
Allah 125, 161, 163, 180-1
Allan 34, 36-7, 51, 80, 399
Allen 80
Allison 97
Almas 254
Alojzij 510
Alps 17, 196, 419, 509
Alsace 196
Alula 529
Alusuisse 110, 127
Alvier 108
Amacher 52, 453
Amarat 310
Amber 203
Amer 417
America 219, 238, 322, 360, 538
American 34, 41, 49, 51, 62, 89, 99, 212, 290-1, 322, 388, 423, 433, 435, 485, 515, 518
Americans 100, 224, 227
Amin 194
Amos 42
Amphitheatre 169
Amsterdam 429
Anambra 13
Anatolia 106, 109, 111, 113, 118, 129, 132, 135, 144, 147, 159, 163, 167, 180, 183, 188, 199, 328, 342, 534, 552
Anatolian 112, 139-140, 142, 187, 342-3
Andersson 218, 220, 501

Andreas 195
Andy 35, 46, 56
Anglican 364
Anglo 245
Angola 534
Angrily 385
Ankara 114, 118-120, 153, 155-6, 158, 165, 174, 182-3
Ann 245-269, 274-8, 280, 283, 285-8, 291-300, 303, 306, 309-310, 319, 322-5, 328, 331, 338-343, 346-350, 353-9, 361, 366, 368, 370-5, 380, 383-4, 387-396, 402-4, 407, 409, 411-3, 415, 419, 429, 432, 437, 440-3, 446-450, 452-3, 457, 460-1, 466, 468, 470-5, 478-480, 483, 485-6, 491-2, 504-7, 522-4, 526, 534-5, 537-541
Anna 408
Anne 100
Annemarie 337
Annie 268
Antediluvian 201
Antiaircraft 347
Antigua 538
Anyuak 336-337

Apapa 18, 24
Arab 301
Arabia 197
Arabian 124, 127, 136, 198, 292-3, 322, 401
Arabic 177, 301, 308, 312, 314, 319, 323, 330, 338, 435, 437, 490, 529
Arbon 321
Arnold 354-355
Arts 503
Ascona 348, 358
Asfaha 428, 491
Ashoka 199
Asia 127, 224, 346, 349, 372-3, 507
Asian 106, 109, 413
Aslanapa 175
Aslehanlar 133, 143
Asmara 331, 494-5, 498-9, 529-533
Assam 231, 285
Astrid 501
Ataturk 116
Athens 343
Auchy 25
Augusta 353
Aunt 450

Aunty 359
Aussie 386, 409, 411
Aussies 359, 412
Australia 9, 37, 44, 219, 266, 286, 304, 350-1, 354-361, 363-4, 366, 369, 383-4, 404-5, 411-4, 440, 484, 498, 500, 518, 522, 539-540
Australian 32, 37, 47, 51, 76, 97, 168, 228, 350-4, 356, 359, 365-7, 406, 408, 412, 432, 470-1, 484, 487, 505
Australians 227, 411, 538
Austria 111, 190, 231, 280, 518
Austrian 354, 503, 511-2, 517
Austrians 227
Aviolat 310, 321
Avon 484
Awami 192-194
Awgu 51, 86
Awka 53, 59-60, 65-6, 68, 83
Axel 470
Ayvallah 237
Ayvallahs 237
Azem 113
Babies 214
Badr 194
Bahini 193, 210, 219

Bahr 304, 312, 332
Bahrain 293
Balair 196, 204, 228, 236, 244, 287, 291-2, 337
Balewa 11
Balkan 502
Balkans 505, 512
Bally 277-278
Balsthal 479
Bangla 219, 250, 447, 461, 472, 483, 539
Bangladesh 52, 191-2, 199, 204-7, 213-4, 216-9, 221-4, 229-230, 233, 235, 238, 240, 244-5, 250-2, 258, 265, 270, 275, 280-2, 284, 290-1, 294, 296, 298-9, 312, 336-7, 348, 351, 357, 374, 380, 387, 412, 437-8, 440-1, 444, 450, 452-3, 465, 468-470, 475, 477-480, 487, 501, 534, 538-9, 548, 552, 555

Bangladeshi 207-208
Bangladeshis 214, 227, 234, 286, 291
Bantu 377
Bar 414

Barbara 62, 65, 83, 508, 513, 517
Barentu 531
Bari 343
Barky 277
Barre 378, 382
Bartolomeo 92
Basel 7, 20, 189, 195-6, 199-200, 204, 287, 291-2, 294-5, 359, 430, 512
Bashir 528
Batumi 182
Baustrag 304, 314, 318, 326, 331
Bayandirlik 115-118, 121-2, 125, 129
Bayindirlik 126
Bazar 212
Bedreddin 495
Bedredin 491, 495, 529
Begbie 51, 97
Beirut 293-294
Beja 417
Belgian 322, 427
Belgium 12, 190, 426
Belgrade 512, 514-5
Ben 361
Beneath 315

Bengalis 223
Beni 417
Benue 26
Berbera 376, 378, 400
Berchtesgaden 190
Bergama 168-169
Bernadette 214, 253, 259, 446-7, 460
Bernarda 207
Berne 21, 109, 127, 164, 167, 188, 194-5, 215, 217, 275, 287, 295, 298-300, 303-5, 319, 339, 344, 354-6, 374-5, 380, 383, 401, 404, 415-6, 422, 428, 431, 437, 441, 452, 457-8, 467, 473, 479, 486-7, 490, 494, 501, 505-6, 513, 518, 523, 527, 529, 531
Bernea 279
Berneadette 253, 447
Bernese 23, 52, 295, 426, 489, 526
Bernhard 94, 441
Betsche 195, 294
Bey 342
Bezirgan 152
Bhola 192
Biafra 11-16, 19-21, 28-9, 34,

37, 47, 52, 58, 61, 64-5, 74, 84-5, 87-8, 91-2, 95-7, 100, 104-5, 108-9, 115, 195, 200, 305, 357, 374, 399, 533, 546, 548

Biafran 19, 23, 27, 34, 36, 49, 56, 61, 67, 70, 72-3, 87

Biafrans 28, 41, 60, 67-9, 73-4, 81, 83, 96, 104

Biel 53, 437

Bielovar 520

Bihar 221

Bihari 219-221, 234, 248, 252, 288

Biharis 220

Biman 217

Bimol 466

Bina 552

Bismarck 98, 103

Blacks 92

Blanchie 249

Blantyre 95

Blotzheim 196

Blue 187, 304, 311, 319, 321, 327, 330, 342, 419

Bob 432

Bobby 515

Bohren 166

Bombay 198, 291-3, 298

Books 9

Bor 333

Boral 537

Borama 386

Boris 515

Bosnia 502, 509, 515, 519

Bosnian 502, 506, 510, 516, 534

Bosphorus 187

Bosporus 111

Bosshart 441

Bracken 350

Brahmaputra 230, 272, 466

Brawand 7-8, 16, 21, 113, 233, 260, 263, 274-5, 388, 390, 499, 517, 519, 540

Brazzaville 90-91

Bregenz 354

Brian 215

Brienzwiler 52

British 26, 34-5, 65-6, 168, 213-5, 221, 314, 326, 332, 359, 376, 378, 386, 399, 405, 481, 518, 530, 539

Brnik 522

Bruderholz 294

Buchs 111

Budapest 518

Buddhist 213
Buds 372
Buffalo 142
Bukra 435
Bulgaria 111, 144
Bullsbrook 485-486
Bundestag 322
Buoyant 316
Burzlaff 413, 484, 538
Burzlaffs 538
Bystanders 334
Cairo 488
Calais 190, 359
Calcutta 200-201, 204-5, 209-210, 235
Calgary 270
California 538
Cameroon 40
Canada 279, 286, 351, 426
Canadian 168, 270, 282, 291
Canadians 227
Canakkale 167
Canberra 414, 470
Caribic 538
Carinthia 517
Caritas 109, 280, 512
Carlo 116-117, 149, 183
Carmel 214, 228
Carmen 512
Carter 18
Cecilia 249, 263, 526
Cessna 326, 335, 340, 388-9
Chad 419
Chairs 131
Chalet 178-179
Championship 515
Chandragona 215-217
Changpur 457
Charles 448-450, 453, 460-2, 470-1, 478, 483, 504, 512, 523, 538, 551
Chef 554
Chenga 444
Chess 515
Chevrolet 234, 248, 268, 390
Children 230, 456
China 12
Chinese 217, 245, 247, 250
Chittagong 209-213, 215, 217-8, 228-9, 231-2, 235, 238-9, 243-4, 250-2, 255, 257-9, 266-270, 272-3, 275-282, 284-5, 287-8, 290-1, 297-8, 336, 350-2, 354, 371, 373, 375, 387, 438-440, 446-7, 457-461, 464, 472, 478, 526, 539, 554-6

Choggidars 240
Cholera 433
Chris 529
Christ 124
Christian 11, 215, 249, 302, 351, 511, 539
Christianity 11, 181
Christians 181, 205, 301
Christmas 29, 94, 164-6, 182, 196-7, 204-5, 292, 296, 350-2, 370-1, 383, 403-4, 407, 415, 446, 470, 528
Chukwuemeka 12
Chur 511
Churfirsten 108
Claude 441-442, 452, 458
Clinic 51-52
Clive 366
Cloe 322
Codfish 361
Cointrin 17
Colombia 50
Colorfully 24
Columbia 546
Comilla 285
Commons 516-518
Congo 91, 219, 336, 487
Conradin 336-337

Constance 196
Coop 298
Cooperation 282, 381
Copenhagen 318
Corfu 343
Corinth 343
Coronado 103
Corps 98
Courthouse 407
Cows 181
Cox 213
Cres 522
Crossers 394
Cyril 249
Czechoslovakia 12
Dallas 189
Dalmatia 519
Dam 216
Damascus 197, 293
Dams 466
Danes 227
Danida 450, 457
Daniel 33, 42, 44, 49, 58, 63, 66, 195, 199, 203-4, 209, 310, 321
Danish 318, 457, 509
Danube 521
Dardanelles 167

Darfur 337, 341
Darling 405
Darods 378
Datsun 365
David 195, 215, 523
Davos 336
Deanery 407
Delhi 199, 298
Deng 9
Denmark 318, 383, 509
Derg 417
Dhaka 199-200, 203, 206-7, 209, 214, 218, 220-1, 223, 225, 227-9, 235, 239, 241-2, 252, 266, 268, 270, 273, 275, 278, 280, 286-7, 290-2, 298, 387, 393, 438-441, 443, 446, 450, 458, 461, 468-9, 473-6, 501, 555
Dias 233
Diaz 92
Dietikon 109-110
Digging 327
Dimitri 305-306, 312, 323, 328, 338
Dinka 301, 493
Dissler 427, 433, 437
Dogra 252, 288

Dolbohanta 378
Doleb 335
Doleib 318
Donald 398
Dosenbach 347
Dover 190, 359
Drau 520
Dubai 197-198, 291-3
Dugite 527
Duk 334-335
Dumlupinar 148, 173-5
Dunant 17
Duncan 352
Dunlupinar 550
Durban 93
Durisol 109-110, 118, 120, 126, 153, 174
Dutch 227, 278, 463-4
Dutchman 60, 278
Dwip 445, 454
Early 49, 106, 164, 295, 323
East 28, 74, 89, 91, 103, 124, 127, 191-4, 199, 207, 221, 235, 255, 322-3, 350, 445, 523
Eastern 21, 167, 183, 520, 553
Edgar 350-352, 362, 365
Egypt 488
Egyptian 304

Egyptians 488
Eid 181-182
Eier 347
Eigil 426
Eileen 359
Ekpoma 24
Elazig 184-185
Elizabeth 93, 249, 412
Elke 493-494
Elmar 427
Elsie 249, 446
Emanuel 34
Embassy 310, 354, 356, 470
Emil 320-321
Emmanuel 42
Enfants 109, 453
England 351, 429, 516-8
English 9, 19, 32, 34-5, 46, 50, 54-5, 59, 63, 66, 75, 83, 113-4, 119, 121, 128, 150, 213, 215, 227-8, 232, 250, 286, 295, 302, 308, 317, 368, 380, 390, 394, 412, 429, 437, 461-2, 483, 506, 508, 515-8, 539
Enugu 16, 19-22, 25, 27, 29-34, 37, 40-1, 43-4, 46-7, 51-3, 55-8, 60-1, 65-7, 70-1, 73, 80, 82-7, 89, 399, 548-9

Ephesus 186
Equator 360
Equatoria 304
Erich 386
Erika 422
Erna 195, 203-4, 215
Ernest 466
Ershad 387, 477
Erzincan 183
Erzurum 183
Eschen 295
Eschenz 195
Eskisehir 119
Eskishehir 153
Essegg 520
Europe 41, 188-9, 219, 312, 349, 352, 506, 522, 538
European 103, 167, 189, 249, 316, 336, 432, 497
Europeans 266, 286, 390, 445, 488
Eva 453
Eve 166, 204, 296, 324, 352, 371, 470, 528
Everest 200
Everybody 265
Eze 83, 89
Faiwil 334-335

Falkenstein 480
Farell 188
Farming 124
Farrel 190
Fatty 149-153, 306
Feist 270, 282, 291, 296, 298
Felicia 50-51
Felix 42
Feni 285
Ferdi 127-129
Ferid 122-123, 128, 136-8, 142, 144, 146, 148, 150-7, 163-4, 170, 175-7, 179-180, 185, 342-3
Ferit 169, 176
Fernando 13
Fhagamo 22
Fiat 380-382, 385
Fiesch 195
Finland 316
Finns 227
Fischer 195, 197, 205, 215-7, 253, 515
Florence 83-84, 89
Flumser 108
Flying 412
Fog 100
Fokker 97, 305, 340, 386
Forrest 367

Forrestfield 527
France 12, 426
Francis 48, 83, 249, 466
Franciscan 508
Frankfurt 487
Fred 37, 76-7
Fredi 412
Fremantle 359, 361-3, 367-8, 405
French 166, 168, 196, 227, 336, 386, 405, 437, 508
Frick 312, 332, 338
Fridays 136, 310, 320
Frisch 473
Fritz 109-112, 166, 174, 263, 274
Ful 308
Fulani 11, 24
Fulbe 419
Furka 189
Gabriel 33
Gaine 526
Galata 187
Gallen 441
Gallipoli 167-168
Gandhi 199
Gandria 116, 183
Ganges 213, 230, 272, 441

Gartner 518
Gash 417, 422-3, 481-2, 495, 532
Gayne 266, 505, 526
Gazaria 459, 463-4, 466
Gdansk 320
Gedaref 421, 430-1, 482
Gediz 169
Geldenis 144
Geldof 432
Genana 389, 401
Geneva 14-17, 52, 105, 210, 218, 221, 278, 287, 298, 300, 303, 312, 319-320, 344, 375, 404, 416, 475, 487, 497, 505-6, 512-3, 516, 523
Genghis 115
Genova 349
George 19-20, 50-1, 277, 296-7, 405, 432
Geraldton 359
Gerhard 31, 41
German 31, 35, 50, 92, 94, 112, 115, 127-8, 139, 141, 150-1, 170-1, 211, 227, 229, 231, 237-9, 241-2, 248, 252, 277, 299, 305, 310, 319-322, 327, 339, 341, 348, 368, 386, 413-4, 437, 470, 493, 506, 512-3, 520, 528, 539
Germans 227, 251
Germanspeaking 182, 347
Germany 112, 116, 188, 190, 231, 252, 322-3, 363, 396, 426, 538
Gertrude 38-40, 53
Ghana 18
Gharb 481
Ghengis 115
Ghezira 321
Gilmans 102
Gina 190
Girba 421
Girlfriends 51
Girrawheen 266, 362, 365, 368-9, 371, 505, 525-6
Giselle 427, 430
Glarus 111
Glatt 348, 370
Glaxo 245, 249, 275, 283, 285
Glenda 296
God 121, 125, 161-2, 205, 249, 360-1, 454, 493
Gods 178
Godwown 555
Goethe 319, 539

Gomes 233, 245-6, 249, 263, 526
Gonsalves 233, 449, 472-3
Gonzales 546
Gonzen 108
Goose 453
Grameen 464-465
Graz 231, 280
Greece 343
Greek 173, 312, 440
Greeks 168, 173
Gretel 162
Grimsel 189
Grindelwald 7, 21, 39, 94, 96, 122, 137, 145, 150-1, 166, 177-9, 263, 274, 295, 339, 348, 350, 358, 372, 414, 479, 490, 499, 538, 546
Grindelwalder 59-60, 411, 526
Gudjon 512
Guido 15-16, 20-3, 25-9, 31-2, 36, 38, 41
Gulf 197, 400, 451, 455, 471
Gulshan 452, 551
Gysin 512
Haalio 178
Habub 425
Hadendoa 417
Hadiid 481
Hag 330
Hagen 205, 224
Hagia 187
Halanga 417
Halfa 421
Halil 163
Hallgren 100
Hamasia 530
Hamburg 171, 367
Hamersley 363
Hamid 115
Hans 166, 252-3, 413-4, 484, 538
Hansel 162
Hansrudi 7, 48-51, 112, 256, 262-3, 268, 366, 380, 402, 452, 505, 517, 519, 540
Hansruedi 473
Harald 13
Harare 94
Harcourt 13
Hargeisa 386, 400
Harry 17, 19, 21
Hassaheissa 330
Hatiya 444, 550, 552
Hatyia 443-444, 450-2, 455, 458, 472-3, 475, 548

Hauenstein 294
Hausas 32
Haussa 11
Haydarlar 147
Hayri 134
Hazel 350, 352, 447-450, 453, 460-2, 470-1, 478, 483, 504-5, 523, 527, 537-8, 551
Healey 518
Hearing 321, 380
Hedi 167, 187
Heidi 14
Heimgartner 427
Heinz 229, 284
Helen 108
Helena 249
Helene 174
Hen 541
Henriette 194
Henry 17, 318
Hercules 214, 270, 272-3, 341, 556
Herzegovina 502
Herzog 196-199, 205-6, 210, 292, 294, 337
Hezekia 34
Hierapolis 186
Highway 408

Hilltracts 440
Hilton 315, 317, 387, 522
Hindu 539
Hindus 194
Hobbs 50
Hobyo 377
Hof 195, 211, 215
Holderegger 297
Holland 190
Holte 490
Homecoming 438
Honda 441
Hondas 452
Hot 135
Hubacher 116-117, 149, 183
Hussein 475, 477
Ibrahim 122, 128-9, 136-141, 145-6, 302, 532
Ice 162
Iceland 515
Icelandic 398, 512
Idah 25
Igbo 11-14, 28, 30, 37, 47-8, 51, 54, 57, 65, 84, 89
Igbos 12, 31
Igode 22
Ihe 38, 52-3
Ikoy 19

Indian 93, 103, 168, 192-3, 195, 198-206, 210-1, 213, 217, 221, 231, 245, 279, 285-6, 353, 360, 365, 394, 399, 405, 407, 438
Indianapolis 49
Indians 286, 351, 417
Instantly 265
Int 231
Intercontinental 206-207, 219, 223-5, 274
Interlaken 16, 166, 189, 339, 348, 358-9, 375, 404, 412, 416, 479
Involuntarily 105
Iran 183
Ireland 505
Irene 493-494
Iris 387
Irish 31, 38, 41, 71, 83, 266
Irishman 54
Ironsi 11
Irshad 475
Isaaq 378
Iseli 320
Isfahani 240
Ishurdi 270, 272-3
Islam 124, 163, 181, 221, 469, 490
Ismail 113, 124-6, 145, 458, 529
Israel 322
Istanbul 110, 112, 127, 153, 164, 167, 174, 186-7, 304, 342-3
Italian 227, 271, 312, 378, 436-7, 530, 532
Italians 376, 530, 532-3
Italy 17, 343, 349-350, 377, 530, 532
Ithnasheri 394
Itneen 435
Izmir 112, 186
Jack 366
Jacob 312, 338
Jakob 312, 332
Jalakala 279
Jamalkhan 248, 254, 266, 277, 296, 298
James 54, 405
Jamuna 272
Jan 60, 510
Janet 249, 447-450, 453, 460-2, 470-1, 478-480, 483, 504-5, 523, 527, 538, 551
Janz 231-233, 280
Japan 219, 450
Japanese 226

Jaques 188
Java 360
Jawhar 376
Jean 178, 432
Jeannie 352
Jebel 337
Jelese 22
Jelinek 506, 513, 516, 518, 557
Jemal 491
Jess 485
Jessie 233, 240, 264, 279
Jessore 206
Jesus 124, 190
Jim 49, 55, 83-4
Jinnah 191
Jkoyi 19
Joachim 413
Johannesburg 91-93
John 71, 75, 79-80, 179, 516-7
Johnny 198
Johnson 11, 34
Joondalup 411
Josefine 422
Josy 422-423, 429, 432, 437, 487, 491
Jovi 327
Jovy 322
Joyce 326, 329-330, 400-1

Juba 302, 304, 318, 320, 326, 333, 335, 337, 339-340, 389, 401
Judy 41, 100-1
Jure 518
Kabul 487
Kadijevic 502
Kalamunda 524-525, 527, 537
Kalinowski 320, 338
Kanuri 419
Kaptai 216, 218
Karim 211
Karl 109, 112, 157, 229, 442, 523
Karlovac 513-514, 519
Karnaphuli 210, 212, 215, 218, 231-2, 235, 440
Kassal 533
Kassala 312, 417-421, 423-7, 429-430, 432, 434, 436, 470, 481-3, 486, 490, 492-3, 495, 498-9, 501, 524, 528-9, 533
Kastro 496
Kathmandu 298
Kathryn 437
Kay 380, 387-8
Kayseri 184, 186
Keller 195, 215

Kemal 116, 146-7, 150, 154-5, 168, 173-4
Kennedy 98
Kenya 9, 90, 103, 304, 318, 332, 335, 338, 376, 389
Keren 530, 532
Kesch 107
Ketterer 109-112, 118, 120, 157, 167, 174-5
Kevin 359
Khan 115, 193
Khartoum 299-300, 303-5, 309-310, 312-4, 318-320, 323, 328, 330-2, 336-9, 341-2, 348, 360, 417, 419-420, 426, 428, 488, 490, 494, 497, 500-1, 527-8, 533, 539
Khulna 280
Khyber 198
Kibo 99-102
Kiir 337
Kilimanjaro 51, 90, 97-101, 103, 389
Killa 287
Kimberley 363
Kingsley 34
Kinshasa 91
Kiraspinar 130, 158, 162, 342

Kirchlindach 195
Klagenfurt 518
Klaus 427, 433, 437
Kleine 166
Klodt 248
Kloten 53
Klus 295, 479
Koch 211, 231-3, 239
Kolk 60
Konya 184
Kordofan 341
Kosti 327-329
Kota 359
Krakatau 360
Kriz 506-507, 519
Kronenberger 512
Kropf 52, 61, 66
Kucan 511
Kucholl 554
Kuehne 367-368
Kuhn 337
Kulna 270
Kurigram 466
Kurt 195-196, 291, 337
Kutahya 167, 173
Kwacakworo 337
Kwate 25
Kyell 490

Lady 266
Lagos 18-19, 21-2, 24, 32-4, 41, 44, 60, 88-91
Laibach 507
Laila 169
Lakshmipur 459-460
Laksimpur 472-473
Lampell 219, 221-2, 225, 227, 229, 234, 238-9, 257, 266, 280-1, 284, 287, 290-1, 375, 380-1, 387, 487
Lanka 299
Laurent 207, 268
Lausanne 277
Lavina 436-437
Law 260
Laying 183
Lebanese 19, 197
Lee 529
Lena 317
Leo 249
Leon 432
Lesmurdie 524, 527
Lewington 366
Liberation 494
Liberia 98, 100
Libya 340-341
Libyan 340-341
Liechtenstein 190
Liestal 196
Lightning 26
Limburger 36
Limmat 110
Linda 322
Lindt 21
Lisinski 522
Ljlja 510
Ljubliana 507
Ljubljana 502-503, 505-7, 510-1, 517, 522-3, 557
Ljubljanica 507
Ljubljanskaborza 503
Lokoja 25
London 190, 217, 245-7, 249, 253, 255, 278, 359, 516
Losinger 304
Lots 37, 139
Lovro 522
Lucien 277-278
Luckily 28, 72, 114, 122, 396, 425, 434, 442, 480, 488
Lucy 50
Lufthansa 487-489
Lugh 401
Lund 318
Luq 389

Lutheran 316
Luxembourg 190
Macedonia 502, 505, 512
Macedonian 506
Madeleine 53
Madie 62, 65
Madressa 394
Maennlichen 166
Magdalena 38-40, 53, 195, 203-5, 215, 294
Maggie 541
Magnusson 512
Mahal 298
Maharaja 201-202
Maharajah 202
Maharani 202
Mahatma 199-200
Mahdi 341
Maher 9
Maizdi 444
Malakal 303, 305, 313-9, 326-7, 329-336, 338-340, 343-4, 545, 553
Malatya 184-185
Malawi 90, 93, 95
Malaysia 354
Malesh 435
Mamoun 488-490

Manhattan 290-291
Manikganj 468, 476-7
Manjaro 99
Manpower 105, 188, 190, 299
Mansoor 387
Marangu 98, 102-3
Margaret 353
Margrit 526
Maria 248
Maribor 513
Marie 352
Marietta 352
Mario 52, 61, 66, 68-9
Marmara 167
Marra 337
Marshall 281
Marte 511
Martha 249, 263, 526
Marti 207, 268
Martine 426
Massawa 531-533
Matatic 522
Matten 404
Maud 214
Mavis 232
Max 166
Maxene 352
Mayardit 337

Maybe 58, 123, 145, 165, 328, 349, 355, 384
Mecca 331, 419
Medani 312, 330
Mediterranean 197, 503
Meghna 230, 441, 444, 450, 452, 457, 459, 466
Mehmet 130, 158
Memories 20, 168, 198, 372
Meneghetti 274-275
Mennel 21, 23, 26, 32-3
Menzingen 207
Merca 394
Mercedes 188, 190
Mercer 278
Mercy 266
Mestre 512
Methodist 34
Metzger 17
Metzler 354
Mexican 320
Mexico 320
Meyenberg 252-253
Meyer 195
Michael 322, 327, 506, 518, 523, 538
Michelin 40
Midwest 24

Migros 111, 114, 298
Mihir 441-442, 450-2, 454-5, 457-9, 463, 467, 471-2
Mike 34, 359
Milan 511
Military 23, 28
Milky 402
Milliken 89
Ministries 87
Mirko 518
Miroslav 320
Mitja 508
Mitsapur 209
Mofiss 458
Mogadishu 375-377, 379-383, 386-8, 393-6, 399-401, 429, 487
Mohamed 129, 306, 341, 490
Mohamedpur 221
Mohammed 124
Mohammedans 161, 179
Mohjeddin 306
Monday 40, 263, 347, 408, 411
Monde 109, 453
Monika 17-21, 27, 36, 49, 75-6, 78, 80-1, 89
Monthly 555
Morning 233

Morris 325
Moscow 190
Moshi 97, 99, 103
Mosque 187
Mowenzi 100
Mozambique 93-94
Mubarak 182
Mubjibur 290
Mucking 45
Muetti 268
Muezzin 126, 161, 176, 178, 547
Muezzins 159
Muhammad 191, 464
Mujibur 193, 214
Mukhtar 131, 133, 145, 148-9, 171, 173-6
Mukti 193, 210, 219
Munich 190, 413, 484-5
Mur 178
Murat 129, 161
Murray 405
Muslim 11, 176, 187, 191, 286, 443
Muslims 32, 181
Mustafa 168
Myanmar 216
Nabadeed 386

Nagel 367-368
Nairobi 103, 304-5, 314, 318, 326, 331-2, 335-6, 338, 340, 387-390, 392-3, 401
Nalchira 472
Nancy 190
Nang 534
Nasidi 60
Naville 52
Nehler 519
Nehru 199
Nepal 205-206
Neptune 360, 454
Nhwafor 84
Nicolas 190
Niger 11, 25-6, 52, 65, 91
Nigeria 11-14, 18, 21, 24, 30, 47, 85, 91, 348, 534
Nigerian 11-14, 17, 19, 22, 24, 27-30, 35, 41, 46, 51, 54-6, 58-9, 61, 64-5, 70-2, 75, 83-4, 88-9
Nigerians 12, 41, 62, 65, 69, 73, 85, 419
Nijhum 445
Nijum 445, 454
Nijumdwip 478
Nil 166

Nile 303-304, 311, 316-9, 321, 326-7, 329-330, 332-4, 336, 339-340, 342, 419
Nilsson 383
Nimeiri 303, 341
Nita 247
Nixon 322
Nnamani 34
Nnamchi 34
Noa 428
Noakhali 450, 457
Nobody 55, 101, 128-9, 182, 427, 434, 469, 488
Noel 322
Nonetheless 226
Northbridge 364
Norwegian 312, 332, 426, 490
Norwegians 227
Nour 341
Nuba 301
Nubian 482
Nuer 301
Nullarbor 363, 365
Nur 306
Nuremberg 190
Nurul 194
Nwafhor 89
Nyala 337
Nyasa 96
Nyasaland 95
Nyassa 96
Oberammergau 190
Oberjoch 166
Oberland 52
Oberoi 201-202
Obrezje 513
Obudu 38, 40
Odumegwu 12
Oerlikon 103, 165, 188, 299, 304, 346-7, 358
Offner 386
Ogaden 378, 382, 386, 401
Ogadeni 378
Ogoja 40
Ogui 45
Oh 155, 178
Ojukwu 12, 74
Okigwe 54, 86
Okonkwo 88
Okoro 35, 46, 56, 89
Omdurman 319, 340-2, 417
Onitsha 65, 83-4
Opara 51
Opel 348, 358
Orphanage 84, 259

Osborne 314, 326, 329, 335-6, 338
Osijek 520
Osman 113
Ostend 190
Oswald 195, 199, 209
Otukpa 27
Oturkpo 50, 60
Oturpo 60-61
Owerri 34
Oxfam 399
Paavo 316-318
Pacific 365
Pag 522
Pajero 531
Pakistan 191-194, 198-9, 208, 219, 221, 223, 232, 235, 255-6, 275, 412, 445, 539
Pakistani 193-194, 206-7, 211, 214, 224, 293, 393
Pakistanis 211, 221, 223, 252, 288
Palestinian 322
Palmolive 248
Pamela 296
Pamukkale 184, 186
Pandit 199
Paris 190
Parmelia 387
Passau 190
Patenga 210, 217, 236, 438
Patience 51, 458
Patricia 84, 366
Patrick 278, 518
Patsy 352
Paul 233, 240, 262-4, 279, 296, 314-8, 326, 329-330, 335-6, 338-9, 408
Paulinus 249, 254, 256
Pawolek 470
Pedro 238, 241, 258-9, 264, 270
Peene 538
Pemberton 353
Penka 31, 41
Pentecost 19
Pepsi 311
Pereira 232, 387
Pergamon 169
Perner 336-337
Persian 197
Perth 9, 350-2, 355-6, 359, 363-5, 387, 405-7, 413-4, 480-1, 483-4, 524-5, 537, 540, 556
Peter 9, 52-3, 386, 453
Peters 99, 102

Petit 298
Peugeot 424
Pfister 18
Pierre 432
Piguet 108, 174
Pilatus 189
Pilbara 363
Piraeus 343
Piz 107
Plants 30
Platt 34, 36
Plenipotentiary 21
Po 13
Poland 12
Pontic 182
Portugal 12
Portuguese 232
Precisa 347
Prof 518
Protestant 109, 249, 266, 505, 526
Queensland 386
Quickly 77, 226, 331
Quoreshi 446, 469, 474-5, 479
Quovo 33
Raedersdorf 512
Rahman 193, 214, 236, 261-3, 290
Rahmann 263
Rainer 229, 231, 284-6, 298
Ramadan 179-181
Rangamati 216, 448-9, 460
Ras 529
Razakars 194
Rdeci 507, 519
Rebeiro 214, 228, 400-1
Regardless 485
Reifenrath 396, 399, 402
Reims 190
Reinach 195
Remo 512
Resting 106
Rhine 7, 20, 189, 196
Rhodesia 90, 93-5, 97
Rhodesian 94
Ribaux 441, 452, 458
Richard 322
Ringgenberg 166
Rita 299
Robert 211, 231-3, 239
Roche 7
Rodrigues 232
Roffique 444, 475
Rolls 202
Roman 195, 215, 440
Rome 314, 343

Ron 270, 282, 291, 296, 298
Ronald 449
Rony 472-474
Rosita 320
Ross 314, 343
Roth 89, 92, 94
Rottnest 407
Roy 466
Royce 202
Ruckstuhl 53
Rudi 222, 260, 353, 361, 366
Rupert 196, 228
Russi 195
Russian 151, 182, 355, 382, 515
Russians 383, 397
Ruth 538
Ryter 538
Saad 341
Saconnex 298
Sadigel 341
Sadikiri 158-159
Saeed 490
Sahara 18
Sahib 202
Sahlili 112
Saidpur 465
Salaam 97
Salauddin 459

Salisbury 94-95
Salva 337
Salzburg 190
Sam 31
Samantha 366
Samuel 21, 316, 329
Sandwhip 473
Sandwip 441, 457-8
Sandy 363
Santschi 262-264
Sara 9
Sargans 108
Sarson 257, 264, 267, 285, 288
Saudi 197, 322
Saurer 279, 321
Sawagi 481
Scandinavian 227, 398
Scarborough 353
Scheidegg 166
Schmid 299, 347
Schneider 430
Schneitz 291
Schuler 523
Schwamendingen 345
Schwarzenberg 108
Scottish 405
Secretly 501
Senet 428, 497

Sennar 330
Seppli 48, 51
Serbia 408, 505, 513-5
Serbian 513-514, 520-1
Severi 305-306, 312, 338
Shaguro 22
Shambel 431, 490, 493-4, 498-501, 528-9, 531-3
Sheik 214
Sheikh 290
Sherifay 423, 426-434, 436-7, 487, 490, 492-5, 498, 500-1, 523, 527-8, 531, 533
Shillong 286
Shintaku 27
Shonkwiler 49
Showak 421
Siad 378, 382
Siddiki 239-240, 242-3, 246, 555
Sidikki 264
Sidman 506, 518, 523
Sidney 383
Sikka 481
Simav 182
Singapora 359
Singapore 359, 384, 415
Sinovas 512

Sir 202, 405
Sisyphus 45
Sivas 183
Skopje 506, 512
Slavery 376
Slavonia 520-521
Slovene 511, 516
Slovenia 502-503, 505-7, 509-511, 513, 515, 517-8, 557
Slovenian 505-510, 513, 519, 523
Slovenjie 507, 519
Smith 266, 383
Smyrna 112
Sobat 318, 335
Societes 375
Sofia 187
Soil 345
Somali 377-379, 381-2, 385-7, 393, 397-9, 402-3
Somalia 375-382, 387, 389, 402, 404, 411, 417, 487, 534
Somaliland 376, 378, 386
Somalis 377, 399
Somebody 308
Somewhere 360
Sonadia 548
Soraya 361

Sorghum 482
Souq 481
Souza 232
Soviet 12, 378
Spain 12
Spanish 50, 512
Spassky 515
Spellman 380
Spirgy 200
Spitzmeilen 108
Sri 299
Stalder 17, 49
Steiner 13
Stella 249
Stewart 89
Stirling 405, 407, 524
Stockholm 501, 510
Strasbourg 190
Stubbings 432
Sturzenegger 238, 259, 270
Stuttgart 188
Styria 231
Suakin 309
Sudan 9, 299, 301-310, 312-3, 315, 319-321, 323, 326-9, 331-2, 336-8, 340-1, 344-5, 348, 357, 374, 415-8, 420-1, 429, 436, 470, 481-2, 487-8, 490, 493-5, 499-501, 523-4, 529, 533-4, 545, 553
Sudanese 301-302, 305, 307-310, 313, 315, 320-1, 323, 325, 327, 331, 337-8, 341, 361, 419-421, 425, 428, 435-6, 488-491, 493-4, 496, 500, 523, 527-9
Sudd 326
Sumatra 360
Sunda 360
Sundarban 280
Sunday 36-37, 54, 56, 58, 70-1, 82, 107, 125, 153, 249, 277, 310, 394, 505, 522, 526
Sundays 58
Supervision 141
Surma 286
Susanne 422
Susie 247, 249-250, 254-5, 262, 297, 350-1, 353, 368
Sustar 510
Susten 189, 479
Sutherland 398
Suzie 375
Sven 219, 221-2, 225, 227, 229, 234, 238-9, 257-8, 266-7, 280-1, 284, 287, 290-1, 375, 380-1, 387, 391-2, 487-8

Swede 218, 380, 383, 510
Sweden 219, 501, 510
Swedes 227
Swedish 58, 219-220, 398, 487, 500-1, 510, 519
Swingerland 279
Swiss 14, 20, 24, 29, 36, 38, 42, 51-3, 55, 61, 98, 103-4, 106, 109-111, 115-8, 120, 123, 127-8, 135, 137, 141, 145, 155-8, 164, 167-8, 171, 174-5, 180, 183, 187-8, 194, 199, 205, 207, 214-5, 217-8, 223-4, 227, 232, 238, 244, 252-3, 268, 274-5, 277-281, 294-5, 298-9, 303-5, 310, 320-1, 323, 336, 339, 343-4, 347, 350, 354, 358, 366, 368, 370, 383, 389, 401, 404, 411, 414-6, 419, 421-3, 426, 428-430, 432, 435-7, 441, 443, 453, 457, 461, 465, 473, 477-8, 488, 501, 504, 506, 511-3, 524, 528-9, 534, 537, 548, 557
Swissair 17-18, 103, 112, 164, 305, 339, 342, 419, 480
Switzerland 7, 12, 14-6, 19, 21-2, 36, 79, 88-90, 103-4, 106, 109-111, 114, 118-120, 132, 137, 156-7, 159-160, 167, 171, 173, 175, 184, 189, 195, 205, 207-8, 214, 216-9, 225-6, 252, 263-4, 268, 270, 275, 278, 288, 291, 297-8, 304, 319-320, 339-340, 342, 344-5, 347-9, 352-4, 356, 361, 404, 412-3, 416, 426, 435-7, 440, 458, 473, 479, 487, 509-510, 515, 523, 527, 537-9, 552
Sydney 365, 384
Sylhet 285-287
Syria 197
Syrian 197
Tadeija 508
Tadeja 506, 509
Tafawa 11
Taj 298
Taka 417-418, 421, 481
Takarir 419
Talata 435
Tanganijka 97
Tanya 413
Tanzania 51, 90, 97
Tanzanian 97, 99
Taylor 546
Teddy 388-389

Teknaf 238
Tensely 456
Tessenai 531
Texan 188
Texans 189
Texas 188, 190
Therese 195, 203-4, 215
Thickly 240
Thirteen 309
Thun 348
Thursday 121, 236, 408
Tigre 491
Tim 383
Tinkerbell 461
Tivoli 509
Tokyo 226
Toli 337
Tom 266, 505, 526
Tommy 277
Tomorrow 159
Toni 205, 224, 344, 473, 479, 486-7, 501, 505, 523, 554
Tonight 262
Topkapi 187
Torn 212
Toronto 279
Totil 481
Trabzon 182

Tracers 66
Trans 91
Tripura 285
Trojan 168
Trojans 168
Tromme 426
Tromostovje 507
Troy 168
Tschiffely 282
Tsegai 533
Tsegay 500
Tugboats 24
Tuor 107-108
Ture 218, 220, 222-3, 501
Turgutlu 112
Turk 134, 182
Turkish 109-118, 120, 123, 125, 128, 131-2, 134-6, 139, 144-5, 153-5, 157, 164-8, 172-3, 175-6, 183, 187, 343, 512
Turks 116, 120, 131-2, 135-6, 143, 163, 173, 181
Tyrol 190
Udi 37, 49, 59
Uganda 302, 318, 332, 335
Ugandan 304
Ugoyi 50
Ugpogu 23

Ukraine 520
Umonovo 45
Umuahia 70-73, 82
Umuhahia 74, 80
Una 350, 352, 362, 365
Uncultivated 442
Undeterred 38, 330
Unnoticed 36
Unterseen 299
Upperland 295
Urdu 192, 293, 393-4, 539
Urs 430
Usak 112
Ussoli 74
Uster 195
Uturu 31, 54, 71, 75, 79-80, 83
Vaduz 189
Vatican 343
Vatroslav 522
Veljko 502
Verena 487, 494, 501, 554
Vice 184, 512
Victoria 94, 363, 408
Victorian 484
Vida 510, 512
Vietnam 336, 534
Villach 518
Ville 190

Villmergen 110
Vinkovski 520-521
Visibility 431
Visp 110
Vogel 196-197, 200, 210, 228, 287, 291
Volkart 232-234, 236, 257-8, 267, 273, 275, 288-9, 297, 555
Volkswagen 312, 319, 325
Vorarlberg 190
Vorpommern 538
Vreni 383, 401, 415, 486-7, 523, 529, 531-3, 554
Vukovar 521
Wachter 422
Wad 312, 330, 423, 426-434, 436-7, 487, 490, 492-5, 498, 500-1, 523, 527-8, 531-3
Wahid 435
Wajale 386
Waldenburger 294
Wallenda 442
Walliston 524
Walter 299
Wanderlust 481, 486
Washington 291
Wau 305, 312, 330, 332, 338
Weber 422-423, 425, 479, 487,

501, 554
Weeks 88
Wenger 344, 383, 401, 415, 473, 479, 486-7, 501, 505, 523, 529, 531-3, 554
Werner 231-233, 241, 258, 264, 280
West 14-15, 17-8, 36, 98, 104, 191-4, 199, 206, 208, 211, 214, 219, 221, 223-4, 235, 252, 255, 288, 337, 353, 359, 363, 406, 419, 445, 511
Westminster 516-517
Wetterhorn 39
Wetzikon 195
Weyand 89
Whear 51, 80
Whitemans 504
Whitty 215
Whitworth 369-370
Wiener 13
Wikipedia 14, 194, 379, 483, 531
Wilhelminian 406
Williams 399
Willy 109-112, 174
Wilson 389
Windhuk 349

Winterthur 110-111, 297
Wittwer 452, 473
Women 465
Wooden 111
Wyss 280
Wyssmann 127
Yahya 193
Yamaha 457
Yaren 159
Yawash 435
Yemen 417, 534
Yohannes 529
Yokine 537
Yona 359
Yugoslav 502, 508-9, 512
Yugoslavia 111, 502, 505, 511, 518-9, 523
Yussef 128
Yussuf 127-129, 464
Yvonne 94
Zaffar 256
Zagi 113
Zagreb 502-503, 506, 512, 514, 519-523
Zak 506, 512, 516-7, 523
Zambezi 94
Zambia 94
Zambian 95

Zanolli 428
Zanzibar 96-97
Zealand 168, 366-7, 375
Zealander 383
Zehnder 110-111
Zeitung 13
Zerfas 37, 76-7
Zia 387
Zigana 182
Zimbabwe 94
Zofingen 252
Zurich 15, 19, 53, 105, 108, 110-1, 164-5, 167, 187-8, 190, 195, 248, 299, 320, 344-8, 355, 367-8, 370, 415, 419, 422, 432, 480, 487, 501, 506
Zuyderhoff 167, 188, 194, 295

www.ingramcontent.com/pod-product-compliance
Lightning Source LLC
Chambersburg PA
CBHW030249010526
44107CB00053B/1642